Taking
WRONGS SERIOUSLY

WITHDRAWN BY THE
UNIVERSITY OF MICHIGAN

WITHDRAWN BY THE
UNIVERSITY OF MICHIGAN

Taking WRONGS SERIOUSLY
Acknowledgment, Reconciliation, and the Politics of Sustainable Peace

TRUDY GOVIER

Humanity Books

an imprint of Prometheus Books
59 John Glenn Drive, Amherst, New York 14228-2197

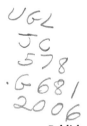

UGL
JC
578
·G68
2006

Published 2006 by Humanity Books, an imprint of Prometheus Books

Taking Wrongs Seriously: Acknowledgment, Reconciliation, and the Politics of Sustainable Peace. Copyright © 2006 by Trudy Govier. All rights reserved. No part of this publication may be reproduced, stored in a retrieval system, or transmitted in any form or by any means, digital, electronic, mechanical, photocopying, recording, or otherwise, or conveyed via the Internet or a Web site without prior written permission of the publisher, except in the case of brief quotations embodied in critical articles and reviews.

Inquiries should be addressed to
Humanity Books
59 John Glenn Drive
Amherst, New York 14228–2197
VOICE: 716–691–0133, ext. 207
FAX: 716–564–2711

10 09 08 07 06   5 4 3 2 1

Library of Congress Cataloging-in-Publication Data

Govier, Trudy.
    Taking wrongs seriously : acknowledgment, reconciliation, and the politics of sustainable peace / Trudy Govier.
        p. cm.
    Includes bibliographical references and index.
    ISBN-13: 978-1-59102-425-5 (hardcover : alk. paper)
    ISBN-10: 1-59102-425-0 (hardcover : alk. paper)
    1. Restorative justice. 2. Reconciliation. 3. Peace—Political aspects. I. Title.

JC578.G68 2006
303.6'9—dc22

                                                                    2006009250

Printed in the United States of America on acid-free paper

Contents

5

6   Contents

Preface

This book is intended for all those interested in the pursuit of sustainable peace whether they be ordinary citizens, practitioners, students, scholars, or activists. It explores the processes of political reconciliation after serious wrongdoing. In the aftermath of violence and oppression, human beings in many parts of the world face the problem of constructing decent relationships. While a highly practical one, this problem is also theoretically profound.

I approach the problems of political reconciliation from a secular point of view. As I understand reconciliation, it is a theme for all human beings on earth. Neither its problems nor its solutions presuppose a theological frame of reference. The plain fact is that people living in the same society need to cooperate; to cooperate, they need to trust; and in the aftermath of violence and oppression, that is difficult. To say that people alienated by wrongdoing are in no position to trust and cooperate is an understatement. Efforts toward reconciliation can be understood as attempts to end alienation and resentment and build relationships characterized by some degree of trust. The problems of reconciliation involve many areas, including psychology, ethics, law, and politics. Attitudes and relationships are not easily explored in quantitative terms; we are looking at the "soft stuff" of human life. But that is not to say we have entered a domain of theology. Notions such as "reconciliation," "forgiveness," and "peace" can be understood without appealing to any tradition of religious faith.

As this work will indicate, many central questions about reconciliation are not context specific. I examine the topic in the context of a number of different countries, specifically Australia, Canada, East Timor, Northern Ireland, Peru, Rwanda, Sierra Leone, and South Africa. Background information concerning each of these particular countries is provided in eight appendices.

I examine central themes from a point of view informed by the study of philosophy. The philosophical aspects of this work are particularly significant with regard to discussions of retributive and restorative justice, individual and collective responsibility, acknowledgement, forgiveness, and the concept of reconciliation itself. As

7

is characteristic of philosophical studies, my discussion includes explanations of objections and responses to those objections.

No sober-minded writer could pretend to answer the many questions that arise concerning reconciliation, and I do not claim to do that. The issues are multiple; central values seem to conflict; and some difficulties seem intractable, as subsequent discussions will show. What I hope to do is to clearly articulate and explore some central problems and influential accounts and show how the same themes and issues present themselves in different contexts. At many points, I state arguments for one or another stance with full awareness that my accounts will be open to challenge from perspectives other than my own.

Despite its ambitious scope, this work necessarily leaves out a number of important questions and themes. One omission is that the international aspect of conflict situations is not emphasized here—even though, in the case of some conflicts (Rwanda and Sierra Leone, for example), those aspects are highly significant. I regret the omission, but can only plead that a discussion has to have some limits. Nor is there any discussion here of the question of reparations for slavery. That topic is a massive one that I was unable to accommodate. I hope, and believe, that my examinations of reparations, redress, and responsibility will interest others engaged with that enormous and fascinating topic.

In references to Internet sources, I have included the date of access. It has been my experience that, for all the timeliness and accessibility of such sources, they have the major drawback of instability. To put it bluntly, the site may disappear. Because of this, I have tried to cite print sources when that has been feasible. The problem of ensuring convenience and stability of electronic sources is a general one that has not been solved, and I can only hope that my use of such sources does not seriously inconvenience any reader.

I have had opportunities to present my ideas on reconciliation on a number of occasions and have benefited from the accompanying discussions. For their questions and comments, I would like to thank audiences in Moscow; Amherst, New York, and Winnipeg, London, Calgary, Vancouver, Hamilton, and Lethbridge, Canada. Thanks for comments and encouragement to Ruben Apressyan, Paul Kurtz, Michael Kubara, Michael Stingl, Gavin Hyde, Wade Snowdon, Katie East, Ben Scott, Joanna Santa-Barbara, Derek Evans, Beverley Tollefson Delong, Nancy Heatherington Pierce, Anna Snyder, Neil Funk-Unrau, Paul Redekop, Lois Edmund, Karl Tomm, Ann O'Hear, Fanie du Toit, Anton Colijn, and Caroline Colijn. I have greatly benefited from the energy, passion, and hard work of two research assistants: Risa Kawchuk and Sarah Laing. The appendix on Sierra Leone was written by Sarah Laing.

Chapters five to ten and all appendices have not been previously published. The first four chapters of this work incorporate elements of jointly published papers on reconciliation, apology, and victim/perpetrator roles. These collaborative papers were based on extensive work and discussion with my colleague and friend Wilhelm Verwoerd. His efforts and ideas appear not only in my footnotes, but also in my ongoing personal reflections about the many questions that arise when we take wrongs seriously.

Chapter One

The Concept of Reconciliation

In societies divided by a bitter past, former antagonists need to work together to build better legal and social institutions than they had before. If they are unable to do so, the divisions of the past will arise again and extend into the future, making the institutions of democracy and peace precarious and unsustainable. Perhaps as a response to widely acclaimed work of the South African Truth and Reconciliation Commission, calls for reconciliation have subsequently echoed around the world.[1]

In Australia, reconciliation has been an important political topic since 1997, when the government report *Bringing Them Home* described the gross and tragic effects of a policy of forced removal that had created a "Stolen Generation" of children. Reconciliation is also an important matter in Canada, where government and society have struggled to cope with revelations of abuse in residential schools attended by Aboriginal Canadians in the period between 1880 and 1969. In Peru, a Truth and Reconciliation Commission was established to study the causes and needs relating to intense and brutal violence during the twenty-year struggle between government forces and the Shining Path movement under the fanatical totalitarian leadership of Abimael Guzman Reinoso. In Northern Ireland, the Good Friday Accord of 1998 set forth terms to end thirty years of violence in sectarian conflicts and was followed by extensive and well-funded community efforts aimed to reintegrate former fighters, redress injured victims, and generally improve relations between Protestant and Catholic communities. Even after the horrific genocide of 1994, the political leadership in Rwanda urged reconciliation between the Tutsis and Hutus, pleading for forgiveness, acknowledging the impossibility of criminal trials for all who had participated in the killings, and seeking community processes of reintegration and reconciliation in a system of *gacaca* courts. In the aftermath of a brutal civil war that raged between 1991 and 2001, Sierra Leone established both a Truth and Reconciliation Commission to address the concerns of victims and the responsibilities of perpetrators and a Special Court to try those bearing the greatest responsibility for the serious wrongs committed. President Ahmad Tejan Kabbah referred specifically to the need for reconciliation, saying:

> I regard the Truth and Reconciliation Commission as one of the most significant pillars of peace, justice and reconciliation ever created in our society. The most important accomplishment of this Commission, it is hoped, will be the reconciling of our population and ensuring that Sierra Leone shall never again experience the evils of the past eleven years.[2]

In 2002, East Timor established a Commission for Reception, Truth and Reconciliation, among the main purposes of which was to attract back to East Timor those who had fled to West Timor and to offer them an orderly and peaceful reception. This commission was intended to "facilitate community reconciliation by dealing with past cases of lesser crimes such as looting, burning, and minor assault" and to make recommendations to the government as to further action "on reconciliation and the promotion of human rights."[3]

LEVELS OF RECONCILIATION

Reconciliation, in its most familiar context, involves individuals. We may, for instance, think of a husband and wife reconciling in the aftermath of a quarrel. In such a case, tears, hugs and kisses, and apologies and forgiveness are features of an intimate emotional reunion. What is sought is the restoration of a close relationship after a period of alienation. Obviously, in political contexts, something broader than individual relationships is at issue. Communities, groups, and, indeed, the whole society are involved. Individuals may play central roles as leaders or as representative figures, and issues of individual responsibility and redress remain important, but the need for reconciliation clearly does not stop here.

The idea of national reconciliation implies a larger scale than that of the community, as is evident when we consider whites and blacks in South Africa, whites and Aboriginals in Australia or Canada, or previously opposed groups in the aftermath of civil violence. In these cases, national reconciliation will involve many thousands of people and their institutions and relationships. The community context is a major aspect of efforts toward reconciliation in the wake of the civil war in Sierra Leone, where persons abducted into the rebel army, often as children, committed gross atrocities in their own villages. In the aftermath of the civil war, the challenge is to have them return and resume a community life. In East Timor, a similar problem arises for persons who may return from West Timor and wish to reenter communities where they committed acts of arson, looting, or assault.

There is often a call for reconciliation in international contexts. After the US invasion of Iraq, some commentators on prospects for "reconciliation" in that country mentioned reconciliation not only with regard to groups within Iraq, but also regarding relations with Kuwait, Iran, the United States, and the United Nations. In the violent society that Iraq has become, such talk seems utopian to the point of irrelevance. But despite implausible assumptions, it points to an important fact: if violence is ever to end in Iraq, relationships will have to be addressed. Another point that arises here concerns the international dimensions of the Iraqi conflict. Any resolution of its many dilemmas would have international dimensions. The same can be said of conflicts in the Balkans (involving, implicitly, NATO, the UN, and the EU), Northern Ireland (involving the United Kingdom, the Republic of Ireland, the EU, and expatriate Irish), Rwanda (involving Uganda, Burundi, and the African Great Lakes region), and Sierra Leone (involving Liberia and Nigeria).[4]

We see, then, that the need for reconciliation can arise at all the following levels:

- Individual
- Family
- Small group or community
- Intergroup or intercommunity
- National
- International

WHAT IS MEANT BY "RECONCILIATION"?

But what does "reconciliation" mean when we move away from the level of individuals? We can readily grasp the idea of two lovers or friends reconciling, or of a former soldier being reintegrated into his or her community. But when we try to think about *reconciliation* in the context of groups and, in particular, large groups, the very meaning of the term can begin to seem unclear. If a society or nation were to achieve reconciliation in the aftermath of intense political conflict, what would that reconciliation be like?[5] Victims of wrongs will be involved; so, too, will those who have committed them. Broader groups, including bystanders, beneficiaries, and third parties, will also be involved. What is meant by "national reconciliation"?[6] Or "political reconciliation"?

Even the prefix "re" in "reconciliation" may be problematic. The prefix suggests coming together again after a break in a relationship—as does the "re" in words like *re*pair and *re*storation. But in many contexts the groups in question never had a decent relationship to begin with. This point applies with particular poignancy to contexts of settler societies such as Canada, Australia, and South Africa. In South Africa, for example, the task of national reconciliation after apartheid cannot plausibly be understood as one of *re*building or *re*pairing relationships of whites and blacks, which had been (somehow) harmonious and equitable in some prior period. Clearly such a presumption would not be historically accurate. There was never a relationship characterized by equity and harmony between blacks and whites in that part of the world. If one wanted to speak of "restoring" such a relationship, one would have to first think of it as an idealization, a fiction based on a notion of what could have been under better circumstances. The same sort of point can be made for other settler societies such as New Zealand, Australia, and Canada. We cannot speak of restoring relationships in any literal sense, given the historically unrealistic nature of the presumption that they were ever decent. To reconcile in such contexts has to mean *building* relationships based on norms of equality and respect; it cannot always mean *rebuilding* them.

Equally perplexing is the issue of what is being sought under the name "national reconciliation." What is the goal? Is there a goal at all? Perhaps reconciliation is better understood as a process than a goal, but that conception still poses a question. The process has got to be aimed at something. What is it? Unity? Harmony? Healing? Apology and forgiveness? Truth about the wrongs of the past? Restorative justice? Retributive justice? Institution building? Or simply coexistence in the absence of violence?[7]

At the multiple levels, ranging from individual to family, community, society, and nation, it makes sense to think of reconciliation in terms of building or rebuilding *relationships*. In an influential work, John Paul Lederach writes:

> Reconciliation, we have seen, is focused on building relationships between antago-
> nists. The relational dimension involves the emotional and psychological aspects of
> the conflict and the need to recognize past grievances and explore future interde-
> pendence. Reconciliation as a locus creates a space for encounter by the parties, a
> place where the diverse but connected energies and concerns driving the conflict
> can meet, including the paradoxes of *truth* and *mercy*, *justice* and *peace*.[8]

Lederach's reference is to Psalm 85:10, "Truth and mercy have met together; peace and justice have kissed." He finds this text profoundly suggestive with regard to reconciliation and its many difficult knots; Lederach states that truth, mercy, peace, and justice are the four elements necessary for reconciliation. Under the notion of *truth*, Lederach includes acknowledgment, transparency, revelation, and clarity. *Mercy*, he takes to allude to acceptance, forgiveness, support, compassion, and healing.[9] *Justice* involves equality, right relationships, making things right, and restitution. (Retributive justice is not mentioned and is not part of his conception.)[10] *Peace* means harmony, unity, well-being, security, and respect.

This account is suggestive, metaphoric, and has been put to practical use by many. For all its importance, however, it does not seem to resolve the deep concep-tual questions posed by the term "reconciliation." Furthermore, the scriptural refer-ence, while suggestive and beautiful, may pose obstacles to secular theorists and practitioners. The emphasis on relationships is highly important and must be accepted, as is Lederach's explanation that in reconciliation people must look both to the *past*, asking what has been done, and to the *future*, asking how can one move beyond the wrongs of the past, having understood and acknowledged those wrongs. People seeking reconciliation are seeking to build relationships of moral equality, relationships that are not overwhelmed by the facts of past oppression and wrongdoing, and relationships that maintain a capacity for cooperation. What sort of relationships are these?

When staff researchers came to write the final report of South Africa's Truth and Reconciliation Commission, they found themselves lacking a definition of the central term, "national reconciliation." Lawyers, jurists, and politicians warned against starry-eyed visions and interpreted reconciliation as coexistence without physical violence. Others, following Desmond Tutu, had advocated a warmer and more intimate notion involving confession and forgiveness and tied to Christian models of the reconciliation of sinful human beings with God.[11] Many people warned about expecting too much from reconciliation processes at the national level; disappointments were inevitable if emotionally rich notions of contrition and forgiveness were imposed on a diverse and divided society. They thought that coexistence would be a more realistic goal.[12]

WORKING THROUGH A SPECTRUM OF INTERPRETATIONS

At this point, it is helpful to work through a spectrum of possibilities.

1. Reconciliation is unity.
2. Reconciliation is harmony.
3. Reconciliation is healing, of individuals and relationships.
4. Reconciliation is forgiveness, following on remorse and apology.
5. Reconciliation is the building of decent relationships.
6. Reconciliation is truth acknowledged.
7. Reconciliation is restorative justice, involving remorse on the part of perpetrators and reparations for victims.
8. Reconciliation is retributive justice, requiring the punishment of offenders.
9. Reconciliation is democratization, requiring the development of legal, electoral, and parliamentary institutions.
10. Reconciliation means that people have stopped using physical violence against each other.

This spectrum begins with emotional richness and "thickness" and moves through to relative "thinness" at the bottom, where there is little emphasis on attitudes and feelings. Shifting from (1) to (10), there is relatively less attention given to attitudes and relatively more attention given to institutional and behavioral factors. We may think of this sequence as a spectrum of possibilities, a spectrum with a thin end and a thick end. The notions of healing and forgiveness appear at the thick end, while those of institution building and nonviolent coexistence appear at the thin end.

As to the first two levels, ideas such as unity and harmony are purely rhetorical and, in any literal sense, would be quite unrealistic in large groups and nations. Any national process involves many thousands of people; the idea that all of these people could be, in anything close to a literal sense, "unified" or "in harmony" is entirely unrealistic.[13] And even if it were possible, such a condition would not be worth the quest; pluralism and differences about beliefs, values, interests, and arguments are desirable in any sizable society.

Moving on to consider levels (3) and (4) on this model, reconciliation would be based on remorse and apology on the part of perpetrators and forgiveness for perpetrators' actions on the part of victims. This has, essentially, been the model assumed by Desmond Tutu and others who presume a religious frame of reference. In such interpretations, attitudes and shifts in attitudes are crucial; a strong interpretation of this sort would require that victims, perpetrators, and their relationship are, in some sense, *healed* when they are reconciled. In the aftermath of violence or oppression, feelings of resentment, hurt, and vindictiveness would be overcome, permitting improved relationships between persons alienated in a conflict. To be sure, when leaders of formerly opposed groups display changed attitudes in actions of apology and gestures of acceptance and forgiveness, their publicized leadership and cooperation can have positive effects on attitudes within the broader society. There are powerful examples: David Trimble and Gerry Adams in some phases of the Northern Irish peace processes, or F. W. de Klerk and Nelson Mandela in the early phases of the transition from National Party to African National Congress in the South Africa of the early 1990s. (These men, after all, won the Nobel Peace Prize *together*.)[14] Given powerful examples of public and publicized forgiveness, one could hardly deny the relevance of remorse, apology, and forgiveness in reconciliation. Furthermore, although these shifts are typically understood as purely individual in kind, they can be related in significant ways to relationships between groups. Yet it is not plausible to understand apology and forgiveness as strictly necessary for reconciliation. These are strong conditions, not strictly necessary, since even those who do not go so far as to engage in apology or forgiveness may form constructive and cooperative relationships.[15]

Moving along in the spectrum we arrive at the question of whether truth provides a route to reconciliation. Truth in this context should actually be understood as shorthand for "acknowledged truth." It is not truth itself that is important for reconciliation; it is the establishment, statement, and mutual acceptance of that truth. Truth itself is irrelevant unless it is both known and *acknowledged* by the people involved. In conflicted societies, the truth about what happened is notoriously difficult to establish. Even what would seem to be purely factual matters are often hotly contested. (Was this person in this village on that day? Did that person issue an order for that act to be done?) People tend to ignore, forget, select, deceive, and self-deceive—all of which makes the discovery of truths about bitter conflicts a difficult matter. Different constituencies have differing interpretations, expressed in powerful emotive narratives of their heroism, victimhood, and role in history.

When thorough research is completed and recognized, or when persons who have committed wrongs acknowledge them and express remorse to victims and the larger society, there are prospects for something richer than truth itself: the acknowledgment of that truth. Acknowledgment is centrally important for reconciliation and the term is often used in explanations and commentaries.[16] More than truth, more than knowledge of truth, acknowledgment involves a public consolidation and articulation of the truth. In contexts of reconciliation, "acknowledgment" refers mainly to recognition and admission on the part of former enemies that they have committed wrongs in the course of a political struggle. Acknowledgment in such contexts involves the admission that certain wrongful acts were committed, that such acts should not have been committed, and that those who committed them were responsible for having done so.[17] To publicly admit that past practices and actions were wrong is to imply that one will not pursue them again.[18] The converse is also true: when people do not acknowledge that they did something wrong, there will be—and will seem to be—a likelihood that they will commit similar acts in the future.

Acknowledgment can plausibly be regarded as necessary for reconciliation, because without it, fear and suspicion will work against the construction of decent relationships. The centrality of *acknowledgment* may explain why national reconciliation is so often tied to *truth commissions*. The proceedings and reports of these commissions provide a public forum for articulating fundamental truths and acknowledging their significance. Acknowledgment, in turn, is significant in relationships because of its connection with relationships and *trust*. Acknowledgment, needed for trust and confidence in functional relationships, involves beliefs and attitudes that crucially affect relationships between previously opposed groups and individuals.

An apparently promising conception is that of restorative justice; on this conception, wrongs are *righted* in a forward-looking way by having perpetrators acknowledge and repent and victims receive restitution and resources for their rehabilitation. The language of restorative justice is often used in discussions of reconciliation processes, that of the South African TRC being a prominent example. Amnesty was offered to some perpetrators, and when that policy was criticized as failing in justice, its defenders said that the TRC was pursuing justice in a nonretributive and appropriate sense; justice should be understood as restorative justice. The ideal is appealing, and there are successful practical implications, but, in political contexts, restorative justice is rather problematic.[19] Often, losses are so profound that significant compensation and repair are impossible. Furthermore, many perpetrators are unwilling to acknowledge wrongdoing and states have often been unable or unwilling to redress the profound harms suffered by thousands of victims.[20]

Restorative justice, though an ethically profound idea and one that is highly relevant in contexts of reconciliation, often fails to fit. When wrongs to victims cannot be repaired, we may turn our attention to the punishment of offenders. This has seemed to many to be a central aspect of building a sustainable peace. At level (8) on the spectrum, we face questions about the relationship between retributive justice and reconciliation. The ending of a culture of impunity, in which people committing crimes against humanity literally expect to get away with murder, is crucial in providing a sense of security and confidence. To many scholars and commentators, it has seemed obvious that what is needed are criminal trials, which should provide a fundamental sign that a period of impunity has ended. Without *justice* in a punitive sense, many who have been harmed will cultivate feelings of grievance and resentment, feelings that are dangerously counterproductive for the building of sustainable peace. The expectation is that trials would serve the function of relieving sentiments of revenge, thereby removing an important obstacle to the building of sustainable peace. Nevertheless, the challenges of reconciliation cannot be fully met in courts since the apparatus of criminal law is slow and expensive. Furthermore, in many contexts of rebuilding, legal institutions are seriously flawed or nonexistent. And given many thousands of persons involved in physical violence and human rights violations, criminal trials must be selective.

A deeper objection lies in the fact that the goal of reconciliation cannot plausibly be understood as that of having the worst offenders tried and punished. Reconciliation is about *relationships* between persons or groups alienated by conflict. It is highly implausible to suppose that simply by imposing hard treatment on selected parties we will succeed in building a positive relationship. At best, we might remove obstacles standing in the way. Highly significant for reconciliation would be the ending of impunity, the beginning of confidence and trust in legal institutions and proceedings, and the reduction of negative feelings such as fear, hatred, and suspicion. To the extent that punitive justice, retributively understood, is part of this picture, it enters in as a *means*, not as a guiding explanation of what reconciliation is.[21]

Moving to level (9) at the thin end of our spectrum, we come to consider accounts of national reconciliation as the building of institutions. These processes would include founding political parties, holding fair and transparent elections, establishing democratic parliaments and consultative bodies, building competent and uncorrupt legal systems, and training military and police in respect for human rights. Such stages of institution building are essential. Thinking in these terms, we may seem to have escaped the intangible realm of human feelings and attitudes. When agents and prospective donors consider such matters, they are likely to have some sense of tangibility and measurability. These are practical things that can be done—and it is crucial to pursue these tasks during efforts to rebuild a society and country. One may arrive, then, at a model of reconciliation as institution building, which can spare practitioners and theorists from addressing notions like grievance, resentment, and hatred or any other "fuzzy-wuzzy" or "touchy-feely" matters. Superficially considered, these activities appear to involve no need to allude to subjective matters such as feelings, beliefs, and attitudes. They are, in a sense, *thin*; they fall near the thinnest end of the spectrum here. Still more reductively and minimally, one may think of reconciliation simply as the cessation of physical violence between the individuals and groups who were involved in the conflict.

However, institution building and the discontinuation of physical violence are better thought of as necessary conditions of political reconciliation than as sufficient conditions.[22] The plain truth is: there are no people-proof institutions.[23] In parliament, the civil service, the judiciary, the military, or the police, people cannot operate as separate atoms. They must communicate and cooperate in order to do their work. It is *people* who construct institutions, *people* who must function inter-actively within them, *people* who will implement and adapt their organizational rules. The holding of an election is, in many respects, a concrete process. But behind measurable aspects such as voting behavior, numbers of monitors, and regulations about procedures and entitlements are beliefs and feelings about the former "enemy"—and confidence about physical security and entitlements to express one's ideas. Into such proceedings enter generalized notions of conflict and human nature itself. In an atmosphere where corruption is the norm, where traditions of repression make people unwilling to articulate differing opinions, or where parties organize on ethnic lines strongly associated with previous divisions, the electoral processes will be flawed. The same may be said of courts, parliament, political leaders, and the civil service. It is social as well as physical structure that has to be built. Social structure requires relationships—which is simply to say that, for reconciliation, attitudes, feel-ings, and expectations matter.

Reconciliation is a matter of coming together again in the *aftermath* of a violent conflict. If violence continues, there is no aftermath and, hence, no context for rec-onciliation.[24] In the aftermath, a first step toward building sustainable peace is a viable cease-fire. Killing and gross abuses of human rights must cease. At that point the wrongs are in the past and the time to respond to the wrongs and reconcile divided groups has arrived. The cessation needed for reconciliation must be sustain-able for national reconciliation to be a meaningful process and goal. But the possi-bility of escaping the domain of feelings and attitudes is more apparent than real. If nothing is done to address grievances and frustration, violence is all too likely to flare up again, and the peace of the cease-fire will have shown itself unsustainable. The absence of physical violence between former enemies is a necessary condition of a stable peace. It is a necessary condition of reconciliation of former enemies. But nonviolence, in this sense of the term, is sustainable only if relationships have improved. If nonviolence exists only in the minimal sense that there is sufficient repression to eliminate or reduce acts of physical violence, one can hardly say that peace is sustainable—or that there is anything like reconciliation. It is exactly because people must live together and work together that reconciliation matters. If past divides persist to structure present and future relationships, there will be little security in the new structures. In all this, relationships are fundamental; it matters how people see each other and how they feel about each other. Thus, even starting at the thinnest end of our spectrum, we are pulled back in the direction of the thick. Even when large groups of people are involved, feelings and attitudes matter.

TRUST, RELATIONSHIPS, AND RECONCILIATION

Sustainable peace requires decent relationships between previously divided and antagonistic people. To live together comfortably and sustainably in a single state or society, people will have to encounter each other, engage with each other, and, for many purposes, work together. Their *relationships* are fundamental in all this, which is just to say that their attitudes toward each other matter and matter enormously. In fact, we can understand political reconciliation as the building or rebuilding of relationships characterized by attitudes of acceptance and nonhostility.

Reconciliation is a coming together after a rift (political violence or oppression) that has undermined the capacity for decent cooperation between the people involved.[25] The process of reconciliation involves the cultivation of an improved relationship so the alienation can be overcome. The context of such reconciliation is, almost by definition, one of alienation and suspicion. That fact makes it difficult for persons harmed to *trust* those who have been their adversaries.[26] Especially when there is no acknowledgment of wrongdoing, there are reasons to suspect that these former enemies could return to inflict harm again. Such feelings are likely to exist within every affected group. If processes are genuinely those of reconciliation, people engaging in them will begin to overcome attitudes of fear and suspicion, and, in so doing, will develop more positive, constructive relationships. If there are effective processes of reconciliation, former enemies will begin to see each other as human beings capable of decent behavior—no longer enemies, but fellow citizens with whom they can live and work. What is crucial for reconciliation is that relationships of animosity and fear be replaced by better relationships characterized by acceptance, respect, and at least some degree of *trust*.

In all contexts, and at all levels, there is a need for reconciliation when relationships have been characterized by harmful practices, wrongdoing, violence, and bitter animosities. Insisting that people get over it and telling them that they *must* learn to live together again because there is no practical alternative simply will not suffice in such contexts. Nor will it be constructive to tell them to dig a hole and bury the past,[27] or to insist that, because they find themselves in geographical proximity, they simply *should* trust each other. Attitudes cannot be created at the snap of a finger or turned on and off like a tap. In the contexts in which national reconciliation is needed, people who are fearful and suspicious have good reasons for these attitudes, which emerge from their past experience and may be deeply entrenched. A developing sense of trust is fundamental in productive cooperative relationships, but that trust cannot be commanded into existence. Trust between former adversaries must be built on demonstrations that wrongs have been *acknowledged* and that efforts at *moral repair* are seriously being pursued by leaders and many citizens.

Trust is a basic and essential element of human relationships and is fundamental at all levels. We need trust because we must interact with and depend on other people—and yet we never have certainty as to what these others will do.[28] We cannot escape the fact that we live in a complex world in which other people's actions affect us considerably. Since we do not live separated from other people, we are always vulnerable to their actions. Typically, we have little control over the circumstances in which we find ourselves and have no way of eliminating our vulnerability to the actions of others. We have no secure knowledge as to what other people will do or how their actions will affect us for better or worse. Our expectations are largely based on experience, which provides us with evidence about individuals, groups, and even human nature itself. Experience provides a fundamental and yet uncertain base since contexts change and people change, both as individuals and in their group behavior.[29] People have some freedom of choice and decision and may act in different ways based on their own motivation and judgment.

Trust is an attitude of confident expectation that most others will act in a morally decent way most of the time. To trust other people in this sense is to believe—*in the absence of certainty*—that they will act in ways that are generally constructive and not harmful to us. If we trust, we can confidently engage in relationships and cooperative arrangements and accept some degree of vulnerability. In societies characterized by the rule of law and minimal violence, people are able to accept the risks of interdependence and social interaction without undue anxiety and fear. They do not regard themselves as having to interact on a regular basis with enemies intent on harming or killing them. Such confidence will not characterize those contexts in which national reconciliation is required. In such contexts, it is an understatement to say that attitudes are unlikely to be trusting and positive. There will be little trust between people divided by bitter conflicts in the past because there will be thousands—perhaps millions—of people whose life experiences have given them strong reasons to fear and distrust those they regard as adversaries. They know from bitter experience that others have the capacity—and the will—to impose pain, suffering, and harm. Their experiences support not generalized social trust and confidence but, rather, fear and suspicion. This is precisely why reconciliation is needed.

The need for some degree of trust between former adversaries becomes all the more obvious when we consider even relatively routine practical matters. Holding meetings? People will come along only if they are reasonably confident that their physical security is not at risk. Fact finding? It makes sense only if a reasonable proportion of witnesses can be believed and documents presented can be regarded as genuine. Courts? Their proceedings will seem meaningful only if judges and officials are regarded as uncorrupt and competent. Treaties? Signing makes sense only if one is confident that the other signatories will keep their word. Monitoring compliance? The monitors have to be trusted. Disarming? It will seem reasonable only if it appears safe; and it will appear safe only if one has reason to believe that the other side will not revert to violence.

A crucial point about trust is that it affects how we interpret actions and events. These things do not have their meaning written clearly upon them. It is people—we ourselves—who respond, interpret, and structure meanings. Whether and how we distrust, or trust, profoundly affects the meanings we construct. When we distrust others, we are likely to feel uneasy and suspicious about them; we may even be fearful as to what they might do. Distrust involves negative emotions about others and fear that they may harm us. When we distrust, we will regard the possibility of harm as one that is significant and must be taken into account when we are making our plans. Such feelings and beliefs are enough to make our relationship uneasy and unproductive. Furthermore, distrust will make us interpret events in negative ways. If materials are said to be lost, we will suspect that they have been destroyed or stolen. If there are calls for a mutual handing in of weapons, we will hear them as attempts to impose weakness on our side. Suggestions that would seem unproblematic within a good relationship ("bring your estimates of numbers to our meeting next week") will seem devious and threatening if the basic framework is one of suspicion.

We interpret events and actions according to our prior dispositions and beliefs. Highly prominent among these are the attitudes constitutive of trust and distrust. Without some degree of trust, it is difficult to improve a relationship; even benign initiatives will be received as suspicious.

We can think of trust at various levels: within families, between friends, within communities, between a community and an individual or group, and between groups in a broader society. The variety of levels is helpful for thinking about reconciliation; as we have seen, it exists for that topic too. These contexts differ in important ways but all involve relationships between people who will have different degrees of confidence in each other and will, as a result, construct relationships accordingly; this means that they will construct relationships based on their prior expectations and attitudes. Trust is not an all-or-nothing thing. Different contexts call for different dimensions and degrees of trust, and evidence supports trust to a greater or lesser degree depending on what is required. For example, trusting someone to mail a letter requires believing only that she is sufficiently capable and motivated to undertake a small task. Trusting her to care for a small child would require much greater confidence because so much more is at stake and a greater range of activities and functions will be involved.

The flexibility of the concept of trust is an important advantage when we seek understanding of reconciliation. Reconciliation involves different aspects in different contexts and trust, too, varies in degree and depth from one context to another while retaining its fundamental meaning. The range and depth of trust varies depending on the context and type of relationship involved. It is for this reason (among others) that an account of reconciliation in terms of trust can be helpful. Reconciliation between husband and wife is different from reconciliation between friends or community groups. In all cases, however, reconciliation centrally involves relationships and the attitudes characterizing them. In reconciliation there is a shift from attitudes of animosity, fear, and suspicion to those of respect, confidence, and acceptance. In the case of an intimate relationship such as that between sexual partners or close friends, the trust required must be deep enough and strong enough to facilitate self-revelation and intimacy. In a less intimate relationship, such as that between neighbors, trust is characteristically less deep—though that might shift if neighborly relationships came to involve an especially morally sensitive activity such as the joint supervision of children.

In contexts of community and national reconciliation, a crucial matter is the intent and capacity to refrain from further violence. But, as we have seen, this is only the beginning. When institutions are to be built and run, expectations about honesty, impartiality, and nonfavoritism will be central as well.

Reconciliation involves the *moral repair* of relationships. This moral repair will always involve the building of *trust* in some form. The focus of that trust marks the range of its expectations, and the degree of trust will vary from case to case. But for decent relationships, trust is always necessary.

The contested concept of national reconciliation can be understood as a repair in which considerations of trust are fundamental. Not only does trust incorporate emotions, beliefs, and attitudes underlying social actions and institutions, it also plays a key role in the construction of the meaning and, thus, in the potential for future cooperation. We can think of reconciliation as the moral repair of relationships, which are fundamental to human beings and social existence in so many ways and at so many levels. To build any kind of sustainable peace, social trust is required.

It is crucial not to confuse the various *means* that may be employed in the quest for reconciliation with reconciliation itself. In practice, the very notion of reconciliation as some kind of *end* or *goal* is somewhat hazardous. It may lead us to regard reconciliation as some kind of end state. That is an illusory notion because, outside fiction, lives and histories do not simply reach a positive goal and remain static. They continue over time; they evolve and develop; there may be further disagreements and ruptures. What is crucial for sustainable peace is not that there be no conflicts between individuals and groups but, rather, that within these relationships, people develop the capacity to handle the conflicts that do arise.[30] Societies sincerely and meaningfully engaging in "national reconciliation" are seeking to amend key relationships so as to shift away from hatred, fear, damaging oppression, and violence to a path of cooperation and trust.

CONTEXTS OF RECONCILIATION

Robert Manne, an Australian political scientist who became interested in reconciliation when learning about the harms done to the "Stolen Generation," distinguished two sorts of contexts in which societies seek reconciliation. One is the *settler society*; another is the society that has been convulsed by *civil war*. Australia, Canada, New Zealand, and the United States would fit into the settler context.[31] Sierra Leone, Peru, and—in very different ways—Rwanda and Northern Ireland would fit into the postwar context. To Manne's framework, we may usefully add a third context, that of the *post-totalitarian society*. Post-totalitarian societies would include post-communist countries such as Russia, Ukraine, and Hungary and former military dictatorships such as Chile and Argentina. In such societies, persons have been wronged by an oppressive state and its agents, including police, spies, the military, and civil servants. Although the term "reconciliation" is used in all these contexts, the issues and dynamics are rather different.

Generally speaking, in settler societies, largely powerless groups, namely, indigenous peoples, have been victimized by others, namely persons who have come to colonize and settle on the land. Characteristically in these situations, harm has gone in *one direction*. Many of the wrongs that will be highly significant for reconciliation have been committed in the fairly distant past; often those charged with responding constructively to them have benefited directly or indirectly from those wrongs. The aftermath of civil war (as in Sierra Leone or Peru) or serious civic violence (as in Northern Ireland) is markedly different because, in those cases, harm and damage have typically flowed in *two or more directions*. Violence has been used by two or more groups against each other and there will be victims, perpetrators, bystanders, and beneficiaries on all sides. Because political struggles usually become more complex as they evolve, civil wars are not merely between two contending groups. What began as two sides becomes further fragmented and complicated—as in Northern Ireland, Sierra Leone, and the Balkans.

In post-totalitarian situations, the picture is both more diffuse and more complex. People were wrongfully oppressed—but it is hard to single out victims and perpetrators because, in various respects, people colluded in their own oppression. Vaclav Havel famously argued that in communist countries such as his own Czechoslovakia (between 1945 and 1989), virtually every adult citizen could be regarded as a perpetrator of oppression; functioning in daily life required complicity with the system in many ways small and large.[32] At the same time, everyone could be regarded as a victim of the system too, given that every human life had been restricted and limited by the impositions of the system. Some referred to post-Soviet Russia as a lake of diffuse grievance, one with so many perpetrators and so many victims that even contemplating "wrongs" was virtually impossible.[33]

The widely cited case of apartheid South Africa is, interestingly, a blend of these three types. South Africa is a settler society; whites came and colonized the southern tip of Africa, ruling over indigenous Africans, oppressing them, and taking their land. This oppression was gross and legally explicit in the apartheid state, with its laws pertaining to voting, residence, internal passes, passports, and civil rights more generally. As resistance to apartheid grew, there was violence, and it was feared that that violence had escalated to the point of civil war. Whether the violent South Africa of the 1980s was or was not in a state of civil war is debated. Given the oppression needed to maintain apartheid, one could also argue that the South Africa that emerged in the early nineties was a post-totalitarian state. Other regions also exhibit a blend: in the Balkans of the early and mid-nineties, there was a situation of civil war in a post-communist context. The civil wars in Peru and Sierra Leone occurred in societies that were post-colonial and had experienced considerable government corruption and incompetence; the same may be said of East Timor. Realistically, however, these cases seem to count more plausibly as civil wars than as contexts in which wrongs have emerged in settler societies.

However different the contexts, it is not inaccurate to generalize to some extent. Certain roles emerge importantly in contexts when societies are trying to reorganize and rebuild in the wake of serious wrongs. Most significant are the roles of victim and perpetrator; to these we may add bystanders, beneficiaries, and interveners.

NOTES

1. Appendixes treat each of these contexts, providing basic background information.
2. President Ahmad Tejan Kabbah, speech, Freetown, April 14, 2003.
3. Fact Sheet 10, UNTAET Press Office, http://www.easttimor-reconciliation.org/CAVR%20Fact@20Sheet-E.htm (accessed March 2004).
4. The international level is not explicitly dealt with in this book.
5. For relevant discussions, see Fen Osler Hampson, *Nurturing Peace: Why Peace Settlements Succeed or Fail* (Washington, DC: United States Institute of Peace, 1996); Kenneth Boulding, *Stable Peace* (Austin: University of Texas Press, 1978); Nicole Negowetti, *Reconciliation: Central Components of Conflict Transformation*. Irish Peace Society, 2003; and David Bloomfield, Teresa Barnes, and Luc Huyse, *Reconciliation after Violent Conflict: A Handbook* (Stockholm: International Institute for Democratic and Electoral Assistance, 2003).
6. There are many possibilities, as subsequent discussions will show. There may be two or more parties; some or all may be individuals; some or all may be groups. As well as individual, community, and national reconciliation, we can think of reconciliation within a single self (e.g., "She finally became reconciled to her lack of success.") and in international contexts, as, for example, between the United States and Japan after the Second World War.
7. Among those noting problems of meaning are Susan Dwyer, in "Reconciliation for Realists," in *Dilemmas of Reconciliation*, ed. Carol A. L. Prager and Trudy Govier (Waterloo, ON: Wilfrid Laurier Press, 2003), and Wendy Lambourne, in "Post-Conflict Peacebuilding: Meeting Human Needs for Justice and Reconciliation," *Peace, Conflict and Development* (April 2004). Lambourne is influenced by Lederach but goes further than many in noting contradictory comments about justice and peace.
8. John Paul Lederach, *Building Peace: Sustainable Reconciliation in Divided Societies* (Washington, DC: United States Institute of Peace, 1997). This account is discussed briefly here because so many have found it so important. I confess to finding it less helpful than many due to its religious overtones and its figurative nature. My italics.
9. Strictly speaking, these are logically distinct in important ways. For A to show mercy to B, A must have some sort of power (usually official) over B. The same does not hold true of acceptance or forgiveness. Mercy is also clearly distinct from healing: one might show mercy without healing; in fact, one might show mercy out of fear and weakness and, by so doing, even inhibit one's healing.
10. Retributive justice is discussed in chapter 7.
11. See Trudy Govier and Wilhelm Verwoerd, "Trust and the Problem of National Reconciliation," *Philosophy of the Social Sciences* (2002):178–205. Verwoerd, who assisted with the writing of the *South African TRC Final Report*, noted that in that process there was no agreement among writers about the fundamental concept of national reconciliation.
12. Compare "Trust and the Problem of National Reconciliation."
13. In fact, conceptions of unity and harmony seem unrealistic even at the interpersonal level, given that people and circumstances change and new challenges will be faced. In marriage, if "two people become one," it has been because the will of one of them (traditionally the man) prevails. This situation is not desirable. People in groups, even the smallest ones, will always have differences; the question of success in their relationships is a matter of how those differences are handled and, crucially, whether they are handled without violence and oppression.

14. There were considerable disagreements and expressions of antagonism later, concerned in part with de Klerk's failure to accept responsibility for serious human rights abuses during the apartheid period.

15. Discussed in Trudy Govier, *Forgiveness and Revenge* (London: Routledge, 2002).

16. Acknowledgment is often alluded to and said to be pivotal, but it is seldom explained. For a preliminary attempt see my "What Is Acknowledgment and Why Is It Important?" in Prager and Govier, *Dilemmas of Reconciliation*, 65–90.

17. Such responsibility may be moral, legal, or both.

18. The Peruvian TRC, for example, stated that its report made it impossible to claim ignorance or incomprehension of the drama that occurred in that country, and that the understanding and awareness of the "shocking dimensions of what happened" make it "indispensable, if we wish to live in a civilized manner in peace and democracy, to make reparations, to the extent possible, for the serious harms that have been caused."

19. This fact was pointed out to me emphatically by Laura Skovel who said, "I was going to do my PhD on restorative justice (in reconciliation). But there isn't any." Interview with the author, Vancouver, March 2004.

20. This topic is explored in depth in chapter 9.

21. These matters are discussed in more detail in chapter 7.

22. Theoretical arguments about groups become relevant at this point. One such argument (not accepted here) is that thick reconciliation is necessarily a religious matter and has no place in a secular state. Another is that since groups are not individuals they, therefore, have no attitudes, emotions, or beliefs. On this theory, no account of *group* or *national* reconciliation can make sense if we interpret reconciliation as a matter of attitudes and feelings because groups necessarily lack such things. This theme is discussed in "Trust and the Problem of National Reconciliation" and also in Trudy Govier, *Social Trust and Human Communities* (Kingston and Montreal: McGill-Queen's University Press, 1997).

23. John Hardwig coined this phrase when discussing the need for trust when relying on experts, scientific or otherwise.

24. This remark is subject to some qualification, as is illustrated in the case of Northern Ireland. See appendix 4, Northern Ireland, for a description and discussion.

25. These comments are adapted, and extended, based on "Trust and the Problem of National Reconciliation."

26. Or whom they have defined as their adversaries.

27. For notions of burying the past, see David Chandler, "Coming to Terms with the Terror and History of Pol Pot's Cambodia (1975–79)," in Prager and Govier, *Dilemmas of Reconciliation*, 307–26.

28. I draw here on my own account of trust as expressed in *Social Trust and Human Communities* and *Dilemmas of Trust* (Montreal and Kingston: McGill-Queen's University Press, 1998).

29. In contexts of reconciliation, this point has positive potential, since the past behavior, during the violent conflict itself, was harmful.

30. Note: by "conflict" I do not necessarily mean "violent conflict." I am assuming that conflicts can be conducted by nonviolent, as well as by violent, means.

31. The extraordinary significance of a history of slavery within the United States is a distinguishing point; this vast problem is not treated in this book.

32. Vaclav Havel, "The Power of the Powerless," in *Living in Truth*, trans. Paul Wilson. (London: Faber and Faber, 1986).

33. This case is discussed in many places including Tina Rosenburg, *The Haunted Land: Facing Europe's Ghosts after Communism* (New York: Vintage, 1996); Janet Keeping, "National Reconciliation in Russia?" in Prager and Govier, *Dilemmas of Reconciliation*, pp. 327–43; and Ryszard Kapuscinski, *Imperium* (Toronto: Vintage Canada, 1995). When I lectured briefly on past wrongs at a summer school near Moscow in July 2005, I found participants (all lecturers in ethics in Russia or another post-communist country) agreeing that the most common response to wrongs of the past was to ignore them.

Chapter Two

Victims, Perpetrators,
Bystanders, and Beneficiaries

In most contexts where reconciliation is sought, each party to the conflict will have its victims and its perpetrators. Reconciliation processes have to deal with persons harmed, commonly called victims. They also have to deal with those who have been agents of harm, commonly called perpetrators. There appears to be a fundamental dichotomy here, between victims and perpetrators. The terminology of "victims" and "perpetrators" has struck thoughtful observers as unsatisfactory in various ways—as potentially polarizing, oversimplifying, and counterproductive. There seems little alternative to using this dichotomous language. Yet clearly the roles of victim and perpetrator are not exclusive; some people are both victims and perpetrators. Neither do these terms exhaust the possibilities; people may also stand in the roles of bystanders or beneficiaries.

The dichotomization of victim and perpetrator roles can usefully be examined from four perspectives: those of logic, morality, social psychology, and prudence.

1. LOGIC, LABELS, AND ASSUMPTIONS

From the point of view of language and logic, the labeling of a person as either a "victim" or a "perpetrator" is often itself an oversimplification. When we use these labels, we suggest that one action of a person's experience is overwhelmingly significant in defining who that person is. Clearly, a person harmed by a wrongful action is, in that sense, a victim of wrongdoing, but equally clearly that person is not only, or merely, a victim. He or she is a human being likely to play many roles in the world—parent, teacher, gardener, musician, and so on. He or she is a person with potential for development and change, and capacities to transcend the victim role. Although victims may struggle with serious injuries and trauma persisting long after the injury was imposed on them, and such after-effects can be profoundly significant, moral and political status as a victim never exhaustively characterizes a person. There is such a thing as the role of a victim, and persons harmed may occupy, and be understood to occupy, that role. The "victim" label can be misleading in suggesting ideas of passive suffering, neglecting more positive capacities. This point has been noted by persons who have insisted that they are *not* victims and that, in virtue of their determination and power, they wish to be regarded as *survivors*.

Critical points can also be made regarding the notion of perpetrator. Labels such as "perpetrator," "offender," "terrorist," and "militant"—even "combatant," "ex-combatant," or "ex-prisoner"—tend to be simplifying and *reductionistic*. For these reasons, such terms are often objectionable.[1] At the time when a person commits an act of political violence or uses lethal force, he or she is an agent harming another person and may be termed a perpetrator, offender, combatant, or militant. This person has taken on the role of being an agent of violence. But he or she is not only this; rather, this person is a human being with many other qualities and capacities.[2] If we consider those who, in the past, have been agents of violence, they may be ready to assume new roles. Labeling them purely and simply as "perpetrators" risks ignoring that possibility. *The Final Report of the South African Truth and Reconciliation Commission of South Africa* strongly cautions against reductionist labeling, stating that it is "essential to examine perpetrators as multi-dimensional and rounded individuals rather than simply characterising them as purveyors of horrendous acts."[3]

The need to reject reductive language was underlined recently by a direct participant in the Northern Ireland "Troubles" who served many years in prison for a politically motivated killing. Introducing himself at a meeting in Belfast, he said: "Hi, I am John. I am a loyalist ex-prisoner . . . but I am also an ex-baby, an ex-ship-yard worker, an ex-football player, and an ex-husband."[4]

The labels "victim" and "perpetrator" often function to encourage polarized thinking. The phenomenon recalls the textbook fallacy of false dichotomy, which can be illustrated by considering nonpolitical examples. Consider, for instance, the contrast between ugliness and beauty. These are contrary notions—"opposites," we colloquially say. We often assume that because qualities are opposites, a person must be characterized by one or the other. But when we make that assumption, we have lapsed into falsely dichotomous thinking. There are intermediate possibilities between beauty and ugliness; moderate attractiveness is an obvious example. Similarly, a person who fails to win does not thereby merit the label "loser," and one who is not a friend does not thereby become an enemy.

In these cases, there is a whole range of phenomena. We can think of this range as a kind of spectrum. There is, for instance, a spectrum of degrees of attractiveness, ranging from ugliness to beauty; there is a spectrum of degrees of success, ranging from abject failure to conspicuous and complete success; there is a spectrum of degrees of friendliness in a relationship, ranging from enemy to close and intimate friend. Encouraged perhaps by "yes/no" or "true/false" thinking that (with qualifications) is integral to logic itself, we too often focus our attention on the contrasting end points of the spectrum and neglect to consider the middle zone. When we think in sharply dichotomous ways, we lapse into a simplistic either/or framework. We forget the all-important middle, assuming incorrectly that the opposites at the ends exhaustively characterize a situation. Such dichotomous thinking is distorting and can be harmful because it leads us to neglect significant possibilities in ways that can inhibit imagination, misrepresent realities, and distort policy. Clearly the victim/perpetrator opposition is not *exhaustive*; there are many persons who are neither victims nor perpetrators.

Nor is this distinction exclusive. Like many oppositional distinctions, the victim/perpetrator distinction fails to be *exclusive* in the sense that there are cases of persons who are both victims and perpetrators. When this happens, a person may be correctly characterized by two contrary characteristics. For example, a person may be a success in some respects and a failure in others; she may be beautiful in some respects and ugly in others. Analogously, a person may be a victim in some respects and a perpetrator in others. In one and the same political conflict a person may be the relative of someone killed and, in that respect, be in the role of a victim of violence; at the same time, as a supplier of explosive materials, he may be in the role of a perpetrator of violence. Victims may become perpetrators out of a desire for revenge. This situation is common in the case of Palestinian suicide bombers who were relatives of persons killed by the Israeli army.

If some perpetrators are, in some respects, victims, then, by the same token, some victims are, in some respects, perpetrators.[5] It is often assumed that *all* victims are passive and bear no responsibility for acts committed during a conflict. But, strictly speaking, this assumption is incorrect. Like other persons, those who have occupied the role of *victim* have many aspects to their character. Let us call the act in which a perpetrator injures a victim the *paradigmatic act*. With regard to the paradigmatic act, the victim may very well have been entirely passive and innocent. She was, perhaps, doing nothing but walking along the street, taking a bus, taking the elevator to her office, or sitting in a pub. But it does not follow from a victim's innocence and passivity with regard to the paradigmatic act that she shares no responsibility for acts and policies in other situations affecting the conflict.

The notion that a victim is *purely and only* a victim may work to endorse a kind of moral arrogance. Focusing on the undeserved nature of the harm and on the suffering that has resulted from it, and encouraged by a culture in which the discourse of victimhood has enjoyed prominence, many persons take on the role of victim and find incentives to concentrate on the paradigmatic act while ignoring its context and background conditions. It is easy to overcommit to the role of victim. Cultural attitudes giving the moral upper hand to victims often function to encourage clinging to a sense of injury and grievance; these sentiments can be seriously counterproductive in the building of relationships with former enemies. Rather than thinking of a *person as a victim*, it might be more accurate to think of the role of a victim as one that persons may occupy, along with other roles.

The paradigmatic act is one in which an agent uses physical force to kill or injure another person who is, in that context, a passive and innocent victim. It is the tragic truth that many such acts are committed when people choose to wage political struggles using violent means. The significance of such acts for victims, perpetrators, and community members is enormous. But even granting this significance, roles within these acts should not be allowed to define the involved persons for the rest of their lives. To extrapolate from the paradigmatic act so as to think that some people are (forever and only) victims and others are (forever and only) perpetrators is to reason carelessly and to underestimate the complexity of conflict situations.[6]

2. THE MORAL PERSPECTIVE: RESPONSIBILITY AND EQUITY

(a) Levels of Victimhood, Levels of Perpetration

There are several levels at which people may suffer harm in the course of political violence. In addition to persons directly injured, usually referred to as *primary* victims, there are the *secondary* victims, those family members and close friends of the primary victims who are harmed by their injury or death. Furthermore, there are *tertiary* victims: persons in the broader community—and the community itself—which may be harmed in various ways.[7] When we think of victims, we tend to think first of primary victims. In apartheid South Africa, for instance, a victim might be a black community leader arrested for helping to organize a community demonstration and tortured in jail. Many such persons were, in fact, killed in jail and never seen again by their family members. Steve Biko, for example, was one of many primary victims (V1) in the struggle against apartheid. Biko left a wife and children; in addition to their loss and grief, these family members were harmed economically and socially by his death. They can be termed secondary victims (V2). Nor does the story end there; there was a loss to black Africans of the talents and energies of this activist leader. Members of this broader community are tertiary victims (V3).

The Australian government's 1997 report *Bringing Them Home* provides many vivid and tragic illustrations of these three levels of victimhood. When an aboriginal or mixed-race child was forcibly removed from parents—as was a common practice for much of the twentieth century in Australia—that child was the primary victim of the removal. Consequences resulting for these children included emotional trauma, cultural denigration, and physical and sexual abuse.[8] Obviously, in these cases the parents from whom the children were taken were also victims, as were other relatives. Parents and relatives were secondary victims, and communities were tertiary victims.[9] The report put the matter this way:

> When a child was forcibly removed that child's entire community lost, often permanently, its chance to perpetuate itself in that child. The Inquiry has concluded that this was a primary objective of forcible removals and is the reason why they amount to genocide.[10]

When we think of the damage resulting from severe political conflict, we tend to think first of primary victims. When we consider secondary and tertiary victims, we can see that harm extends outward from these people to affect others affiliated with them.

Less widely recognized is the fact that we can also distinguish different levels of perpetration, or agency. Just as we can distinguish V1, V2, and V3, we can distinguish P1, P2, and P3. We can begin with the *direct* or *primary* participants in a conflict in terms of their intent and causal role in bringing about harmful actions. Two sorts of persons fall into this category: agents on the ground and those who directed them—that is to say, militant agents and leaders. The militants are those persons who engage physically in acts of force or violence. Such agents may commit assaults, pull the triggers on guns, place bombs under buses, or blow themselves up in public places, killing and injuring other people while doing so. In contexts of political violence, such acts are typically regarded by militants and their leaders as justified; they are committed intentionally and voluntarily. In support of militants, and essential to their actions, are their leaders, financers, and organizers. These persons make decisions about strategy and tactics and play a close role in obtaining support from the community on whose behalf they believe themselves to be fighting. Insofar as they have sponsored, planned, and directed the actions of the militants, they share responsibility for them.[11] Thus, agents on the ground and their leaders can be regarded as primary perpetrators (P1s) of acts of violence.

At a secondary level are persons who are close to the violent action but are neither the immediate agents nor the instigators of it. In legal language, these persons may be said to "aid and abet" the direct actions of militants. They may, for example, drive getaway cars, shelter attackers immediately before an attack or when they are "on the run," provide food to persons being trained as militants, offer advice to recruiters, deliver guns or explosives, and so on. In the case of suicide bombers, these secondary perpetrators may make videos to be shown after the militant is dead. Such people are active members of a group engaged in conflict; they identify with the goals of that group and they know how the violent struggle is being waged. They know about the actions, approve them, and support them. Because of their knowledge and approval, it is appropriate to say that such people intend that the actions of militants occur. When involved in supporting a specific action—say the bombing of a nightclub—these people do not qualify as primary perpetrators. They are neither the leaders who planned the operation nor the militants who carried it out. Nevertheless, they share goals and intentions with these people, and, through their supportive actions, they causally contribute to the bombing. By aiding and abetting, they share moral responsibility for the act. Such people can be called *secondary* perpetrators (P2s).

In any political conflict, behind primary and secondary participants are many others who support the struggle of the group in various ways. Some will also endorse the violent means used to wage the struggle. Thus, we come to see a larger circle of *tertiary* participants (P3s) in the political struggle. At this stage, issues of moral responsibility are complex. Many members of the community will identify with their side and support it, believing that their own community or group has a *just cause* against its opponents. Substantial numbers will go further, supporting the idea that the group is justified in employing *violent means* to pursue what it regards as a just cause. Without this support, the violent struggle would not, in fact, be a political one. Community support is necessary, and those who supply it contribute to the struggle and bear some responsibility for actions taken within it. Their support helps to facilitate it; without that support, the violent struggle could not be waged at all. Thus, given this contribution, these "backers" *share moral responsibility* for the actions committed by militants and planned by leaders. Thus, we can see that a considerable number of people, though not P1s or P2s, are, nonetheless, involved in supporting actions of violence and bear some degree of moral responsibility for those acts. These people can be regarded as tertiary participants (P3s). Tertiary participants *share the intention* of the group engaged in violence and make a *causal contribution* to its efforts; accordingly, they bear some degree of moral responsibility for the acts committed by P1s and assisted by P2s.

Given the need for support from a broader community, violent acts in a political conflict do not and could not result solely from the acts and efforts of primary and secondary agents. Many people at higher and lower ranks of community life and organization share responsibility for them and qualify as tertiary participants. These people are not involved with carrying out, directing, or closely assisting particular acts of violence.[12] However, their contributions are no less intentional, and no less essential from a causal point of view. The support of many persons in a broader politically committed community facilitates violent actions on the ground. Group culture supports and makes possible the context in which violent acts are undertaken within a political struggle. Many people who are not primary or secondary participants in a political conflict contribute to the antagonistic cultural patterns underlying it.[13] Tertiary participants maintain the customs, discourse, and practices that support the antagonistic divisions underlying the violent conflict. They support their side in the conflict and may be complicit with its conduct in many ways: by participating in antagonistic discourse, making financial contributions, supporting educational and religious programs of a sectarian or divisive nature, privately cheering deaths on "the other side," or simply being silent when hatred and violence are advocated and undertaken within their community or group.

The claim that persons who were neither militants, nor leaders, nor close collaborators are, nevertheless, *participants* in a conflict and share some *responsibility* for acts committed within it tends, for various reasons, to be contested.[14] (Motives could be suspected here; we might ourselves be participants sharing responsibility in this sense, and have an incentive to deny our involvement.) Perplexing issues arise in many cases. One relevant point is that support for political violence may take the form of acts of omission—people may facilitate actions by not objecting when others advocate them, or do nothing to inhibit or prevent the activities of P1s and P2s.

Another consideration is that people who broadly support the struggle may be in circumstances of partial ignorance, self-deception, or denial with regard to what is being done for the cause, ostensibly on their behalf. They may approve in a general way of violent means used on their behalf, and yet not know in advance about some particular action of which they would disapprove if they were fully informed and thought carefully about the matter. A person might, for example, support a cause and support a violent struggle in general, without knowing that the militants and leaders active in the cause are planning to bomb a specific nightclub at a specific time. She might claim, in the aftermath, to have known nothing about this act, to have had nothing to do with it, and to bear no responsibility for it. In one sense, her defensive claim would be correct. Given her ignorance, she is not morally responsible for that particular act, because it cannot reasonably be argued that she intended that that act be committed or causally contributed to it as a particular act. But that is not the end of the story. If, within the community that is waging the struggle, this person has supported the cause as just and endorsed violent means as a way of pursuing that cause, she has contributed to the violence more generally speaking and bears a degree of moral responsibility for that violence. Thus, such a person qualifies as a tertiary participant in violent acts in general, though not of some particular act.[15]

While explicit discussion of primary, secondary, and tertiary agents is rare, the fact of widely shared moral responsibility has been acknowledged in some contexts.[16] Consider, for example, the case of apartheid South Africa. Policemen who brutally interrogated and in some cases killed black activists would be regarded as primary perpetrators. These men did what they did using state resources and with the support of an ideology and a state insisting that black activists were terrorists and communists who endangered the survival of the white community. Their immediate superiors, who gave orders and ran the institutions in which these acts were done, would also be regarded as primary perpetrators, as would the higher officials who directed them. Those who willingly gave support on the scene—doctors who were in attendance when prisoners were being tortured, for instance—can be regarded as secondary perpetrators. And the broader mainly white community that supported an apartheid regime and voted in elections to maintain its continued political power would be tertiary participants.

At the South African TRC Military Forces hearing, former major Craig M. Williamson said:

> Our weapons, ammunition, uniforms, vehicles, radios and other equipment were all developed and provided by industry. Our finances and banking were done by bankers who even gave us covert credit cards for covert operations. Our Chaplains prayed for our victory and our universities educated us in war. Our propaganda was carried by the media and our political masters were voted back into power time after time with ever increasing majorities. It is therefore not only the task of the members of the Security Forces to examine themselves and their deeds. It is for every member of the society we served to do so.

When he speaks of "our," Williamson is alluding to the South African army as it was involved in fighting against African National Congress forces based in neighboring countries. We can see that the circle of secondary and tertiary participants was rather large in this case. Consider, for instance, the bankers. Williamson asserted that bankers issued *covert* credit cards for the fighters. Those credit cards were intended to be used to fund *covert* operations across the borders. If we assume this much, then in issuing the credit cards, the South African bankers knowingly and intentionally functioned to support the war between the South African apartheid government and black border states supportive of the anti-apartheid African National Congress. The bankers bear moral responsibility for *knowingly* issuing those credit cards, which were a *causal contribution* to the war being waged by the apartheid state. Given this intention, and given that the credit cards were causally relevant in helping the fighters to work for their cause, the bankers can rightly be said to share moral responsibility for actions committed by the South African army in the context of that war. They were tertiary or even in some cases secondary participants. The same sort of argument can be made for the businesspeople, chaplains, and media—and, by extension, South African citizens who voted for the National Party during this period.

Without the support of tertiary and secondary participants, a violent struggle could not be waged as a *political* conflict. Causally, it is inaccurate to suppose that agents on the ground are the only persons responsible for actions in which victims have been harmed. Such a stance also involves moral error. To criminalize and stigmatize agents on the ground—and only them—amounts to scapegoating and constitutes a serious injustice. This view was expressed by General C. Viljoen, former head of the South African Defence Force.

> I still maintain it is unfair that the operators be exposed as the chief perpetrators of atrocities and violence in general when the politicians and strategy managers hide behind their status and positions. *The iniquity of our past was of a political nature first.*[17]

In making this claim that the conflict over South African apartheid was political, Viljoen is stating that it was a conflict that involved groups in a violent struggle over political power and the nature of state institutions. Within this conflict, an individual committing a violent act against another individual was acting politically with the backing and resources of many others in his or her community. If these others had not supported this person, he or she would not have acted in that way. In many cases, such actions would have been simply and literally impossible.

(b) Considering Bystanders and Beneficiaries

Important questions arise about the relationship between tertiary participants and two other roles often referred to in contexts of aftermath, those of bystander and beneficiary. Although there are typically many tertiary participants in a violent political conflict, not *everyone* in a given community counts as a tertiary perpetrator. Some people do not participate in struggles because they are not in a full sense moral agents; young children or persons suffering from dementia to the point of losing their understanding of the world would fall into that category.[18] Others do not participate because they do *not* support what their community is doing in the conflict; they express that lack of support by speaking out. They oppose actions that are undertaken on behalf of their community or seek roles as mediators and peacemakers. Others living in a context of political conflict may fail to participate because they are not members of the communities in contention. They may have recently arrived on the scene from elsewhere or for some other reason may not identify themselves with any of the contending groups. All such uninvolved people may be termed bystanders in a neutral sense of that term.

The term "bystander" is often used with decidedly nonneutral implications. There is an established negative sense in which the bystander is a person who *merely* stood by when he or she could have acted so as to prevent wrongs. Such a person may be deemed a guilty bystander. A guilty bystander is one who, with minimal risk to himself or herself, could have intervened so as to prevent a serious wrong, but failed to do so. Instead, the guilty bystander failed to act, often in a public environment where the violence was visible, and allowed serious wrongs to be committed. The notion of a bystander in this negative sense is modeled on the notorious Kitty Genovese case. In New York, in 1964, Kitty Genovese was raped and murdered while she screamed desperately for help. Thirty-eight people who witnessed the crime did nothing whatsoever to intervene, failing even to take the minimal step of making a telephone call to police.[19]

Many persons who would claim status as neutral bystanders may be regarded as guilty bystanders. For instance, it might be argued that persons who had the capacity to protest apartheid policies but did not do so in effect *supported* those policies by their failure to act. They were bystanders in a guilty sense, bystanders whose inaction helped to make apartheid seem legitimate. If guilty bystanders, by their failure to intervene in any way, facilitate wrongful actions, should they be deemed tertiary participants? This suggestion has been made and has a certain plausibility. In the end, however, it should be resisted for logical reasons; a *bystander* is not a *participant*.[20]

As used here, the word "bystander" is intended to have its neutral meaning. When that meaning is not intended, the expression "guilty bystander" will be used. Bystanders, in the neutral sense, are persons who did not participate in wrongdoing and share no moral responsibility for it. A person may be regarded as a guilty bystander if he or she was in a position to intervene, with little personal risk, to prevent a wrong, but failed to do so. As a guilty bystander, a person can be deemed morally responsible for his or her failure to intervene. Guilty bystanders share some responsibility, but are not to be identified with tertiary perpetrators.[21]

The role of beneficiaries, like that of bystanders, must be logically distinguished from that of tertiary participants. One helpful way of appreciating the distinction is to consider the factor of time. As causal contributors to a political struggle, tertiary perpetrators must be involved at the time, or prior to the time, when the acts are committed. (One cannot assist in the causation of actions after they have happened.) By contrast, beneficiaries of oppressive policies sometimes receive their benefits later, many years after wrongs were committed. Consider, for instance, such countries as Canada and Australia. A citizen born in 1965 could not possibly have been a tertiary perpetrator in the takeover of aboriginal lands, given that those takeovers happened long before her birth. She can, however, be said to be a beneficiary of these actions, insofar as she lives in a country in which a settler population was able to acquire the land and settle according to its own legal and cultural practices. We can see, then, that many beneficiaries are not tertiary participants.

However, it is possible for the roles of beneficiary and participant—whether primary, secondary, or tertiary—to overlap. They can overlap in the sense that some persons may occupy several of these roles at once. Although not all beneficiaries are participants, some participants are also beneficiaries. For example, settlers who came to countries such as Canada and Australia to take over indigenous lands can be deemed to be participants in policies of colonization and also beneficiaries of those policies. Similarly, in apartheid South Africa, many white persons who supported apartheid practices and were, in that sense, tertiary participants were also *beneficiaries* of the system. (For example, white South Africans were able to employ black people at low wages and enjoy an extremely high standard of living.)

(c) The Issue of Scapegoating

In the aftermath of political violence, primary perpetrators—in particular, militant agents on the ground—may be the only persons labeled as perpetrators. Often such persons are socially shunned, have criminal records, and are barred from many occupations and opportunities. In effect, they are scapegoated. This scapegoating results from insufficient acknowledgment of the various ways people have participated in the violence. Wanting to recover from bitter troubles, people who understand themselves as never having shared any involvement in the conflict are all too ready to exonerate themselves by blaming these others, whom they brand as criminals or terrorists. At the same time, former leaders in the struggle, who were also primary perpetrators, may have become respected political figures. Leaders may have been needed in the process of reaching a political settlement and, as a result, they may have acquired a political role that restored them to respectability. They can be members of government, sit in parliament, and appear on television as respected commentators while, at the same time, many of those whom they recruited as militants are castigated as men of violence with blood on their hands. Burdened by criminal records and years of restricted opportunities to develop careers and relationships, former militants are often stigmatized in the aftermath of a conflict.[22] Such differential treatment is clearly unfair. Such singling out is inaccurate, misrepresents causal and moral responsibility, and is clearly objectionable from an ethical point of view. It results in a discounting and undermining of the human dignity and worth of many persons.

3. THE PERSPECTIVE OF SOCIAL PSYCHOLOGY

Arguments against the criminalization and unfair scapegoating of certain primary perpetrators are also supported by social psychological research into the causes of political violence. The central message of a chapter on "Causes, Motives and Perspectives of Perpetrators" in the *South African TRC Final Report* is that the most plausible and coherent explanations for involvement in violent political conflict are *not* to be found in the realm of individual psychology. Involvement is not a matter of psychological dysfunctions or abnormalities. Rather, the most fertile explanatory ground is provided by the complex interplay of political frameworks, social identities, and specific situations.

The message of this key chapter can be illustrated by taking as an example a typical white member of the South African security forces, referred to in Craig Williamson's statement quoted above.[23] Let us recall Williamson's references to the roles of industry, bankers, chaplains, educators, politicians, and voters. Given these considerations, it is unlikely that a search for *understanding* of a security policeman's brutal use of force against a black South African will focus simply on the policeman's individual personality traits. To merely ascribe his actions to his being some kind of sadist or psychopath or to his having an authoritarian personality type would be highly simplistic because it would fail to consider the social and political context in which those actions occur. Nor will references to the man's rage, frustration, or revenge be relevant if we are seeking to understand his dark *political* actions. Rather than focussing on individual traits, we would need to begin by locating the specific actions of this policeman within a broad *political* framework. That framework would include the legacy of the Anglo-Boer War, the Cold War, and processes of decolonization in Africa.[24] In the struggle over apartheid, these are the historical conditions that effectively framed and fueled political violence by Afrikaners against black Africans. Afrikaners, the group standing behind this policeman, saw themselves as fighting under the banner "defense of an Afrikaner homeland against communist-inspired black terrorists." To understand the actions of a typical white security force member in apartheid South Africa, one would need to untangle his intertwined *social* identities. These would likely include a racial and racist identity as a white South African under apartheid; an ethnic identity as an Afrikaner; a religious identity as a member of the powerful Dutch Reformed Church; a male identity as a man who grew up in a patriarchal culture, with its macho values further deepened by the militarism; and a citizen identity as a patriot and good soldier.

In its *Final Report*, the South African TRC stated that these political frameworks and social identities functioned as preconditions for the violence carried out by many security force members. The painful story of political perpetrators does not end there, however. The report goes on to state that "if there is a single dominant message emerging from psychological research over the past fifty years, it is a tale that emphasises *the persuasive power of the immediate situation*." Without denying possibilities of resistance by individuals, it is claimed that certain situations provide triggers of violence. Consider, for instance, the typical white, Afrikaner, Christian, and militarized security policeman in a situation where he is actually faced with a black person held in detention for demonstrating against the apartheid state. In this situation, like most of his colleagues, the policeman would likely deem himself to be *authorized* to use physical force (through being ordered or implicitly encouraged to do so, or because he was functioning in a context in which there was tacit approval). Because the black person has been *dehumanized* to the point where he is regarded solely as a terrorist or communist enemy, the policeman is likely to use extreme force. Often he will feel pride in doing so, thinking of himself as "doing his duty." Similar comments apply to another situation that occurred often, and tragically, in black townships. A group of young people returning from a political rally see someone they believe to be an *impimpi* (informer); or they see a white person whom they have come to regard as an oppressor and a *settler* who stole their land. Someone shouts, "let's necklace him." Soon "ordinary" young people, together, engage in an act of extraordinary violence—one that, in different circumstances, they would not have dreamed of committing.

Though these examples are taken from the South African context, similar social psychological insights clearly apply elsewhere. To consider just one other example, during the "Troubles" in and about Northern Ireland, there were many people who became immersed in centuries of Irish-British conflict and developed strong Republican or Loyalist social identities. Those identities were deepened by membership in military or paramilitary organizations. Many of these people—often teenagers— were unable or unwilling to resist the persuasive power of immediate situations in which physical violence appeared to be the most realistic action against a dehumanized enemy. A crucial point here—and one that is denied by those who criminalize only primary perpetrators—is that many of the "boys" or "lads" would most likely not have become engaged in violence at all had it not been for this political context.

This plea for a deeper understanding of the behavior of violent political agents does not mean that all efforts to evaluate actions and hold people accountable for them should simply be given up. The relevance of contextual factors does not prove that individual moral responsibility should be relinquished as a relevant concept. People do make choices, and there is room for considerations of degrees of moral responsibility when wrongs are committed in violent political struggles. The point made by the South African TRC is that a complex interplay among political frameworks, social identities, and immediate situations underlies the use of extreme force in political conflicts. While emphasizing the historical context of violence and the many situational factors influencing individuals, the commission stopped short of taking a fully deterministic position. It did not assert that people were *compelled* to act as they did. Noting that some options of resistance remained open, the report stated that

> it is dangerous to regard situational forces as inevitable, since there are always possibilities of resistance, it would be as much of an error to see resistance to situational forces as *merely* freedom of choice, strength of character, or individual moral maturity.[25]

In other words, there *were* possibilities of resistance; the idea that agents will *inevitably* commit serious acts of violence is resisted. But it would be a mistake to reflect on such situations *only* by attending to options that were open to individuals and fail to consider social and situational factors. Such factors were relevant in important ways.

A similar and highly relevant statement was made by Christopher Browning, a leading Holocaust scholar and author of the widely read book *Ordinary Men*. In that work, Browning used extensive documentary evidence to argue that many "ordinary men" chose continued involvement in duties that involved personally engaging in the massacres of Jews—even though these men could have opted out with immunity. Browning emphasized that *there were choices* for many agents involved in Nazi killings. One could choose not to engage in mass killings of Jews and still survive as an individual and even as a soldier. The punishment for such refusal was not death or even demotion. Given the powerful Nazi regime, the prevalence of extreme anti-Semitic propaganda in German culture over many years, and the ongoing war, the circumstances were highly unusual. When these ordinary men did choose to kill Jews en masse, there were circumstantial factors relevant to their making such a choice. Having argued this point, Browning added that "explaining is not excusing, understanding is not forgiving."[26]

In other words, historical and situational factors may help to explain *why* people do certain things, but to say that they have this explanatory role is *not* to say that such actions are excusable or inevitable. Despite the horror of this historical context, some choices remained for individual agents.

But the crucial point here is not one about choice, or about excuses or even forgiveness. Rather, it concerns the stigmatization of primary perpetrators. Once we acknowledge the vital roles of political frameworks and social identities in political violence, it becomes more difficult to disown militants and former militants as having political blood on their hands and, in this respect, being especially and singularly morally culpable, while others further removed from the violence bear no responsibility for it. Although the acts of militants are likely to be more dramatic and conspicuous than those of other persons, they are by no means the only morally significant acts in contexts of political violence. To think of them that way would be a considerable oversimplification.

An awareness of the vulnerability of ordinary people to the persuasive power of certain situations argues against a rigid notion of the evil perpetrator. Once we become sensitive to the pull of situations, it becomes more difficult to point arrogant moral fingers at individual militants. The humbling point should be, "If I were placed in the same situation, with the same set of social identities, it could have been me."

4. PRUDENCE AND PRACTICALITY

So far as political violence is concerned, the perspectives of social psychology are vital in order to develop effective measures to *prevent* further violence. If certain contextual factors make political violence likely, one needs to understand those factors to avoid perpetuating the violence. So far as reconciliation is concerned, sustaining a cease-fire is obviously a key point. A better understanding of these factors could encourage reconciliation processes that concentrate instead on building improved relationships between affected individuals and groups. To reduce the persuasive power of situations, what is needed is a culture characterized by inclusiveness and openness. There must be room for disagreement, debate, and sensitivity to various forms of dehumanization. Scapegoating is incompatible with these attitudes.

It is crucial to consider roles of perpetrators and victims from a pragmatic perspective. Whatever else may be involved, in terms of institutions, resources, and social healing, sustainable peace requires an ongoing and secure cessation of political violence. Minimally, reconciliation requires that previously opposed parties do not resume the use of physical force against each other. If political conflict continues, it must be waged by nonviolent political means.

Persons who have acted as militants in a political conflict have often built their lives around fighting for the cause. Many were recruited at a young age and have built their sense of meaning and self around the political struggle in which they have been engaged. Engaging in a violent struggle that is accepted by their community as necessary for its survival is likely to provide a rich and deep sense of identity and purpose. When such a struggle ends, there is a serious risk of these former militants being left in a radically disoriented position, with no firm sense of identity or role. Given that such persons have become accustomed to seeking goals by violent means, it is an understatement to say that such a situation will be unstable. If these persons are not reabsorbed into society, there is a serious risk that they will resume activities harmful to others. Some may reengage in political violence while others resort to criminal acts. Responding to the needs of former militants is a crucial practical matter.[27]

In Northern Ireland, both Republican and Loyalist groupings include many former militants, often referred to as "ex-combatants." In some cases, their terms were long and substantial chunks of their adult lives were spent in hard and isolated conditions. After the Good Friday accords of 1998, many such persons came to identify themselves as "ex-prisoners." In Northern Ireland, persons with criminal records are restricted in their opportunities. As militants or former militants in a political conflict diminishing in intensity, they no longer have the community support that they once did. A major aspect of reconciliation is to arrive at the point where acts of violence are regarded as criminal, rather than political. For that goal to be achieved, new roles and identities will have to be found by those persons who previously built their lives around the political struggle. If these prospects are not open, the resumption of political or criminal violence will stand as an ongoing and serious temptation.

Reductionism, objectionable from a logical and ethical point of view, is refuted by the facts of some striking and inspiring cases. A man who might have bombed a bus or committed an act of execution at the height of a political struggle may gain professional training and commit himself to community leadership, accomplishing many valuable things in the aftermath. Some ex-militants and ex-prisoners have become dedicated community leaders, a phenomenon that exposes the limitations of reductionism and powerfully illustrates the human potential for moral change. There are powerful examples of ex-prisoners from Northern Ireland who have gained considerable skills in mediation and conflict resolution and have traveled to Bosnia, Kosovo, Macedonia, Moldova, and elsewhere to work with youths in those areas.[28] They have developed skills and insights that enable them to make effective contributions in these troubled areas, where their efforts have been well received. If a person is to accomplish such things, he must be able to engage in interactions with people who receive him as a human being with creative abilities and capacities and who do not reductively regard him as forever a "perpetrator," "offender," or "terrorist." Clearly, labeling, polarizing, and stigmatizing are unlikely to be helpful in providing for the relationships needed in contexts of political reconciliation. Nor will such hypocrisy and scapegoating go unnoticed by primary perpetrators. Such attitudes and policies will be resented and will contribute further to alienation and discontent.

And yet the tendency to denigrate primary perpetrators remains powerful. The striking achievements of some who have become community leaders may not be attainable by others. The danger of stigmatizing and alienating agents of violence is clear; when primary perpetrators survive a violent conflict and are left with no income or role in its aftermath, they become, and remain, a threat to sustainable peace.

FURTHER COMMENTS

It is understandable that persons in civil society will mark physically violent acts as having crossed a certain important threshold. There are deep reasons for singling out paradigmatic acts and regarding them as particularly threatening to personal security and rule of law. The special significance of such acts is well stated by Joseph Liechty and Cecilia Clegg in a recent book on sectarianism in Northern Ireland.

> Any act of violence shatters the web of relating, not only at the physical but also at the psychological level. It shatters it in a way that makes trusting very difficult and the way back very long, because the perpetrators and/or their group can become an unconscious symbol of threat and hurt for those traumatized.[29]

Reflecting on paradigmatic acts, we might reach the conclusion that it is the primary perpetrators of such acts and, in particular, agents on the ground, who constitute the major threat to physical security in the aftermath. It will seem a plausible corollary that these are dangerous and fearsome people and that sustainable reconciliation will require their isolation. Even after considering the arguments presented here, many may wish to claim that if militants and ex-militants are ostracized when society is rebuilding, they are getting just the treatment they deserve. In paradigmatic acts, there is nearly always a clear and sharp moral distinction between the passive innocent victim and the guilty violent perpetrator. But roles that characterize paradigmatic acts should not be assumed to hold for all other contexts. To play the victim role once is not to play it always and everywhere. To play the perpetrator role once is not to play it always and everywhere. If we fail to appreciate that point, we have fallen into logical and ethical errors that will be counterproductive for the building of constructive and trusting relationships.

In extreme cases, some may believe that militants in a violent political conflict have committed evil acts that will taint them forever. From the nature of these acts, some may infer that the militants are morally irredeemable—unforgivable in an absolute sense—and could never reform or contribute meaningfully to a reconstructed society. To this line of thought, there are two fundamental objections. Even when an act is gravely wrong, the logical distinction between the *act* and the *agent* remains valid.[30] Furthermore, we must recall the distinction between an act committed in a context of a political conflict and an ordinary crime. When a political conflict is resolved or altered, the motivation for violent acts within it will be undercut. In contrast, the motivation for ordinary crime is unaffected by alternations in the political context.

The seriousness of paradigmatic acts helps to explain the common desire to shun those who have committed them—even those who have acted with community support. A more detailed consideration of moral responsibility suggests that the shunning of primary perpetrators and them alone is not justified. Over the medium and longer term, castigating and ostracizing attitudes are likely to undermine reconciliation and endanger the security of all persons in the society—including the many victims of the previous political violence.

While the needs of victims should be acknowledged and respected, recognition for victims does not require that former militants be regarded as unforgivable and irredeemable. Empirically, there are examples of persons who were agents in a violent struggle and went on to lead constructive lives in its aftermath. From a moral point of view, commitment to norms of human dignity and rights carries with it a commitment to the possibility of moral change in any human being. Whatever one might say about the nature or justifiability of the militants' violent acts, to regard them as incapable of moral change is to disregard their humanity.

A simplistic focus on individual agents or perpetrators may be encouraged by the individualist workings of the criminal justice system, the sensationalism that often characterizes media reports, and the all-too-human desire to deny shared responsibility. Against such individualization, the point is that polarized oppositions between victims and perpetrators exemplify a kind of antagonistic thinking that amounts to a sort of intellectual imprisonment. The concern for accuracy, even at the cost of complexity, was hauntingly captured in a statement by Paul Russell, who said, "If truth is the main casualty in war, then ambiguity is another. . . . One of the legacies of war is a habit of simple distinction, simplification and opposition . . . which continues to do much of our thinking for us."[31]

If primary agents are not reabsorbed into society, there is a considerable likelihood of their reverting to the lives for which they had been trained. Whether such persons reengage in political violence or resort to criminal acts, those acts will also have their victims. Failure to reintegrate ex-combatants will create more victims—

and it might even revictimize some of the same persons harmed in the original conflict. Thus, even if one presumes that the primary focus should be a concern for the needs and interests of victims, that concern will lead directly to a need to properly understand and reintegrate ex-combatants.

Any simplistic polarization of "victims" and "perpetrators" will be a handicap, so far as processes of reconciliation are concerned.

NOTES

1. One might argue that any word can become a label and work in a reductionistic way. (This suggestion was made by Risa Kawchuk.) For example, "mother" and "housewife," though having positive or neutral meanings in some contexts, may be applied and interpreted as exhaustively describing who women are. When this happens, these words function as reductive and limiting labels—and that is objectionable. Obviously, the same is true for descriptive terms such as "disabled," "diabetic," or "obese." People who have these characteristics do not *only* have these characteristics, and these characteristics should not be understood as definitive of their identities. For the issues of "victims" and "survivors," see (for example) the *Truth and Reconciliation Commission of South Africa Final Report* (Cape Town: Juta and Co., 1998), I: 58–59. The commission ultimately decided to use the word "victim," but acknowledged that many described as victims might prefer to be described as survivors. In fact, many of the victims had played such a crucial role in the struggle that "even the term 'survivor' might seem an inadequate description" (p. 59).

2. This point has been strongly urged by Desmond Tutu, who repeatedly emphasizes that we must distinguish the sinner from the sin. See, for example, *No Future without Forgiveness* (New York: Doubleday–Random House, 1999). A similar idea has been urged in a secular framework in Trudy Govier, *Forgiveness and Revenge* (London: Routledge, 2002).

3. *South African TRC, Final Report*, 5:259.

4. Reported to me by Wilhelm Verwoerd, who was in attendance at this workshop.

5. These claims are, of course, logically equivalent.

6. This has been the experience of Wilhelm Verwoerd, in the context of facilitation work in Northern Ireland.

7. This point is standard in reconciliation literature. See, for instance, David Bloomfield, Teresa Barnes, and Luc Huyse, ed., *Reconciliation after Violent Conflict: A Handbook*, (Stockholm: International Institute for Democratic and Electoral Assistance, 2003).

8. See the appendix on Australia for further details.

9. The Australian report suggests a similar view—that it is true both that persons in the broader community were harmed as individuals and that the community itself, as a collectivity, was harmed.

10. *Bringing Them Home*, http://www.austlii.edu.au/au/special/rsjproject/rsjlibrary/hreoc/stolen.

11. This would be true whether we speak of *moral* or *legal* responsibility.

12. By acts of violence, I mean acts of physical violence such as the assault, physical torture, battery, wounding, or killing of persons. Also included would be severe cases of property violence such as the destruction or severe damaging of homes, buildings, bridges, and roads. Not included are minor acts of property violence such as writing graffiti on fences.

13. A similar analysis of shared responsibility is given in Joseph Liechty and Cecilia Clegg, *Moving beyond Sectarianism: Religion, Conflict, and Reconciliation in Northern Ireland* (Dublin: Columba Press, 2001).

14. That has been my experience when speaking about the topic.

15. The notion of affected ignorance applies here. One might argue that if a person is supportive of a cause and its means, generally, and yet avoids information that could inform her as to the specifics of acts committed by its agents, she is in a state of *affected ignorance* and bears some responsibility for that. I have been assisted in these reflections by the work of Tracy Isaacs, who does not, however, share responsibility for the application of her reflections here. In addition to correspondence, the key paper by Isaacs is "Individual Responsibility for Collective Wrongs," in *Bringing Power to Justice*, ed. Joanna Harrington, Michael Milde, and Richard Vernon. (Montreal and Kingston: McGill-Queen's University Press, in press), pp. 267–308.

16. The notion that responsibility for perpetration should be extended beyond primary agents is also presented in Bloomfield et al., *Reconciliation after Violent Conflict*. It is not explained in the same manner as here. The editors move from primary agents directly to consider the responsibilities of bystanders and beneficiaries. Thus, they omit consideration of what are called here secondary and tertiary perpetrators. (The approach of perpetrator/ bystander/beneficiary was also taken by the TRC in South Africa; see its *Final Report*, 1:132–34).

17. *South African TRC, Final Report*, 5:277. My emphasis.

18. Child soldiers are a special case and will be considered in chapter 8. As immature and vulnerable persons, child soldiers can be regarded as having been compelled to carry out actions for which they do *not* bear moral responsibility.

19. B. Latane and J. M. Darley, *The Unresponsive Bystander: Why Doesn't He Help?* (Englewood Cliffs, NJ: Prentice-Hall, 1970).

20. To see the distinction, consider, for instance, persons of Chinese origin in the context of the Northern Ireland situation. If such persons are not members of either Catholic/Republic or Protestant/Loyalist communities, and play no role in either community with regard to the conflict, they are bystanders in the neutral sense of that term.

21. The suggestion has been put to me in several discussions; however, while accepting that the guilty bystander bears responsibility, my inclination is to resist it. The roles of "bystander" and "participant" *are* genuinely contrary in the sense that one cannot play both at once.

22. The question of whether such prisoners were political was, of course, strongly contested during the Troubles in Northern Ireland. See the appendix on Northern Ireland for relevant information.

23. This chapter, contained in volume 5 of the *Final Report of the South African TRC*, was written by Professor Don Foster.

24. For relevant details, consult appendix 8, South Africa.

25. Ibid., p. 292. My emphasis.

26. Christopher Browning, *Ordinary Men* (New York: HarperCollins, 1992).

27. The problem of reintegrating ex-combatants is explored in detail in chapter 8.

28. There are also, of course, negative examples. See chapter 8 and appendix 4, Northern Ireland, for examples.

29. Liechty and Clegg, *Moving beyond Sectarianism*, p. 145.

30. Discussed in Govier, *Forgiveness and Revenge*, chapter 5.

31. Cited in Antje Krog, *Country of My Skull* (Johannesburg: Random House South Africa, 1998), p. 99. I owe this reference to Wilhelm Verwoerd.

Chapter Three

Acknowledgment: Its Potential and Challenges

In the introduction to his book *A Miracle, A Universe*, Lawrence Weschler describes a conference at which participants struggled to come to terms with the concept of acknowledgment. Weschler says:

> Fragile, tentative democracies time and again hurl themselves toward an abyss, struggling over this issue of truth. It's a mysteriously, powerful, almost magical notion, because often everyone already knows the truth—everyone knows who the torturers were and what they did, the torturers know that everyone knows, and everyone knows that they know. Why, then, this need to risk everything to render that knowledge explicit? The participants . . . worried this question around the table several times—distinctions here seemed particularly slippery and elusive—until Thomas Nagel, a professor of philosophy and law at New York University, almost stumbled upon an answer. "It's the difference," Nagel said haltingly, "between knowledge and acknowledgement. It's what happens and can only happen to knowledge when it becomes officially sanctioned, when it is made part of the public cognitive scene."[1]

CALLS FOR ACKNOWLEDGMENT

Emphasizing the importance of acknowledgment for reconciliation, Human Rights Watch stated the point in bald terms.

> It is impossible to expect "reconciliation" if part of the population refuses to accept that anything was ever wrong, and the other part has never received any acknowledgement of what it has undergone, or of the ultimate responsibility for that suffering.[2]

A recent handbook on reconciliation states:

> The acknowledgement of what happened is a way of breaking the vicious circle of impunity: silence and amnesia are the enemies of justice.[3]

45

Such statements have been echoed around the world.

An international conference on post-truth commission processes, held in Lima, Peru, in 2003, was called "From Denial to Acknowledgement." Speaking there, Salomon Lerner Febres, president of the Peruvian Truth and Reconciliation Commission, stressed that when societies are in transition, it is crucially important to establish processes to seek and state the truth. Febres said:

> The search for truth after a conflict . . . can constitute a second, precious opportunity for societies. . . . Bringing to light the truth is not only a way of acknowledging victims and identifying perpetrators and harms; it can also be a way to discover ourselves."[4]

> With the submission of its report to the country, the TRC believes that *if it had ever been possible to claim ignorance* or incomprehension of the drama that occurred in the early years of the conflict, *it is no longer possible to do so.*[5]

In Australia, a national Sorry Day was established to acknowledge and honor the stolen generations of Aboriginal children.[6] The Australian prime minister, John Howard, has not been willing to issue an official *apology* for the past practices; however, he has made and endorsed statements of *acknowledgment*.[7] A motion of acknowledgment was passed in the Australian parliament in August 1999, moved by Howard.

In a 1996 report on Canada's Aboriginal peoples, a Canadian Royal Commission stated that the situation of Aboriginal peoples was the single most important human rights issue confronting Canada. The report called for apologies as a form of acknowledgment and a step toward compensation for "the affront to dignity, self-respect and self-determination" implicit in many relocations. In 1991, the Canadian Human Rights Commission had recommended government apologies for various aspects of native/white relations in Canada, including forced relocations, the brutal system of residential schools, the treatment of veterans, and the exploitative failure to take treaty commitments seriously.[8] In its survey of relations between Aboriginal peoples and those who came later to settle in their territory and found the nation of Canada, the report notes that official Canadian history tends to downplay or even ignore the role and perspectives of Aboriginal people. It calls for *acknowledgment* of these peoples and cultures, of the wrongs done to them, and of their contribution to Canadian history and society.

> The government of Canada, on behalf of the Canadian people, must acknowledge and express deep regret for the spiritual, cultural, economic and physical violence visited upon Aboriginal people, as individuals and as nations, in the past. And they must make a public commitment that such violence will never again be permitted or supported.[9]

And later, with regard to healing, the report stated:

Healing will begin in earnest only when governments *acknowledge* that relocation practices, however well-intentioned, contributed to a denial of human rights. *Acknowledging* responsibility assists in the necessary healing process because it creates room for dialogue about the reasons for relocation. . . . Aboriginal people need to know that governments accept responsibility for relocations and recognize their effects. *Recognition and responsibility* are the necessary first steps to overcoming the many adverse effects of relocations.[10]

The acknowledgment of past wrongs and of the persons who had suffered from them was also a primary goal of South Africa's Truth and Reconciliation Commission. In his introduction to the *TRC Final Report*, Archbishop Desmond Tutu alluded to Ariel Dorfman's well-known work *Death and the Maiden*, which explores a torture victim's temptation to exact revenge on the man who tortured her. She has him tied up when he admits that what he did was wrong. Then, says Tutu, "his admission restores her dignity and her identity. Her experience is confirmed as real and not illusory, and her sense of self is affirmed." A central purpose of the South African truth commission was to "acknowledge the tragedy of human suffering wherever it has occurred," whether victims were black or white.

Alex Boraine, deputy chairman of the South African TRC, makes similar comments, explaining that it is not the truth itself that is important, but, rather, the *human working of the truth*, the truth that is humanly, socially, and politically acknowledged. In other words, acknowledgment is the crucial thing.

Knowledge must be accompanied by acknowledgement of accountability. Public acknowledgement that thousands of South Africans had paid a very high price for democracy affirmed the human dignity of the victims and survivors. It was an integral part of the healing of South African society.[11]

After the work of the TRC in South Africa, it would no longer be possible for white South Africans to deny what had happened under apartheid, to dismiss the wrongs, and to excuse themselves by saying, "I did not know." Andre Du Toit, an academic commentator, said that truth in the form of acknowledgment was a key moral conception of that country's TRC. The commission's banner, displayed at hearings, was "Truth, the Road to Reconciliation." The underlying assumption was that knowing and publicizing the *truth* about what had happened was a needed step in building improved relationships.[12] Du Toit comments usefully on the relationship between truth and acknowledgment. Bringing out the truth about abuses of the past is a matter of publicly articulating known facts as facts—facts now established, recognized by public bodies, and no longer reasonably deniable.

Acknowledgment is more than truth and more than knowledge. In the aftermath of political violence, there is a need not only to *know* the *truth* about what happened but to articulate and recognize that knowledge. This requires acknowledgment as contrasted with denial. Denial, states Du Toit, amounts to a display of power on the part of those who have committed wrongs. In refusing to acknowledge what they have done to others, these persons display their political power and impunity. Their denial amounts to a denial of the human and civic dignity of the victims of wrong-doing and, as such, to a further violation of them. Victims will be fearful of persons who, by their denial, indicate an expectation of acting with impunity. Du Toit's account begins to explain why acknowledgment is important: acknowledgment of dignity and legal status begins the restoration of civic status to persons previously treated as though they lacked it.

WHAT IS ACKNOWLEDGMENT?

There are many contexts in which we speak of acknowledgment. We may acknowledge the receipt of a message by letting the sender know that it arrived. We may acknowledge objections to our arguments by allowing that they exist, explaining what they are, and describing the lines of a reply. We may acknowledge the presence of another person passing in the street by nodding or saying "good morning" to him or her. We may acknowledge the contributions others have made to our work; here acknowledgment is typically the public statement of their names with gratitude for the contribution. We may acknowledge our own deficiencies, our addictions and diseases, our need to reform. But it is not these forms of acknowledgment that are most significant for reconciliation. In reconciliation, two kinds of acknowledgment are paramount: the acknowledgment of wrongdoing and the acknowledgment of the human beings who have been harmed by it.

In the aftermath of political violence, reconciliation—almost by necessity—occurs in a context where serious wrongs have been committed.[13] People in many countries have been marginalized, deprived of legal and social benefits, assaulted, wounded, tortured, and killed in contexts of oppression and political violence. Calls for acknowledgment are, in the first instance, *calls for those responsible for committing such wrongs to recognize and admit having done so, and to articulate or represent that admission in a public forum* so that it becomes an enduring part of the public history of the state and society. The public admission and expression amount to acknowledgment. Because acknowledging that one has committed wrongs is not generally a pleasant thing, this is a kind of *aversive* acknowledgment. Aversive acknowledgment, in this sense, has fundamental presuppositions: that the acts in questions were wrong, that the persons charged with committing them did in fact do so, and that they were responsible for doing so.

The second form of acknowledgment, also fundamental in contexts of reconciliation, is acknowledgment that the persons who were harmed possess human worth and dignity and merit full and equal human rights in their state and society. This may be called *existential* acknowledgment. Racist and colonial attitudes or ethnic or religious prejudice often served as an underlying "justification" or excuse for wrongful treatment of people regarded as less than fully human. Thus, acknowledgment of the moral dignity and equality of denigrated persons and the cultural groups to which

ONE face policies, citizenship, duty

they belong is an essential element of reconciliation. Persons insulted as "primitives," "barbarians," "savages," "vermin," or "cockroaches" must be acknowledged as human beings, as citizens meriting respect and full legal status. +++

In this context, aversive acknowledgment and existential acknowledgment are closely connected. To acknowledge that denigrating and wounding policies were wrong is, in effect, to admit that the harmed persons affected deserved better. As human beings that merited equal consideration with others, these people should not have been treated as they were. In this respect, acknowledgment of wrongdoing implies acknowledgment of their dignity, rights, and civil status. If these people had been treated as full members of the society, such wrongs as discrimination, cultural denigration, physical abuse, and compulsory relocation would never have occurred.

At the conference described by Weschler, participants discussed a situation in which many people knew that certain individuals had been torturers under a military regime, but those widely known facts had not been publicly acknowledged. In other words, those facts were not openly admitted and taken into account. To acknowledge them would mean spelling out what the practices of torture were, saying who ordered or condoned them, and naming the persons who carried out those practices. That would mean public exposure of those who had been torturers or had ordered and supported the practice. Such acknowledgment would, presumably, be the first step toward ending the practices. If the practices are not acknowledged, people will see no need to terminate them. Weschler referred to a context in which knowledge existed and was widespread prior to its being publicly articulated. But not every case has this feature. There are many contexts in which the truths in question are not generally known prior to the inquiry. Often research is required and findings are made; then, acknowledgment is made for claims that are discovered, as distinct from facts that were known prior to investigations.

Whether it is discovered or preexisting, knowledge is presupposed by the demand for aversive acknowledgment. To urge that a group or institution acknowledge wrongdoing is to assume that such wrongdoing did actually occur, that the fact of its occurrence is known, and that this fact should be publicly articulated. Acknowledgment is the admission or statement of wrongdoing to the public. Acts that should not have been committed were committed; it is these acts that were committed; these were the agents; and these were the persons harmed. These realities, once acknowledged, can no longer be ignored or denied.

Acknowledgment, in this sense, can be contrasted with denial. But since denial may take many forms, there is no instant clarification to be found through this contrast. Denial can be a matter of *deception* in the form of lying—as when a government knows full well that it has directed police to undertake a campaign of repression but denies having done so when asked. Frequently, denial takes the more complex form of *selective attention*: people ignore certain aspects of their world that they would prefer not to attend to. In Canada, the notion of "two founding peoples" (French and English) illustrates denial in this second sense; the Aboriginal presence prior to the arrival of French and English is ignored and implicitly denied. Those who assert that Canada has two founding nations are not exactly *lying*. (When people lie, they assert to others a claim they believe to be false, with the intention of getting those others to believe it.) The problem with the language of "two founding nations" is that no attention is paid to undisputed (indeed indisputable) facts. Aboriginal peoples occupied what is now Canadian territory before European traders and settlers arrived; interactions between Aboriginal peoples and Europeans have been central to the history of Canada; the land of Canada was Aboriginal land. Yet the "two founding nations" expression fails to incorporate any recognition of those fundamental truths, which are *ignored*. In this case, denial amounts to ignoring something known to nearly everyone.

Denial based on ignoring is based on selective attention and can amount to self-deception. Sometimes, known facts are ignored by choice; we choose to ignore so that we can construct a more satisfying story for ourselves. When we deceive ourselves, we attend selectively and omit or reinterpret evidence that would count against what we want to believe. Self-deception depends on attention selected for some purpose; we know something but choose to ignore what we know and choose not to pursue the topic further because we suspect that the further information we would obtain would be uncomfortable for us. (We do know enough to give us this suspicion.) Self-deception can be a matter of individual psychology. Indeed, its complexities are great at that level; the paradox of self-deception in individuals has absorbed philosophers for at least forty years. It is asked: how can we deceive ourselves, if what is required is that we believe one thing and yet (in some sense) know the very opposite? These phenomena can also be social. Groups can be said to deceive themselves when their members assist each other in "conveniently" ignoring or "forgetting" unpleasant aspects of their histories. In a recent article on ignoring, Annette Baier remarks on the phenomenon of selective social attention as it exists within groups.

> These phenomena, of sensible selective attention, of selective recall, of imperfect record keeping or cover-up of our own past selective control, are normal human phenomenology, both for individuals and for groups. Nations attend to some calls on their attention more than to others, write selective histories, and rewrite them as establishments and ideologies of change. Also, social mechanisms of many kinds assist individuals in their individual self-deceptive activities, especially when these are coordinated with the maintenance of the preferred collective memory that is needed for a group's self-esteem. War veterans' memories of what slaughter they participated in or witnessed may be uncomfortable memories both for them personally and for the national record. Psychiatric services help soothe and play down such memories as could be disruptive. In a free nation, the press, the film industry, and the book trade can serve as important curbs on this smoothing over of the blemishes on our shared past, can serve to revive uncomfortable memories and to stir up painful awareness of what we would understandably prefer to forget, or to continue to ignore.[14]

Both within groups and as individuals, we may choose to ignore unpleasant facts and events that we would rather not consider. The chosen picture of reality seems to serve us better, in the sense of making us more happy and comfortable, because certain emotionally negative matters have not been incorporated. In groups and as individuals, we have a powerful capacity to deny what we do not wish to avow. To attend to unpleasant facts about suffering and damaged individuals would mean amending our favored narrative about our identity and place in the world. In contexts of reconciliation, calls for acknowledgment are calls to admit what we have done to others so as to construct an honest and equitable relationship with those injured by wrongdoing.

The phenomenon of ignoring is interesting in several respects. Ignoring things does not mean simply being in a state where one does not know about them. Quite the opposite is the case: to *ignore* something we must first have some *awareness* of it. To consider a highly mundane example—removed from reconciliation contexts but perhaps useful for that very reason—consider the householder who ignores cobwebs in a high corner of a room. To ignore their presence, she must first know that these cobwebs are there—she has, perhaps, noticed them while dusting a nearby bookshelf. Unable to reach them, too lazy to fetch a chair, she decides to ignore them. In other words, to ignore them, she must first notice them and then decide to put them out of her mind—not think about them any further and not do anything about them. There is a choice made, a choice that requires a moment of knowing what it is that one decides to ignore. Clearly, there are elements of deliberateness in the case: there is that moment of conscious awareness on which the decision to *ignore* is based. Once we have decided to ignore something, ignorance of further facts will usually result. If she continues to ignore the cobwebs in the corner, the householder will then fail to have further knowledge about them; for example, she will not notice whether they attract dust, entrap small flies, or grow into a state of greasy ugliness.[15] And so it is that selective attention in the form of ignoring leads to ignorance about those things that we have decided to ignore. Having decided to ignore the cobwebs, the householder becomes ignorant of a number of facts about them, facts that were and remain quite accessible to her, facts that she easily could have come to know and could have remembered. Instead of acquiring that knowledge, she chose to ignore.

To remark that some phenomenon has been *ignored* is to suggest that it should not have been ignored but should, rather, have received attention. The householder who ignores cobwebs might be criticized for doing so; one might presume that she should have dusted more carefully. If we point out that someone has ignored cobwebs in her house, there is already a suggestion of failure in the mere claim that she has ignored them.[16]

Yet not all ignoring is culpable. In fact, some ignoring is a necessity. As finite human beings, we are incapable of attending to every phenomenon and event, of directing our attention to every aspect of what is presented to us in our lives. Some things we never notice at all, so we cannot be claimed to ignore them. But many other things we may notice briefly and then dismiss as not meriting our further attention. We must do this in order to cope with the world; we cannot attend to everything and cannot even attend to everything we notice. Selective attention is an unavoidable feature of the human condition for individuals and groups alike. People may disagree, and quite reasonably disagree, about what merits attention. Consider, for example, the case of a museum of local history that fails to display in its exhibits memorabilia relating to the history and winnings of a popular local soccer team. Some might criticize the museum for ignoring and failing to display such memorabilia, while others would defend its decision, arguing that the soccer theme is relatively unimportant.[17] Clearly, such a museum cannot acknowledge *all* local stories and achievements. Choices must be made; there will be a selection, and people may rightly ignore certain stories and artifacts.[18]

So ignoring is not always culpable. And yet, some cases of ignoring *are* culpable. In contexts of reconciliation, attention to people and relationships is crucially important. Given their importance for building trust and overcoming alienation, statements and policies of acknowledgment have great significance. Denial is almost certainly harmful to people, and it is because harmful denial is so common that calls for acknowledgment are so ubiquitous. Such calls for acknowledgment assume that denial and ignorance are inappropriate and damaging. For most of us, reflecting on the suffering of others is painful—especially if we who share responsibility for causing that suffering are urged to admit our role and accept the implied costs. In these contexts, people often have a powerful incentive to protect themselves by attending selectively to history and ignoring unwelcome aspects of their stories.

We may ignore the protestations of those who suffer in the aftermath of wrongs, fail to listen, and fail to hear and understand. We may become so oblivious to cries and protestations, to reports of abuse and suffering, that we ignore the evidence and act as though the harmed people barely exist at all. We can choose to ignore many facts, problems, and cries of pain. Then, as a result of ignoring, we know little about these others with whom we are in relationships flawed by denial. If wrongs are claimed, if we are called upon to acknowledge and reconcile, we then plead that we did not know. At this point, the choice presupposed in ignoring is highly salient. We *did* notice something; we *did* know something. We knew enough to know that we wanted to avoid paying attention to a situation, choosing instead to ignore it. We chose to ignore evidence and failed to discover truths that we could have suspected and did suspect—truths that would be unsettling because they would be incompatible with favored views of our communities and selves. We knew enough to know we did not want to know more. So, in this crucial sense, our lack of knowledge was chosen— it was willed and willful. If we can truly say now that we did not know, we can say that because, at some time in the past, we chose to ignore and not to learn more.

At this point, where the rights and well-being of other human beings is concerned, it is fair to regard inattention and ignoring as wrong in themselves. Ignoring the suffering of other people is far more serious than ignoring cobwebs on the ceiling or the story of the local soccer team. It is morally objectionable because it allows us to deny any obligations to damaged people. It allows us to hold back from asking whether we share responsibility for the acts and policies that caused this harm and suffering. It enables us to avoid asking whether we should take on some responsibility for responding to the damage that has been done.[19] Ignoring the suffering of others, we may avoid knowing whether we are in any sense responsible for that suffering; we have ignored evidence that could have led us to that knowledge. In addition to being morally culpable, this sort of "affected ignorance" may be criticized as being extremely unwise. It is unwise because it is imprudent. Our resulting insensitivity and lack of awareness undermine the possibility of constructing better relationships in the aftermath of wrongdoing. Harmed persons, often angry and resentful, receive no assurance that their concerns are being heard and the damaging policies will cease.

In a recent book, *States of Denial*, Stanley Cohen argues that denial is common for human beings and is a more normal condition than its opposite, acknowledgment itself.[20] Cohen, who has lived both in South Africa and in Israel, has worked with Amnesty International on appeals for aid. Those appeals communicate vivid information about suffering and go on to request help for efforts intended to diminish the suffering. Their intent is often that help be given in the form of financial donations. Thus, the context of Cohen's reflections on the phenomenon of denial is not one in which reconciliation is the central issue or even an issue at all. Cohen is considering cases in which relatively safe and secure citizens are presented with evidence about the suffering of people in distant countries. There is usually no implication that these people have themselves caused this suffering or share moral responsibility for it. What interests Cohen is the human response to this sort of information. Will people ignore it? Or will they acknowledge it, acknowledging in the strong sense of actually responding to the appeal for help?

According to Cohen, denial involves matters of cognition, emotion, value, and action. Acknowledgment, as the converse of denial, involves the same things. To Cohen, acknowledging that some wrong has been committed means more than accepting certain claims and avowing one's knowledge of them. Acknowledgment also involves feelings, values, and rectifying actions. Those who would deny unwelcome facts seek to maintain a social world in which undesirable and uncomfortable situations go unrecognized as such. Those things are ignored or reinterpreted so as to seem normal. Cohen allows that all human life involves some denial; it is impossible to pay full attention to everything. He even allows that in some cases—such as personal struggles with debilitating diseases—denial can be constructive and helpful. But in political life, where people can and do suffer enormously as a result of the action or inaction of others, Cohen states that denial cannot be condoned. People with positive illusions about themselves, their groups, and their role in the world can be enabled by denial to commit terrible atrocities.[21] Although, for leaders, "pessimism of the head" and "optimism of the heart" may amount to a good combination, Cohen states emphatically that social justice should never be entrusted to "these pseudo-stupid optimists, with their positive illusions and creative self-deceptions."

Just as there are varieties of acknowledgment, there are gradations of denial. People may deny altogether that a wrong has occurred. They may, as an initial stage, admit that the wrong has occurred, but insist that it is an isolated incident and not typical. They may acknowledge that this sort of thing used to happen and was wrong and inexcusable, but claim that they have corrected the problem and it does not happen anymore.

Cohen describes how political wrongs such as those committed during the Holocaust may be an *open secret* in societies and communities, which can show a bizarre combination of literal denial and ideological justification of the acts. About German concentration camps, people admitted to having noticed certain things such as Jewish neighbors disappearing overnight. Many people came to accept such things as normal and asked no further questions. They suppressed and ignored their suspicions—sensing that if they had asked some questions they would have had to ask more. If they had investigated and had come to understand what was going on, there would have been implications for action, implications incompatible with going on with "normal" life, something to which most people cling with desperate affection. Albert Speer, who Cohen calls the most intensely studied case of "I didn't know" since Oedipus, was an inner member of Hitler's circle. Speer admitted in his trial that he had been intimately knowledgeable about details of Hitler's regime. Nevertheless, he maintained that he was ignorant of the extent or even the very existence of genocide against the Jews. Of this denial, Cohen says, "His mantra was constant: 'he should have known,' 'he could have known,' but 'he hadn't known.'"[22] Speers admitted to having a moral blindspot about the Jews in Germany, saying revealingly: "I was blind by choice but I was not ignorant."[23]

On the so-called final solution, Cohen concludes that "people were easily taken in but also took themselves in."[24] The authorities did their best to spare ordinary citizens the pain and trouble of thinking; they largely protected citizens from direct confrontation with the atrocities and clear evidence for them. In return, people did their government the favor of not trying to learn anything about the matter. Thus, the quest to exterminate European Jews came to be an open secret in German society. The open secret involved logical inconsistencies and self-deception by individuals and the broader society. About the German Jews who had been their neighbors and colleagues, Cohen states that it was as though people were saying, "We know they are no longer alive, but we do not believe they are dead." The mind was in a kind of uneasy limbo. One might know something, but not be able to accept it or admit it. Though real, knowledge of such matters was denied and, for years after the Holocaust, denial of these policies and acts continued to be the norm.

Shifting from Germany to apartheid South Africa, Cohen cites the example of Leon Wessels, who was a deputy minister for law and order in a National Party (apartheid) government of South Africa.[25] Testifying before South Africa's Truth and Reconciliation Commission, Wessels admitted that he had been involved in a kind of denial. He had ignored suspicions and failed to look for further facts or speak out effectively against abuses. Wessels said:

> I do not believe the political defence of "I did not know" is available to me, because in many respects *I believe I did not want to know.* . . . In my own way, I had suspicions of things that had caused discomfort in official circles, but because I did not have the facts to substantiate my suspicions, or I lacked the courage to shout from

the rooftops, I confess that I only whispered in the corridors. . . . It may be blunt, but I have to say it . . . the Nationalist Party did not have an inquiring mind about these matters.[26]

In this statement, Wessels acknowledged his prior denial and willful ignorance about the sorts of actions the National Party was committing. As is suggested by his words "I confess," in making the admission, he was acknowledging that his denial amounted to a further wrong.

During the apartheid years, many white South Africans would have been in the position described by Wessels. They would have had the sense that acts of heavy repression such as brutal treatment, torture, and killings were being committed in the name of protecting the state, under the leadership of a government for which they themselves had voted. Most white South Africans chose not to pursue such matters, not to ask questions, and not to inquire about what was going on and what was being done in the name of protecting their state and society. Reflecting on that situation, the question to ask is not "what did they know?" Rather, we should ask three other questions. "What could they have known?" "What should they have known?" "What did they do to avoid the knowledge that they should have had?"

WHY IS ACKNOWLEDGMENT IMPORTANT?

In an essay in the *New York Times*, Emir Suljagic describes his reaction to the acknowledgment, before the International Criminal Tribunal for the former Yugoslavia (ICTY) at The Hague, of war crimes committed by Bosnian Serbs in Srebrenica in July 1995. Suljagic says:

I am a Bosnian Muslim from Srebrenica, where more than 7000 Muslims were killed by Bosnian Serbs in July 1995. I survived because at the time of the massacre I was in Potocari, some 15 miles away from most of the execution sites, working as an interpreter for the United Nations. My uncle, my 70-year-old grandfather, my best friend and almost all of my schoolmates were killed. Two officers in the Bosnian Serb army, Momir Nikolic and Dragan Obrenovic, last month pleaded guilty before the war crimes tribunal at The Hague for crimes against humanity, admitting they helped plan the Srebrenica massacre, the worst atrocity committed in Europe since World War II.[27]

Appallingly, there are 7,500 bags of body parts that the International Commission for Missing Persons for the former Yugoslavia has collected. Yet Suljagic states that he had never previously heard a Bosnian Serb admit that the Srebrenica massacre happened at all.

In the Serb half of Bosnia, most people claim that the killings in 1995 never took place. When pressed, they sometimes say that the Muslims killed one another in a fight over whether or not to surrender to the Serbs, or that all of those killed were soldiers. Last year, the Bosnian Serb government issued a report claiming that only 2000 Bosnian Muslims were killed in Srebrenica. And of these, the report said, 1800 were soldiers.

The confessions at The Hague included detailed descriptions by one man of how he had helped to organize the mass execution, burial, and cover-up that army superiors had ordered him to carry out. This confession, says Suljagic, "punches a big hole in the Bosnian Serb wall of denial." Nevertheless, some of the officials involved in the conspiracy are still at large and hold positions in the Serbian army; one person is even a member of the Serbian parliament.

Suljagic finds the acknowledgment that the Srebrenica massacre had occurred profoundly satisfying, even though he recognizes that it is unlikely to result in deep changes in Serbian Bosnia. He says:

> But the confessions have brought me a sense of relief I have not known since the fall of Srebrenica in 1995. They have given me the acknowledgement I have been looking for these past eight years. While far from an apology, these admissions are a start. We Bosnian Muslims no longer have to prove we were victims. Our friends and cousins, fathers and brothers were killed—and we no longer have to prove they were innocent.

Suljagic's statement illustrates the importance of acknowledgment for victims of atrocity and abuse. This acknowledgment did not come from any official Serb leader or group. Rather, it came from two individual Serbs who confessed before an authoritative third party—the international tribunal at The Hague.

Being seriously wronged has profound and prolonged effects on people. If others deny that the harming actions have occurred, those harmed are likely to feel a fundamental sense of unreality as a result. A fundamental part of their history will be unrecognized, meaning that, in many social contexts, they will not be able to represent themselves and be accepted as they take themselves to be. The fact that identities are in fundamental ways social underlies the importance of acknowledgment. When significant events have occurred but go unrecognized, others are treating those events as though they did not even occur. And when that is so, they are, in significant respects, denying the experience, and even the identity, of killed and damaged persons. Suljagic finds it a relief that he and other Bosnian Muslims can stop trying to prove that there were massacres at Srebrenica, where Serbs killed many of their relatives and friends. Given the acknowledgment, through a confession at an international tribunal, that these things really did happen, Bosnian Muslims are relieved of the bitter choice between acting as though atrocities never occurred and persisting in attempts to prove that these terrible events were real.

Acknowledgment that these things were done and were wrong expresses a commitment to *values*: the wrongful acts should not have been done to these people, who deserved better. This acknowledgment is aversive—and implicitly existential as well; it implies recognition of the dignity and moral status of people who have been wronged.

That is part of the explanation for why some groups find acknowledgment highly satisfying—even when it stands alone, in the absence of apology and compensation.

The case of the Acadians provides an interesting example here. Evicted by the British from lands in Canada's maritime provinces in the eighteenth century, the Acadians were dispersed after "Le Grand Dèrangement." Estimates are that between ten thousand and eighteen thousand people were affected. Yale University professor John Mac Faragher has called this compelled displacement an early case of ethnic cleansing.[28] The Acadians, rural settlers who had come from France, were removed by the British because they refused to swear loyalty to the British crown during a time when Britain was at war with France. Most were displaced to the thirteen colonies of what would become the United States. Many families were separated, with members never seeing each other again. The conservative philosopher Edmund Burke spoke out against these deportations at the time. The Acadians were mostly unwanted in the places to which they were deported. Some hid successfully in Nova Scotia. Later, many returned closer to home where their descendents to this day preserve elements of the francophone heritage while being successful members of Canadian society. Many descendants of the Acadians remain convinced that their ancestors did not deserve their fate and wish to have the wrongs acknowledged.

The Acadians received an acknowledgment of the wrongs of this relocation in the fall of 2003 when Canadian governor-general Adrienne Clarkson signed a proclamation as the Queen's representative in Canada. It recognized the wrongs suffered by the Acadians and proclaimed July 28 as a commemorative day to publicly acknowledge both the wrongs committed during "Le Grand Derangement" and the subsequent contributions of Acadians to Canada. The proclamation stated, "The Government of Canada reiterates its acknowledgment, in the most official way possible, of the historical fact of the Acadian deportation." Why? To help Acadian Canadians celebrate their achievement; and because it is a part of Canadian history that should be included in history books and museums. Some Acadians had sought an apology, but what they received was an acknowledgment. In the Acadian case, the acknowledgment was deemed to be important for setting the historical record straight. It was put forward in an attempt to provide an authoritative statement about past policy, saying that that policy had not been appropriate. The acknowledgment allowed that the Acadians had not been traitors and were wronged when their houses and barns were burned and their families dispersed. On this interpretation of events, the Acadians were victims, not wrongdoers.

This case illustrates that a historical record is more than a chronicling of facts. It is based on interpretations that include *value judgments*. The story of the Acadians has come to include the recognition that people *should not* be forcibly removed from their homes, dispersed, separated from their families, and so on, on the basis of religious and ethnic affiliation. An acknowledgment that such a practice was *wrong* implies a commitment that it, and similar things, will not be repeated.

Another case of acknowledgment is that of the Japanese Canadian community, which was forcibly relocated away from the west coast of Canada during the Second

World War. Representatives struggled for acknowledgment and received it in 1988 under the Conservative government of Brian Mulroney. There was some financial redress in the form of compensation for lost property; however, no apology was issued in the case. The Redress Agreement between the government of Canada and the National Association of Japanese Canadians stated:

> The acknowledgement of these injustices serves notice to all Canadians that the excesses of the past are condemned and that the principles of justice and equality in Canada are reaffirmed.
>
> Therefore the Government of Canada, on behalf of all Canadians, does hereby:
>
> - acknowledge that the treatment of Japanese Canadians during and after World War II was unjust and *violated principles of human rights as they are understood today;*[29]
> - pledge to ensure, to the full extent that its powers allow, that such events will not happen again; and
> - recognize, with great respect, the fortitude and determination of Japanese Canadians who, despite great stress and hardship, retain their commitment and loyalty to Canada and contribute so richly to the development of the Canadian nation.[30]

This acknowledgment was seen as highly significant by the community to which it was offered. It was an allowance and a statement of recognition by the government—and, by implication, the Canadian state and society—that what the Japanese Canadian community had suffered was real, that what was done to them was wrong, and that there was no justification for the government policy.

Acknowledgment offers a kind of *vindication* to victims, a public articulation amounting, in effect, to an official recognition that they were wrongfully harmed by others and did not deserve the treatment they received. Having received an acknowledgment from appropriate authorities, people are likely to have a sense of relief because their claims are no longer being denied.[31] People seek vindication in the aftermath of wrongdoing because, when they have been victimized, more than physical pain is involved. Their status and worth has been challenged; the implication of abusive practices is that "these people" deserve no better. Acknowledgment "unstates" that implication, offering, to the contrary, a message of social status and entitlement to something better, a legitimization of their claims. If wrongful practices have involved the humiliation of victims—which is often the case—acknowledgment is the beginning of their restoration to full dignity. Conversely, the denial that anything has happened amounts to a "second wound." In the aftermath of wrongdoing, the message of denial is that not only can these people be abused and wounded, but those abuses and wounds are not even sufficiently significant to merit public attention. The first wound is the harm of the original wrongdoing. The second is the insult of denying the first, with the implication that it does not matter. To imply that it does not matter is to imply, all over again, that these damaged people deserved no better than the treatment they got and that they were of lesser worth. When acknowledgment is offered to persons harmed by wrongdoing, their experiences are recognized and named for what they are. What damaged people have experienced is given a social status; these facts about their history will no longer be avoided, ignored, or denied as though these events had never happened.

One might ask *why* this acknowledgment, this public naming, is so important. An important aspect of this naming is identity and status, which are largely social in nature. In social relationships, individuals and groups require recognition to be what they take themselves to be. The question is not merely about what "happened," in some passive way. Rather, it concerns what some people knowingly and responsibly did to others. Names and language matter in human relationships. Think, for instance, about the public disputes and debate about the application of terms like "terrorist," "insurgent," "militant," "suicide bomber," "martyr," "soldier," "combatant," "ex-combatant," and "freedom fighter." Also notable are the many disputes about how a society's history textbooks treat past events. The textbook is perhaps the ultimate vehicle for public acknowledgment. How one's history is stated and named is a crucial point, because different terms and conceptual frameworks express different assumptions and values and have different implications for relationships, actions, and policies.

In many contexts where wrongs are relatively recent and feelings are raw, there is a real possibility that similar wrongs could be committed in the future. Statements of acknowledgment serve as a form of reassurance and a basis for the establishment of some degree of trust. Acknowledgment of wrongdoing implies a commitment that no such thing will be done again. In this way, acknowledgment provides a basis for the beginnings of confidence in persons with whom they have to live again in the aftermath of bitter conflict.

We can perhaps appreciate the impact of acknowledgment on trust by reflecting on its converse. What is implied by *denial*? Denial implies impunity for those who have committed wrongs. For those harmed, impunity spells continuing danger. If wrongs are committed and then denied, the implication is that they may legitimately remain unmarked, that they were of slight significance, and that those harmed are of little worth. These implications suggest a strong likelihood that such deeds could be committed again, at which point victims would suffer again and perpetrators would continue to enjoy impunity. If there is no acknowledgment, fear and suspicion will almost certainly persist. Nothing has been done to assert contrary values or to assure victims that there will be no further offenses. By contrast, acknowledgment offers a basis for overcoming fear and suspicion and building better relationships characterized by some degree of trust. When persons responsible for committing these actions offer acknowledgment to those damaged, they commit themselves to refrain from doing similar things again. Clearly, words and forms of acknowledgment do not *ensure* that such changes in policy and action will result. But they do provide a crucial beginning, a first and necessary step in the direction of positive change, and a reassurance that can be pivotal for the establishment of trust.[32]

Acknowledgment in this context will be most significant when it comes from those responsible for committing the wrongful acts. It is, after all, the harming individuals and groups—those who are the perpetrators—who have conveyed the messages of insult and humiliation. If these people withdraw their denigrating message, it can be as though the message is taken back—withdrawn, "unstated."[33] It will remain true that the harmful acts have been committed and have damaged or destroyed individuals, communities, and groups, but through acknowledgment and commitment, their impact can be lessened.

As the example of Suljagic illustrates, acknowledgment does not always come from the individuals and groups who committed the wrongs. At the time when Suljagic wrote for the *New York Times*, the fact of the Srebrenica massacre had just been acknowledged by two individuals who confessed before the international tribunal at The Hague. This body is widely accepted as credible and authoritative; it played a *third-party role* in the case. Although this acknowledgment is highly significant for Bosnian Muslims, it does not have the same significance that an official Bosnian Serb acknowledgment could. Fundamentally, the withdrawal of a profound insult can be achieved only by those who communicated it. In addition, there is the crucial matter of reassurance and trust. Many thousands of Bosnian Muslims live in close proximity to Bosnian Serbs. Insofar as those Serbs, through their political organizations, continue to deny any responsibility for such atrocities as the Srebrenica massacre and live out deceptions involved in that denial, they have offered the Muslims no assurance that they will not do such things again. Third-party acknowledgment, while important in its own right, is less able to offer assurance that perpetrators will not commit similar wrongs in the future.

We can reflect on the importance of acknowledgment from two points of view other than those of the victims. These are the perspectives of the broader society and of the perpetrators. Given what has been said about victimized persons, it is relatively easy to construct an account of the benefits of acknowledgment to the larger society. From the societal perspective, acknowledgment can be deemed constructive and important because it provides an articulation of fundamental values and a commitment to uphold those values. The public discussion required to explore and resolve those demands is likely to be helpful for a society, providing occasions to reflect on contested narratives and interpretations and to address differences about facts and values. In many cases, historical wrongs were an expression of fundamental moral flaws in the society—racism being an obvious example. Acknowledgment can amount to a public recognition and exposure of an important and neglected underside of history. The articulation of values tied to respect and human rights is a basis for the development of morally equitable cooperative relationships. Reflecting on the past and acknowledging wrongs provides a foundation for reconstructing state and society. Statements and acts of acknowledgment provide a society occasion to say, in effect, "what was done in the past was wrong; it will not happen any more; these are not the values we now hold."

The perspective of persons responsible for the wrongful actions tends to be quite different, particularly in the case of relatively recent conflicts. In such cases, resistance to acknowledgment by perpetrators is common. It can constitute a major obstacle to reconciliation. Calls for "acknowledgment" have a certain passivity and abstractness that invites us to ignore what should be an obvious fact. If some individuals and groups are going to receive acknowledgment, *other individuals and groups will have to grant it*. The topic of acknowledgment begins to look quite different, however, if we consider it from that standpoint.

THE POINT OF VIEW OF PERPETRATORS

For reconciliation, the most crucial and powerful acknowledgment will come from the individuals and groups who committed the wrongs.[34] For acknowledgment to work for victims and society, individuals and groups who committed wrongs will have to admit, publicly, that they did so. To *acknowledge* wrongdoing in this context means owning up to having made mistakes—not just mundane mistakes, but serious moral errors—and to acknowledge culpability and responsibility for those moral errors. That is not an attractive prospect. Admitting that one has committed serious wrongs is likely to seem humbling, even humiliating. It may involve fundamental revisions in one's conceptions of identity and history. Thus, acknowledgment is often resisted. There is likely to be a clinging to denial. Failure to consider difficulties of acknowledgment from the point of view of perpetrators amounts to a serious gap in the theory of acknowledgment.

To put the question bluntly, what can perpetrators gain by acknowledging what they did? How could they be persuaded to offer acknowledgment to victims and the broader society? One might urge that people should acknowledge as a way to be honest with themselves, better understand themselves, and enjoy the benefits of honest dialogue and cooperative relations with their former enemies. One might claim that acknowledgment by perpetrators can, in the best circumstances, provide for the ending of enmity. One could suggest that, in some circumstances, such acknowledgment can provide a basis for forgiveness, which would be beneficial for relationships of moral equality. One might suggest that people who have committed such acts as rape, torture, maiming, and killings are bound to feel *guilty* at some level (even though they deny it), and their acknowledgment could relieve their feelings of guilt.

But there remains the fundamental problem—that of perpetrator denial. The plain fact is that people do not characteristically think of themselves as committing wrongs. They rarely set out to do so and would not be likely to admit any such intention. Rather, they believe themselves to be risking their lives for a good cause, protecting their community, standing up for religious or ethnic values and traditions, fighting against an evil enemy, waging a just war, liberating their people and nation. In other words, wrongful acts—even atrocities—are not typically regarded as such by those who have committed them. In the aftermath of serious conflicts, when people identify strongly with their cause and the militants who acted for it, there is characteristically a tremendous unwillingness to acknowledge having done anything wrong. This is likely to be the case even in the wake of killing, abduction, mutilation, pillaging, and widespread rape.

Denial, in this sense, is nearly ubiquitous among perpetrator individuals and groups. To give only the beginnings of a list, such denial is widespread among Serbs, Croats, and Bosnian Muslims in the former Yugoslavia; Republican and Loyalist ex-combatants in Northern Ireland; whites in South Africa; Hutu-power advocates and supporters in Rwanda; Indonesians in regards to East Timor; and the military and political parties engaged against the Shining Path guerrillas in Peru.

In this context, denial takes some familiar forms. People claim that they did nothing wrong.

"What you say happened did not happen at all." (*Straight denial*)

"Something a little like this happened, but it wasn't what you think." (*Alternative interpretation*)

"We did these things, but when you understand the context, they weren't wrong, given the situation we were in. Actually, they were justified." (*Proffered justification*)

"What we did wasn't nearly as bad as what our enemies were doing to us." (*Excuse*)

"Those things happened and were wrong, and some of our people did them. But these were *a few bad apples*. It wasn't a general policy; it was an *isolated incident.*" (*Scapegoating*; *attempt to shift responsibility onto an isolated few*)

Such denials can be sincere, insincere, or—what seems most likely most of the time—sincere in some respects and insincere in others. People are often unwilling to acknowledge because they do not believe themselves to have done anything wrong. To those that they injured, their resistance will seem frightening and will be a cause of suspicion and an obstacle to cooperation and trust. To themselves, it may seem essential to their identity and life story. It may appear that the "other side, in seeking acknowledgment, is, in effect, wanting the "top dog" position in the aftermath of the conflict; these people requesting acknowledgment may seem to be seeking a *moral victory*.

If they grant acknowledgment, admitting that they committed wrongful actions, people may feel that they are thereby relinquishing their own narrative and sense of rightness and justification. When victims and societies seek acknowledgment of wrongs, perpetrators may feel that they risked their lives in a dangerous struggle and are now being asked to disavow their own efforts. They are being pressed to eat a most indigestible humble pie—to confess that, rather than being courageous and heroic, they were morally wrong. Many persons who have been agents of violence and regarded as wrongdoers do not see themselves in that light and will frankly state that, if similar circumstances were to arise, they would do the same thing again.[35]

Narrative divisions about a conflict situation are nearly always accompanied by differences about what was right and what was wrong. Often heralded as the first step toward reconciliation, acknowledgment can become a stumbling block. Third parties such as courts, governments, the United Nations, and international groups may be able to provide acknowledgment when those who have committed the wrongs will not grant it. Another potentially helpful factor here is that of mutuality. In many conflicts, wrongs have been committed on several sides, and the admission of this by all the relevant parties may diminish resistance to acknowledgment.[36]

NOTES

1. Lawrence Weschler, *A Miracle, A Universe: Settling Accounts with Torturers* (New York: Penguin, 1990).

2. Human Rights Watch, Africa Watch 1992, quoted by Brandon Hamber in "How Should We Remember? Issues to Consider When Establishing Commissions and Structures for Dealing with the Past," INCORE Occasional Papers. http://www.incore.ulst.ac.uk/home/publication/conference/thepast/hamber.html (accessed March 2004).

3. David Bloomfield, Teresa Barnes, and Luc Huyse, *Reconciliation after Violent Conflict: A Handbook* (Stockholm: International Institute for Democratic and Electoral Assistance, 2003), p. 23.

4. International Center for Transitional Justice (ICTJ), "The Peruvian Truth and Reconciliation Commission Backgrounder," http://www.wola.org/andes/Peru/truth_comm/background.htm (accessed May 2004).

5. *Peru Truth and Reconciliation Commission, Final Report: General conclusions.* Translated from Spanish by the International Center for Transitional Justice (ICTG), http://www.ictj.org. The points quoted are numbers 162 and 163 in the summary. My emphasis.

6. http://www.hansard.act.gov.au/hansard/1998/week03/527.htm (accessed January 2004).

7. The willingness to acknowledge while refusing to apologize points to an interesting theoretical question. What is the difference between acknowledgment and apology? I am inclined to say that (a) all moral apology involves moral acknowledgment; (b) not all moral acknowledgment involves moral apology; and (c) over and above acknowledgment, apology implies (i) acceptance of *responsibility* for the wrongdoing; (ii) expressed *sorrow* for the wrongdoing; and (iii) a commitment to *practical amends*.

8. This material and several of the following paragraphs have been adapted from my earlier article, "What Is Acknowledgement and Why Is It Important?" in *Dilemmas of Reconciliation*, ed. Carol A. L. Prager and Trudy Govier (Waterloo, ON: Wilfrid Laurier University Press, 2003), pp. 65–90.

9. *Royal Commission on Aboriginal Peoples, Final Report*, vol. 1, *Looking Forward, Looking Back* (Ottawa: Ministry of Supply and Services, 1996).

10. Ibid., 513.

11. Alex Boraine, "Truth and Reconciliation in South Africa: The Third Way," in Robert Rotberg and Dennis Thompson, eds., *Truth vs. Justice: The Morality of Truth Commissions*, ed. Robert Rotberg and Dennis Thompson (Princeton, NJ: Princeton University Press, 2000), pp. 141–77.

12. Andre Du Toit, "The Moral Foundations of the South African TRC: Truth as Acknowledgment and Justice as Recognition," in Rotberg and Thompson, *Truth vs. Justice: The Morality of Truth Commissions*, pp. 122–40.

13. I say "almost by necessity" to allow for the remote possibility that all sides are fighting for a just cause, using just means, and just means only.

14. Annette Baier, "The Vital but Dangerous Art of Ignoring: Selective Attention and Self-Deception," in *Self and Deception: A Cross-Cultural Philosophical Inquiry*, ed. Roger T. Ames and Wimal Dissanayake (Albany, NY: State University of New York Press, 1998), pp. 53–72.

15. Apologies here to persons who consider cobwebs to be things of intricacy and beauty.

16. Outside the context where we remark on this in order to give a philosophical example, that is.

17. In this case, the issue is selective attention and ignoring. Ignoring here does not amount to denial unless we amend the story so that people would have a protective incentive not to display—as, for example, if the local team had a history of embarrassing losses or had been involved in racism or sexual abuse.

18. In some cases, given the requirements of a social role on a particular occasion, it is even obligatory to ignore certain facts. For example, a man on a hiring committee will be obliged to ignore the fact that one of the job applicants is the first cousin of his wife; if he cannot ignore the fact, when deliberating about decisions, he should resign from the committee.

19. Themes of responsibility are considered in chapters 7 and 8.

20. S. Cohen, *States of Denial: Knowing about Atrocities and Suffering* (Cambridge, UK: Polity Press, 2001), p. 51.

21. Ibid., p. 58.

22. Ibid., p. 85.

23. Ibid., p. 86.

24. Ibid., p. 141.

25. For relevant background information, see appendix 8, South Africa.

26. Leon Wessels, quoted by Cohen, in *States of Denial*, p. 128. My emphasis.

27. Emir Suljagic, "Truth at The Hague," *New York Times*, June 1, 2003.

28. Judy Stanford, "Journey's End: Proclamation Gives Sense of Closure to Many Acadians," *Advertiser* (Lafayette, LA), August 1, 2004.

29. My emphasis. Note that these actions and policies were not claimed to be wrong by standards of human rights applicable *at the time*. (It is stated that what was done *then* counts as wrong according to standards we endorse *now*. This way of putting the point allows for the possibility that the policies did not count as wrong according to the moral standards of the time at which they were implemented.)

30. Financial redress was given. Twenty-one thousand dollars was awarded to each Japanese Canadian person who had personally suffered forced relocation. Twelve million dollars was given to the Japanese community for educational and cultural activities. The govern-

ment contributed twelve million dollars toward the creation of a Canadian Race Relations Foundation, with the Japanese Canadian community to contribute an equal amount. See appendix 2, Canada, for further background information.

31. Acknowledgment may be given by different individuals, groups, or institutions. For our purposes, the most important distinctions are between (a) those groups or individuals responsible for committing the wrongs, (b) the state, and (c) international bodies. The state may have been involved with perpetrating groups through supporting them, condoning their activities, or failing to act effectively to prevent them, or it may have functioned as a third party. The same might be said of international bodies; however, these more typically stand in a third-party role.

32. Some degree of trust would be involved in even accepting the acknowledgment as genuine, of course. Compare Trudy Govier, *Dilemmas of Trust* (Montreal: McGill-Queen's University Press, 1998).

33. Wrongs cannot be undone, and even speaking of "righting a wrong" is somewhat metaphorical. This question is discussed further in chapter 9.

34. As noted earlier, third parties may offer acknowledgment and (as in the case of the Bosnian Serbs and the tribunal at The Hague) this can be highly significant to victims. Still, acknowledgment by persons responsible for committing these actions who are, in that sense, perpetrators is the most significant in terms of vindication, reassurance, and foundations of trust for victims.

35. In discussing issues of perpetrator acknowledgment in Belfast in the fall of 2003, I was told this by persons on both the Republican and the Loyalist sides of this conflict.

36. These things having been said, I make no pretense to offer a complete account of how to persuade perpetrators to admit to having committed wrongs.

Chapter Four

The Apology Initiative

Among responses to wrongs of the past, public apology enjoys a prominent place. In fact, in the final decade of the twentieth century—before the September 11 attacks, the "war on terrorism," and the invasion of Iraq—issues of past wrong and public apology were so prominent in public discourse that several commentators dubbed the period "the age of apology." As this label may suggest, there came to be considerable doubt and cynicism about the practice. Pierre Trudeau once said that political apologies were an attempt to fix history, which was an impossible thing to do. He concluded that there was no point to the practice. Actions cannot be undone and the events of the past cannot be made to "unhappen." Furthermore, individuals and groups affected by serious wrongs have had their lives and feelings altered by what happened. Their history and development in the aftermath cannot be reversed by words of apology uttered by some political figure. Although these comments are thought provoking, in the end, Trudeau's dismissal is based on a mistake. Properly understood, apologies do not look only to the past. They are an important gesture toward reconciliation and a repair of relationships, which means that they look to the present and the future.

Striking public apologies include those of the Japanese government, apologizing to Korean "comfort women" who had been forced into providing sexual services to soldiers during the Second World War; that of British prime minister Tony Blair, who apologized to the people of Ireland on behalf of the role of Britain in the nineteenth-century Irish potato famine; that of US president Bill Clinton to the people of Africa for the practice of the slave trade; numerous apologies by Pope John Paul II for practices and attitudes of the Catholic church; and the apology extended by Ontario premier Mike Harris to the Canadian Dionne quintuplets for government exploitation of their childhood and abuse of a trust fund that had been established on their behalf.

AN ACCOUNT OF MORAL APOLOGY

Dictionary entries for "apology" reveal three basic senses. An "apology" may be a *defense* of one's position (as in Plato's *Apology* for Socrates or Cardinal Newman's *Apologia Pro Vita Sua*). Second, a sort of apology may accompany an *excuse or explanation* of one's actions, as in "Sorry I was late, but I was interrupted just as I was leaving." Third, there is the *moral apology*, which is an expression of admission and sorrow for having done something harmful or wrong. An example of a moral apology would be "I apologize for hurting your feelings with that tasteless joke; I shouldn't have said that." In contexts of reconciliation, moral apologies are significant. Many are public apologies for acts that have caused significant harm. Moral apologies are not required for insignificant acts such as phoning the wrong number or spilling soup on a freshly washed floor.

People often say "sorry" in contexts that do not require a full moral apology and, strictly speaking, do not require apology at all. In some cases, we say we are sorry simply to express our sympathy. For example, if a friend breaks her leg, we might say, "Oh, I'm so sorry that happened to you." Our sorrow and sympathy are often genuine in such cases, but the use of the word "sorry" does not mean that we are offering a moral apology. The context does not require that we admit any responsibility or make amends, and there is no admission of fault in the case; in these contexts, "I'm sorry" is an expression of sympathy. Sometimes, even when we are not responsible for the harms experienced by others, we may say "sorry" casually, without, in the strict sense, apologizing for anything we have done. (For that reason, it is an error to think of apologizing simply as a matter of saying "sorry.") Another kind of example is found in cases where we have not acted intentionally or voluntarily, but have interfered with or inconvenienced someone else. For instance, we may say "sorry" when we mistakenly pick up another person's suitcase rather than our own at the baggage collection. Sometimes what we apologize for is not even an action; we may, for instance, say "sorry" for brushing against someone on the bus when the contact was not initiated by us at all but, rather, was caused by the sudden swerving of the bus. Saying "sorry," in these ways, is significant for social life. It indicates sensitivity to possible inconvenience or discomfort on the part of the other person and serves as a sort of social oil, or smoothing of potential friction. But none of these cases amount to moral apology. Moral apologies are appropriate when a person or group is responsible for wrongdoing.

In a context in which reconciliation is sought, a moral apology is a serious matter, an initiative toward the improvement of relationships. If a person is expressing a moral apology, then all the following elements are present.

1. The person *acknowledges* committing *wrongful* acts.
2. The person says he or she is *sorry* for committing these acts.
3. The person acknowledges that he or she bears *moral responsibility* for committing these acts.

4. In accepting responsibility, the person does *not seek to justify or to excuse* the acts in question.
5. The person invites forgiveness or some other reconciliatory response from those to whom the apology is addressed.
6. The person, in acknowledging that the acts in question were wrong, implies that those harmed by the wrongful acts *deserved* better treatment.
7. The person, in apologizing, explicitly or implicitly communicates a *commitment* that these and similar wrongs *will not be committed again* by himself, herself, or the group represented.
8. To the extent appropriate, the person implies a commitment to offering to those wronged some form of *practical amends*.

In a full-fledged moral apology, the central aspects are *acknowledgment* to the person harmed that one is responsible for doing something that was wrong, the expression of *sorrow*, and a commitment to reform and practical amends. A moral apology amounts to a renunciation or disavowal of the wrongful acts. One who apologizes for something implies that it was wrong, and his commitment to its being wrong implies that he is resolved not to do such a thing again. In this way, a moral apology may serve as a request for a softening of attitudes or even for forgiveness. To acknowledge that what one did was wrong is, by implication, to acknowledge that the persons harmed did not deserve what was done to them. To apologize for an act is to accept responsibility for having committed that act and to admit that the act was wrong. To apologize is *not* to seek to justify the act by arguing that it was right after all; nor is it to claim that that act was excusable, so one was not really at fault.[1]

Like reconciliation itself, apology looks *backward* to what has been done and *forward* to commitment to reform, practical amends, and a better relationship.

Commitments to refrain from perpetrating such wrongs again and to offer practical amends are forward-looking elements of apology. The presence of these elements indicates that it is an oversimplification and, indeed, a mistake to think of apology as being only about the past. To be sure, if no wrongs were committed, no one would be responsible for committing them, and there would be no need for an apology. Clearly, moral apology is about the past—but it is not only about the past. It is about the future too, due to its implied commitments to reform and to practical amends. To offer an apology is to seek to improve a relationship in the wake of wrongdoing; one offers the apology in the hope of receiving some positive response from those to whom it is offered. That, too, shows an orientation to the future.

Given the forward-looking aspects of apology, we can see that there is something misleading about regarding an apology as an event or "speech act." To be sure, an apology will be presented on some particular occasion, and its issuance on that occasion will be an event—often a rather short event. However, the implementing of the implied commitments will extend into the future. Given this extension, one might even regard the apology as initiating a process. This ongoing aspect of apology will be especially significant when institutions are involved; in such cases, many persons and practices will need to change in order to avoid having the wrongful acts committed again.

To apologize, to admit fault and wrongdoing, is to humble oneself and make oneself vulnerable to the other. There is often a power shift involved: one who had power to harm is now opening himself or herself to the other, resulting in vulnerability to rebuff. In discussing apology, Martha Minow says:

> Full acceptance of responsibility by the wrongdoer is the hallmark of an apology. Equally important is the adoption of a stance that grants *power to the victims*, power to accept, refuse, or ignore the apology. The victims may in addition seek punishment, offer forgiveness, or conclude that the act falls outside domains eligible for forgiveness. In any of these instances, *the survivors secure a position of strength, respect, and specialness.*[2]

When wrongs were committed, the party apologizing was more powerful than those harmed; in apologizing, this party reverses the power situation, rendering itself vulnerable to the responses of the other.

In writing about apology, Nicholas Tavuchis described how an apology can serve to inspire forgiveness and, in this way, constitute the beginning of a repaired relationship between parties alienated by harmful conflict. Tavuchis emphasized the emotional element in apology and argued that, in interpersonal cases, apology gains its potential through the expression of sorrow and remorse. When an apology is wholehearted and complete, and received as such by the person wronged, there has been a significant achievement. Tavuchis admitted to finding something rather puzzling about this process. He understood apology as a speech act and posed the question of how a speech act could do so much. "The helpless offender, in consideration for nothing more than a speech, asks for nothing less than the conversion of righteous indignation and betrayal into unconditional forgiveness and reunion."[3] What allows such a shift to happen? Tavuchis found something puzzling about the ability of a speech act to inspire forgiveness. He called that the *mystery* of apology and suggested that the answer lay in the expression of emotion by the person apologizing. Perhaps that person's emotion would serve to evoke feelings of sympathy and empathy in recipients, who would then be moved to change their feelings away from resentment in the direction of acceptance. On this interpretation, emotion is what makes apology work; Tavuchis suggested that emotion can be seen as the engine of apology.

In the aftermath of serious wrongdoing and harms, a moral apology expresses recognition of the victims' dignity and moral worth, and respect for their feelings of resentment. In offering to those harmed a moral acknowledgment that their resentment and sense of grievance are not misplaced, a moral apology offers to them a kind of *vindication*, a recognition that they were in the right. Through that moral acknowledgment, apology can make it easier for injured persons to amend their attitude to those who have harmed them, regarding them with less anger and resentment, perhaps, in some cases, even with forgiveness. In effect, the person who apologizes is doing what he or she can to cut off the ramifications of the deed. One might think of him or her as taking the initiative, moving to stand next to the injured persons so as to look at the wrongs through the eyes of those harmed.

The idea that moral acknowledgment is central to moral apology was suggested by Jean Hampton. In an influential discussion, Hampton claims that, in wronging others, wrongdoers imply that these persons are of little or no moral worth and that their interests and needs do not have to be considered. One response to the mystery of apology is to point to the profound insult that serious wrongs imply; the message is that harming these persons simply does not matter. Because such a message is profoundly insulting, having it withdrawn is profoundly important. The taking back of a message of worthlessness means a lot to most human beings.[4] The fact that a perpetrator or perpetrator-spokesperson expresses respect for harmed persons gives them some reason to overcome their anger and resentment and begin to change their attitudes toward those who harmed them. Such a response may not happen, of course, but the apology is an invitation to it. In this way, acknowledgment might explain what Tavuchis called the mystery of apology.

Insofar as moral apologies express acknowledgment of the human dignity and moral worth of victims, as well as respect for victims' feelings of resentment, they can provide reason for an emotional shift on the part of victims. The power of apology lies not in any ability to undo the wrongs of the past (which is manifestly impossible), but rather in its offering of moral acknowledgment and commitments to reform and practical amends. A complete and heartfelt apology retracts or cancels messages of denigration that may have been implied by the wrongs committed. For these reasons, apology is often profoundly significant to victims.

Writing about law and culture in Japan and the United States, Hiroshi Wagatsuma and Arthur Rosett emphasize the aspect of moral acknowledgment and its relevance to processes of law. They argue that injuries through which victims have been humiliated can be repaired only by apology and not by monetary compensation in the absence of apology. Commenting on their work, John Haley cited evidence that apologizing properly and early and offering some redress may serve to prevent lawsuits. Haley's evidence concerns cases of failed medical procedures. Further evidence on this matter has been put forward by Jonathan R. Cohen, who has studied the procedures put in place at the Veterans Affairs Medical Center in Lexington, Kentucky for dealing with the aftermath of medical errors.[5] The Lexington center adopted the practice of admitting medical mistakes to patients, apologizing for them, and doing what was possible to correct any systemic practices that had led to problems. The results were improved practice, confidence within the institution that people were doing the right thing, increased trust between patients and the medical center, and fewer and less costly lawsuits. Although people may be afraid to apologize on the grounds that doing so will leave them liable to expensive legal claims, there is respectable evidence to the contrary. Cohen says:

> I am not reducing apologies to mere matters of economics or suggesting that parties make insincere apologies solely for strategic advantage. Apology should be

rooted in *responsibility and remorse* rather than in economics and strategy. It is the *ethical response* to injuring another, irrespective of the economic consequences. However, I think that parties often fail to make apologies out of their fear of adverse consequences and thereby fail to seriously consider both the potential risks and benefits of apology. . . . The Lexington VA's experience helps refute the skeptic's view that apology necessarily entails financial suicide. Rather, it indicates the opposite: apology can be to the apologizer's financial benefit.[6]

REPRESENTATION, COLLECTIVES, AND THE INSTITUTIONAL CASE

As this example illustrates, there are important apologies that are collective in nature. It is not a mistake of logic or attribution to think of an institution or collective as being responsible for wrongdoing, apologizing, seeking to amend relationships, and making amends. Collectivities may engage in practices that bring great harm to people, practices such as violence, torture, discrimination, marginalization, and other forms of ill-treatment. Given that serious wrongs are committed by collectivities, it would be a serious limitation—and a mistake—to think of apologies only in the context of the actions of individuals. Institutions may have been responsible for wrongs in various ways. They may have had policies that sanctioned or even required certain wrongful acts. Persons within the institution may have been involved as primary, secondary, or tertiary perpetrators—or as guilty bystanders. They may have failed to prevent wrongs within their jurisdiction, even though they knew that such wrongs were being committed. In institutional contexts, a group of people may consider what they, *collectively*, have authorized, done, and permitted. They may reflect on what, if anything, they wish to do with regard to those harmed by their actions and practices. Often, an obvious first step is that of apologizing— acknowledging the wrongs, committing to reform and amends, and hoping to build a better relationship with those who were harmed. In collective and institutional contexts, however, expressions more formal than "sorry" are common.

(a) The Spokesperson Role

Crucial to apology is moral acknowledgment, which can be offered by collectivities as well as individuals. In collective cases, persons who issue apologies have a spokesperson role. Spokespersons are in many cases apologizing for actions and policies that were not implemented by them personally. Understanding apology as a form of moral acknowledgment is helpful in offering a constructive interpretation of public apologies that are collective in nature. *Acknowledgment does not necessarily require emotionality.* While the ability of institutions and collectivities to feel (and thereby to sincerely express) emotion is limited—and may be denied altogether— their ability to *acknowledge* is not in doubt.[7] In fact, with respect to acknowledgment, collectives are often in a better position than individuals—given their resources and status. A state, for example, can construct a museum, issue official statements, or establish memorial days—acts that individuals, as such, rarely have the power to do.

To issue a genuine and serious apology, a group has to reach a consensus on the basic elements of that apology. A spokesperson can rightly represent the collectivity only if it has conducted appropriate deliberations to establish that the acts in question were wrong, that they were done by its agents without justification or excuse, and that, in light of these acknowledged responsibilities, the group is committed to reform and practical amends. The spokesperson role presupposes that there is a consensus within the collective on the content of the apology so that, in issuing it, the spokesperson genuinely does represent the group.

Ludwig Wittgenstein offered a striking example of how a single drawing could be seen in either of two ways. From one perspective, his drawing seemed to be a duck with a long bill; from another, the lines that constructed the bill seemed to be the ears of a rabbit. The drawing could be seen as either a duck or a rabbit, but not both at once. The image is useful when thinking about apologies in politics. There is a kind of duck/rabbit aspect to many cases. We can see the apology as individual: here is a person making a speech, admitting wrongs were done, and saying he is sorry. Alternatively, we can see the apology as collective: here (for example) is a hospital speaking out and admitting the inadequacies of its procedures, acknowledging fault to the victim for its mistakes, and committing itself to reform. From the individual perspective, we may look at the spokesperson and ask what is happening; we feel puzzled because this person, as an individual, does not seem to have done anything wrong in the case. It was along these lines that some criticized British prime minister Tony Blair's apology for the nineteenth-century Irish potato famine—"Blair didn't do anything; he wasn't even alive at the time," some critics said. This criticism is based, in part, on the gap in time between the nineteenth and twentieth centuries. However, it also assumes, mistakenly, that there can be no valid spokesperson role so far as apologies are concerned.

As the apology is delivered, one sees an individual who presents himself or herself publicly to issue a statement and perform a "speech act." That person's body language will be interpreted as the expression of an individual offering an apology, just as he or she might do in an interpersonal case. But if we think in this way, we are forgetting the collective perspective and ignoring the fact that this person is acting in a spokesperson role. He or she is issuing a statement of moral acknowledgment and indicating commitments on behalf of a group. What is needed for an authentic and sincere group apology is not the *individual agency* of the spokesperson and his or her *personal and tearfully expressed remorse*. Rather, the authenticity of the apology requires a valid representational role based on consensus within the collective and the implementation by that collective of the commitments implied in the apology. If a present spokesperson does not express his apology emotionally, the genuineness of the apology should not be doubted purely on those grounds. For example, when Pope John Paul II apologized for the Crusades and the Inquisition, he may or may not have felt personal sorrow about these distant actions on the part of the Church. As far as the genuineness of these apologies is concerned, that is not the key element. Rather, the key point is whether he represented a solid conviction within the Church that such practices were wrong and should not be repeated.

(b) The Persistence of Collective Entities

In the case of wrongs in the distant past, the entity represented by the spokesperson must be the same entity that committed the wrongful acts. In the case of many collective apologies, that agent is the state.[8] With Blair's apology, it would be the United Kingdom, which did exist in the nineteenth century. (Among the factors leading to the potato famine were the policies and practices of this very country.) As prime minister and leader of the government of the United Kingdom at the time this apology was offered, Blair (assuming appropriate consultation with his cabinet colleagues) was in a position to speak for his country and dissociate the government and practices of the 1990s from the attitudes and practices of the 1820s. Far from being absurd, as was alleged by some critics, this apology seems to have facilitated cooperation between the United Kingdom and the Republic of Ireland in the processes leading up to the 1998 Good Friday Accord.

Reflecting on state apologies, Janna Thompson raises the question of how it can be appropriate for officials of state to apologize for wrongs of the distant past. Thompson sets this problem in the more general context of relationships between states, emphasizing that such matters as treaties and incurred debts can pass obligations from one generation to another.[9] If, for example, a state signed a treaty some decades ago, it acted as an agent in so doing. A state is an entity that endures over time and can make and keep long-term commitments; as such, it can make treaties that last longer than the lives of particular individuals. In the case of treaties between states, there is an assumption that contractual arrangements and the obligations that accompany them will generally persist even as governments change and individual citizens die and are born. Were this not so, states could not make treaties at all.[10] Citizens of a given state have an obligation to ensure that it acts appropriately with regard to any burdens imposed under past treaties. Relations between states are conducted on the presumption that they can both make and keep long-term commitments. This presumption is integral both to treaty making and to international law itself. The link between a *present* state and citizens and obligations flowing from state policies in the *past* may be understood along these lines.

Applying such reasoning to the case of state or institutional apologies, even though an individual representative might not have been alive when wrongful policies were implemented, the collectivity in question has a life longer than that of the individual. It is quite uncontroversial that people cannot act before they are born and it is equally uncontroversial that, as individuals, people are not morally responsible for actions that they did not intend and did nothing to cause. But these features do not show that the idea of collective apologies, issued by spokespersons, is based on some deep mistake.

(c) The Question of Emotionality

An expectation that expressions of emotion will make up for wrongdoing and that such emotion is the key to sincerity may very well lead to faked emotionality. The phenomenon of exploiting "crocodile tears" in public life was satirized in a recent novel about public apology by Jay Rayner.[11] In an interview, Rayner said of people presenting public apologies:

> They have to look authentic. What an apology does is lend emotional authenticity. Blair is brilliant at this, and Clinton was brilliant at it—look back to one of his ear-liest ones, I think it's Tuskegee, it's an apology to a bunch of African-American men who were experimented on by the American government. And then the '98 apology for the Rwandan genocide, which followed an apology for slavery that had only taken place three days before. People forget this one. And it preceded his apology for Monica Lewinski. He became very very good at it. As a nice, god-fearing lib-eral, I went into this thinking, well why shouldn't the body politic behave in the same way as person relations behave, why shouldn't those two things mirror each other? But the further I went, the more I concluded that the apology was actually a route to not dealing with the offense, rather than dealing with it.[12]

Sensing that some people were good at putting on an emotional act and even felt better after doing it, Rayner came to a generally cynical stance regarding public apologies, expressing them in a highly satiric novel about a restaurant critic who became the Chief Apologist for the United Nations. He got his job largely because he was so wonderfully good at displaying emotion in public.

Rayner's novel is thought provoking and highly entertaining. However, several of his amusing criticisms seem to be based on misunderstanding. The *sincerity* of a collective apology lies not in the emotionality conveyed or felt by the spokesperson but rather in the consensus that legitimates his spokesperson role. Ultimately, the practical test of the *significance* of the apology is in its commitment to make reforms and practical amends, not in the atmosphere of tearfulness in which a spokesperson presents it. In fact, Rayner's comment indicates some appreciation of these facts. One of his objections to apologizing for wrongs of the *distant* past is that, because they are so distant, there is not much practical that can be done in the way of reme-dies or practical amends. The problem with many apologies, Rayner says, is that they are "completely useless."[13] We may ask *why* apologies are useless (if they are). The answer is that useless apologies are those where there are no prospects for fol-lowing through on one's words and no plausible commitments to make reforms and practical amends. If we see the matter in this light, we immediately acquire the resources to move beyond cynicism. The clear implication is that public apologies will not be useless so long as there is follow-through of an appropriate kind.

What is crucial in collective cases is not emotionality (which can be faked) but moral acknowledgment, the legitimacy of the spokesperson role, and the implemen-tation of commitments. Failure to shed individual tears and cry out individual sorrow does not mean that a person is failing to express a sincere apology in a public collective case.

APOLOGIES AT THE SOUTH AFRICAN
TRUTH AND RECONCILIATION COMMISSION

A prominent case at the hearing of the South African TRC was that of the Medical Association of South Africa (MASA). This group had some fourteen thousand members, so, in considering this case, we are discussing an apology on behalf of a large and organized collectivity. At issue were MASA policies with regard to apartheid and the behavior of doctors who, over many years, had helped to create a climate of serious human rights violations in South Africa. In some cases, district surgeons had actually assisted in the torture of detainees and had then failed to testify accurately in court about the damages that those detainees had suffered under torture. As a substantial institution, MASA had more financial and physical capacity to make amends for its practices than would individuals acting on their own. In addition, with thousands of members and policies for licensing and monitoring those members, its attitudes would be manifested in many regulations and practices. To reform, many changes would be required. If South Africans who were directly or indirectly victimized by doctors were to change their attitude toward them and begin to trust the medical profession in the aftermath of apartheid, extensive changes would be needed. Damaged persons would have to be reassured that the medical profession as a whole was taking these wrongs seriously and that a commitment to change and make amends was really there. They needed assurance—reasons to believe that MASA would not simply lapse into its bad old ways.

The need for sustained institutional effort was recognized by MASA, as is apparent in the following statement:

> The transformation of MASA of which I speak is an ongoing process. A significant event along the way was the unconditional apology for the past wrongs of the Association that was made in June 1995. We stand by every word that was spoken in that apology. . . . The apology was a necessary step along the road we are traveling, but it was only a step. Our wholehearted participation in the work of this Commission is yet another step on this road, but again only a step.
>
> There is much that remains to be done. We intend to participate fully in the work of the proposed over-arching Health and Human Rights Organization. We propose to enlarge and to strengthen the office and the activities of our ombudsman, our public protector. Our peer review system has already been sharpened and structured much more effectively than it ever was before. We are currently engaged in a program designed to promote structured ethics education in all the medical schools in this country, and we are planning formal structured training for prisons' health service personnel.[14]

Clearly, the implementation of such reforms is no short and easy matter.

A remarkably less effective apology before the South African TRC was that of former president F. W. de Klerk. In a highly significant appearance, de Klerk said:

> Let me place once and for all a renewed apology on record. Apartheid was wrong. I apologize in my capacity as leader of the National Party to the millions of South Africans who suffered the wrenching disruption of forced removals in respect of their homes, businesses, and land. Who over the years suffered the shame of being arrested for pass law offenses. Who over the decades and indeed centuries suffered the indignities and humiliation of racial discrimination. Who for a long time were prevented from exercising their full democratic rights in the land of their birth. Who were unable to achieve their full potential because of job reservation. And who in any other way suffered as a result of discriminatory legislation and policies. This renewed apology is offered in a spirit of true repentance, in full knowledge of the tremendous harm that apartheid has done to millions of South Africans.[15]

On the face of it, this striking statement by a former state president sounds like a sincere and credible apology. However, grave problems emerged during the subsequent questioning of de Klerk by the TRC staff and commissioners. By the end of the day of hearings, Archbishop Tutu, literally in tears, expressed his deep disappointment with de Klerk's performance. The African National Congress issued an angry press statement in which it rejected de Klerk's apology "with contempt." What went wrong?

Several features of moral apology are relevant here. One problem was that questioning revealed the highly selective nature of de Klerk's acknowledgment of responsibility for the wrongs committed under the auspices of National Party governments, including his own. Another was that his statement displayed no commitment at all with regard to practical amends. A third was that his role as a spokesperson for the National Party, and the status and role of that party as representing white South Africa, was unclear.

De Klerk's responses to questions at the South African TRC revealed a contradiction between his initial (apparent) acknowledgment of responsibility for the moral wrongs and material harms imposed on nonwhite South Africans and his later highly selective acknowledgment of responsibility for gross human rights violations. There was a glaring gap between his "full knowledge of the tremendous harm that apartheid has done to millions of South Africans" and his persistent denial, in response to questions, of any responsibility for—or even knowledge of—widespread, systematic torture and severe ill-treatment by state agents. This denial made a mockery of his "spirit of true repentance." De Klerk accepted that the security legislation and the state of emergency that had been established under the National Party government of the South African State created circumstances that were conducive to state agents committing human rights violations against their opponents in the struggle over apartheid. However, even after detailed and written testimonies of consistent and widespread human rights violations by police and defense personnel, de Klerk maintained that such acts were never authorized by the state and were never endorsed by official government policy. He said, "It has never been the policy of the government, the National Party, that people should be murdered, should be assassinated." Torture, murder, rape, and abduction are, indeed, deplorable and detestable acts; that much de Klerk would admit. But none of those acts, committed by soldiers, police, paid informers, or anybody else operating under government auspices, were actually done under official instructions. De Klerk maintained that there was no government official or body responsible.

As presiding chairperson, Archbishop Desmond Tutu noted that some highly placed police and army employees had actually admitted wrongdoing and had applied to the TRC for amnesty. In response, de Klerk stonewalled. He sometimes denied the allegations, saying in effect that "we never did it, accepted it, or recommended it." He sometimes offered excuses: torture in jails happens all over the world, after all; besides which, the ANC had also been guilty of violence against persons in its camps; this was, in any case, a context of violent struggle. He firmly insisted that it had never been government policy to murder, torture, rape, abduct, or abuse antiapartheid activists. De Klerk expressed *regret* that these horrors had been perpetrated, but he *did not apologize* for them.[16] (To regret something is not to acknowledge responsibility for it.) De Klerk and the group that he should have represented (the National Party government of South Africa during the 1980s) did not acknowledge that it had committed or shared responsibility for these wrongs.

Vagueness about any practical or material amends made de Klerk's apology seem even more insincere. The lack of an explicit commitment by his political party to a process of practical amends stood in stark contrast with some other institutional apologies such as those by MASA, as described above.

De Klerk's appearance was a highly public one, in a public context, with extensive media publicity. The public dimension is, of course, very important in understanding this apology. As with many public apologies, de Klerk was concerned to protect his personal self-image and the reputation of the National Party. "We abolished apartheid and we are proud of it," he said.[17] In part, it was true. It was de Klerk and his National Party government that had reached the conclusion that there was no way to defend the apartheid state militarily and it would, therefore, be better to negotiate with the liberation forces. It was this government that had negotiated with Nelson Mandela when he was still officially a prisoner. And it was this government that had arranged his release from prison and had given up its power after the elections in 1994. De Klerk and his party could rightly claim a positive role and a positive image. The problem was that they wanted to avoid acknowledging responsibility for the grave human rights violations that they, as a governing party, had authorized and condoned over many years. De Klerk wanted to take a position of *pride* (we ended apartheid) while refusing to acknowledge wrongs (we admit responsibility for gross violations of human rights) for which *shame* would be appropriate.

A further problem was that de Klerk had an inadequate and unclear mandate to speak for the National Party. Members of the older (pretransition) party, such as former South African president P. W. Botha, were not present at the hearings, and they had not authorized de Klerk to speak on their behalf. In fact, Botha publicly criticized some of de Klerk's statements, thus immediately revealing the limitations of de Klerk's mandate to serve as a spokesperson for the National Party. A further confusion in the matter lay in the fact that there were, in an important sense, two National Parties. The older National Party was pro-apartheid and had governed the country for decades prior to the commencement of negotiations with the ANC. The new National Party served as the official parliamentary opposition at a time when the ANC was the governing party in South Africa. In 1997, when de Klerk testified, he was a member of the new National Party, which had reconstituted itself so that it was not officially a pro-apartheid party. Although he was accompanied by some members of the reformed National Party, de Klerk insisted on being the only one to answer questions. It was unclear to what extent he represented a consensus within the new party; nor was it clear how the new party was related to the old party.

Tragically, this was a case of an apology gone wrong. The subsequent denials compromised acknowledgment. There was no commitment to practical amends. The public format seemed to indicate cover-up rather than sincere admission. And, crucially, de Klerk's mandate and status as spokesperson were unclear. There was promise in the initial statement. But the impact of this botched apology was negative in the end. The millions of South Africans hurt by apartheid were hurt again by this partial and ultimately ineffectual effort. Instead of "pouring balms on the wounds of many," as Tutu had wanted apologies to do, de Klerk's compromised apology served only to rub salt in those wounds.

GENERALIZED DOUBTS ABOUT PUBLIC APOLOGIES

The Argument from Overload

It is sometimes argued that there were thousands, perhaps millions, of wrongs committed in the past, and if public apologies are required for some of these wrongs, they are required for all of them. To apologize for all the wrongs of the past would simply be impossible. Hence, it may be claimed, there is futility in the whole endeavor of apologizing for the wrongs of history. We cannot overcome them and there are far too many to even try. To take historic wrongs seriously is to overwhelm ourselves. Instead, we should move forward.

An overload argument of this type was a central element of Pierre Trudeau's resistance to the notion that his government should apologize for the wrongs committed by Canadian governments in the past. Trudeau said that "once you start apologizing for one bad act of history, you'd never stop."[18] A press advisor to Indira Gandhi used the same sort of argument to resist the suggestion that India should apologize to the Kashmiris. One would need, he said, to list "all the apologies that could be tendered, starting with God for creating man."[19] A similar theme was echoed by a Scottish columnist who mocked Christians trying to apologize for the Crusades nine hundred years after they happened. This columnist asked rhetorically:

> Should the French go down on their knees to show they repent Louis XIV's terribly laying waste of the Rhineland or the suffering caused by the insatiable ambition of Napoleon? And should the Germans cover themselves with sackcloth and ashes on account of the horrors of the siege of Paris in 1871? It is all nonsense: you might as well apologize to the elephants of the Paris zoo eaten by hungry Parisians during that siege.[20]

The argument here seems to be that public authorities cannot apologize for everything and for that reason they should not try to apologize for anything.

The argument may seem persuasive. If there is no follow-through, the apologies will be empty gestures. And yet, if there is follow-through, one will be overwhelmed by the obligations following from the acknowledgment of past wrongdoing; one risks being so overwhelmed that it becomes impossible to cope with present and future problems. The Argument from Overload can also be given a moral interpretation: it can serve as a reminder that it is unfair for the burden of the past wrongs of several generations to be placed on a single generation, that of the present.[21] Underlying the Argument from Overload is the perfectly valid point that people—whether individuals or collectivities—should not be burdened with more moral duties than they can possibly carry out. The philosophical dictum that "ought implies can" applies here. We have obligations to do only what we can do; if it is not possible for us to do something, we have no obligation to do it. Clearly, it would be objectionable for a government or other institution to be so preoccupied with apologies and redress that it diminished its capacity to manage current problems. If that were to happen, wrongs of the past might be mitigated, but further wrongs would be committed in the present. For all these reasons, there are valuable reminders to be found in the Argument from Overload.

But ultimately, the Argument from Overload is not compelling. It amounts to the quite unreasonable claim that because a consistent and thorough response to *all* serious wrongs would be impossible, a state or institution should respond to *no* such wrongs. In other words, because it would be *overload* to deal with *everything*, one should deal with *nothing*. Clearly, this line of reasoning is flawed. The proper response to overload is not that one should do nothing but, rather, that one is facing a management problem and needs a basis for distinguishing between cases and contexts.[22]

A Fallacy of Presentism?

Some have claimed that there is a systematic error of logic and interpretation involved in the identification of past wrongs. According to these critics, it is a systematic fallacy to employ the values of the present when judging the actions and policies of the past.[23] Many past actions that are now regarded as wrong by persons identifying or affiliating with victims can be argued *not* to be wrong according to this doctrine. Practices of colonization, assimilation, and missionization may serve to illustrate this point. The governments of Canada and Australia in the nineteenth and early twentieth centuries believed that a Christian European belief system and way of life were clearly superior for all human beings; they established policies to educate and assimilate indigenous people according to those values. When they sought to suppress the language, culture, and even family relationships of these people, they were doing what they thought was right. They were not setting out to "commit wrongs." Similar reasoning can be applied to such past practices as patriarchal marriage, the economic and physical authority of men over women, the use of captive persons as slaves, the denial of the vote to men without property and to all women, discrimination against persons of color, and the sterilization of the "mentally incompetent."[24] Were all these practices morally acceptable, simply because the people who carried them out believed them to be so?

The idea that it is a mistake to judge the past by the values of the present provides a response to many demands for apology: one simply refuses to grant that the actions in question were wrong. One says, instead, that they were right, because they were judged right by the standards of the time at which they were committed. If these actions were not wrong, then no wrongs were committed and there is, accordingly, no need to apologize.

The word "presentism" is often used to express the view that it is a systematic mistake to apply *present* values to interpret and evaluate the policies and actions of the *past*. To say that presentism is a fallacy is to say that such an imposition of values amounts to a logical and moral mistake. It gives predominance to the present in a way analogous to the way *racism* makes one race predominant and sexism makes one sex predominant. Presentism is deemed to be a mistake because it makes one *time* (our own, the present) paramount so far as the validity of value judgments is concerned. The healthy and sensible reminder to be extracted from these ideas is that one should be cautious about applying systemic generalities to the lives of other people. We may misinterpret the actions and narratives of past persons if we anachronistically seek to understand their lives in terms of our own times. According to our present-day values, such practices and ideologies as slavery, colonialism, apartheid, and patriarchy are wrong. But, if value judgments are relative to time, then we should not paint every character and action within these systems with the same moral brush. Subtleties and individual variations exist and these should not be forgotten.[25] Public apologies should be worded so as to avoid cavalier generalizations about individual characters and lives.

The idea that presentism amounts to a fallacy is a type of relativism over time; this view could be termed historicism. The more familiar version of relativism is cultural relativism over space. A major problem with cultural relativism is that people within a given culture do not all agree on questions of value. Given variety within cultures, we cannot successfully appeal to cultural practice as the criterion of moral correctness. The same point about variety within a given culture can be made for variety within a given time period. It is a mistake—though a common one—to think that people at a given time all agreed on the practices of their day. Aristotle wrote in defense of slavery; he was moved to do so because others had argued against it. Immanuel Kant supported the subordination of women; his friend Theodor Gottlieb von Hippel argued passionately against it. When the Americas were conquered, there were opponents who spoke out against the brutality used against indigenous peoples. During the slave trade, the Quakers argued passionately against it. Thus, there is ample evidence to show that it is possible for people to think in ways that are unorthodox in terms of their time and culture. Criticizing the moral practices of one's own time is more than possible: it is actual. As a general doctrine, presentism is too sweeping to be plausible. Furthermore, when present people reflect on what to do with regard to harmed and aggrieved persons in their time, they should act according to their best *present* values.[26] Appealing to presentism, then, is not a cogent basis for dismissing apologies for past wrongs.

Cynicism

Apologies are often regarded as empty gestures, mere words, which can be offered lightly to provide an easy way out of responsibility. The Canadian writer Mordecai Richler wrote a highly skeptical essay about the "Age of Apology," saying that it was a time of "oily sincerity ... [and] glib, opportunistic tears."[27] Citing with approval Pierre Trudeau's resistance to public apologies, another columnist, Bruce Wallace, stated cynically that "regrets for past atrocities cost nothing on their own, they can make people feel better, and best of all, they are other people's mistakes you are apologizing for."[28] Yet another columnist alluded to the "safe permanence of the bureaucrat" and claimed that "the empty words of organizational apologies" amounted to *too little* after *too much*. "Sorry we overfished your cod . . . made whores of your women . . . murdered your millions." This critic argued that saying "sorry" was so far from being enough in cases where large institutions had committed serious wrongs that it was absolutely useless.[29]

These selected remarks are by journalists and writers who are not serious scholars, activists, or victim advocates. Nevertheless, they merit attention because they vividly illustrate a cynical attitude that is quite common. Here, as in many other contexts, it is important to come to terms with cynicism. Apologizing is one thing people can do to try to improve relationships in the aftermath of wrongdoing. As such, apologizing is a practice with important potential for reconciliation. Given that there are relatively few such practices, widespread cynicism and skepticism about apology seem regrettable and not to be encouraged. We risk dismissing a practice that has potential for amending attitudes and improving relationships. It is too easy to indulge oneself in facile cynicism while dismissing statements of public apology as easy and empty verbal gestures, acts undertaken casually in response to social pressure and political trends, failing to indicate genuine resolve and commitment, and lacking in credibility.

Skepticism about the merits of public apologies can be useful in some ways. It can, for instance, serve as a reminder that one should watch for follow-through in the implied commitments to reform and practical amends. If a person issues an apology under pressure, if his or her acknowledgment is not sincere, if there is no resolve in a group that is allegedly represented, and if there is no realistic commitment to reform or practical amends, then what is presented as a public apology is no more than an empty verbal gesture. In such cases, skepticism would be warranted; it is undoubtedly true that some apologies are lacking in sincerity and commitment and, for that reason, unlikely to be useful in processes of reconciliation. What we have to remember is that these negative circumstances do not always obtain.

Ostensibly, apologies are addressed to victims of wrongdoing. However, individuals and groups may issue apologies for reasons having nothing to do with victims—because it seems to offer them a cheap way out, makes them look good, or is politically expedient in some context. In such cases, to apologize is indeed hypocritical and may be merely "trendy"—or worse. Empty apologies can actually be harmful to victims if they raise hopes in order later to dash those hopes because there is no follow-through on implied commitments. However, from the fact that some apologies are defective, it does not follow that all have these defects.[30] A cynical interpretation can be imposed on any action at all and can thus be superimposed on *any* public apology. However, nothing is thereby proven.

An interesting recent twist on cynicism about public apologies is the argument that leaders such as Bill Clinton and Tony Blair have apologized for long-ago wrongs in distant places precisely because, in those cases, the practical implications will be minimal. Referring to a number of public apologies including those of Blair and de Klerk, and Bill Clinton's apology (in Uganda) for American involvement in the slave trade, commentator Neal Alexander stated that political leaders apologize for historically distant acts because, in those cases, little would be expected in the way of practical amends.

> Those expecting an apology for war crimes committed in Vietnam, Argentina, or Nicaragua in the past few decades will continue to be disappointed for some time to come, and it will be a very icy day in Hell when George Bush junior expresses any remorse over the current orgy of pillage and destruction in Iraq.[31]

Alexander allows that not every public apology should be cynically interpreted. He states that cynicism is not warranted if the apologies in question are offered at the right time and in the right context. Alexander's comments about effectiveness and significance suggest that *right* times and contexts would be those in which the implied commitments had some practical significance. The problem about apologizing for wrongs in the distant past is not simply a matter of a large number of years having elapsed. Rather, it is the correlative fact that the time frame lessens the likelihood of significant follow-through.

In 1986, the United Church of Canada offered a public apology to Aboriginal Canadians for having regarded them as heathen people in need of conversion and assimilation into a European civilization. The United Church statement included an acknowledgment of wrongdoing and a request for forgiveness.

> We did not hear you when you shared your vision. In our zeal to tell you of the good news of Jesus Christ we were blind to the value of your spirituality. We confused Western ways and culture with the depth and breadth and length and height of the gospel of Christ. We imposed our civilization as a condition for accepting the gospel. We tried to make you like us and in so doing we helped to destroy the vision that made you what you were. . . . We ask you to forgive us and to walk together with us in the spirit of Christ so that our people may be blessed and God's creation healed.[32]

In response, the Aboriginal community within the United Church acknowledged that the apology had been offered but reserved judgment on whether to accept it. One way of interpreting this reserve is to see it as a kind of "wait and see" attitude; in effect, this community was saying "We will wait and see what you are doing to follow up on this apology."

CONCLUDING COMMENTS

Although apologies can be flawed in significant ways, they can mark a significant phase in processes of reconciliation. Generalized skepticism and cynicism about serious moral apologies is not warranted, and it would be unfortunate to arrive at such views, since that would amount to a rejection of a potentially important strategy for improving relationships. Clearly, words of moral apology do not do everything. But they can do something, and something of value.

Acknowledging widespread cynicism about public apologies in a recent piece, Neal Alexander notes a "formal element" that marks a shift in public debate and attention.

> The present vogue for apology cannot responsibly be dismissed as simply so much "contrition chic" or PR flannel, for the very gesture of making an apology incorporates a vital formal element which tends, almost independently of the intentions of the apologist, to set in motion the interconnected processes of mourning, accusal, and (sometimes) atonement. By saying "I'm sorry," an individual is not closing a book or drawing a line under a dispute; rather s/he is inviting an exacting dialogue through which the consequences of her actions might be examined and redressed. It is in this sense that apology may, in Brooks' words, "raise the moral threshold of a society."[33]

Speaking in particular of his own society, that of Northern Ireland, Alexander acknowledges that questions about sincerity, legitimacy, and remorse abound, so far as political apologies by parties in the Troubles are concerned. And yet, he says, it is possible to see the formal element of apology at work even in this troubled context. For as a society people are already involved in the processes of mourning, accusal, and atonement, which make up the difficult work of reconciliation. In this respect, it is worth stressing that reconciliation is itself a process rather than a state; the end of reconciliation is to remove the necessity for its own existence, to erode the enmity without which it has no purpose.[34]

When made seriously—expressing *moral acknowledgment* and reflecting a solid conviction that the acts in question were wrong, and followed by *reform* and appropriate policies of *practical amends*—apologies mark an important step in building and repairing relationships. Failing to apologize may indicate denial or a dismissal of victims' concerns. Individuals and groups using individuals as authorized spokespersons may issue apologies; and these apologies may mark an important phase in processes of reconciliation.

Moral apologies are a form of moral acknowledgment. As such, they convey respect. A corollary is that, in contexts where they are needed, their absence implies disrespect. Moral apologies convey commitments to reform and practical amends and, in so doing, provide some basis for trust in the aftermath of wrongdoing. A corollary is that their absence conveys a lack of such commitment and, thus, no basis for developing trust in the aftermath. The corollaries would be reinforced if an individual or a group was asked to apologize and refused to do so. In such an instance, there would be no initiative to renounce the wrongs of the past. So far as reconciliation is concerned, an important opportunity would have been missed.

NOTES

1. This chapter draws on Trudy Govier and Wilhelm Verwoerd, "The Promise and Pitfalls of Apology," *Journal of Social Philosophy* (Spring 2002).

2. Martha Minow, *Between Vengeance and Forgiveness: Facing History after Genocide and Mass Violence* (Boston: Beacon Press, 1998), p. 115. My italics.

3. Nicholas Tavuchis, *Mea Culpa: A Sociology of Apology and Reconciliation* (Stanford: Stanford University Press, 1991), p. 35.

4. An especially strong person with a keen sense of his or her own moral dignity might maintain dignity in the face of repeated affronts and thus not need any recognition of his or her worth. There are people like this and, for them, vindication may have little significance. Nevertheless, resentment in the wake of wrongdoing is an extremely common response—and one expressive of our sense that we deserved better. The point connects with the social aspect of acknowledgment, discussed in chapter 3.

5. Jonathan R. Cohen, "Apology and Organizations: Exploring an Example from Medical Practice," *Fordham Urban Law Journal* 27 (2001): 1447–82. Thanks to Neil Funk-Unrau for bringing this paper to my attention.

6. Ibid., p. 1459. My italics.

7. I would argue that feelings and attitudes *can* be attributed to collectives, on the basis of their statements, policies, and deliberations. However, this is a minority position and I will not insist on it here.

8. Janna Thompson has effectively emphasized this point.

9. Janna Thompson, "Apology, Justice and Respect: A Critical Defence of Political Apology," paper presented at a conference on Apology in North Carolina in October 2004. Thanks to Thompson for providing me with a copy of this paper and for e-mail discussion of some related themes.

10. I would add here that if a state were to find the treaty unsuitable at a later date, there

would still be a prima facie obligation to abide by its terms unless it could negotiate an end or amendment to the previous arrangements.

11. Jay Rayner, *Eating Crow* (New York: Simon and Schuster, 2004). In the United Kingdom this novel was published under the title *The Apologist*.

12. "The Apologist," interview with Jay Rayner, in *The Vacuum* (December 2004). Published by Factotum, 11-114 Donegall Street, Belfast BT1 2GX, UK. Thanks to Sarah Laing for bringing this newsletter to my attention.

13. Ibid.

14. Transcript of the South African TRC Health Sector Hearing, Cape Town, June 18, 1997. *South Africa Truth and Reconciliation Commission, Final Report*, 5:387–88.

15. Transcript of Political Party Submissions, Cape Town, May 14, 1997. The appearance of de Klerk on behalf of the reformed, or new National Party was the first in a series of follow-up hearings in which the TRC questioned representatives of various political parties on submissions presented to the TRC in August 1996.

16. The passive tense is a way of disguising agency and denying responsibility, as suggested in expressions like "had been committed," "were raped," "were killed," and so on.

17. Transcript of Political Party Submissions, Cape Town, May 14, 1997.

18. For relevent background, see appendix 2, Canada. Trudeau was quoted by his one-time aide Tom Axworthy, as explained in Bruce Wallace, "The Politics of Apology," *Maclean's* 33 (1998).

19. K. Subrahmanyam, "A Sorry Situation: Apologies at a Discount on Poll Eve." *Times of India* online, http://www.timesofindia.com/today10edit4.htm (accessed February 9, 1998, by Nicholas Tavuchis).

20. Allan Massie, "A Sorry Response to Injustice," *The Scotsman*, September 3, 1998.

21. I am indebted to Wilhelm Verwoerd for these observations.

22. For an example of such reasoning see D. Graham, *Trick or Treaty?* (Wellington, New Zealand: Institute of Policy Studies, 1997). In this book, the minister in charge of the Treaty of Waitingi negotiations (New Zealand) describes the difficult process of addressing the large number of longstanding grievances of Maori during a period of tight fiscal discipline. A key decision was to settle the claims within a substantial, but fixed "fiscal envelope" (one billion New Zealand dollars over a ten-year period), divided into different percentages, according to agreed-upon criteria.

23. I first came across the term "presentism" (in this sense) in 1992, in the context of comments about whether Columbus's "discovery" of America should be celebrated or should, rather, be castigated as a colonial act that led to catastrophe for the indigenous people of North America. The argument that present values should not be applied to the acts and policies of the past is often made but, taken as a completely general position, this claim is seriously flawed.

24. The list can be extended almost indefinitely, a fact that itself should provoke skepticism about the doctrine of presentism.

25. For example, even in the residential schools in which Aboriginal Canadians were notoriously victims of cultural, physical, and sexual abuse, there were some caring persons, some decent relationships, and some cases of genuine learning.

26. For a detailed argument in this regard, see M. Nussbaum and A. Sen, "Internal Criticism and Indian Rationalist Traditions," in *Relativism: Interpretation and Confrontation*, ed. M. Krausz (Notre Dame: University of Notre Dame Press, 1989), p. 299.

27. Mordecai Richler, "Please Forgive Me, but I Must Write About All These Apolo-

gies," *Toronto Star*, April 12, 1998, p. F3. Thanks to Nicholas Tavuchis for providing me with a copy of this and several other skeptical essays.

28. B. Wallace, "The Politics of Apology," *Maclean's* 111, no. 3 (1998): 33.

29. P. Currier, "Sorry about Writing This, But . . . " *Globe and Mail*, August 10, 1992, p. A16.

30. A critique of generalized cynicism is offered in Trudy Govier, *Social Trust and Human Communities* (Montreal: McGill-Queen's University Press, 1997), chapter 11.

31. Alexander, "Sorry for Your Troubles."

32. "Apology to Native Congregations, 31st General Council of the United Church of Canada, August 15, 1986," as reproduced in *Why the Healing Fund? The United Church Response* (United Church of Canada, 3250 Bloor Street West, Etobicoke, Ontario, Canada M8X6Y4).

33. Alexander, "Sorry for Your Troubles."

34. Ibid.

Chapter Five

Forgiveness Revisited

orgiveness and reconciliation are closely associated, particularly in religious discourse. It is surely helpful for reconciliation if those wronged are able to forgive the persons who have injured them and, in so doing, overcome their resentment and sense of grievance. Often, reconciliation has been interpreted as involving forgiveness in a crucial role. Nevertheless, forgiveness and reconciliation are quite distinct, and the distinction is of considerable importance.

People may reconcile, in the sense of reestablishing a degree of trust and some capacity to cooperate. They may live without committing or inciting acts of violence against each other. They may refrain from urging or committing acts of revenge. And yet, in these cases, they may not arrive at the point of full-fledged forgiveness. In such contexts, there is reconciliation in the absence of forgiveness. Given that this is possible, we can see that forgiveness is not a necessary condition of reconciliation. There are also instances of forgiveness without reconciliation. For example, an abused woman may forgive her ex-husband and yet be unwilling to reconcile with him to the extent of living with him again and reestablishing their relationship. Such unwillingness could be predicated on the fear that he might lapse and abuse her again. Thus, she could forgive him for injuring her, and yet not trust him to the point of being willing to reconcile. This case illustrates the fact that forgiveness is not a sufficient condition of reconciliation. We see, then, that it is possible for people to reconcile without forgiving and to forgive without reconciling. Forgiveness is neither necessary nor sufficient for reconciliation. The distinction between forgiveness and reconciliation can also be appreciated from another perspective. Forgiveness is something victims may do, whereas reconciliation involves a relationship between victims and perpetrators. To put this point another way, forgiveness is undertaken from the perspective of one role, whereas reconciliation involves two.[1]

Despite this conceptual distinction, it would be taking logic too far to insist that there is no connection at all between forgiveness and reconciliation. Clearly, if people overcome their anger and resentment and, in that sense, forgive, such changes of attitude will remove important barriers.

The assumption that political reconciliation requires forgiveness is widespread. Its prominence is almost certainly due to the leadership and influence of Desmond Tutu and the work of the Truth and Reconciliation Commission of South Africa, which operated under his leadership.

DESMOND TUTU'S ACCOUNT OF RECONCILIATION AND FORGIVENESS

In his book, *No Future without Forgiveness*, Tutu describes the work of the South African TRC and powerfully articulates his conviction that forgiveness is the key to sustainable peace in South Africa and around the world. Tutu reminds his readers that South Africa's transition from apartheid to democracy seemed astounding, both to insiders and to outsiders. Observers of the apartheid state had been virtually unanimous in anticipating a bloodbath when the racist system was defeated. Instead, there occurred a largely nonviolent transition process; a well-conducted electoral transition of power from the National Party to the African National Congress; and a well-funded and widely publicized set of hearings by the Truth and Reconciliation Commission.[2] South Africa took an innovative path to regime change. The TRC heard testimony from victims, perpetrators, and others; offered selective individual amnesties based on clearly specified criteria; and recommended reparations for victims of gross violations of human rights. The TRC approach was distinctive with regard to its hearing of victims, acknowledgement of wrongs, and association with the African notion of *ubuntu*. *Ubuntu* is a conception of human nature according to which human beings depend on each other for their very existence. With its emphasis on the importance of relationships, this conception of human nature is credited with making reconciliation seem more essential to human existence and, for that reason, with facilitating it.

In this context, Nelson Mandela provided strong leadership and a powerful example. Mandela's appointment of a commission that included Tutu (retired Anglican Archbishop of Cape Town) as well as several other ordained Christian leaders as commissioners was quite striking. As Tutu understands it, the fact that the President appointed him chairperson indicated that the tasks of the TRC were understood as being not only political but also spiritual in nature. In his book, Tutu comments that few objected to the heavy spiritual and Christian emphasis of the Commission. If journalists questioned him about matters such as the use of prayers in opening ceremonies and his wearing of a purple bishop's cassock when presiding over hearings, Tutu simply told them that he was a religious leader, was obviously known as such when he was selected to head up the TRC, and was not about to pretend he was otherwise.

Tutu's account of his work with the South African TRC reveals a combination of political astuteness with a strong faith perspective. In his book, Tutu quotes prayers and inspirational messages that he expressed in the context of his work with the TRC. Christian theology is cited at many points. For example, theological premises are used to argue against the idea that perpetrators are moral monsters and to defend the claim that no one should be regarded as beyond redemption. Tutu also credits theology with the insight that this is a "moral universe" in which the truth will eventually emerge. He emphasizes the Christian teaching that all human beings are brothers and sisters under God, saying, for example that "the victory was for all of us, black and white together—the rainbow people of God."[3] He cites the story of Adam and Eve as an illustration of the human tendency to avoid responsibility and blame others for what went wrong. (Adam blames Eve; Eve blames the snake.) Tutu states that, for Christians, the death of Jesus Christ amounts to "proof positive" that "love is stronger than hate, that life is stronger than death, that light is stronger than darkness, that laughter and joy, and compassion and gentleness and truth, all these are so much stronger than their ghastly counterparts."[4]

His religious faith provided Tutu with a firm basis for hope and optimism, attitudes that were fundamental in coping with the many tales of horrifying brutality and indifference that were told at the hearings of the TRC. In the conclusion to his book, Tutu appeals to religious faith for an interpretation of history. He says that God chose South Africa to be an example for all humanity of how people could overcome grievances and move forward to a more positive future of peace.[5] God, Tutu says, had a sense of humor when he did this. (The comment suggests that Tutu himself has quite a sense of humor!) Tutu expresses his conviction that in other parts of the world—Rwanda, Sudan, Ireland, Israel, Palestine, the United States, and elsewhere—the South African example of the power of forgiveness in politics could be followed to good effect. Tutu says:

> Our experiment is going to succeed because God wants us to succeed, not for our glory and aggrandizement but for the sake of God's world. God wants to show that there is life after conflict and repression—that because of forgiveness there is a future.[6]

A fundamental idea underlying Tutu's belief that forgiveness in politics is the key to a peaceful future is that if people do not overcome their resentment and animosity—if they engage, instead, in campaigns of revenge or quests for retribution—they will be trapped in cycles of violence and counterviolence. Victims, frustrated and furious, will struggle to the top to overcome those who wronged them. Then, in the top position, they will wrong the perpetrators,[7] and the cycle of violence will continue. How is humanity to escape from the vicious cycle of grievance, revenge, and counterrevenge? Tutu argues that escape is possible if victims use their moral capacity to forgive, and implies that it is not possible otherwise.

At the Truth and Reconciliation Commission hearings, and in arranged meetings, there were prominent cases in which victims were able to meet with perpetrators, who acknowledged their wrongdoing, expressed remorse, apologized, and asked for forgiveness. In these cases, many individual victims were willing to forgive those who had wronged them in the struggle over apartheid. As TRC chairperson, Tutu passionately endorsed the relational transactions, commending the resilience of the human spirit and the generosity of victims, and noting what he regarded as a wonderful human capacity for forgiveness. Dramatic cases of victims and perpetrators shaking hands or hugging were publicized in the press. In one such case, Neville Clarence, who had been blinded by a car bomb planted by the ANC, shook hands with Aboobaker Ismail, who sought amnesty as a perpetrator in the case. Clarence said he wanted all South Africans to be able to work together for the common good. Tutu comments:

> The picture of the two shaking hands was blazoned on our TV screens and splashed on the front pages of our newspapers. It said more eloquently than words what the whole process of healing and reconciliation was about. It stood out as a superb icon for the Truth and Reconciliation process.[8]

In other words, the reconciliation of an individual victim and perpetrator, based on acknowledgement and forgiveness, could symbolize the reconciliatory aspects of the TRC process. This case involved *acknowledgement* (usually referred to as confession, due to the religious discourse that was so common), *apology*, and *forgiveness*. It culminated in a handshake indicating reconciliation. For Tutu, the two individuals shaking hands, after apology and forgiveness, was a model of what reconciliation would mean. Individual victims would encounter individual perpetrators, and remorse would be followed by forgiveness—and reconciliation. We can see that Tutu understands reconciliation in terms of this sort of scenario. He notes that apologizing and asking for forgiveness will require courage and humility on the part of perpetrators. One would hope that victims would respond to apologies by forgiving the culprits—and many did. Some said they would not forgive.

Strangely, his faith perspective allows Tutu to interpret even the refusals along optimistic lines.

> Of course there were those who said they would not forgive. That demonstrated for me the important point that forgiveness could not be taken for granted; it was neither cheap nor easy. As it happens, these were the exceptions. Far more frequently what we encountered was deeply moving and humbling.[9]

This kind of confidence can be harmful, however, and at this point, we find evidence of a faith-based approach that seems resistant to counterevidence. It might have been illuminating to scrutinize such cases more carefully to see what reasons and emotions led these people away from forgiveness.

In the final chapter of his book, Tutu describes trips abroad, during which he spoke and preached about the positive potential of forgiveness in politics. He visited Rwanda and preached at a rally in a stadium. Despite the horrors of the recent genocide there, people were still able to dance, sing, and laugh—all of which struck him as amazing. Tutu preached about the danger that the Hutus would shift from being underdog to top dog and engage in further retribution against the Tutsis who, resenting this, would struggle to become top dog again.[10] He seems to have envisaged the choice for Rwanda as one between *justice* (by which he meant criminal justice, retributively construed) and *forgiveness* (which would be the path to reconciliation and a sustainable peace). Forgiveness and reconciliation should be chosen "rather than their opposites," he says.[11] This comment suggests an unfortunate either/or framework. While superficially plausible, such a dichotomized conception is seriously misleading because it omits intermediate or mixed possibilities. Tutu reports that his message was not so well received in Rwanda—a fact that is not altogether surprising given the circumstances of that country. The Rwandan president replied that even Jesus would not forgive the devil, stating that extreme atrocities were unforgivable. However—and again, the perspective of faith seems relevant to his interpretation—Tutu is, nevertheless, able to interpret his reception in Rwanda somewhat optimistically. Skepticism in Rwanda did not give Tutu cause to reexamine his position. Rather, he notes that people did at least listen to him. He credits this fact to the power of the South African example and the fact that bloodshed there was largely avoided. Instead of a generalized civil war, there was the most substantial, public, and thorough truth commission ever—accompanied by publicized instances of apology and forgiveness. Tutu describes positive receptions he received in Germany, Ireland, and Jerusalem, again attributing his influence to the interest of the South African example.

CRITICISMS OF TUTU'S CONCEPTION OF RECONCILIATION AS FORGIVENESS

Several recent books on the South African Truth and Reconciliation Commission have expressed criticisms of this account of reconciliation as forgiveness. Even while the hearings of the TRC were proceeding, some objected to the prominence within it of Christianity and Christian accounts of forgiveness in its proceedings. We have seen Tutu's response to such criticism: he was chosen, as a religious leader, to head up the TRC. Indeed, reading Tutu's account, one can see that his faith orientation gave him a core of optimism, energy, supporting confidence, and determination. But even when acknowledging this fact, there are problematic aspects. One has to ask whether faith can make a person take difficulties too lightly. Faith may lead a person away from scrutinizing problems and objections and appreciating their significance. There may be a fine line between faith that supports practical confidence and faith that leads to the disregarding of serious criticisms and difficulties.

Obviously, secular observers will be unable to accept Desmond Tutu's faith that a benevolent God exists and is working through human history, using South Africa as an example of how people can forgive and find thereby a path to peace in the aftermath of brutal wrongdoing and serious grievances. A secular analyst will not believe that such a God exists in the first place. Even granting the existence of God, it is a problem how one could know his intentions. And one would certainly want to question why one country, above others, should have been selected to have a special historical role.[12]

Desmond Tutu is, without question, one of the great moral leaders of the twentieth century. His stature and accomplishments are such that one feels quite uncomfortable criticizing his account. Nevertheless, there seem to be significant questions about Tutu's position on forgiveness and reconciliation in South Africa. One problem concerns the basic logical point that forgiveness and reconciliation are distinct, as we have seen. Reconciliation does not strictly require forgiveness and forgiveness does not guarantee reconciliation. But the matter goes beyond questions of logic and definition. It has been argued that reconciliation in South Africa should never have been interpreted as something for victims to bring about by forgiving their perpetrators. In a recent book, Louise and Kader Asmal and Ronald Suresh Roberts argue that the TRC was wrong to encourage forgiveness as it did, saying that this approach put pressure on victims. They maintain that instead of being pressed to forgive, victims should have received redress and resources to address the gross socioeconomic inequalities of South Africa.[13] Asmal, Asmal, and Roberts argue that people should not be asked to forgive in a context in which their grievances have not been addressed. These authors share a concern expressed by others that, under Tutu's powerful leadership, forgiveness was so strongly urged that some victims were intimidated and not able to fully express their anger and frustration. Some victims maintained that the TRC, in the person of Tutu, was presuming to forgive perpetrators on their behalf, preempting their unique status as persons entitled to forgive those who had injured them.

In another recent book, Martin Meredith addresses problems about reparations. Though he commends the acknowledgment provided through the *TRC Final Report*, Meredith emphasizes the resistance of many South Africans to the Commission's urging that they should reflect on their roles and responsibilities under apartheid and work to repair the damage wrought by the system. Meredith quotes an open letter to President Mandela and Archbishop Tutu, written in April 1998 by Jon Qwelane. He said:

> Is it not simply amazing that black South Africans are the only people in the entire history of humankind expected to hug and kiss their oppressors, and to love them unconditionally like brothers and sisters, while the new-found family members give nothing in return except scorn, derision, and absolute contempt for our dignity as a people?[14]

Qwelane, a magazine editor, accused Mandela and Tutu of pursuing reconciliation in a one-sided way by placing too much emphasis on the responses of victims, who were supposed to forgive.

Having worked through several books critically appraising the South African TRC, one commentator concludes that neither the strengthening of democracy nor the healing of victims seems to require *forgiveness*.[15] Given the conceptual distinctness between forgiveness and reconciliation, these conclusions should not be surprising. But, given Tutu's charisma and influence, and his powerful emphasis on forgiveness as the route to reconciliation, they were surprising. (Was forgiveness simply a red herring in all this?)

Richard Wilson, an anthropologist who studied the dynamics of punishment and revenge in selected South African townships, has voiced particularly harsh criticisms of the TRC's emphasis on forgiveness. Wilson alleges that the TRC selectively favored cases in which victims were willing to forgive, biasing its proceedings and publicity in favor of forgiveness while silencing those who were resentful and vengeful. He maintains that retribution, whether achieved through formal courts of law or informal township courts, provides a more reliable and acceptable approach to reconciliation than forgiveness.[16]

A more theoretical concern about forgiveness has received relatively little attention by analysts. This issue concerns the discourses of individuals and of groups and amounts to an issue of logic. The problem is that the publicized cases of successful reconciliation in South Africa were nearly all about relationships between *individuals*. Tutu's view is that a sequence of "acknowledgement, apology and forgiveness" at the *individual* level provides the road to reconciliation. And yet, Tutu also tells us clearly that reconciliation, in just this sense, is the key to a future of sustainable peace in politics, where relationships between *groups* are concerned. There is a substantial gap between these levels: it is one thing for an individual black activist to reconcile with his torturer and quite another for blacks, as a group, to reconcile with Afrikaners—or for black activists to reconcile with the police, army, medical profession, or some other group. As Tutu himself tells us, cases of individual victims forgiving and reconciling with individual perpetrators were publicized so as to serve as "icons" representing the work of the TRC. But this leads to a fundamental question. How do the stories of *individual* victims forgiving *individual* perpetrators model relationships between groups? This question can be addressed in part by arguing that relationships between individuals and relations between groups are connected in various ways. For example, one might claim that stories of individual reconciliation serve to inspire many people and thus affect groups. However, the case needs to be made—and the issues here are complex.[17]

Tutu does not really define forgiveness, probably because he presumes that it is a notion familiar from common experience and embedded in Christian theological traditions. Given the many emotional challenges in the political environment of the TRC, matters of definition and distinction may seem pedantic and even redundant. However, crucial questions arise. It is not always clear whether Tutu recommends forgiveness only as a response to confession and apology or recommends it even in their absence.[18] If forgiveness requires sincere confession (or acknowledgment) and confession will not be regarded as sincere in the absence of reparations, then some criticisms launched against Tutu's approach could be rebutted—but then he would be recommending forgiveness in far fewer cases. Tutu usually defends forgiveness without referring to reparations—but in one short passage toward the end of his book, he links them.

> If someone steals my pen and then asks me to forgive him, unless he returns my pen the sincerity of his contrition and confession will be considered to be *nil*. Confession, forgiveness, and reparation, wherever feasible, form part of a continuum.[19]

In the final analysis, the notion that forgiveness by victims should be predicated on confession and reparation by perpetrators does not fit with Tutu's account. Nor, for that matter, would this conception of forgiveness apply to the widely acclaimed forgiveness that Nelson Mandela extended to supporters and civil servants of the apartheid state. Mandela forgave without receiving reparations and even without receiving any acknowledgment that he, or South African blacks generally, had been wronged by the state and white society.

WHAT IS FORGIVENESS?

The fundamental elements of forgiveness may be summarized as follows:

(a) one overcomes any anger, resentment, and vindictiveness that one has felt in response to being wronged;
(b) one relinquishes any sense of grievance and injury resulting from that wrong;
(c) one locates the wrong in the past, as distinct from the present and future;
(d) one allows to the wrongdoer a fresh moral start; and
(e) one comes to accept the wrongdoer as a human being with positive potential, capable of entering with oneself into a relationship of moral equality.

Defined in this way, forgiveness does *not* presuppose a framework of religious belief. Forgiveness may be motivated entirely by secular concerns, and it can be explained in entirely secular terms. Its point is the management of attitudes and relationships, and these are entirely within the natural world. The account here says nothing about original sin, Jesus, the suffering of Christ on the cross, the existence of God, the need for reconciliation between an alienated humanity and a divine spirit, or any other transcendental matter.

Forgiveness is a relevant and important phenomenon in the empirical world. Its importance emerges in the context of an entirely mundane set of social facts. We live in a shared world in which our actions affect other people. We wrong each other in various ways and, after such wrongs, have choices to make about our responses. Forgiveness, in this sense, is a matter of changing feelings and attitudes away from bitterness in the direction of acceptance so that we can go forward in relationships with those who may have wronged us. Forgiveness is an attitudinal shift, one that concerns our approach and responses to other people in this world, and to the wrongs they have committed against us, again in this world. From a purely practical point of view—again, having nothing to do with theology and its presuppositions—forgiveness can be argued to be a highly commendable response to wrongdoing insofar as it replaces negative feelings and relationships with more constructive ones, allowing people to move beyond alienation and wrongdoing.

Forgiveness is a matter of how we respond to other people. In particular, it is a matter of how we respond to those who have harmed and injured us. Although we speak about unforgivable *acts*, strictly speaking, it is *people* whom we forgive, or do not forgive. (No *act* ever apologized, expressed remorse, or asked for forgiveness.) In forgiveness, certain values are presupposed. Suppose, for instance, that Fred has stolen Susan's car. He later returns it to her, apologizes, and asks for her forgiveness. Fred's apology implies moral acknowledgment: his stealing the car was wrong, and he was morally responsible for doing it. Susan's forgiving him indicates her acceptance of these implications that the act was wrong, that the person who committed it can be distinguished from his act, and that this person is worthy of being accepted back into a relationship of moral equality.

Forgiving someone does *not* mean *condoning* what that person did. Quite the contrary is the case. The offering and accepting of forgiveness presuppose that wrongs were committed and the person to be forgiven is accountable for doing these things. To condone actions is to adopt a soft attitude to them, implying that one thinks they were possibly right. Although observers might confuse forgiving with condoning, the two are importantly distinct and are, in fact, logically incompatible. To forgive is not to condone, because forgiving involves opposing. What is opposed is not the person but the action committed. In forgiving, a person is dissociated from the wrongs he or she committed, and is reaccepted into a relationship of moral equality despite those wrongs. Thinking back to Susan and Fred, if Fred maintains that he was actually *justified* in taking the car (perhaps Fred is an anticapitalist who deems property theft to be a commendable act of protest), he will not be prepared to be *forgiven* for what he has done. He does not think he has done anything wrong. If Fred does not think he has acted wrongly, he is likely to find Susan's offer of forgiveness offensive.

A central feature of forgiveness is that it takes *time*. To say "I forgive you" is not tantamount to forgiving, and processes of reconciliation will not be served if people are encouraged to say "I forgive" in contexts where there has been little change in attitude.[20] Saying does not make it so; saying is not doing in this case.[21] Forgiving a wrong that has had some impact on one's life requires attention, reflection, and effort. What is needed is a kind of reworking of one's emotional states. A person who has been pressured to say "I forgive you" before authority figures or in a public context has not necessarily forgiven. A person has not forgiven unless her feelings, attitudes, and actions have changed in the relevant ways. To put the matter in plain terms, forgiveness usually requires a certain amount of emotional work. In cases where wrongs have been serious, the resulting pain and disabilities are likely to intrude on many moments of the victim's days and nights. Those who seek to direct or manipulate forgiveness are likely to find *incompleteness* in the result.

ACCEPTING FORGIVENESS

Accepting forgiveness requires acknowledging that one was *responsible* for committing *wrongs* against those who have offered to forgive. If one does not grant the presumption, one will find the offer of forgiveness patronizing and insulting. An illustrative story in this context is that of the white South African householder whose gardener, hitherto a loyal and competent servant, came to him one day to announce that he was leaving his job and returning to his family in the countryside. As the man bade his employer farewell, he looked him straight in the eye and said, "I forgive you." The employer was mystified; he did not think he had done anything wrong. The employer could not accept his gardener's forgiveness because he could not grant a fundamental presupposition of that forgiveness. He did not acknowledge having done anything wrong. He had had good relations with this man and, in his own eyes, had treated him well over many years of employment.[22] Forgiveness is a response to wrongdoing. In the context of wrongdoing, we may see a certain opposition between the wrongdoer and the victim. But for forgiveness to be accepted by a wrongdoer, that opposition must already have ended, at least in one highly significant respect. To accept the forgiveness, the wrongdoer must *acknowledge* that what he or she did was wrong. Thus, the acceptance of forgiveness is based on moral agreement between wrongdoer and victim.

A further matter related to acceptance of forgiveness is that of the fresh start.[23] One who forgives an offender offers to that person a *fresh start*, which is to say, a social identity based on equal moral status, an identity that is not that of "offender" or "perpetrator." To accept forgiveness, a person must be able to accept the offer of a fresh start. At this point, a necessary element of accepting forgiveness is believing that one is *capable* of making that fresh start. To accept forgiveness, a person must not only acknowledge having been responsible for wrongdoing; he or she must, in addition, have a self-conception that incorporates a capacity for moral transformation. Acknowledgment of wrongdoing is required for acceptance of forgiveness, but if that acknowledgment results in complete discouragement or demoralization, there will be a sense of unworthiness and, as a result, an inability to accept forgiveness. This line of thought suggests that the acceptance of forgiveness may require something like *self-forgiveness*.[24] The person who has committed the wrongs must believe himself or herself to be capable of embarking on a new path in order to accept the fresh start offered in forgiveness. In a political situation, people will accept forgiveness only if they can envisage for themselves new roles in the aftermath—roles unaccompanied by that sort of wrongdoing.

FORGIVE AND FORGET?

Thinking about forgiveness requires caution since some familiar expressions related to forgiveness are rather misleading. Among these is the common expression "forgive and forget," which is used so often that it amounts to a cliché. Reflecting on "forgive and forget," we can see that it is silly if interpreted literally. It is surely not correct to think that all who forgive will forget, just because they have forgiven.[25] It is not forgetting that is a corollary of forgiveness; rather, it is the cessation of a particular kind of remembering—remembering in a bitter, grudging, and grievance-cultivating way.[26] Clearly, a person can forgive something without forgetting it. Though Susan may have forgiven Fred for stealing her car, that does not mean she will forget that the car was ever missing. The point of Susan's forgiveness is that she will cease to feel angry at Fred for what he did and will no longer have a bitter, resentful attitude about it. Thus, she will not cultivate a sense of grievance based on this incident. If her cognitive functioning is normal, Susan will surely remember that Fred took the car. Famously, Nelson Mandela forgave the white South Africans whose elected government had consigned him to spend twenty-seven years of his adult life in jail for opposing the unjust and racist system of apartheid. It would make no sense at all to think that, because he forgave, Mandela actually *forgot* all the years he spent in jail. Clearly, Mandela did not forget that he was ever in prison or that he had arrived there because of the judicial system of a brutal and unjust apartheid regime. Quite the contrary, in the year 2000, Mandela held a large millennium party on Robben Island, the site of much of his imprisonment.[27]

"TO ERR IS HUMAN, TO FORGIVE, DIVINE"

There may seem to be little that is objectionable in the famous phrase "to err is human, to forgive, divine"—provided we interpret the expression metaphorically. But, if the expression is understood to express the claim that forgiveness is up to God and God alone, it leads to problematic questions. If God exists, then He or She will have the ultimate discretion about how to judge human beings when (and if) Judgment Day comes. In the nature of things—if this is, indeed, the nature of things—God will have complete knowledge on which to base those judgments. Human beings cannot have complete knowledge; therefore, God's judgment would be better than human judgment. Unlike mere humans, God would presumably be in a position to understand the motives and intentions of wrongdoers, and to understand their vulnerabilities, needs, and degrees of responsibility. God would also have the perfect moral perspective from which to determine degrees of right and wrong, and the perfect perspective from which to comprehend the suffering and needs of the victims of wrongdoing. The God of traditional theology would clearly be the best authority on forgiveness.

The problem here is that these theological elements provide no practical guidance about what we human beings should do about our own fractured relationships. Ethically and politically, as individuals and groups, we conduct our relationships right here on the mundane earth. On this earth, we are in no position to know God's intentions and are only escaping responsibility if we seek to shove tough problems off into heaven. The hypothesis that there is an all-knowing and supremely virtuous God who is the best judge of whether people should be forgiven provides no practical guidance in the mundane world. In this world (the only one that matters for politics), we are in no position to know what God would do or whether we should do the same. One might argue that God will forgive all and that, accordingly, humans should forgive all. Alternately, one might argue that God will forgive only those who repent, so humans should forgive only those who repent. Or one might argue that God will knowingly forgive and that, accordingly, human beings need not bother themselves about forgiveness since the whole issue can be left to God. Another possible interpretation would be to argue that God's perspective cannot possibly be understood. Thus, we are responsible for working out our own solutions from our own positions and perspectives in the real empirical world. To do so requires careful reasoning from the best moral principles we can work out for ourselves, based on our practical needs. But this sort of theological position amounts, in effect, to the same thing as developing a secular position on forgiveness. It is the secular position that is adopted here.[28]

"TO UNDERSTAND ALL IS TO FORGIVE ALL"

Another poetic but ultimately misleading expression is "to understand all is to forgive all." This expression seems to amount to the assertion that when all the factors involved in the commission of a wrong are understood, our understanding will lead us to the conclusion that there is no blame or responsibility in the case. The moral agent will turn out to be fully excusable and thus fully forgivable for his or her acts. The expression "to understand all is to forgive all" may be understood as expressing the following argument:

1. To understand all is to excuse all.
2. To excuse all is to forgive all.
   Therefore,
3. To understand all is to forgive all.[29]

The corollary is clear: if one fully understood why people do what they do, one would always forgive them for it. (In other words, if you really understood, you would forgive. If you do not forgive, there is something you have failed to understand.) Full and complete understanding would lead to full and complete forgiveness—the clear suggestion being that to forgive all would be a desirable thing. Applying this argument in the context of political wrongs, one would say that when we *fully understand* why people acted as they did (say, in a time of war), we will learn that what they did was *fully excusable* and not blameworthy and should, accordingly, be *forgiven*. Because the argument is completely general, it would seem to show that everything should be forgiven. One might regard this stance as useful for reconciliation. It is, however, flawed, and amounts to a denial of accountability.

Both premises are oversimplified and incorrect. The first premise is incorrect because fully understanding does not amount to fully excusing: understanding may be the understanding of reasons and motives that are compatible with responsibility and for that reason do not fully excuse. The second premise involves a basic mistake about forgiveness, ignoring the fact that in the absence of moral responsibility and wrongdoing, there is nothing to forgive. If one were to conclude that certain persons (for instance, abducted children forced to become soldiers) were *coerced* into performing atrocities, one would have concluded that they were *fully excused* and in this sense *not morally responsible*. But these unfortunate people would not require forgiveness, since there would have been no wrongdoing in the case.

THREE FORMS OF FORGIVENESS

Forgiveness can be bilateral, unilateral, or invitational.

In cases of *bilateral* forgiveness, the perpetrator acknowledges in some way that he has done wrong; he apologizes or in some other way expresses remorse; the victim, in response to that acknowledgment, then forgives. Because the victim forgives in response to acknowledgment offered by the offender, bilateral forgiveness involves both parties. Bilateral forgiveness is *conditional* in the sense that shifts in attitude on the part of the victim are a response to the acknowledgment offered by the offender.

In cases of *unilateral* forgiveness, there is no acknowledgment or repentance on the part of the wrongdoer. He or she may be absent or even dead, or may be present and unrepentant. When forgiveness is unilateral, the victim forgives not as a response to acknowledgment by the perpetrator but for other reasons of her own. These often include a sense that, for the victim herself, it will be best to overcome feelings of anger and resentment so as to cultivate a more constructive and healthy attitude to the world and move ahead in life. Unilateral forgiveness is *unconditional* in the sense that it is not based on any expression of acknowledgment offered by the offender, but is, rather, an initiative undertaken by the victim, based on her needs and goals.

An intermediate type of forgiveness may be called *invitational* forgiveness. Like unilateral forgiveness, this shift in attitude is accomplished without prior acknowledgment by the perpetrators; in this respect, it is unconditional. But like bilateral forgiveness, invitational forgiveness has a relational element. It can be regarded as an invitation to the offender, an initiative that may elicit acknowledgment, remorse, and apology. To forgive in this invitational sense is to convey, through one's words and gestures, that one would be willing to engage with the perpetrator in a relationship of moral equality; one would be willing to move past the wrongdoing and beyond the roles of victim and perpetrator in the direction of reconciliation. Invitational forgiveness does not presuppose acknowledgment by the perpetrator, but it does presuppose that his or her act was wrong. Otherwise, there would be nothing to forgive. To suggest that one is willing to forgive is to invite the acknowledgment that wrongs were committed. Interestingly, Nelson Mandela's forgiveness is best interpreted as invitational. It was not bilateral, since, prior to his forgiving, the whites of South Africa had not acknowledged wrongs committed against him and his people. Unlike bilateral forgiveness, this forgiveness was unconditional and was expressed prior to any such acknowledgment. However, Mandela's forgiveness cannot plausibly be regarded as unilateral, in the sense of being something that he did for the benefit of his own personal mental health. It clearly had a relational aspect: he sought a response from South African whites.

In his account, Desmond Tutu usually seems to envisage what is here called bilateral forgiveness. He usually speaks of apology, acknowledgment, or confession by the perpetrator and forgiveness as a response by the victim to the perpetrator's initiative. However, Tutu also allows for unilateral forgiveness, saying, for example, that "ultimately acknowledgement by the culprit is indispensable—not completely so but nearly so."[30] At one point, Tutu says that confession and contrition by the culprit make it easier to forgive, but that these are not strict requirements of forgiveness. He cites the example of Jesus on the cross, saying that Jesus did not wait until those who were nailing him to the cross had asked for forgiveness. He was ready to pray for their forgiveness as they drove in the nails. Tutu adds that if confession by the culprit were, strictly speaking, a requirement for forgiveness, then a victim would not be able to forgive until the culprit confessed. This restriction would be highly problematic since the victim would be locked into the culprit's choice. Clearly, Tutu allows for both bilateral and unilateral forgiveness and is prepared to recommend both, and recommend them highly. He does not, however, articulate a full view on these matters. He does not say which type of forgiveness is morally preferable or whether (within his frame of reference) either is obligatory. Most of Tutu's examples are about bilateral forgiveness, though unilateral forgiveness receives high praise. He also gives an example that can be plausibly interpreted as one of invitational forgiveness. Allowing for potential difficulties with regard to the acceptance of forgiveness, Tutu says, at one point, that "the victim may be ready to forgive and make the gift of her forgiveness available, but it is up to the wrongdoer to appropriate the gift— . . . He does this by acknowledging the wrong he has done, so letting the light and fresh air of forgiveness enter his being." In this case, it would seem that the victim offers forgiveness to a wrongdoer who, at that point, has not acknowledged wrongdoing but is, in effect, invited to do so. If the perpetrator *accepts* the victim's offer of forgiveness, then, in doing so, he does acknowledge.[31] An invitation has been extended and accepted.

There should be relatively little controversy about bilateral forgiveness, since forgiveness, in that sense, presupposes acknowledgment by perpetrators. If wrongdoers have acknowledged wrongdoing, forgiveness by victims seems clearly beneficial. For victims, it is beneficial because they are enabled to overcome negative feelings of resentment and animosity, live their lives in the present and future as distinct from the past, and move beyond the victim role. For perpetrators, acknowledgment will enable them to accept forgiveness and thereby receive social reinforcement of a more positive conception of themselves, and move beyond the perpetrator role to engage in relationships of moral equality with victims and the broader community. From the community perspective, the ending of animosity and beginning of improved lives and relationships is clearly constructive and positive.[32]

As we have seen, however, acknowledgment by perpetrators is often absent. When forgiveness is widely recommended, it is not reasonable to assume that there will be perpetrator acknowledgment in every case. One must consider some other form of forgiveness. Victims are often urged to forgive unilaterally for their own sake. They are urged to forgive in the interests of improving their mental health and their ability to go forward in life, leave the victim role, and escape emotional ties to the perpetrator. In other words, victims are often urged to forgive in the interests of their own wellbeing and mental health. Though virtually faddish in some therapeutic circles, unilateral forgiveness is more contestable than bilateral forgiveness. Unilateral forgiveness may have positive potential for peace and reconciliation; it can hardly be denied that if resentment and hostility are overcome, the likelihood of violence resuming will diminish. And yet, unilateral forgiveness has been strongly contested by some critics. One problem is that the relational element of forgiveness has disappeared. Forgiveness is undertaken by the harmed person without any initiative or reciprocation from the perpetrators. To many, unilateral forgiveness has seemed too "therapeutic" and self-focused, expressing too little concern for the perpetrator. Because unilateral forgiveness is one-sided and nonrelational in this way, some critics have seen it as entirely self-oriented and even somewhat selfish. In the therapeutic frame of reference, forgiveness can seem to be a matter of good mental hygiene, defensible as a kind of self-help, but lacking ethical or relational implications. Other critics allege that victims are often urged by therapists and religious leaders to forgive prematurely, in ways that underestimate the significance of the wrong and restrict the development of self-respect on the part of victims. It may also be alleged that unilateral forgiveness is too soft on perpetrators, who are forgiven in the absence of any acknowledgment, apology, or expression of remorse.

Highly relevant to contexts of political reconciliation is *invitational* forgiveness. One forgives in the hope of inspiring acknowledgment and apology. One does not require acknowledgment and apology first, but is attentive to the relationship and seeks a conciliatory response. Like bilateral forgiveness, invitational forgiveness is relational in intent. Like unilateral forgiveness, it does not presuppose prior acknowledgment. For reconciliation, invitational forgiveness seems extremely relevant, given its attention to relationship and willingness to take a positive step without absolutely insisting on reciprocity. Invitational forgiveness can be seen as a unilateral initiative toward bilateral forgiveness and can even be compared to unilateral initiatives toward bilateral disarmament.

PROSPECTS FOR MUTUAL FORGIVENESS?

When discussing forgiveness, it seems impossible to avoid a polarized framework of victim and perpetrator, injured party and wrongdoer, innocent and guilty. The notion of forgiveness requires such a framework to some extent. If there is no wrong and no wrongdoer, there is no one to be forgiven, and if there is no victim of wrongdoing, there is no one to provide forgiveness. Yet here as elsewhere a polarized framework may limit our understanding, imagination, and opportunities. In both individual and group contexts, most conflicts involve wrongdoing on both sides. (Often there are more than two sides and there have been wrongs committed by all sides.) Even the briefest consideration of civil conflicts in such places as Northern Ireland, the Balkans, Sri Lanka, and Sierra Leone will serve to establish this point—which is, in any event, quite obvious from the point of view of common sense and ordinary life. Even in the case of individuals, it will often happen that a victim in one context is a perpetrator against his own victimizer in another context.

What can be said about forgiveness then? Should it not be mutual? It seems reasonable that when each of several parties has committed wrongs, people should forgive each other. To put the point pedantically, one party would apologize, another would receive the apology and offer forgiveness and then, in turn, offer its own apology, thereby acknowledging its own culpability and fallibility and its own capacity to offend. In scenarios of mutual forgiveness, we could envisage people acknowledging their suffering, their wrongdoing, and aspects of their shared humanity.[33] Based on shared suffering, responsibility, and mutual acknowledgment, transactions of mutual forgiveness would seem to have enormous potential for reconciliation. The situation has been terrible and all have done wrong, so wrongdoing can be acknowledged on all sides. These people can forgive each other. Mutual forgiveness would seem to have everything to recommend it. There would be no moral arrogance on the part of victims presuming their own passivity and innocence, no "holier than thou" attitude, no scapegoating, and no pointing of fingers. And yet, there would be acknowledgment; mutual forgiveness does not amount to a mutual decision to "dig a hole and bury the past."[34]

Strangely, *mutual* forgiveness, in this sense, is rarely discussed by writers on forgiveness. Discussions of forgiveness are usually couched in a victim/perpetrator framework where one is wronged and the other has committed wrong. The complicating possibility that both parties may be both wronged and committers of wrong—both victims and perpetrators—is omitted from consideration. And yet, this situation is a highly realistic one, both interpersonally and in political contexts. Karl Tomm, a therapist experienced in counseling same-sex couples, warns that the absence of polarity is difficult for many people to appreciate because they are so accustomed to thinking in terms of a right/wrong, victim/perpetrator dichotomy. The temptation to dichotomize and polarize inhibits creative thought about forgiveness. In Tomm's experience, same-sex couples have been handicapped in moving forward from their conflicts because, like most people, they would like to be able to think in terms of dichotomized expectations (which, for heterosexual couples, are available within the traditionally polarized roles of husband and wife). Alienated same-sex partners cannot find such expectations in their experience and culture. Tomm's therapeutic experience suggests to him that people are most comfortable when they can reason in a framework of clear dichotomies and roles. Nuances, ambiguities, and multiple possibilities are often hard to understand. If Tomm is correct, prospects for mutual forgiveness may be weak, given that, in those frameworks, all parties are wronged and are wrongdoers.

Frameworks that are simple, in the sense of being dichotomous, may be cognitively and emotionally satisfying but they are typically insufficient to do justice to the subtleties of the facts.[35] A dichotomized and polarized framework in which one person or group occupies only the role of perpetrator and another occupies only the role of victim is unlikely to be accurate to the realities of conflict situations. A more qualified and complex understanding of these roles could facilitate mutual forgiveness, a shift that, if one could bring it about, would be profoundly significant for reconciliation.[36]

FORGIVENESS AND AUTHORITY:
THE PROBLEM OF DIRECTED FORGIVENESS

In the immediate aftermath of serious wrongdoing, those harmed are likely to feel pain, anger, and grievance. They may struggle to overcome their injuries and go on with life as best they can. Forgiveness has been strongly urged by many religious leaders. In contexts where reconciliation is sought, their interventions have usually been welcomed. To the extent that these interventions inhibit the cultivation of grievances and expression of hatred, they may save many lives. From this perspective, it would seem highly unreasonable to criticize such interventions. Nevertheless, there are concerns when religious and other authorities seek to facilitate forgiveness through manipulative practices directed toward victims. Given that forgiving typically takes time—emotions and attitudes have to be examined and struggled with—urging victims to rush into forgiveness may be manipulative. If so, such practices are objectionable. Although one can appreciate the fact that religious leaders were not cultivating hatred and a sense of grievance, it remains troubling to think that seriously damaged people might forgive (or "forgive") simply because authoritative leaders have told them to do so. We can call this the problem of directed forgiveness.

In the wake of the civil war in Sierra Leone, there is an urgent need for social and political reconstruction. Victims have been told to forgive those who have perpetrated atrocities. President Kabbah has voiced an appeal to victims, saying, "I am convinced that with successful disarmament it is only by such an act of forgiveness and reconciliation that peace can return to Sierra Leone." [37] The Reverend Joseph Humper, head of the Sierra Leone Truth and Reconciliation Commission, has also strongly urged forgiveness. There has been an energetic attempt in Sierra Leone to reintegrate ex-combatants. Reintegration means *re-acceptance*, or acceptance back into communities in which many people were grievously victimized during the civil war. Ex-combatants can be reintegrated only if communities (including victims) are ready to accept them, and it would seem that such re-acceptance would be greatly facilitated by forgiveness.[38] Victims' forgiveness might be regarded as essential for the social reconstruction of this devastated country; thus, the religious mandate of forgiveness could be seen as playing an essential role.[39]

In 2000, audiocassettes of the Anglican minister Dale Lang were circulating in the country and being played to victims of the Sierra Leone civil war.[40] Dale Lang's son Jason was killed in a high school shooting in Taber, Alberta, Canada, in the spring of 1999. Immediately after Jason's death, Lang announced that he forgave the young man who had killed his son. Lang spoke out because he was a Christian, he said—and his religion taught him to forgive. For several years after Jason's death, Lang spoke frequently about the case, preaching in favor of forgiveness on religious grounds, telling groups how his Christian beliefs had helped him respond to the tragedy in a constructive way, and warning about the adverse effects of bullying in schools. Lang strongly urged forgiveness as the constructive response to terrible wrongs. While his determined efforts against bullying and violence have been impressive, Lang's forgiveness struck some observers as strange and implausible. It came very quickly after Jason's death; Lang seemed to feel no need for time to work on his feelings. Forgiveness seemed to be almost an automatic response. It was as though he had needed only a very simple line of reasoning: "I am a Christian; Christians forgive; therefore, I forgive." It is rather alarming to think of this simplistic response being promoted in Sierra Leone in the aftermath of an extraordinarily damaging civil war.

Indeed, there seem to be some strange problems that arise with regard to the advocacy of forgiveness in Sierra Leone.

"We are forgiving the ex-combatants for the sake of God."

"We are forgiving them because the government says so."[41]

"People say we should forgive, but how can we forgive? One man at the amputee camp told me that the rebels are now being integrated into the army. They are going around in the streets and asking people, "please forgive me," and handing out candies. That's not enough."[42]

"I know the man who did this to me [performed an amputation]. He's in the Sierra Leone army now. But I'm thinking of my children and we need peace. I forgive him."

"Well, let God fight for me."[43]

When we recall the atrocious wrongs experienced by many victims in Sierra Leone, such comments inspire doubt. One cannot help but suspect that victims' forgiveness in Sierra Leone is halfhearted at best.

Sometimes, of course, forgiveness is altogether absent, despite the directives of religious and political leaders. One writer, based in Sierra Leone with a western

NGO, tells a story about a man whose hands had been cut off by rebels. Later, when he saw the man who had wielded the machete against him, he ran up behind him, "grabbed him with his stumps," and then sank his teeth into the man's neck.[44] Such frustrated fury is understandable. Given that such intense and bitter feelings work against reconciliation and peace, it is quite understandable that leaders would seek to moderate them. But it is misleading to say that someone with injuries that serious and feelings that intense should simply be able to forgive his attacker—even if an authoritative figure told him to do it.

A directive to forgive may be felt by many as a harsh and authoritative order.[45] In their crudest form, such directives may threaten people, insisting that their salvation depends on forgiving. Victims, who may be in the mood to undertake furious acts of vengeance, are asked—or even directed—to forgive because it is their religious obligation to do so. What is requested in these contexts? Given the frequent absence of perpetrator acknowledgment and even of perpetrators themselves, most likely it is not *bilateral* forgiveness. It is more likely that directed forgiveness is *unilateral* or *invitational*. We will assume here, somewhat charitably and in the interests of simplicity, that it is *invitational*.[46] In other words, victims are directed to overcome their resentment and hatred and to accept former perpetrators. If, as is often the case, it is religious leaders who are urging this forgiveness, the reason is likely to be simply that such forgiveness is a religious obligation.

There are, however, several reasons for doubts about directed forgiveness. The many problems include the following:

1. *Inappropriate Burden.* Duties seem to be wrongly assigned here. The directive to forgive places the moral burden on *victims* rather than perpetrators. This allocation of burden is especially problematic if victims are directed to forgive perpetrators who have not acknowledged doing anything wrong.

2. *Further Insult.* When there has been no acknowledgment by offenders, to insist that victims *must* forgive is to add another injury to the initial victimization. Even when their intentions are good, those seeking to direct forgiveness seem to downplay the suffering of victims in their pursuit of the broader social goals of reintegration, peace, and reconciliation. To victims, directives to forgive feel like nonacknowledgment—especially if those directives are issued only a short time after highly traumatic events.

3. *Insufficient Autonomy.* Directed forgiveness seems disrespectful of the autonomy of persons. Each person's feelings and attitudes about what happened to him or her are his or her own, just as each person's story and sense of self are individual. While it may be appropriate to try to *persuade* others to forgive, *directing* them to forgive wrongly preempts their responsibility for their own feelings and attitudes.[47]

4. *Corroded Rhetoric*. The result of directed forgiveness is likely to be a corroded rhetoric in which the notion of forgiveness loses much or all of its meaning.[48] When powerful and influential leaders issue directives, people may respond by mouthing forgiveness because that's what they are told to do. Yet, their mouthings are tokenistic and, so far as genuine shifts in emotions and attitudes are concerned, are likely to indicate little. "Yes, I forgive them" is likely to amount only to "I *say* I forgive because that's what I've got to do." Corroded rhetoric of this type is likely to evoke cynicism and further resentment. If people mouth forgiveness merely because they are pressed (or even forced) into doing so but continue to be angry and resistant, their resentment, in the long term, is likely to increase as a result. Thus, efforts to direct or manipulate forgiveness may be counterproductive in the end.

5. *Incompleteness*. If people are directed to forgive, they are likely to do so only partially—if at all. This incompleteness makes it unlikely that there will be attitudinal changes allowing for improved truth. Directed forgiveness is likely to be incomplete and, for that reason, is unlikely to contribute to reconciliation.[49]

CHOICES

In response to arguments against directed forgiveness, it might be argued that leaders are right when they try to direct it, because the alternatives are terrible. What if the alternatives to directed forgiveness are resentment, bitterness, and incitements to violence? Think of the many nationalist leaders who have exploited a sense of grievance within their group and have incited people to hatred and revenge. Often, it is just such urgings that cause cycles of violence and counterviolence, alternations of top dog and underdog, in human history. Given these ominous possibilities, it may seem that urging forgiveness is sensible and benign. Reconciliation requires social reintegration, which requires the cooperation of victimized persons. It could be argued, on these grounds, that forgiveness by victims is simply essential to progress in the direction of peace. Presumably, that is what Tutu had in mind in insisting that there is no future without forgiveness. He was rejecting "the opposite," The operative assumption here is that, without forgiveness, there can only be continued conflict and renewed violence. From the standpoint of practical consequences, it could be argued that whatever *can* be done to encourage forgiveness *should* be done.[50] One might almost want to say, "*So what* if victims are burdened, feel unacknowledged, and have some of their autonomy tampered with by leaders?" One might say, "Well, *so what* if the rhetoric of forgiveness loses a little of its luster? It is all for a good end (or goal) and these would be means (or strategies) justifiable by the ends in question." One might urge that these means would be justifiable given the urgent need for peace, which, in aftermath contexts, is the most urgent end of all.[51]

If directed forgiveness did provide an effective means of reconciliation—and the only such means—we would find here a problem of means and ends, a problem about whether a questionable means can justifiably be used when one is pursuing a morally worthy goal. We would face a profoundly difficult ethical dilemma. However, this dilemma does not arise. We have seen that, to provide for reconciliation, directed forgiveness is neither sufficiently authentic nor sufficiently enduring.[52]

There is, however, an even more fundamental problem with this account. Ultimately, the idea that people should forgive because it would be terrible if they were to seek revenge can be seen to presume a *false dichotomy* between revenge and forgiveness. The alternatives "forgiveness or revenge" are opposite in the sense that they are mutually exclusive. But, in the sense that they are not exhaustive options, they are not opposite. One can refrain from revenge while at the same time not going so far as to seek or advocate forgiveness. There is a spectrum of attitudinal possibilities ranging from forgiveness to revenge; that is why the distinction between forgiveness and revenge is not exhaustive and the revenge/forgiveness dichotomy is a false one. There are ways of refraining from revenge that do not amount to achieving forgiveness. In fact, people refrain from revenge for many different reasons. They may hold back from relationships and suspend judgment. They may tolerate others and coexist peacefully with them without going so far as to forgive them. They may believe in the rule of law and seek justice through criminal law. In the final analysis, it turns out to be a mistake to defend forgiveness by arguing against revenge.

NOTES

1. Or more.
2. For further details, see appendix 8, South Africa.
3. Desmond Tutu, *No Future without Forgiveness* (New York: Random House, 1999), p. 86. Another insider account of the work of the South African TRC is Alex Boraine, *A Country Unmasked* (Oxford: Oxford University Press, 2000).
4. Tutu, *No Future without Forgiveness*, p. 86. Even when one is reading with a critical eye and from the perspective of an agnostic, this inspirational rhetoric is hard to resist.
5. These comments suggest to me that Tutu does think that God is working in human history. There are obviously problematic aspects to this view even if one grants that God exists. Notoriously, a God who works through and in human history would seem to bear some responsibility for its enormous evils, including those of genocide and apartheid. Perhaps Tutu is in some way speaking metaphorically in these comments. I doubt it, however. Therefore, I take them at face value.
6. Ibid., p. 282.
7. Or, as can be argued for the Jews, they will use their power to wrong others, not the original perpetrators. Tutu's comments about Israel and the Palestinians suggest that he would agree with this remark; strictly speaking, however, the observation is mine, not his.
8. Tutu, *No Future without Forgiveness*, p. 154.
9. Ibid., p. 271.
10. See appendix 6, Rwanda. This concern was not by any means unrealistic.

11. Tutu, *No Future without Forgiveness*, p. 260. It is a brief comment. However, Tutu's use of the word "opposite" hides an extremely important problem. One might urge that seeking revenge and retribution in courts of law be avoided; however, to avoid revenge and retribution does not require going so far as forgiveness. One might choose an intermediate option. Because they ignore other ranges of possibility, the forgiveness/revenge and forgiveness/retribution dichotomies are false ones.

12. And yet, many of the arguments for acknowledgment, apology, and forgiveness can be defended from a secular point of view. I argue this case in my book *Forgiveness and Revenge* (London: Routledge, 2002).

13. Kader Asmal, Louise Asmal, and Ronald Suresh Roberts, *Reconciliation through Truth: A Reckoning of Apartheid's Criminal Governance* (New York: St. Martin's, 1997).

14. Martin Meredith, *Coming to Terms: South Africa's Search for Truth* (New York: Public Affairs, 1999), p. 318.

15. John-Paul Ferguson, "Democracy in a Land of Resentment," http://muse.jhu.edu/journals/said_review/v-2-.2ferguson.html (accessed November 2005). Reparations are discussed in chapter 9.

16. Richard Wilson, *The Politics of Truth and Reconciliation in South Africa: Legitimizing the Post-Apartheid State* (Cambridge: Cambridge University Press, 2001). A key paper articulating Wilson's position is discussed in my *Forgiveness and Revenge*, 37–39. Issues of retributive and restorative justice are explored here in chapter 7.

17. Discussed in detail in chapter 5 of *Forgiveness and Revenge*.

18. Interestingly, Tutu seems to envisage all three types and one more, but he does not clearly distinguish them. This point is explained further below.

19. Tutu, *No Future without Forgiveness*, 273. See note 26.

20. Argued in *Forgiveness and Revenge*, chapter 3, and elsewhere.

21. Argued in *Forgiveness and Revenge*, chapter 3. The point is that "I forgive you" is not a performative speech act in the way that "I promise you" is.

22. This story was told to me by a student in a seminar at Rhodes University in Grahamstown, South Africa, in March 1997.

23. The notion of forgiveness as offering a fresh start was suggested by Jean Harvey in "Forgiveness as an Obligation of the Moral Life," *International Journal of Applied Ethics* (1995): 211–21.

24. A cautionary note must be expressed at this point. Given that many people are all too ready to deny responsibility for their actions, brand all guilt as neurotic and misplaced, or deny any awareness of wrongdoing, the idea of *self-forgiveness* is open to serious abuse. To be morally acceptable, self-forgiveness must involve acknowledgment of one's own wrongdoing and a sincere resolve to avoid repeating the offense. It is not morally acceptable if it is predicated on denial. A useful discussion of self-forgiveness is found in Margaret Holmgren, "Self-Forgiveness and Responsible Moral Agency," *Journal of Value Inquiry* (1998): 75–91.

25. The fact that forgiving does not require forgetting is noted by Tutu on page 271 of *No Future without Forgiveness*.

26. I am indebted to Wilhelm Verwoerd for this conception.

27. Nor, for that matter, does forgetting entail forgiving. If one ceases to remember a wrong, one will thereby cease to resent the person who committed it, but this will not amount to forgiving that person. One will not have worked to overcome one's resentment; nor will other conditions of forgiveness, such as reacceptance of the wrongdoer, be implied by mere forgetting.

28. Religious perspectives on forgiveness are explored in appendix 1 of my book *Forgiveness and Revenge*.

29. Clearly, this argument is deductively valid. I am rejecting it because I am rejecting both premises.

30. Tutu, *No Future without Forgiveness*, p. 270.

31. Ibid., p. 273.

32. I have argued these points in more detail; see especially chapters 3 and 5.

33. I am presuming that mutual forgiveness would typically be bilateral, on both sides, although it could make sense to think of it as invitational as well. Unilateral forgiveness does not make much sense in this context.

34. The expression is borrowed from David Chandler, who in turn borrowed it from the debate over acknowledgment concerning the Khmer Rouge killings in Cambodia. See David Chandler, "Coming to Terms with the Terror and History of Pol Pot's Cambodia," in *Dilemmas of Reconciliation*, ed. Carol A. L. Prager and Trudy Govier (Waterloo, ON: Wilfrid Laurier Press, 2003), pp. 307–26.

35. Karl Tomm is a family therapist based at the University of Calgary. I am indebted to him for conversations about this matter.

36. These matters follow on discussions in chapter 2 and will be further developed in chapter 6.

37. This comment, and the information about the Dale Lang audiotapes, is taken from Lorna Dueck, "Hell Has Had Its Turn," which appeared in the *Toronto Globe and Mail*, May 4, 2000. Dale Lang's forgiveness is discussed in my *Forgiveness and Revenge*. Despite her own avowedly Christian perspective, Dueck expresses skepticism about the use of Lang's tape in this context. She acknowledges that forgiveness, especially of the near-instantaneous variety, would be inappropriate in this case. The idea that Christian theology provides a complete set of reasons for forgiving anybody anything, regardless of specific acts and circumstances, is extremely simplistic and can be understood as such both from within and from outside of serious Christian thinking. Thanks to Janet P. Schmidt and Lois Edmund, both of Winnipeg, for useful discussions of this matter.

38. Efforts to reintegrate ex-combatants in Sierra Leone are described in chapter 8.

39. This is a line of reasoning that I attribute to persons seeking to *direct* forgiveness in this and similar contexts. We could question it, obviously. One might insist that reintegration presupposes not forgiveness but something more like tolerance and restraint from inciting acts of revenge.

40. Reported by Dueck, "Hell Has Had Its Turn."

41. Cited in Jeremy Ginifer, "Reintegration of Ex-Combatants," http://www.iss.co.za/pub/monographs/No80/Chap2.htm.

42. Carol Fouke Mpoyo, "Looking for Justice, Forgiveness, Survival, and Peace in Sierra Leone." Church World Newsroom, July 13, 2002.

43. Quoted in Austin Merrill, "Sierra Leone June 18—Amputees Get New Home, New Life," *International Monitor Institute*, http://www.imisite.org/index_news.php?id=221.

44. David Millikan, "Forgetful Forgiveness in a World of Atrocities," http://www.shoot-themessenger.com.au/9909/c_forg.htm (accessed April 15, 2005).

45. Allegations that people are attempting to direct, or even command, forgiveness also arise in other contexts of reconciliation—notably those of South Africa and Rwanda. Several people have reported to me cases of such attempts in Canada. These cases typically involve a member of a Christian family who has been sexually abused by another family member. The

victim is told that she should forgive for Christian reasons; it was she who was wronged but, nevertheless, it is up to her to take this important step to repair relationships within the family. (Thanks to Karl Tomm, Lois Edmund, and Jan Schmidt for discussions of these cases.)

46. This is a charitable assumption, I think. The argument stated here can also apply to unilateral forgiveness. This application will be developed later. Given that religions, including, most significantly, Christianity, urge repentance by offenders as well as forgiveness by victims, this interpretation makes sense.

47. If the directives are put forward virtually as God-derived commands, with the implication that persons who do not forgive will fall into a spiritually alienated state, there is a serious violation of autonomy. In fact, orders to forgive could even be said to amount to manipulation in the form of *spiritual abuse*. (I owe the notion of spiritual abuse to Lois Edmund.)

48. The problem of corroded rhetoric is discussed in chapter 10.

49. Here I refer back to the interpretation of reconciliation in terms of the establishment or reestablishment of trust (see chapter 1). At this point, we must ask whether it is even *possible* for someone to forgive simply because another person, whom she regards as authoritative, directs her to do so. I find the matter odd and suspect that this may not be possible, but will not argue that point here.

50. And, on this view, if that involves spiritual abuse, it is just too bad.

51. Means and ends are discussed further in chapter 6.

52. I rely here on arguments from chapter 1.

Chapter Six

Fairness and Mutuality

THE PERILS OF VICTOR'S JUSTICE

The expression "victor's justice" alludes to the fact that parties who win a military victory are able to set up courts to try accused persons on the other side, which they are able to define as clearly being the "wrong side." The Nuremberg and Tokyo trials in the aftermath of the Second World War are often criticized as being examples of victor's justice. The Allied powers that arranged and staffed these trials were victorious powers, and the trials were, in an important sense, one-sided. They addressed the issues of war crimes, but only those committed by the losing powers. (Though many thousands of German and Japanese civilians were killed in the firebombings of Dresden and Tokyo and the atomic bombings of Hiroshima and Nagasaki, these acts were not addressed in postwar trials.) Thus, the postwar trials did not provide for *mutual* acknowledgment of wrongdoing; the victors were not compelled to consider the possibility that they themselves might have been responsible for wrongful acts during the war.

Because it constitutes a failure of evenhandedness, victor's justice is widely agreed to be problematic. In victor's justice we find selectivity in the application of relevant laws and norms. Although wrongs were committed by several parties, criminal proceedings are applied only to one, or only to a select subset. Problems here can be seen, from another perspective, as failures of *mutuality*.

With regard to reconciliation, most contemporary contexts differ in significant respects from those in which the Nuremberg and Tokyo trials occurred. While those trials dealt with an international conflict, more recent conflicts have largely been *within* nation states. And yet that fact does not lessen the temptations—or diminish the perils—of victor's justice. There remains a danger that the winning group or groups will assume power and seek to impose sanctions on the losers—and only them. Impartiality and mutual acknowledgment remain important in these contexts, not only in legal processes but also in contexts of investigation, acknowledgment, and reparation. Given the need to develop cooperative relationships within a society, selectivity and bias may be even more undermining in national contexts than in international ones.

In a situation of victor's justice, one group presumes the authority to judge others while remaining itself immune from scrutiny. After a period of political violence, it is extremely unlikely that any involved group will be "pure" in the sense of having committed no human rights violations or other wrongs. (If some group were "pure" in this sense, then it would presumably have nothing to fear from the investigations of truth commissions, courts, or other bodies and would feel no need to exempt itself from these proceedings.) If investigations of alleged wrongs are selective, they will be perceived to be so and the procedures and institutions involved will lack credibility. Selective procedures will make authorities and institutions seem more committed to power and image than to fairness and the rule of law, thereby undermining trust, credibility, and prospects for improving relationships. Those on the "losing" side will feel singled out by biased processes—"witch hunts" are often alleged in such cases. People are likely to be suspicious and resentful if they believe that they are being penalized for acts that others have committed with impunity.

A fundamental goal in contexts of national reconciliation is to understand why abuses occurred so as to prevent them from happening again. If investigations are selective and partial, the understanding will be incomplete and recommendations for reform are likely to be so as well. Failures of mutuality in the acknowledgment of wrongdoing will undermine efforts to establish an impartial judicial system capable of ending impunity and providing for the rule of law. For all these reasons, selective and nonmutual forms of acknowledgment mark flaws in processes of reconciliation. Mutuality is a key condition for their success. As used here, the term "mutuality" refers to the evenhanded and appropriate acknowledgment of wrongdoing by all relevant parties in the wake of a bitter conflict.

Collectively, wrongs may occur with regard to the "cause" defended by a group or with regard to the *means* employed to pursue that cause. *Individually*, people on all sides may suffer wrongs as *victims* or commit wrongs as *perpetrators*. Thus, there are four aspects we can distinguish when reflecting on the rights and wrongs of a given conflict.

(1) *cause* or goal;
(2) *means* employed;
(3) harms suffered by individual *victims*;
(4) wrongs committed by individual *perpetrators*.

The first two aspects have to do primarily with collectives; the next two largely concern individuals. A given individual may be considered at both the third and fourth levels, being both a victim and a perpetrator. The understanding of reconciliation processes is enhanced if these distinctions are kept in mind.

Considerations are complex at each stage. Often one finds arguments in which considerations from one stage are cited as relevant to those at another. For example, a group that is fighting for what it regards as a just cause (for example, liberation from an oppressive governing power) may very well argue that it needs to employ means that would prima facie be illegitimate in order to achieve a military victory. However, the issue of *cause* and the issue of *means* are logically distinct, even when they are connected.

AN ILLUSTRATIVE STORY: SOUTH AFRICA, 1998

In the early 1990s, the African National Congress, the main group struggling against the apartheid regime in South Africa, faced allegations that severe human rights abuses were being committed in its camps in Angola, Zambia, and Tanzania. It was alleged that abuse, torture, and extrajudicial executions were being committed against persons suspected of collaborating with the apartheid government. In response to these charges, the ANC initiated an investigation into its own conduct in the form of a three-man commission of inquiry headed by Louis Skweyiya. This commission reported that there had been serious abuses in the camps, abuses that amounted to staggering brutality. Nelson Mandela accepted the claims of this commission and acknowledged that the ANC leadership bore collective responsibility for the abuses. Neither he nor the commission itself named any individuals as responsible. In response to further criticisms on the matter, the ANC leadership appointed a second investigative commission. Comprised of independent figures not linked to the ANC, this commission was chaired by S. M. Motsuenyane. Its report, issued in August 1993, stated conclusions similar to those of the Skweyiya Commission. However, this second report did not stop with collective responsibility; it named individuals.[1] In reponse, the ANC leadership said, "We accept its findings that periodically abuses did occur within the ANC camps, but acknowledge that it was *not established that there was any systematic policy of abuse*."[2] The ANC leadership stated that it was making efforts to establish a rigorous chain of command and authority that would prevent further abuses.

Given the enormous human rights abuses that the South African state was perpetuating under apartheid, the ANC was understandably frustrated by attention given to human rights violations within its own ranks. Its negotiating partner, the National Party (NP) had, after all, run a state in which every institution and aspect of daily life embraced a commitment to apartheid, which had been pronounced a crime against humanity. The South African state, under successive NP governments, had committed abductions, rape, torture, and killings of activists and suspected activists. Concerning the Motsuenyane Report and its context, the ANC's National Executive stated:

> The violations referred to in the Report can in no way be equated to the activities
> of the apartheid state, which were gross, systematic and a product of a policy which

transgressed not only South African law but virtually the whole range of fundamental rights protected in international law. It must always be remembered that the international community has condemned the practices of apartheid as a crime against humanity, akin to slavery, extending far beyond any notion of single acts taken against individuals. Apartheid's violations were based on a denial of national rights where torture, ill-treatment and violence were instruments of state policy.

In recent years when there have been investigations into the abuse of rights that have happened in other national liberation struggles, like Chile or El Salvador, violations committed by the liberation forces have comprised only a minute proportion of the number of total transgressions by illegitimate and authoritarian regimes. There is no reason to believe that the situation in South Africa is any different.

Only a broad national Truth Commission will establish whether this is in fact true. We further maintain that in no way can the lapses in authority and control that did occur in the ANC camps be compared to the systematic pattern of human degradation and suffering that apartheid consciously created. There was never a deliberate and preconceived policy of abuse in the ANC. In fact, conscious efforts were made to ensure protection even under the difficult circumstances of responding to South African government infiltration into our ranks, assassination of our leaders, and the daily torture, harassment and dislocation of our supporters.

Thus, the ANC sought to contextualize its own abuses—which, it insisted, were limited, given the historical context in which they were committed.

It was this sense of relative disproportion in the attention given to its own abuses as compared to those of the apartheid state that led the ANC National Executive to call for a Truth and Reconciliation Commission. Such a commission would investigate violations of human rights from all quarters, hear the stories of victims and perpetrators *whatever race or group they belonged to*, and propose recommendations that could provide for better, nonabusive policies. It would ensure appropriate compensation for victims and "work out the best basis for reconciliation." Thus was the idea of the South African Truth and Reconciliation Commission born.

In its *Final Report*, issued in the fall of 1998, the South African TRC found that human rights violations had been committed by the apartheid state between 1960 and 1994. In seeking to defend its apartheid institutions, the South African state had committed many serious violations of human rights. The liberation groups were recognized by the TRC to have been fighting for a just cause: they were, after all, seeking to overthrow a grossly unjust system in circumstances where political repression had made nonviolent means virtually impossible.[3] Thus, with regard to *just cause*, there was a fundamental difference between liberation groups and the apartheid state. At the level of *means*, there were also significant differences. Nevertheless, the South African TRC found that there had been some gross violations of human rights by all parties involved in the struggle against apartheid, including the ANC.

The TRC commended the ANC for having investigated some of its own abuses through the Skweyiya and Motsuenyane Commissions, calling this step unprecedented. It found, nevertheless, that the ANC had been responsible for serious human rights violations in four major categories.

(a) There were violations committed by the armed unit of the ANC in the course of both planned and unplanned offensive operations.
(b) There were violations against persons regarded as spies, informers, and collaborators.
(c) There were violations against other parties in the course of the "mass struggle" in the 1980s.
(d) There were violations against other groups (mainly members of the Inkatha Freedom Party) after the legalization of the ANC in South Africa in February 1990.[4]

Unplanned operations sometimes caused civilian injuries and deaths, which were counted by the TRC as gross violations of human rights. (The assumption made here was that if a noncombatant person is killed in the course of a violent conflict, he or she has been a victim of serious human rights abuse.) When one considers the period under scrutiny, 1964–1990, and the fact that South Africa had, at that time, a population of some thirty to forty million people, the approximately one hundred thirty civilian deaths attributed to the ANC seems very small. Furthermore, those noncombatant deaths occurred mainly in actions directed against state and military targets. The TRC recognized that the ANC had, indeed, tried to minimize civilian casualties. For example, during the 1980s, the ANC had used land mines in some rural areas. When civilian deaths due to land mines began to exceed military deaths, the ANC ended its landmine campaign in those areas. With regard to identified "spies," "collaborators," "enemies," and "defectors," the TRC found that there had been cruel treatment and summary executions by ANC agents. These were extrajudicial killings, which amounted to gross violations of human rights.

The *TRC Final Report* of 1998 allowed that there were areas of ambiguity in some contexts in which abusive actions by the ANC were alleged. One problem was that some agents who identified themselves as belonging to the ANC were, in fact, outside the control of its leadership. Another was the extent to which the ANC had been involved in "black-on-black" violence in many South African townships in the late 1980s and early 1990s, at which time there was intense conflict between it and the Inkatha Freedom Party (IFP). There was also uncertainty about the causes of that violence; the ANC claimed that the South African government had used the IFP as a tool to provoke it. The TRC acknowledged that there were many gaps in understanding of these matters but found, on a balance of probabilities, that some killings and abuses in these bitter struggles were attributable to the ANC. The ANC insisted that it had never defined members of the Inkatha Freedom Party as legitimate targets. Nevertheless, the TRC had heard testimony to the contrary.[5]

Many members of the IFP were killed by ANC members during this struggle.

The UDF (United Democratic Front), which was allied to the ANC, attacked youth and others affiliated with the IFP. In his testimony to the truth commission, Daluxolo Luthuli stated:

> Militant youth who were affiliated to the UDF were very active in black areas. Through violence and intimidation they were forcing people to support them in their efforts to make the country ungovernable. People who did not support the comrades were abused in many ways by these comrades. People's courts were held and the sentences which were meted out by youngsters were often inhumane and barbaric. People were commonly sentenced to hundreds of lashes, forced to parade naked through townships and killed by necklacing. Inkatha and its supporters were labelled as collaborators of the white government and were, in the view of the comrades and UDF, enemies. It was common for Inkatha leaders and supporters to be attacked and murdered.[6]

In the fall of 1998, the TRC informed the ANC of its findings and showed the ANC the relevant sections of its *Final Report* to provide an opportunity for response. The result was an uproar within the ANC, which contested the findings and eventually went to court to attempt to prevent the release of the report. Ironically, the very party that had called for and established the TRC was extremely dissatisfied and frustrated with important elements of its results. The ANC's submission to the TRC, contesting the findings, has a strongly emotional tone. Reading it, even years later, one can almost feel the anger and defensiveness jumping off the page. The ANC seems to have expected from the TRC some kind of exoneration. After all, it had fought and won the struggle against apartheid, which was a crime against humanity; it had committed far fewer offenses than the state against which it was struggling; it had established two commissions to investigate itself; it had been careful about civilian deaths resulting from military actions; and it had established a truth commission with a general mandate to consider the struggle and its contexts in terms of victims and perpetrators in all races and in all groups. And, nevertheless, the ANC—now the governing party—found itself on the receiving end of criticisms from that commission. It stood accused of gross human rights violations.

In its angry response, the ANC accused the TRC of criminalizing its struggle for liberation and delegitimizing the struggle against apartheid. The ANC defended its liberation struggle in strong terms, insisting that it had been far superior to its enemies and far more morally upright than other liberation groups (who themselves, in turn, in nearly all cases, killed far fewer people than the states they were opposing.) The ANC stated firmly that it was rightly proud of its role in ending apartheid and proud, too, of the fact that it had taken the unique step of investigating its own human rights abuses through the Skweyiya and Motsuenyane Commissions. The criticisms amounted, the party said, to a betrayal.[7]

One contested issue was whether the killing of noncombatants during a war amounts to a gross violation of their human rights. The ANC argued that killing, as such, does not itself amount to a "gross violation of human rights" when committed by the *right side* in a *just war*—by their very nature, wars involve killing people, including (regrettably) even some noncombatant people. If all such killings were deemed, legally and morally, to constitute gross violations of human rights, then war itself would constitute a gross violation of human rights and, as such, would be delegitimized.[8] That, the ANC claimed, would be "absurd," especially in the context of people fighting a war against a system that itself amounted to a massive violation of human rights.[9] The ANC argued that international law authorizes recourse to war under some circumstances; apartheid had been pronounced a crime against humanity; and the ANC had tried to follow the Geneva Conventions of 1949 and the related 1977 Protocols for the humanitarian conduct of warfare.

The ANC questioned the TRC's interpretation of international humanitarian law, claiming that:

(a) Civilians are "necessarily and inevitably" killed during the conduct of warfare.
(b) "Spies do not enjoy the rights of prisoners of war."
(c) "Resort to the penalty of capital punishment is permissible in the context of a war situation."
(d) "Irregular wars of liberation against foreign, colonial, and racial oppression, as opposed to regular wars conducted by States, are recognised as legitimate forms of warfare."[10]

With regard to the first point, the TRC seems to have presumed that neither Just War Theory nor the Geneva Conventions permit *any* killing of "protected persons."[11] The Geneva Conventions were intended to promote respect for the life and physical safety of persons located within war zones but not themselves participating in the war. (These persons are said to be "hors de combat.") The Geneva Conventions were formulated not as "other things being equal" (prima facie) restrictions but rather as *absolute bans*, which was, in effect, what the TRC assumed in its reasoning.[12]

The occurrence of torture, abuse, and extrajudicial executions of suspected collaborators and spies in ANC camps had been the subjects of the Skweyiya and Motsuenyane reports. In this area, TRC findings against the ANC were based on the testimony of victims and persons applying for amnesty—including many ANC members—and on prior acknowledgments by the ANC, according to the results of the earlier reports. The ANC leadership had acknowledged the abuses, denying only that they were systematic. ANC members had themselves testified to the TRC about such matters. Thus, the TRC was shocked when the ANC reacted as strongly as it did to findings in this area; after all, the evidence had come from the ANC itself.

On the subject of these abuses and violations, the ANC did not deny that they occurred, but it did offer excuses. It claimed that it was conducting a guerrilla war under extraordinarily difficult circumstances and that there really were spies and collaborators. From the ANC perspective, these persons had to be "dealt with" in contexts where no normal courts were available. Unlike its opponent, the ANC did not have the power and resources of a state to control its agents. For these reasons, it argued that it should not be held to account in the way a state could be held to account.

In its October 1998 reaction to the TRC report, the ANC went so far as to accuse the commission of shifting the blame for the political violence away from the apartheid regime to the democratic movement. It called on the TRC to recognize *the truth* that the struggle we waged helped our country to avoid the death of millions of civilians and radically reduced the hostility of the majority of our people towards those who belonged to the "oppressor nation" as well as their black partners who were bribed or intimidated to participate in the commission of the apartheid crime against humanity.[13]

While one might wish to grant many of these points, the ANC's written response to the TRC nevertheless seems emotional and defensive. Some of its reasoning seems logically flawed. Consider, for example, the following aspects:

"We were better than them, so we were without fault."

"If you criticize *us*, you legitimize *them*."

"It delegitimizes our *cause* if you attack us for the *means* we used in pursuing that cause."

"We investigated ourselves, so we were good—so you should not criticize us."

"We were much more righteous than other liberation groups; therefore you should not criticize us."

There is flawed logic here. Being better than someone else does not provide evidence that one has done no wrong. A criticism of one group is just that—not a legitimization of some other group. Doing some good things, and being superior to other comparable groups in some respects, does not provide evidence that one is faultless.

The ANC's legal challenge to the publication of the *Final Report* failed to prevent its publication and the report was released in late October 1998. On February 25, 1999, Deputy President Thabo Mbeki gave a speech about the TRC in the South African Parliament. Mbeki saluted the TRC for its work in discovering and exposing truths about human rights violations, tracing missing persons, encouraging reconciliation between perpetrators and victims, cultivating a spirit of remorse among those who had done wrong, and identifying some persons entitled to reparations. However, he expressed reservations about the findings of the TRC.

One of the central matters at issue was and remains the erroneous determination of various actions of our liberation movement as gross violations of human rights, including *the general implication that any and all military activity which results in the loss of civilian lives constitutes a gross violation of human rights*. The net effect of these findings is to de-legitimise or criminalize a significant part of the struggle of our people for liberation and to subtract from the commitment made in our Constitution to "honour those who suffered for justice and freedom in our land."

While praising the TRC for some of its work, the ANC government did not change its position that some findings against the ANC itself were fundamentally mistaken.

It is sobering to recall that during this conflict between the ANC and the South African TRC, Nelson Mandela was the president of South Africa. This man was one of the greatest moral leaders of the twentieth century. Apparently even he found mutuality a challenge. The story of this conflict between the South African Truth and Reconciliation Commission and the ANC—the very party that had brought this ambitious and highly influential TRC into being—is one of challenges in the area of mutuality. It illustrates a fundamental set of problems that go far beyond the borders of South Africa.

In fact, issues of mutuality can be found in virtually all contexts in which national reconciliation is required. In the aftermath of a violent conflict, *selective* attention to wrongdoing will inspire suspicion and resentment. Processes of reconciliation will not be credible and convincing if they are one-sided. Evenhandedness, lack of bias, and impartiality are essential. Selective attention to alleged offenses will not provide a basis for fair institutions, public confidence, the rule of law, or the ending of human rights abuses. This means that empowered groups engaged in processes of reconciliation must be willing to admit fault in themselves as well as in their former opponents.[14] Thus, mutual acknowledgment is clearly important. And yet it is very difficult to achieve in practice—even when the circumstances that should provide for it are close to ideal. In South Africa, the ANC moved a great distance in the direction of mutuality but eventually found it too painful to acknowledge its own serious violations of human rights, even when findings were based on evidence that it provided.

To briefly consider another example, in Peru, the Shining Path guerrilla group committed serious atrocities. So, too, did government forces and other contending groups.[15] The Peruvian truth commission estimated that some sixty-nine thousand people had been killed between 1980 and 2000. Of these, approximately 50 percent were killed by the Shining Path guerrillas and 30 percent by the military and police. (Other deaths were due to a smaller guerrilla group, peasant self-defense groups, or were unattributed.) Though the government can clearly be said to have had a *just cause* in fighting against the Shining Path, given the murderous ideology of that group, it was found by the truth commission to bear a very grave responsibility for its *means* of waging the struggle. Persons in the military responsible for grave abuses were living freely in the society when the commission submitted its report, and the commission urged that some of them be prosecuted for human rights violations. These recommendations were badly received by persons on the government side. A common response was to accuse the commission of left-wing bias, to claim that the commissioners were Marxist in an attempt to deny credibility to the report, and to allege that the findings failed to honor people who had fought heroically against a fanatical and totalitarian ideology that had to be defeated.

THE STRANGE CASE OF SAM HINGA NORMAN

In Sierra Leone, rebels could initially claim justice in their *cause*, given that they were fighting against a highly corrupt government and seeking equality of opportunity and education for disadvantaged youth. Nevertheless, the rebels used grossly barbaric *means* in waging the struggle.[16] In response, forces allied with the government also used atrocious means, resorting to such practices as the abduction of children, the burning of villages, and the intimidation of the civilian population by the use of torture, rape, and sexual violence. Eventually, all involved groups committed serious wrongs in the course of the struggle in Sierra Leone. Individuals were profoundly harmed: there were many deaths, maimings, and injuries that resulted in separated and dislocated families and handicapped and suffering people. Many were victims and many of these, including child soldiers, were also perpetrators.[17]

The Special Court for Sierra Leone sought to try representative individuals who were most responsible for the grossly abusive acts undertaken during the war. They were unable to try key persons on the rebel side. Rebel leaders Foday Sankoh and Sam Bockarie died. And it is rumored that another key rebel leader, Johnny Koroma, also died. Charles Taylor, a key leader, sought and received sanctuary in Nigeria; eventually he was turned over to Sierra Leonese authorities in the winter of 2006. Three persons indicted had actually fought to defeat the rebels. One was Sam Hinga Norman, who had been a deputy defense minister and later a minister of internal affairs in the Kabbah government. Hinga Norman was indicted on eight counts for crimes against humanity, war crimes, and other severe violations of international humanitarian law. He was accused of unlawful killings of civilians and captured combatants; inhumane acts; looting and burning; terrorizing the civilian population and imposing collective punishments; and the conscripting and use of children under the age of fifteen in the hostilities.[18] At the time these acts were committed, Hinga Norman was the national coordinator of the Civil Defence Force (CDF) and, as such, was a principal force in organizing and supporting that group. He was also the leader and commander of a militia called the Kamajors, a group of traditional hunters who supported the Kabbah government against the rebels.

In its indictment, the Special Court stated that Hinga Norman is "by his *acts or omissions . . . individually criminally responsible because he planned and ordered the acts, or aided and abetted in them.*" In addition, or alternatively, Hinga Norman would be criminally responsible as a *leader* who was accountable for the acts of his subordinates; he *knew* or *should have known* about such acts and did not act to prevent them.[19]

The idea of indicting this man, widely seen as the person who had managed to defeat the rebels, struck many as outrageous. There were certainly anomalies. Hinga Norman was regarded as a hero who had been on the right side and played a key role in ending vicious violence by rebel forces. He was in the government of President Kabbah who must (or so one would think) have had many of the same associations and liabilities but was, nevertheless, not indicted by the Special Court. Furthermore, the attempt of the Special Court to be evenhanded in its prosecutions was thwarted by its early inability (later corrected) to take Charles Taylor into custody and by the deaths of several key rebel leaders. There was an effort to be evenhanded, but realities undermined that effort, with an anomalous result.

Peter Penfold, a former UK high commissioner in Sierra Leone, wrote skeptically about criminal process of the Special Court, saying:

> Without Taylor and with Sankoh's death, plus the previous death of the infamous RUF commander, Sam Bockarie and the reported death or disappearance of the AFRC junta leader, Johnny Paul Koroma, the only person of note being prosecuted by the Special Court is Chief Sam Hinga Norman. He is the former Minister of Internal Security and erstwhile coordinator of the Civil Defence Forces (CDF), the groupings of indigenous civil militia who fought against the rebels and helped restore the legitimate democratic government of President Tejan Kabbah. Thus the impression is given that Norman is the person most responsible for the awful atrocities committed during the rebel war, an impression which even Norman's detractors do not accept. No one denies that some members of the CDF committed excesses in their struggle to restore peace and democracy but these were far fewer than those committed by the rebels.[20]

The Sierra Leone Truth and Reconciliation Commission estimated that the RUF (rebel forces) committed over 60 percent of the atrocities in the civil war, with the army committing 16 percent and the CDF 6 percent.[21] When the CDF was the highest profile group in prosecutions, the trial process gave a highly misleading picture of the conflict. Arthur Abraham, a historian of Sierra Leone, noted that Hinga Norman was in the Kabbah government and was a friend and associate of President Kabbah. Arguably, if Hinga Norman was associated with the Kamajors, then Kabbah was also associated with them and should share command responsibility for some or all of their actions. Abraham asked whether Norman's arrest would mean that the President himself might be arrested by the Special Court. He also raised the question of what message the Special Court was sending to other African persons who might seek some day to defend peace and democracy by taking up arms against brutal rebel forces. Abraham went so far as to say:

> Though set up with good intentions, I believe that [the Special Court] is undermining the fragile peace which has been achieved in Sierra Leone. The role of the US government in all this is particularly incongruous . . . at the very time when they are pushing the work of the Special Court, they have signed an agreement with the Sierra Leone government *exempting* US citizens from being sent to the International Criminal Court [to be tried for] committing atrocities and human rights violations.[22]

The trial of Sam Hinga Norman began on June 3, 2004. He is being tried along with two other leaders, Moinina Fofana and Allieu Kondewa. At the trial's outset, Hinga Norman dissolved his legal team, stating that he wished to defend himself. In defense, he denied the authority of the court and argued, in addition, that he was not in a position to control the actions of the Kamajors. He further argued that the CDF was likewise outside his control and that because it had arisen spontaneously in opposition to the rebels it was not, strictly speaking, an armed faction at all. By the fall of 2005, Hinga Norman had founded his own political party from his jail cell and was working with remnants of rebel forces against the government of which he had been a key member. There were political parties and civic groups organizing in his support throughout Sierra Leone. The Steering Committee to Elect Hinga Norman (SCEHN) stated that it had many working partners. Far from regarding Hinga Norman as a war criminal who needed to be tried in the interests of establishing democracy and the rule of law, his supporters deemed him to be an important leader for the future.[23]

This perplexing case suggests limits to mutuality and evenhandedness. Given the near absence of significant indicted rebel leaders and the further fact that command responsibility was arguably shared with President Kabbah himself, the indictment and trial of Sam Hinga Norman struck many people as unfair to the point of perversity.

There are real risks here: if a commitment to impartiality in the interests of rule of law results in impressions of unfairness and the (selective) mistreatment of heroic figures, it may create resentment and resistance, which can threaten the stability of the peace. One can only hope that the rally of supporters for Hinga Norman will not be a destabilizing force in Sierra Leone. Ominously, however, the potential is there.

THE TEMPTATIONS OF POLARIZATION

While clearly necessary for reconciliation, mutuality requires complex reasoning and important concessions. In contrast, polarization, predicated on a sense that "we were right and they were wrong," seems intellectually clear and, for many, will be more satisfying psychologically. After risk and sacrifice, one will not want to admit fault. Rather, one will wish to regard oneself as heroic, justified, and right. In a violent political struggle, a group and its leadership will adopt an ideology of the just and necessary struggle within which people bravely risk and sacrifice their lives for legitimate ends. In this context, winning will seem to be everything. After all, when one is risking life, limbs, and loved ones for a political cause, it is very easy to lapse into thinking that the cause is so urgent that it will justify *any* means. The group's sense of righteous solidarity will make it hard to admit fault—as many stories of reconciliation confirm.

Even apart from the context of violent political struggles, most people find it difficult to acknowledge wrongdoing and fault. Although the fallibility of human beings is a matter of basic common sense, it can be very difficult to fully appreciate the following straightforward argument and conduct one's life accordingly.

Human beings are fallible.
I am a human being.
Therefore,
I am fallible.

Constructing an analogous argument on the group level, the same point can be made.

Groups of human beings are fallible and can make mistakes.
We are a group of human beings.
Therefore,
We are fallible and can make mistakes.

Most of us do not like to admit that we have made mistakes—much less that we have committed serious moral wrongs in pursuing what we take to be a just cause. In contexts of national reconciliation, the path of mutual acknowledgment is difficult to follow. The more familiar path is one of denial and selective attention: these responses are likely to feel natural and easy. In addition, denial and selective attention serve to reinforce the solidarity of the group.

People who have fought in a political conflict usually believe that they have struggled in defense of a just cause and that, since the cause was just, so were the actions undertaken in its defense—even acts of brutality. Encouraged by the widespread belief that the just cause can be clearly identified and that violence is the best way to pursue it, they regard their struggle not as morally flawed but as obligatory and heroic. It is hard to be clearheaded and logical in such contexts. A nonpartisan observer may note that simplifications and hasty inferences abound. Acts are easily confused with agents, and the claim that a group did something wrong is easily confused with the idea that that group did everything wrong. Many will have a sense of solidarity and identity based on the belief that they were fighting for a just cause. They are convinced that they were *right*—and will have a deep (though fallacious) tendency to conflate *being right* with *doing no wrong*.

CLARIFICATIONS

(a) Distinguishing Mutuality from Moral Equivalence

A "one just victorious" presumption underlies the pursuit of victor's justice. Though it is nearly always flawed, such thinking often feels "natural" and "right" to people who had heavily committed to one side or another in a conflict. We are inclined to presume two sides in such a conflict, with one side being the winner and the other side being the loser. We presume that if things have gone as justice requires, the winner is in the right and the loser is in the wrong. Thus, the winning side will be deemed the one just victorious and—as a corollary—the losers will bear the imposition of the penalties. All victims on the one just victorious side will be considered innocent persons. Contrastingly, all perpetrators on the losing side will be deemed villainous agents of harm. In this kind of polarized model, the one just victorious side is assumed to be thoroughly and completely right: it had a just cause, won a fair military victory in the violent struggle, and has now rightly come to a position of power from which it can impose its will on the losers. Through its victory and its virtue, the one just victorious side will be entitled to investigate wrongdoing by the losers, penalize individual perpetrators belonging to that group, and compensate innocent victims on its own side. One might call this "victor's reconciliation."

The one just victorious model is easy to understand and is familiar from fictional narratives in such contexts as the stereotypical western movies in which there are clearly differentiated good guys and bad guys.[24] (Our guys are always good guys.) But clearly this model is too simplistic to be plausible in detail. When parties engage in a violent struggle in a highly complex world, the likelihood of ambiguously just causes and illegitimate means is high.

So far, the discussion has been about groups and their fallibility, whether at the level of cause, of means, or of both. However, considerations about *individual* responsibility and harm are also crucial to processes of reconciliation, whether in the form of trials, truth commissions, workshop processes, or programs of acknowledgment and compensation. It is not realistically possible to avoid all need to explore the circumstances and needs of individuals—whether they are persons harmed, militant agents, or both. We need to reflect on individuals and cases will vary, often in complex ways.[25] The challenge of mutuality for theory and practice is that when we depart from the simple structure of the one just victorious framework, we find considerable complexity and ambiguity. That is not to say that moral and legal judgments become impossible or unnecessary. Rather, it is to say that they become less certain and more qualified than we might wish or expect.

A risk at this point is that of lapsing into a framework of *simplistic moral equivalence*, in which it is presumed that no meaningful moral distinctions can be made. It is easy to conflate these two claims:

(i) All parties committed some *wrongs.*

(ii) All parties were equally *wrong (or* equally *right) and are thus morally equivalent.*

Claims (i) and (ii) are logically distinct and should not be conflated. To say that each of the involved parties—call them X, Y, and Z for purposes of exposition—is open to criticism is *not* to say that X, Y, and Z are *equally* open to criticism. For example, party X might have committed a relatively small number of wrongs while fighting for a just cause; party Y may have committed a large number of wrongs while fighting for an unjust cause; and party Z, while playing a small role in assisting party X, might have committed many minor wrongs in the course of doing so. In an aftermath in which groups X, Y, and Z were involved in reconciliation, acknowledgment would be needed from all three (through their leadership) in order for mutuality to be achieved. That is *not* to say that there would be a moral equivalence between these groups.

When we come to consider individuals within all three groups, there would almost certainly be both victims and perpetrators—though there is no reason, a priori or empirically, to expect that victims and perpetrators should distribute themselves equally among these groups. Mutuality of acknowledgment would mean requiring that *all* parties—X, Y, and Z—should reflect on, and if appropriate, admit to any wrongs they have committed, and that they should do this regardless of their relative power as a result of the military or negotiated settlement. Ideally, each group would acknowledge the existence and needs of victims in other groups as well as the degrees of responsibility among militants and leaders. Such acknowledgment would contribute a sense that all sides were acknowledging wrongs and that there was mutuality and a kind of evenhandedness. It would not amount to moral equivalence.

In its proceedings and deliberations, the South African TRC can be plausibly interpreted as having sought mutuality. The ANC, however, interpreted its quest for mutuality as an endorsement of moral equivalence. The commission treated victims and perpetrators equitably regardless of their political affiliations, exploring the causes and means used by the apartheid state and its various agents and by the various groups fighting against that state. To judge, as the South African TRC did, that the ANC had been responsible for *some* violations was *not* to claim that the ANC was morally equivalent to the apartheid state. When the TRC called for its collective acknowledgment of (some) illegitimate means, the ANC reacted as though the TRC had made a finding of moral equivalence between it and its pro-apartheid opponent. Yet the TRC is more plausibly interpreted as seeking mutuality. It did not presume or conclude that there was moral equivalence between the contending groups.

In the aftermath of the struggle in Northern Ireland, one experienced practitioner said, "we have all deeply harmed one another."[26] His remark is doubtless true, and in many respects it is profound. Yet more must be said. Individuals involved in reconciliation processes will have their own particular stories to tell; individuals found accountable by courts or commissions will have particular circumstances, motives, and causal stories needing to be considered; individuals claiming compensation will have their own specific and particular needs. Although the individual stories will, at significant points, be interlocked with group narratives, the details and nuances of particular cases will be relevant to their determination. Sensitive and equitable judgments will be impossible without them. A generalized sense of moral equivalence based on the rough idea that each group had some justice and some injustice on its side, and that victims and perpetrators were everywhere to be found, would satisfy no one.

(b) Just War, Just Cause, and Just Means

The distinction between the *cause* for which a group is fighting and the *means* it uses to pursue its cause is clear from a logical point of view and firmly entrenched in just war theory. Nevertheless, it is easy to lose one's appreciation for that distinction. As we have seen, in its dispute with the TRC, the ANC interpreted criticisms of its *means* as delegitimizing its *cause*.

Within just war theory, a distinction between just cause and just means is a fundamental element, and from a practical point of view, the distinction between cause and means is useful and important. In the real circumstances of the contemporary world, neither international law nor just war theory suffice to provide reliable and coherent *general criteria* to clarify who has a just cause and who does not. Nevertheless, some individual cases are clear. Apartheid in South Africa was a crime against humanity and had to be opposed. The Khmer Rouge in Cambodia slaughtered hundreds of thousands of people in their quest for a pure communist state; they had to be defeated. The same can be said of the fanatical Shining Path guerrillas in Peru, the rebels in Sierra Leone, and the genocidal Rwandan regime in 1994.[27] In these cases, it is relatively easy to make an intuitive judgment that one party or grouping had a just cause and the others did not. Other cases—the Balkan and Sri Lankan conflicts, for example—are less clear-cut.

Even if a group were to be justified in using *some* violent means in pursuit of its goals, it is not thereby justified in using *any and all* violent means. Although this distinction is clear enough in concept, it poses considerable difficulties in practice. Norms pertaining to combatants and noncombatants, prisoners of war, and powerful modern weaponry are by no means easy to apply during the fearful turbulence of a violent conflict.[28] The nature of contemporary weaponry is one aspect of this failure. Another is the practices of nonstate and state agents who seek and often receive extensive support from persons who would seem otherwise to qualify as noncombatants. In the real circumstances of this world, it is unlikely that any participating party will satisfy the moral requirements of just war theory with regards to its means. It is even less likely that it will conform to the international legal standards specified by the Geneva Conventions and 1977 Protocols.

If the Geneva Conventions and related Protocols are interpreted in an absolutist way—as they usually are—they are far stricter than just war theory itself. There are no legitimate exceptions. On this interpretation, the likelihood of satisfying conditions of just means in conducting a modern war is close to zero because one would have to kill absolutely no persons except for combatants. According to these strict standards, any party resorting to violence to defend its cause would be almost certain to have committed violations at the level of means. Mutuality in acknowledgment will mean that all parties who engaged in the violent struggle will have wrongs to acknowledge.

To acknowledge violations and wrongdoing in the aftermath of the violent conflict means acknowledging the fallibility of one's own side and, potentially, the fallibility of one's own self.

(c) The Collective and the Individual

Most of what has been said so far involves groups. As has been pointed out, reconciliation processes will also have to consider individuals. Relationships are crucial to reconciliation; relationships are, first and foremost, between individuals, although they also exist between groups.

Individuals may be considered as persons harmed by violence and suffering in its aftermath, as perpetrators responsible for committing wrongs, or—in some cases—from both perspectives. In deliberating about such matters, it is crucial to recognize that considerations about *individuals* do not emerge straightforwardly from considerations about *groups*. For example, a group may have been alleging a just cause on the basis of a mistaken or even cynical manipulation of information while a particular individual fighting within it may have sincerely and even reasonably believed its claims. The leaders of the apartheid state in South Africa knew better than to believe that the ANC was a communist organization. However, some young white conscripts, subjected to propaganda about the communist threat to the state, may well have believed it and, as a result, may have sincerely thought themselves to be fighting for a just cause. To fail to observe the distinction between the group level and the individual level is to lapse into a logical fallacy known as the *fallacy of division*. A *group* may have characteristics that do not belong to each of its members considered as *individuals* and, for that reason, premises about the qualities of a group do not provide sufficient evidence for conclusions about the qualities of individuals within it.

Fallacy of Division:

Group G has characteristic x.
Individual I is a member of Group G.
Therefore,
Individual I has characteristic x.

Because aspects of a group do *not* transfer automatically to each of its individual members, an argument along the lines above is fallacious and cannot support its conclusion. For example, a group might be motivated by a cynical pursuit of power and resources while some individuals within it are unaware of these motivations and idealistically support a rhetoric imputing more benign motivations. Conversely, a group may be pursuing a just cause while an individual within it has signed up for reasons having little to do with that cause.

It is also a logical mistake, called the *fallacy of composition*, to argue directly from premises about individuals to conclusions about groups.[29]

Fallacy of Composition

Individual I has characteristic x.
Individual I is a member of Group G.
Therefore,
Group G has characteristic X.

Many examples can be constructed to illustrate this basic distinction. An individual may be heroic although the group for which he is fighting is cynical and exploitative; to infer the group's moral qualities from his would be a mistake, amounting to the fallacy of composition. A group may "win" a struggle, though many individual members have been seriously harmed by it and can be argued, in that respect, to have "lost."

In the Balkan wars, the Serbs, collectively, committed serious wrongs including ethnic cleansing and, at Srebrenica, massacres. There were also many thousands of Serbian victims of wrongs. The Serbs lost much in these struggles—both individually and collectively. The collective and individual losses are, of course, connected. But, nevertheless, they have to be distinguished. Indeed, the fundamental distinction between groups and individuals is important at many stages of reconciliation processes. A group may be blameworthy for having knowingly employed brutal and cruel means in a struggle while, at the same time, some individuals within that group are not blameworthy at all, due to the fact that their participation in cruel and indiscriminate actions was coerced. The point can be made most readily when considering children abducted and forced into soldiery, as in Sierra Leone, Uganda, or Sudan; in these cases, groups and leaders (as individuals) were guilty of atrocities while a number of individual combatants, because they were coerced, were not guilty.

Truth commissions and courts have to recognize such subtleties in order to carefully interpret evidence and apply relevant standards of law and morality when deliberating about responsibility, harm, and compensation in the aftermath of a struggle. How individuals and groups share responsibility for violent acts and suffer harm in their aftermath will affect their potential for engaging in processes of reconciliation. The factors relevant to judgments about individuals include the harm done to them; their suffering, needs, and resources; and their legal and moral responsibilities for wrongful acts committed during the conflict. Mutuality between groups engaged in a conflict must prepare the way for mutuality and equity in the consideration of individuals—whether victims, perpetrators, or both.

NOTES

1. Bronwen Manby, "South Africa's Truth Commission: Background to Issues of Accountability in South Africa," Human Rights Watch, http://www.article19.org/docimages/650.htm.

2. "NEC Response to Motsuenyane Commission Report: African National Congress National Executive Committee's Response to the Motsuenyane Commissions's Report," http://www.ancorg.za/ancdocs/pr/1993/pr0829.html. My emphasis.

3. The judgment that nonviolent means could not have achieved the result of overthrowing apartheid is, in my opinion, questionable—though few seem to share this view. However, Desmond Tutu has credited the overthrow of apartheid more to nonviolent activism such as consumer boycotts than to the violent struggle. I cannot explore the fascinating and deep questions about nonviolence as a force for resisting oppressive power here. The TRC *Final Report* allows—as is common—that nonviolent alternatives would not have worked in

the case and that violence was therefore necessary; however, not *all* the particular violent acts committed by the ANC were necessary (or legitimate).

    4. Truth and Reconciliation Commission of South Africa, *Final Report*, vol. 2, chap. 4.

    5. Ibid., "Conflict with Inkatha," p. 9.

    6. Ibid., p. 10.

    7. "Submission of the African National Congress to the Truth and Reconciliation Commission in Reply to the Section 30 (2) of Act 34 of 1996 on the TRC: Findings on the African National Congress," http://www.anc.org.za/ancdocs/misc/trcreply.html.

    8. This conclusion may seem acceptable to many horrified by the realities of contemporary wars. Indeed, I myself find it rather tempting. But I cannot explore the matter here. It was assumed by the ANC, and granted by the South African TRC, that the violent struggle against apartheid *was* legitimate in the sense that the ANC was fighting for a just cause in a context where there were no realistic alternatives to violence. It was also assumed by both parties that *not all* means were acceptable simply because the cause was just. The difference was whether, given the justice of the ANC cause and the fact that many more wrongs were committed by the apartheid state than by liberation forces, the wrongs committed by the latter should have been mentioned in the TRC report.

    9. Some may feel that we have here the beginnings of a strong argument that contemporary war, as such, can never pass the standards provided for in international law.

    10. Submission of the African National Congress, p. 5.

    11. Does *any* killing of a civilian in time of war amount to a gross violation of that person's human rights? When war is waged, are engaged parties entitled to kill some civilians (provided they attempt to minimize these deaths)? Are they, in pursuit of the just cause jeopardized by enemy agents, entitled to subject suspected spies to rough interrogation and extrajudicial execution when appropriate? The ANC assumed "yes," while the TRC assumed "no." The contrary conclusions are the result of the fact that the TRC interpreted the Geneva Conventions as stipulating absolute bans. The Geneva Conventions represent an international legal consensus arising from a widespread conviction that means of warfare should be limited so that they do not impose unnecessary losses or excessive suffering, and so that the distinctions between civilian populations and combatants are observed.

    12. Article 3 of the Fourth Geneva Convention states that

in the case of armed conflict not of an international character occurring in the territory of one of the High Contracting Parties, each Party to the conflict shall be found to apply, as a minimum, the following provisions:

    (1) Persons taking no part in the hostilities, including members of armed forces who had laid down their arms and those placed *hors de combat* by sickness, wounds, detention, or any other cause, shall in all circumstances be treated humanely, without any adverse distinction founded on race, colour, religion or faith, sex, birth, or wealth, or any other similar criteria. To this end the following acts are and shall remain prohibited *at any time and in any place whatsoever with respect to the above-mentioned persons*; (a) violence to life and person, in particular murder of all kinds, mutilation, cruel treatment and torture; (b) taking of hostages; (c) outrages upon personal dignity, in particular humiliating and degrading treatment; (d) the passing of sentences and the carryout of executions without previous judgment pronounced by a regularly constituted court, affording all the judicial guarantees which are recognized as indispensable by civilized people.

(Italics are mine.) Just war theory, while similar to the Geneva Conventions insofar as it insists on the combatant/noncombatant distinction, appears to be more flexible and lenient with regard to the killings of noncombatants. Just war theory does not strictly disallow *all* killings of civilians during war. It incorporates the view that some such killings are permissible, provided they are not disproportionate and that serious efforts are made to minimize them. (The principle of double effect is commonly cited at this point.)

13. Submission of the African National Congress, p. 9.

14. The point holds for groups and will—though the point is a distinct one—hold for many individuals too.

15. Truth and Reconciliation Commission of Peru, *Final Report*, General Conclusion, volume 7, translated from the Spanish by the International Center for Transitional Justice, http://www.icty.org (accessed May 2004).

16. For background and further details, see appendix 7, Sierra Leone.

17. Indeed, the Special Court and Truth and Reconciliation Commission of Sierra Leone made clear and sustained efforts to provide for this mutuality. The prosecution of Sam Hinga Norman was, however, problematic in unusual ways, given that he was widely regarded as a hero for his role in defeating the rebels.

18. Sam Hinga Norman, "Case Summary," Special Court for Sierra Leone, http://www.sc-sl.org/norman-casesummary.html (accessed October 2005).

19. "The Prosecutor Against Sam Hinga Norman: Indictment," Special Court for Sierra Leone, Case no. scsl-01-1, http://www.sc-sl.org/normanindictment.html.

20. Peter Penfold, "Is This Justice? Sierra Leone's Special Court Drags On," ZNet Africa, http://www.zmag.org/content/showarticle.cfm?SectionID=2&Item1 (accessed November 2005), pp. 1–2.

21. Cited by Penfold in ibid.

22. Arthur Abraham, "Sierra Leone: Post-Conflict Transition or Business as Usual?" News from the Nordic Africa Institute (2003), http://www.nai.uu.se/newsfromnai/arkiv/2003/abrahameng.html (accessed November 2005). My italics.

23. "As the Political Tempo Heats Up . . . Hinga Norman Now Said to Be Ultra-Cautious in Sierra Leone," Awareness Times: Sierra Leone News and Information, October 14, 2005, http://news.sl/drwebsite/publish/article_200565.1.shtml (accessed October 2005).

24. In fairness to the genre, it should be noted here that some western movies have more subtle plots.

25. Whether any party has a just cause will be debatable; whether the means employed meet legal and moral standards will also be debatable. The point is that these are distinct questions. It is possible to use illicit means to pursue a just cause and it is also possible to use licit means in the pursuit of an unjust cause. The moral and legal accountability of individual agents, and the harms done to victims, are further, distinct questions. The latter two questions are explored in chapters 8 and 9.

26. Quoted to me by Wilhelm Verwoerd.

27. For relevant background information, consult appendix 5, Peru; appendix 6, Rwanda; and appendix 7, Sierra Leone.

28. To say the least; this is a highly charitable way of stating the point.

29. For a further account of the fallacies of composition and division, see Trudy Govier, *A Practical Study of Argument*, 6th ed. (Belmont, CA: Wadsworth, 2005), p. 317–19. For an application of related themes to the topic of reconciliation in particular, see Trudy Govier and Wilhelm Verwoerd, "Trust and the Problem of National Reconciliation," *Philosophy of the Social Sciences* 32, no. 2 (2002): 178–205.

Chapter Seven

Justice and Peace

A rather common argument against reconciliation processes is that they wrongly give peace priority over justice. The general theme here is that in order to achieve peace in the wake of serious wrongs, one must relinquish efforts in the direction of justice. The problem is often illustrated by the amnesty provisions that were part of the establishment of the Truth and Reconciliation Commission of South Africa. By those provisions, any person who had committed severe human rights violations while an agent in the political conflict over apartheid could apply to the TRC Amnesty Commission for immunity from civil and criminal prosecution. If the Amnesty Committee found that the acts had, indeed, been of a political character, and the agent in question had fully disclosed to the commission information about them, the commission would grant amnesty. The South African TRC did not provide for blanket amnesty given to all persons in any given category. Rather, amnesty in this context was individualized.

The South African amnesty provisions have been defended on various grounds. Crucially, it is argued that the political transition would not have been possible without some amnesty provisions; no government will hand over its power if it thinks that its people will wind up in criminal court as a result. In South Africa, the much-debated amnesty was almost certainly the price of civil peace and the necessary means of avoiding a civil war that could have cost hundreds of thousands of lives. Furthermore, extensive criminal trials of all persons alleged to have committed serious human rights violations would not have been practically possible. Even for South Africa (a relatively rich country overall, despite the poverty of its black majority), financial and legal resources were limited and not adequate to the task. Furthermore, disclosures by persons testifying as perpetrators provided information needed for victims, for the commission itself, and for the broader goal of understanding the conflict over apartheid. In many contexts where there is a transition to democracy in the wake of oppression or civil war, the justice system is in no condition to provide for judicial reliability because it is well-known that dishonesty and corruption have characterized its previous operations.

The issue of "peace versus justice" remains prominent in discussions of the work of the South African TRC. Its amnesty provisions were one of its most controversial features and have been widely discussed both inside and outside South Africa. The amnesty provisions have not generally been copied by more recent truth and reconciliation commissions. In the aftermath of civil violence in East Timor, Sierra Leone, and Peru, for example, no general provisions for amnesty have been established. In Sierra Leone and East Timor, truth commissions have been instituted so as to coexist with criminal trials of persons deemed to have been the most serious offenders. And yet, in the aftermath of widespread civic violence, prosecutions are necessarily quite selective. It is a practical impossibility to try all persons who have committed gross human rights violations. Though the point seems to be neglected in some discussions of criminal prosecutions for gross human rights violations, it must be recalled that the dictum "'ought' implies 'can'" applies here as elsewhere. If a state *cannot* prosecute all violators of human rights, then it cannot be true that such a state *ought* to do so. And yet the rhetoric of "bringing them to justice" often seems to ignore the point that, in many circumstances, it is simply not possible to conduct criminal trials of all perpetrators. Regardless of international law and categorical statements of human rights groups, when such a thing is not *possible*, it clearly cannot be obligatory. If there is, realistically, no feasibility of criminally prosecuting and trying all violators of human rights, then there is an important sense in which it is not a violation of "justice" to fail to do so. On this understanding, justice does not seem to conflict with peace after all.

To consider whether "justice" is in conflict with "peace," we must first think about justice itself.

ASSUMPTIONS ABOUT JUSTICE

The argument that justice cannot be sacrificed for any peace worth having is based on certain specific assumptions about what justice is. It is nearly always assumed in such arguments that *justice* is punitive justice, the justice of punishing perpetrators after a criminal trial conducted within an appropriate legal system. To achieve "justice," in this sense requires "bringing the perpetrators to justice"; this is understood to require that offenders be brought to a court of law where they may be tried and, if found guilty, convicted and sentenced. Justice will be done if they are punished according to the findings of the law. That is to say, "justice will be done" if wrongdoers are made to pay for their wrongdoing by being punished and suffering the castigation and hard treatment they deserve. In this argument, such punishment is nearly always presumed to be necessary for *retributive* reasons. In other words, the idea is that those who commit wrongs *deserve* to pay for them; justice will be done if—and only if—they are punished (provided that they have been found guilty according to due legal processes). The belief that justice is a necessary condition of peace turns into the idea that perpetrators of wrongs must be tried and punished before any peace worth its name can be achieved.

This requirement of trial and punishment is grounded, in part, on the expectation that the punishment of perpetrators will bring satisfaction and a sense of closure to the victims, presumably offering them vindication, acknowledgment, and a sense that "justice has been done." Criminal trials can also serve to articulate and emphasize legal norms—typically norms of human rights that were violated in contexts of civil war or oppression. In articulating and emphasizing such norms, criminal trials can serve as important steps toward the ending of a culture of impunity (in which people could literally get away with murder) and the transition to a society based on the rule of law.

The main problem with this account is that a highly misleading rhetorical reduction occurs when *justice* is interpreted in punitive, retributive terms so as to require only that wrongdoers be tried and punished. Justice should not be reduced to penal justice; nor should it be assumed that penal justice must be understood in retributive terms. Furthermore, in the aftermath of a prolonged civil war or oppressive regime, the number of persons sharing responsibility for violations will be far too numerous for all to be prosecuted. In most such situations, the class of primary perpetrators will be large and, in addition, there are bound to be many secondary perpetrators and tertiary participants who share some responsibility for the violations committed. Further complicating matters, among those people responsible for violations will be many who are, at the same time, victims.

Rhetorical demands that "justice must be done" and that people must be "brought to justice" often seem to be commonsensical, ringing out as uncontroversially true. Nevertheless, we can see that such calls are far from unproblematic. Apart from the impossibility of trying even a substantial subset of the persons involved, extensive financial and legal resources are required to conduct trials and such trials are often very slow. Furthermore, complex challenges are presented by the need to sort out the mitigating factors of circumstance and the sometimes overlapping character of victim/perpetrator roles.

ONE DEBATE ABOUT WAR CRIMES TRIALS

Helena Cobban has written several thoughtful articles about the extraordinary dilemmas with regard to prosecutions of persons accused of primary responsibility for the Rwandan genocide. Citing costs, delays, and alienation of Rwandans from the ad hoc international tribunal based in Arusha, Kenya (ICTR), Cobban argues that the Western perspective, insisting on a legal response, has been oblivious to the enormous problems of the Rwandan case. Cobban said:

> What happened in Rwanda was a human tragedy of unimaginable dimensions. It was a collective frenzy of hatred and killing in which the bonds of community that

normally are directed toward the sustenance of human life were directed instead towards the extermination of an entire social caste.[1]

In the aftermath of this frenzy, the costs, delays, and legalistic details of formal court proceedings struck her as inappropriate to the point of absurdity. Contrasting the role of international criminal justice envisaged for Rwanda with community processes in Mozambique, Cobban wrote approvingly of the latter. It did not involve legal trials of persons accused as perpetrators. Instead, local communities employed a variety of indigenous cultural approaches. Cobban argued that the Rwandan context called for *therapy and healing*, rather than the application of Western-style *law*.[2] In her view, in the aftermath of horror and devastation, war crimes trials staged by the international community were not serving the people of Rwanda.

By 2002, the ICTR had spent about *one billion* dollars and had tried *ten people* in connection with the Rwandan genocide. These costs struck all observers and commentators as grossly disproportionate to the accomplishment of the court. Rwanda is an extremely poor country and nearly all of its citizens were profoundly damaged in some way by the events of 1994 and subsequent years. The funds that supported criminal trials for a few persons could have been used instead for much-needed social and educational programs that could have benefited thousands of people. Noting the simplistic rhetoric of "justice" in the context, Cobban maintained that many who had killed in the genocide had done so in highly coercive circumstances and were themselves traumatized and severely damaged by the events of 1994. (In effect, this is the argument that many who were perpetrators were, in some respects, also victims of circumstance.) Cobban argued that for such persons *healing*, not legal process, was required. She accused the international community of funding the ICTR in an attempt to cover its own failure to intervene to prevent the genocide. She commented caustically that instead of sending troops that could have prevented atrocities, the international community waited until 800,000 people had been killed. At that point, it deployed lawyers.[3]

Cobban's call for *healing* rather than *justice* was roundly criticized by Kenneth Roth and Alison DesForges, whose responses illustrate the rhetoric of "justice first." Despite enormous costs, great delays, and the alienation of the Rwandan government and people from the ICTR, Roth and DesForges called for continuing the pursuit of criminal trials and legal justice in the Rwandan case. Against Cobban, they claimed that even in the face of overwhelming odds, it remains fundamentally important to assert and establish norms of legal accountability. They argued that the international community needs to emphasize that people cannot, with impunity, incite and commit genocide and mass murder. Roth and DesForges said:

> But it is precisely at a time of atrocities—or when a tyrant contemplates committing atrocities—that a policy of trial and punishment is essential. Justice reinforces social norms and deters some would-be perpetrators.[4]

Unlike many simplistic appeals to justice, this statement goes beyond the presumptions of retributivism. Roth and DesForges did not offer the retributive argument that perpetrators were wicked people and wicked people deserve to suffer for their crimes. Rather, they refer to the reinforcement of norms and the deterring of would-be perpetrators. What they say is, accordingly, consistent with theories of punishment other than retributivism. The idea of reinforcement of norms would fit into a moral education theory of punishment; obviously, the deterring of would-be perpetrators would fit into a deterrence theory. But even granting these qualifications, Roth and DesForges nevertheless simplify the notion of "justice" in the Rwandan case. They assume that justice would be *penal justice* and conclude, for that reason, that justice would be served by having a few selected accused persons undergo a *criminal trial* and suffer *punishment* if convicted.

Roth and DesForges are experienced observers of the Rwandan situation and are knowledgeable affiliates of the highly respected human rights group Human Rights Watch. But despite their considerable experience, they seem to lack political realism in their comments on the overwhelmingly difficult case of Rwanda. They fail to acknowledge the fundamental practical difficulties that would be involved in prosecuting many thousands of perpetrators in the context of an underdeveloped and ill-equipped judicial system. Nor do they indicate any sensitivity to the theoretical problems about selectivity in prosecutions, time and scarce resources, circumstantial considerations, and persons who are both victims and perpetrators.

Cobban responded to Roth and DesForges by objecting to the rhetoric in which the word "justice" is uncritically used to refer to Western-style *legal* institutions (she saw this as "legalistic prejudice") while the language of *healing* is assumed to have negative implications, referring to something soft, sentimental, and lacking credibility. Citing her own experience of the dilemmas of life in Lebanon in the wake of its severe civil war, Cobban said:

> Highly paid lawyers from rich secure countries are perhaps the last people on earth from whom to expect an understanding of such dilemmas. And people in the human-rights community should avoid pandering to legalistic prejudice.[5]

Cobban repeated her view that it was *healing* that was needed in the Rwandan context. She believed that workshop leaders, psychiatrists, counselors, and church people would be more useful than lawyers.

WAR CRIMES TRIALS IN HISTORICAL PERSPECTIVE

In the Nuremberg trials after the Second World War, German Nazi leaders were charged and convicted of war crimes under courts established by the victorious Allied Powers. Many hoped that these trials would serve as a precedent to establish norms of conduct and responsibility. These trials have been acclaimed by some but criticized by others, who have pronounced them to be a case of victor's justice. The circumstances of Nuremberg were highly unusual, so far as political aftermaths are concerned.

Nuremberg was an exceptional circumstance that allowed geopolitical forces to coalesce around the idea of a criminal prosecution of surviving leaders. Among the factors that can be mentioned are the following: the claim of the victorious powers that the losing side embodied an evil ideology; the public pressure for some sort of punitive action against those believed responsible for waging such a devastating war; the consensus among leaders that Germany (and Japan) must not be held collectively responsible in the manner of the peace settlement after the First World War; the closely related geopolitical idea in the West that not enough had been done to protect the victims of Nazi persecution before and during the war itself; and the overall sense that the reconstruction of world order around moderate lines would be helped by a dignified trial of German defendants as opposed to the impression created by a vengeful process of summary execution.[6]

Some idealistic observers anticipated that the Nuremberg trials would establish a valuable precedent for criminally trying persons responsible for committing atrocities. There was an expectation that justice at Nuremberg would serve to inspire the development of international legal institutions, meaning that persons who committed acts of genocide, crimes against humanity, and violations of the Geneva Conventions would be held responsible for what they had done.

The spirit of Nuremberg has been a source of inspiration to many. Activists seeking to defend the appeal to conscience in protest of nuclear weapons development and other policy issues often cite the Nuremberg judgments.[7] Yet, in a fundamental respect, the idealistic expectations of activists have been frustrated. For fifty years after Nuremberg, there were no international war crimes trials. That situation changed with the establishment of the ICTY, the international tribunal for crimes committed during the civil wars in the former Yugoslavia. After the bitter wars in Bosnia, Croatia, Serbia and Kosovo, under the auspices of the Security Council of the United Nations, the ICTY was established as an ad hoc international tribunal in The Hague. This tribunal was established for the purpose of trying persons accused of committing crimes against humanity and war crimes during the Balkan wars between 1992 and 1995. Slobodan Milosevic, former president of Serbia, was charged with sixty-six counts for crimes committed in Kosovo, Bosnia, and Croatia. The alleged crimes were crimes against humanity and violations of the laws and customs of war—including murder, deportations, and persecutions.[8]

Milosevic, who had insisted on conducting his own defense, objected to the jurisdiction of the court on a number of grounds. Prominent among them was the matter of selectivity. The tribunal was ad hoc in the sense that it was established in order to deal with particular offenses in this particular conflict. The ICTY was international in its institutional framework and funding but not international in its mandate, which was to consider offenses in a select geographic area during a select time period. No American or Western European could have been charged by the ICTY with international criminal acts. Thus the ICTY could not have dealt with allegations against American leaders for acts committed in Vietnam, Iraq, or Guatemala. The same is true of the criminal tribunal for Rwanda, the ICTR. Its mandate is to consider acts during the Rwandan genocide of 1994—not to consider crimes against humanity that might have been committed elsewhere—say in Burundi, the Congo, the Sudan, Uganda, Iraq, or Somalia.

A significant problem of selectivity regarding trials for war crimes and crimes against humanity has arisen from the fact that the international community, through the United Nations, established ad hoc tribunals for some serious conflicts and not others. Given their veto power in the Security Council, the major powers of Britain, France, Russia, China, and the United States would be extremely unlikely to have their leaders and agents facing such trials.

The awkward intersection of international factors and nationalist sentiments in Serbia has been a significant factor in recent Serbian politics. One observer described the "international legal paradigm" for transition and commented that Balkan countries were not able to choose whether to employ amnesties, lustration laws, truth commissions, reconciliation mechanisms, reparations, or domestic trials. An approach was forced upon them: that of international law, through the ICTY.

> Serbia's post-Milosevic governments had to deal with the UN Security Council's predilection for international law and forum: a functioning international criminal tribunal and an international community pushing for the transfer of suspects to its jurisdiction. Hence the widely held perception in Serbia that the ICTY is a form of justice selectively imposed on the country from outside, a victory for "Serbia's enemies." In the last several years the Tribunal's official statements, indictments, as well as formal and informal pressure for cooperation have become an important factor and persistent intervention in day-to-day politics. This inevitable ICTY meddling in local politics has made it difficult for moderates to accept the court as legitimate and has provided a convenient excuse for nationalists to preclude genuine debate about dealing with the past, framing it in defensive and ideological terms.[9]

A wider jurisdiction is claimed by the International Criminal Court, which is developing as this book goes to press and may soon hear its first case. The ICC is not an ad hoc tribunal and will seek to be universal in its jurisdiction. In principle, the ICC will be able to prosecute any person from any country. However, in practice, not all countries support the ICC. The United States, Russia, and China have been prominent resisters. The United States insists that its leaders and military personnel cannot be subject to the jurisdiction of any international criminal court. Although the United States energetically supported the ICTY and the ICTR as ad hoc tribunals for geographically restricted areas and conflicts, it has resisted any idea that American citizens could be held accountable in any international court.

The United States does not accept that such a court should have authority over Americans and has sought exemption from the jurisdiction of the ICC by pressing countries to sign treaties guaranteeing that they will not prosecute agents for any offenses committed by US leaders, soldiers, or other personnel. Given this quest for exemption, the commitment of the United States to the rule of law internationally is weak at best. The notion that law should apply to others but not to oneself is, of course, contrary to the notion of the rule of law and even to the notion of law itself. International law will have limited credibility if some powerful countries are immune to its requirements. The position of the United States government in the period poses significant challenges to the prospects of the International Criminal Court. The US position appears self-serving and highly objectionable at a time when serious abuses at the Abu Ghraib prison in Iraq have been publicized around the world and hundreds of prisoners continue to be held in indefinite detention by the United States outside its own borders at Guantanamo Bay and elsewhere.

Nor has the failure of anything even approximating universal jurisdiction escaped the attention of important defendants in international tribunals. Such persons often cite the ad hoc nature and limited jurisdiction of these tribunals in attempts to demonstrate their partiality and illegitimacy. Milosevic, for example, argued that the ICTY had no legitimate jurisdiction to charge him for offenses as Serbian leader during the Balkan wars. He accused the tribunal of implementing victor's justice. A primary element in his argument was that, due to its geographically restricted mandate, the ICTY was incapable of acting *equally* among nations and was, therefore, a partial, discriminatory, and illegitimate tribunal. Milosevic submitted that the ICTY was established by the Security Council of the United Nations, which, he said, is an undemocratic body (given that the five major powers can exercise a veto over its decisions). He asked, rhetorically:

> Can a criminal tribunal for Yugoslavia which ignores pervasive violence by the United States and diverts public awareness from U.S. conduct and legitimizes by silent acceptance aerial and missile assaults on civilians and illegal weapons used against one country after another making its repetition expected before it occurs contribute to the hope for the rule of law or justice or peace?[10]

Milosevic went on to claim that the ICTY was only "another arrow" in the arsenal of the United States. He contended that the tribunal was being used, politically, by a major power. It would be a naïve error, he claimed, to understand the ICTY as an instrument of international law, which would conduct *impartial* proceedings and *justly* punish persons found to be guilty of violations.

This man hardly counted as a credible authority so far as international law and crimes of war were concerned. He played a major role in inciting the Balkan wars of the 1990s and he participated in ethnic cleansing and the establishment of murderous concentration camps. Nevertheless, his points about selectivity do merit some consideration. In fact, more credible observers have endorsed some elements of his position. Aryeh Neier, for example, is a prominent human rights advocate and supporter of the ICTY. He believes that it can play an important function in affirming human rights and the force of international legal norms. Nevertheless, Neier maintains that the ICTY was established for the wrong reasons. When images of grossly emaciated Muslim men held in Serbian-run detention camps were widely shown on television, there was considerable shame and embarrassment in Western countries about the fact that the international community, in general, and the United States, in particular, had not intervened to prevent widespread killing and abuse. The ICTY, Neier submits, was established as a gesture *after-the-fact*—a gesture that was intended to save face for the Clinton administration in the United States, which had been severely criticized for its failure to intervene. In other words, the ad hoc tribunal was established because it served the interests of one major power, a power that was in a position to apply to others principles of international law it would not accept as applicable to itself.[11]

Richard Falk, a prominent American legal theorist, stated:

> International experience to date suggests that an international tribunal of the Nuremberg type will only be brought into being if it is geopolitically convenient for the governments of the leading states, an observation that casts some shadows across the current efforts at The Hague and in Arusha.[12]

These limitations in jurisdiction undermine the credibility of claims that prosecutions and convictions serve the cause of *justice* and can contribute to the establishment of international legal standards and the rule of law.

The rule of law requires that all agents within the territory to which the law applies be covered by the norms of the law. In the international context, achieving a situation characterized by the rule of law would mean, minimally, that leaders and agents of *all* states would be candidates for prosecution were they to violate international criminal law in course of using violent means to wage political struggles. To achieve the rule of law, in this sense, would be an enormous accomplishment. It is an understatement to say that no such thing exists at present. The rule of law, internationally, would clearly require that agents of power such as the United States, Russia, and China—which have not supported the ICC—be as liable to prosecution as the agents of minor states and nonstate groups. In a situation where there is rule of law, no agents are immune from the scope of the law on the basis of their geographic location or political affiliation. To the extent that the International Criminal Court can develop into an institution with broader capacity than that of the ad hoc tribunals, there exists a potential for overcoming some of the problems of fairness and impartiality. Obviously, no such situation exists at present. Even the most idealistic and committed observers would acknowledge that it seems far from imminent. Nevertheless, there are those who believe in a progressive human history and are prepared to assume that political evolution will eventually produce a "fully articulated international legal order," one that is "global in scope, evenhanded in application, and effective in operation."

Falk, while wishing in a way to embrace this hopeful perspective, acknowledges that there are powerful criticisms of it. Critics have argued quite persuasively that often what has been regarded as "progress" amounts, on analysis, to nothing more than the most powerful countries using the rhetoric of law and justice to serve their own interests. Nevertheless, Falk says:

> It is important not to become irresponsibly cynical in light of these disappointments, but it is also equally important to take account of prevailing ideas about

security among governmental elites and the patterns of international practice in recent decades. Realism tends to be the prevailing orientation toward the formation of policy by the leadership of most states. It puts state interests at the top, and tends to regard respect for international law and morality as instruments of propaganda rather than as providing policy guidelines that clarify national interests. Such realism, especially as an ideological orientation of elites in the American setting since 1945, view(s) the restraining claims on behalf of a Nuremberg worldview as "legalistic" or "moralistic," as misplaced and dangerously sentimental given the structure of international society.[13]

Those who have supported prosecutions for violations of international law see such steps as means of enforcing norms of action (albeit selectively) in the short and medium term. Over the longer term, such enforcement is expected to contribute to a more universal and less selective enforcement and thus, over time, to the international rule of law. The prosecution and conviction of (some selected) persons who have committed serious crimes of war can be argued to serve the goals of universalism because it can be regarded as a step on the road to something more universal. Better to try and convict *some* mass murderers than *none*, one may plausibly insist. This claim can be made independently of a commitment to retributive punishment. Here as elsewhere, the argument that because one cannot do *everything*, one ought to do *nothing* can be rejected as bad logic.[14]

INDIVIDUALS, GROUPS, AND LEGAL ACCOUNTABILITY

With very few exceptions, criminal trials are of individuals. Nations, nonstate groups, corporations, and committees do not appear before courts as collective units. Even when people are named in the same indictment for the same offenses, they go on trial as individuals. The assumption behind this practice is that group entities are not, as such, morally and legally accountable. Such entities are not conscious, do not have minds, cannot deliberate and choose what to do and, therefore, cannot satisfy the legal conditions of mens rea (having a guilty mind). On such grounds it is often argued that collective entities cannot be morally or legally responsible for their actions. In legal proceedings, responsibility is *individualized*. That fact is regarded by some as correct in its own right and as contributing positively to reconciliation.

For example, Richard Goldstone, the first prosecuting judge at the ICTY, later to serve on the Constitutional Court of South Africa, defended such individualization forcefully. In the aftermath of the Balkan wars of the 1990s, it was crucial, Goldstone said, to demonstrate that certain *individuals* had committed offenses and that these people were, as individuals, responsible for what they had done. Goldstone believed firmly that this point needed to be legally established: by identifying individuals, one could prove that it was not the Serbian nation, or the Serbs as a people, or simply "Serbs" who had done these things. Rather, it was specific individual people who happened to be Serbs and who claimed to be acting on behalf of the Serbs. Goldstone claimed that individualization of responsibility would serve the interests of reconciliation between ethnic groups in the former Yugoslavia (Serbs, Croats, and Bosnian Muslims). Pinning responsibility on specific individuals should shift ideas away from prejudice and guilt by association.[15] Seeing the trials and hearing some of the evidence, people would learn that it was not "Serbs" who did bad things but particular individual people who happened to be Serbs. A few persons, not the whole group, are found to be legally guilty of war crimes. The individualistic aspect of the trial would, on Goldstone's view, contribute constructively to reconciliation by working against stereotyping and notions of collective guilt and responsibility.[16] Louise Arbour, Goldstone's successor at the ICTY, expressed a similar point of view. In the press release in which the ICTY announced its indictments of Slobodan Milosevic and four others, Arbour explained that the indictment was made against neither the *state* of the Federal Republic of Yugoslavia nor against the *people* of that state. Arbour said:

> Whatever the differences amongst the citizens of the FRY and the differences they may have with other nations, I believe that they will expect their leaders who have abused their trust to come to The Hague to respond to these accusations.[17]

With due respect to the stature and contributions of these two persons, this view seems to presuppose an overly simple individualistic account of causes and responsibilities in contexts of violent political conflict. Indeed, it turns out to have been too optimistic, largely for that reason. Iavor Rangelov, a researcher based in Belgrade who has studied transitional justice in Serbia, articulated an observation for which there had been considerable evidence.

> One of the mantras of international lawyers in justifying the Tribunal has been that the prosecution of select individuals serves to exonerate those not mentioned in the indictments. Ultimately, they have argued, the idea was to preclude attributing "guilt by association" and collective criminalization of the Serbian nation. Yet people in Serbia have largely remained unconvinced by this mandate to punish a few individuals on the top, thereby exculpating the collective. Processed through the framework of nationalism and victimization, the ICTY is turned into a landmark victory of "the enemies of Serbia," those who have repeatedly demonized and humiliated Serbs. In the hearts and minds of many, "Serbs on trial" is equivalent to "Serbia on trial," individual criminal responsibility notwithstanding.[18]

The point is that many Serbs supported their side in the wars and were not led by the activities of the international community and the ICTY to amend their nationalist narrative. They made sense of history in terms that offered an account of what was at stake for Serbs in the breakup of Yugoslavia, regarding their nation and its leaders not as perpetrators but, rather, as persecuted victims.

Most non-Serb commentators would dissent from the Serbian nationalist narrative; they regard the brutal actions undertaken by Serb groups and individuals during the 1990s as serious wrongs. Since many Serbs supported the nationalist cause, there is something to be said for a more collective approach, in terms of factual accuracy, if not legal practicality. Secondary and tertiary perpetrators should be considered, in addition to primary perpetrators. Whether they are leaders, supporters, or militant agents on the ground, persons engaging in a violent political conflict act *politically*. By definition, a *political* conflict is one between groups. That means, effectively, that a larger community or group beyond leaders and militant agents is supportive of the goals and, generally, the means used to reach them. That broader group provides support necessary for waging the struggle in the ways in which it is waged, and those who are participants at this level—tertiary participants—share some responsibility for what is done.[19]

So far as reconciliation is concerned, what eventually matters most are the relationships between many individuals and many constituent groups. The central focus of reconciliation processes is to shift such relationships away from anger, hatred, and grievance in the direction of acceptance and trust so as to build the capacity for collaboration and sustainable peace. From a perspective within which trust and relationships are emphasized, the individualistic and necessarily selective character of legal proceedings is problematic. Apart from considerations about mutuality and fairness, there is the absolutely critical problem that circumstances permit only a few of the responsible persons to be prosecuted within an appropriate legal system. Such *selectivity* poses moral and political difficulties because of perceptions of unfairness. One can understand why not everyone responsible for violations is prosecuted in a society undergoing transition. After all, selectivity in this sense is a feature of the workings of law even in well-run civil societies. Not all murderers are apprehended; of those apprehended and prosecuted, not all the guilty ones are legally convicted. But such limitations hardly amount to an argument for not apprehending and prosecuting murderers at all.

In the sensitive contexts in which people use legal trials to seek reconciliation, the *appearance of justice* is highly important. People call out for justice and many understand it as a necessary precondition of peace. In the rhetoric of political debate, anyone objecting to "justice" is placed in a difficult position. How can one plausibly claim to be "against" justice? How can one deny that "justice must be done"? Yet, in concrete terms, what is achievable in courts of law, under these difficult circumstances, seems rather removed from justice in any general sense of the term. It is penal justice, not the *justice* of reparations to victims, not restorative justice, not socioeconomic justice, and not distributive justice. And even within the framework of penal justice, only a selected few of the many persons who share responsibility for serious wrongdoing can be subjected to a legal trial, and this consideration is significant. When leaders are selected as the most responsible persons, that makes sense; however, leaders can lead only if there are others who follow them willingly. Given that in *political* conflicts many people share responsibility for wrongs committed, it is a considerable simplification to presume that "justice" will have been "done" when a select few of them are legally prosecuted. In some contexts, there are convincing practical answers to questions about just which persons are indicted and put on trial. For example, some key persons may be impossible to apprehend. But theoretically, the matter remains problematic. Insofar as a sense of fairness affects confidence and the willingness to reconcile, selectivity is highly significant.

When selective legal trials are undertaken as a means to reconciliation, there is a significant chance that the situation will seem unjust. If those prosecuted are militant agents relatively low on the hierarchy, there will seem to be unfairness in the case because leaders, organizers, and recruiters are not prosecuted. If those prosecuted are leaders, high in the hierarchy, things are (and will seem to be) more fair. However, one may question the apparent immunity of their senior advisors, colleagues, and supporters. Even if prosecuted persons include both leaders and agents on the ground—as has been the case at the ICTY—one may still wonder how just *these* particular individuals were unlucky enough to be selected for indictment and trial.

If key individuals charged with war crimes trials are distinguished and detached, morally, from their nation or group (as Richard Goldstone and Louise Arbour expected would be the case), the interests of reconciliation may be served. One may hope that people will follow the trials and the legal reasoning and understand the sentencing and punishment of key individuals. They might then arrive at the conclusion that "it is not all those people—not *all* Serbs, not *all* Hutus—who did those things to us; it is only these people, these particular individuals, who stood out as markedly bad and wicked compared to the rest." If people did think in this way, their distinguishing of responsible individuals from the larger group would illustrate an important respect in which legal trials could contribute to reconciliation. But there remains an important sense in which individualization of responsibility remains simplistic and, as such, is ethically problematic. Only a small percentage can be tried. When many who share responsibility go untouched while selected others are subjected to trial and punishment and castigated as evil, proceedings will not seem fair. Furthermore, those on the losing side are apt to object to trials—as do the Serbs. They may still believe that their side was in the right and that those who led it and fought for it—by whatever means—were heroes in the struggle.

When many people have been hurt by many others, the legal trials of a few may soothe some feelings. Certainly, that is the expectation with regard to the role of criminal trials in reconciliation. However, at best, legal trials constitute modest steps in that direction. To the extent that they do so, it may be at the cost of perpetuating a falsely individualistic understanding of conflict.[20]

A BALANCE OF CONSIDERATIONS

It is in the context of these issues and debates that international or internationally assisted trials need to be considered.

Notwithstanding these many difficulties, there is still much to be said in favor of war crimes trials. From the point of view of international jurisprudence, the ICTY and the ICTR have helped to build international legal capacities, both with regard to legal personnel and in the content of the law itself. As they are applied to new cases, the relevant international laws have been further articulated. For example, conditions of legal accountability have been developed; *rape* is now included as a crime of war; and the ICTR has struck new legal ground in making one conviction based on *media incitement* to genocide. The Special Court in Sierra Leone has pronounced the recruiting of *child soldiers* to be against international legal norms. When the ICC begins to consider cases, further significant developments with regard to international law may be anticipated. If there is ever to be a viable and effective international framework with regard to human rights and violent political conflict, these efforts will be an important stage in the development of that framework.

In most contexts of war and systematic oppression, there have been expectations of impunity. On the basis of past experience, leaders and many followers have expected to be able, literally, to get away with murder—and worse. If they have been functional at all, judicial institutions have been unwilling or unable to prosecute the many persons who have committed acts of torture, abduction, battery, rape, and mass murder in the pursuit of their political goals. Without enforcement, there has simply been no operative law for these extremely serious acts. Conducting criminal trials of even some of the persons suspected and accused of such serious offenses can express the resolve to develop and sustain an operative law. It can function to *end that culture of impunity* and to convey forcefully the message that these acts are impermissible and that those who commit them are liable to prosecution and punishment. If the "no impunity" message can be conveyed convincingly, it can contribute to a sense of security and confidence. Persons who might have considered performing or directing similar brutal violence may be deterred from doing so when they see that such actions can be prosecuted and can lead to harsh punishment. In this way, criminal trials may serve the interests of deterrence and function to prevent future abuses.

When properly conducted and publicized, criminal trials can increase awareness and understanding of relevant principles of human rights law and international standards. The criminal trial of a high level perpetrator can send a clear message that, contrary to what leaders and participants might have claimed as their own justification, people *did* commit atrocities and these actions *did not* become morally legitimate simply because leaders and agents were committing them in the name of a just war. The investigations made in conjunction with legal proceedings can reveal important information about acts, agents, and the context of the events examined. Convictions can articulate norms and acknowledge relevant legal and moral standards, thus providing some of the acknowledgment that is so important and that persons responsible for violence may be unwilling to provide.

Some speak as though the public can learn from trials, learn about past history and how serious abuses come to occur. It is possible that historical understanding of some key events may emerge from trials of leaders and other selected perpetrators. Still, there is a problematic aspect to the idea that war crimes trials can teach us a history lesson. The proper function of a *legal trial* is to determine whether the accused person is guilty or not guilty of having committed the acts for which he or she has been indicted. That is to say, the proper function of a legal trial is highly specific. Important historical truths may, indeed, emerge from legal trials, and if such truths are effectively publicized, a public that is attending to the trials can learn from them, as seems to have been the case with the trial of Klaus Barbie in France and the issue of collaboration with the Vichy regime during the Second World War. But the teaching of history cannot be a major purpose of criminal trials. Legal process is jeopardized, to say the least, if a trial is turned into a lesson in ethics or in history. If due legal process is to be served, there should be no intent and certainly no guarantee that trials will teach people the "lessons" of history. If a trial is held in order to prove some point about who was wrong and who was right and what a given event or sequence "means" in terms of its moral message, then one has reached the territory of show trials. Any legal trial that is turned into a platform from which lessons from history are taught has exceeded its proper role, which is to determine the legal guilt or innocence of the person who is on trial based upon the facts and laws that apply in his or her case. If the conduct and public discussion of a particular trial inspires the broader public to reflect on the past, that is well and good. But that cannot be the chief reason for the trial.

As we have seen, limitations in legal and financial resources make selectivity in prosecutions inevitable. For many observers, awareness of such selectivity will tend to undermine a sense that "justice is done." Even when the selectivity is not pernicious but emerges from unavoidable factors such as the death of key parties, the impossibility of apprehending people, or the inadequacy of resources for witness protection, those factors may not be generally understood.[21]

The phenomenon of selectivity will almost certainly be aggravated by the fact that in the aftermath of civil war and oppression, societies are unlikely to have effective and reliable legal personnel and facilities. If, as is typically the case, the local system of criminal justice is damaged or unreliable, international funding and personnel will be required. Societies emerging from violent political conflict will almost certainly have limited resources for recovery and reconstruction. Given pressing needs in terms of health, education, and rebuilding, they are likely to be reluctant to expend large sums of money on legal trials for more than a few of the most spectacular cases. In some contexts (such as the aftermath of apartheid, communism, or military dictatorship), though a legal system may be relatively intact, concerns will arise about its integrity. Judges, lawyers, and the law itself are likely to be tainted by association with the former power structure. These factors will generate a need for international involvement—both in terms of personnel and in terms of financial resources.

As illustrated both with the ICTR and with the ICTY, international involvement with courts to try selected war criminals was needed, but nevertheless led to problems. Most significantly, the physical remoteness of these courts makes it difficult for people to know what is going on at the trials. There is a risk that they will find the trials simply irrelevant or even alienating—having a sense that people from other countries, far away, are using irrelevant standards to pass judgment on a few selected people (who may even seem to be martyred) from a conflict rooted in local conditions. As Helena Cobban emphasized, international norms and personnel may seem foreign and inappropriate, giving rise to an alienated sense that a damaged and vulnerable local community has become a platform for arcane reflections and arguments about matters remote from the lives of people who suffered in the conflict. Rwandan frustration with the ICTR's proceedings in Arusha was a factor that influenced the United Nations to assist in establishing courts in Sierra Leone and East Timor that would operate in the countries, employ a significant percentage of national personnel, and leave a courthouse and trained personnel in the country when its deliberations were over. Even so, there have been criticisms of the Sierra Leone court due to the fact that the prosecutor and top personnel are American. And there is certainly the potential for other problems. The salaries and lifestyles of the international personnel whose expertise will be necessary in the case may be conspicuously and offensively luxurious in contexts where local people who lived through the conflict are desperately poor and living in rubble.[22] There may be a sense that the international community is using or even exploiting the aftermath to (expensively) pursue goals of developing legal norms within the system of international law while, at the same time, pressing local needs are not addressed.

If accused persons are found guilty, they may be regarded as martyrs by sympathizers on their own side, as illustrated in the Milosevic case. These sympathizers, for various reasons, will seek to discredit the findings of the court. They may continue to regard the policies and actions of their leaders as necessary and right under the circumstances. Trials at the ICTY did not demonstrate to his former supporters that Milosevic and others were guilty of heinous offenses; in fact, many Serb nationalists have found in the proceedings at The Hague only further evidence to support their conviction that their country was an especially persecuted one that was victimized by the great powers and the international community. On this view, the United States and other Western countries bombed it with impunity over policies in Kosovo and now use the ICTY as a tool of further persecution. To some nationalist Serbs, Milosevic appeared a martyred hero. Popular observers rallied to the nationalist cause, and even some academic observers have constructed theoretical defenses of their country and former leader.

A striking example of the latter phenomenon is that of Jovan Babic, a philosopher based in Belgrade. Babic is by no means an ill-educated nationalist. He attends international meetings and has published in English, arguing against the very idea of international trials for crimes of war. Though his account is theoretical, readers may sense that, underneath the abstract argumentation, there are echoes of frustration and defensive nationalism.[23] Babic claims that international law does not have the requisite institutional structure to qualify as genuine law. On his view, such a structure would require world government. And thus, Babic concludes that what is commonly referred to as "international law" does not even amount to law in any sense in which the term is legitimately used. Babic states:

> It appears to me that international law is not, and cannot be, law in the fundamental sense of the word. International law lacks the institutional structure (such as sovereign states have) necessary for its application, and instead appeals to the moral—and moralizing—sentiments of those who are, or think they are, powerful enough to take their moral feelings at face value and transform their moral judgments into legal ones. What is more, the very phrase "international law" contains in itself a certain tension: it would really be a kind of law if a World State existed, and consequently it would not be "international."[24]

If there is, strictly speaking, no such thing as international law, then it would follow that there are no such things as war crimes in violation of international law. There are, Babic submits, only *crimes* and not a special category of crimes that amount to *war crimes*. People who commit criminal acts should be tried according to the laws of the territory in which those acts were committed and not in any *other* court.

Babic argues that such war crimes trials illustrate nothing more than the power of dominant countries.[25] The disillusioned conclusion can only be that "*Defeat* is a crime." Babic maintains that third parties to a conflict have no right to appeal to so-called international law. He states that participants in such a conflict waged war in their own territory and for their own purposes, purposes likely to be inadequately understood by outside parties.

> Thus, international prosecution of so-called war crimes, *except according to conventions that states have freely signed on*, is legally invalid. It represents a morally suspect *paternalistic* act, which can earn some sort of justification only as a political act, and only on the condition that real attackers and insurgents go to trial. Such a prosecution isn't then truly international; it's simply the court of the victorious side.[26]

Babic's arguments are cited here, not in the belief that they are correct but, rather, because they illustrate how prosecutions of the selected few may be deeply resented and may seem like grievances to persons with a patriotic impulse to defend their leader and their group.[27]

Counterarguments can be stated, of course. One response to Babic's position is that even in the absence of international police and systematic enforcement, international law operates effectively in contexts of business, travel, and diplomacy—and, in fact, most states have signed on to fundamental provisions with regard to human rights and the humanitarian laws for the conduct of war. The international realm is not, after all, a state of nature. People communicate, trade, and travel across borders millions of times each day.

Departing from this kind of fundamental objection and reverting to a situation in which we acknowledge that there are both national laws and international laws, we arrive at other issues that may affect the sense of "justice" in contexts of reconciliation. When some accused persons are tried nationally and others are tried internationally—as in the cases of Rwanda and Sierra Leone—anomalies result. Under international law, there is no provision for capital punishment. Thus, international tribunals are not authorized to sentence convicted persons to death—a fact that strikes many survivors of serious violence as appalling and unfair. In the Rwandan case, for example, persons tried and convicted of genocide within Rwanda were sentenced to death and executed. By contrast, there was no possibility of capital punishment for persons tried before the ICTR. If one assumes that it was the most serious offenders who appeared before the ICTR, as distinct from Rwandan courts, one's sense of anomaly only increases: those who are (potentially) the most serious offenders cannot be sentenced to death while those who are (potentially) lesser offenders can be. Similar anomalies characterize the situation of the Special Court in Sierra Leone. They may be expected to continue with the ICC. Without defending here the institution of capital punishment, it must be acknowledged that when international legal institutions do not authorize capital punishment, even for persons convicted of extremely serious crimes, their standards of legal justice will seem strange to persons accustomed to brutal widespread violence. Survivors will ask why convicted perpetrators should continue to live when they have been responsible for the killing of so many other people.

Nor is the absence of the death penalty the only such anomaly. When accused persons are kept in custody under international authority, they will be in a situation of relative advantage: they are fed, sheltered, kept warm, and—within reasonable limits—kept healthy. There is, for instance, the case of an accused before the ICTY who wanted his trial to continue through the winter. Warm and well-fed when he was in captivity in The Hague, this man feared that he would freeze or starve to death if acquitted and sent back to his village in the former Yugoslavia before spring.[28] To cite an even more gross discrepancy, persons suffering from HIV-AIDS who are awaiting trial before the ICTR are provided with the drug cocktail that will preserve their lives while thousands of Rwandan women infected with HIV-AIDS as a result of rape during the genocide receive no such treatment.

Victims may receive acknowledgment and vindication when some perpetrators are found guilty and subjected to punishment. Indeed, that is a goal, one often referred to as the "satisfaction" or "closure" of victims. And yet, given the need to observe due process, the results can be frustrating for victims. An accused person may receive, or seem to receive, better treatment than victims themselves. Worse yet (from this point of view), an accused person may be found to be legally innocent because it has not been possible to gather sufficient evidence for his or her conviction. While the possible satisfaction and sense of vindication of victims should be counted as a reason favoring war crimes trials, their possible frustration should also be counted as a factor against such trials.

CONCLUDING COMMENTS

War crimes trials are important for the development of international law and international legal institutions. For all that has been said here, it is not reasonable to *oppose* such trials—even though it is nearly always difficult to conduct them in an efficient, cost-effective, nonselective, and fair way. We must hope that the work of the ICTY, ICTR, and ICC will ultimately contribute to a situation of rule of law, respect for human rights, and the end of impunity, even in situations of serious political conflict. But to support trials for these purposes is one thing; to understand them as the means or even one major means toward reconciliation is quite another. The notion that victims will be satisfied when perpetrators are punished and that these shifts will pave the road to decent and trusting relations between former enemies is naïve and seriously flawed. At best, criminal trials of some of the most conspicuous offenders provide a partial route toward diminishing resentment and increasing confidence. While profoundly important in its own right, the legal story is not the story of reconciliation.

NOTES

1. Helena Cobban, "The Legacies of Collective Violence," *Boston Review* (April/May 2002), http://bostonreview.ne/BR27.2cobban.html (accessed November 29, 2004). By 2004, the ICTR had spent an estimated 1.2 billion dollars and had twenty persons on trial and another 22 awaiting trial; 10 persons indicted were still at large (Frontline Bulletin, PBS, http://www.pbs .org/wgbh/pages/frontline/shows/ghosts/today [accessed November 29, 2004]).

2. Cobban acknowledged the lack of credibility of the Tutsi government due to its failure to acknowledge and address its own offenses—which are serious.

3. The same argument has been made concerning the ICTY, the international criminal tribunal for the Balkan wars of the 1990s.

4. Kenneth Roth and Alison DesForges, "Justice or Therapy?" *Boston Review* (Summer 2002): 51–52. These commentators are by no means naïve persons speaking without experience. Kenneth Roth was the executive director of Human Rights Watch and a former federal prosecutor in the United States. Alison DesForges was a senior advisor to Human Rights Watch, had been an expert witness for the ICTR, was a historian of Africa specializing in Rwanda, and was the author of *Leave None to Tell the Story: Genocide in Rwanda* (New York: Human Rights Watch, 1999).

5. Cobban, "Legacies of Collective Violence."

6. Richard Falk, "Accountability for War Crimes and the Legacy of Nuremberg," *War Crimes and Collective Wrongdoing: A Reader*, ed. Alexandr Jokic (Oxford: Blackwell, 2001), p. 121.

7. Described effectively by Falk, ibid., pp. 113–39.

8. He was charged as having direct and command responsibility (not as having directly performed these acts himself); in other words, as one who had instigated, ordered, or had aided and abetted in planning, preparing, or executing these acts.

9. Iavor Rangelov, "International Law and Local Ideology in Serbia," *Peace Review* 16, no. 3 (2004): 331–37, p. 332.

10. Transcript provided by the Dutch newspaper *NRC Handelsblad*, wysiwyg://htp// www.nrc.n//Doc/Milosevic/milosevic!html (accessed November 26, 2001). I have also benefited from Guy Lesser, "War Crime and Punishment: What the United States Could Learn from the Milosevic Trial," *Harper's* (January 2004): 37–52.

11. Aryeh Neier, *War Crimes: Brutality, Genocide, Terror, and the Struggle for Justice* (New York: Times Books, 1998). Neier is the former executive director of Human Rights Watch and the president of the Open Society Institute. He is making essentially the same point about Yugoslavia that Cobban made about Rwanda.

12. Richard Falk, *Accountability for War Crimes*, p. 130.

13. Ibid., p. 118.

14. I have explored such arguments in greater depth in "Prosecuting Crimes against Humanity: Rule of Law and the Selectivity Argument," January 2002, unpublished. Slobodan Milosevic died on March 11, 2006. The trial was discontinued.

15. Richard Goldstone, comments, Conference on Dilemmas of Reconciliation, Institute for the Humanities, University of Calgary, June 1999. Richard Goldstone was the chief prosecutor for the ICTY and the ICTR, August 15, 1994–September 1996. Further comments about his conception of the impact of such trials may be found in an interview of Goldstone by Harry Kreisler, Institution of International Studies, University of California, Berkeley, http://globetrotter.berkeley.edu/Goldstone/gold-con0.html (accessed December 7, 2004). In that interview, Goldstone expressed the idea that trials could help to end many years of hatred between groups, hatred stimulated by the fact that demands for justice had been frustrated. He claimed that trials would provide a sense of acknowledgment and healing.

16. The fact that there are primary, secondary, and tertiary perpetrators provides grounds for questioning this individualization of responsibility. Individualization is distorting in that it omits the shared and collective aspects of responsibility and, in this regard, risks scapegoating a few primary perpetrators.

17. Louise Arbour, ICTY press release, May 27, 1999.

18. Rangelov, "International Law and Local Ideology," p. 332.

19. As argued in chapter 2.

20. For reasons argued in chapter 2.

21. As in Sierra Leone, where Foday Sankoh died. For details, see appendix 7, Sierra Leone.

22. For a relevant comment in that context, see appendix 3, East Timor.

23. On my reading at least.

24. Jovan Babic, "War Crime: Moral, Legal, or Simply Political?" in Jokic, *War Crimes and Collective Wrongdoing*, pp. 57–75; cited passage is on p. 63.

25. Ibid. The phenomenon of selectivity and the fact that, in particular, US and British leaders are not subjected to trials for crimes of war functions to support that position.

26. Ibid., p. 68. The argument would be that Serbia was defending its territory against aspiring separatists in Kosovo and (perhaps) against NATO attacks. My emphasis. Note: this qualification, which is not discussed in the essay, is highly important.

27. This is the main point argued by Rangelov, "International Law and Local Ideology."

28. Lesser, "War Crime and Punishment," *Harpers*, January 2004. Serbian attitudes with regard to these trials are also interestingly discussed in Lawrence Weschler, *Vermeer in Bosnia: Cultural Comedies and Political Tragedies* (New York: Pantheon Books, 2004).

Chapter Eight

Issues of Reintegration

The pragmatic and theoretical limitations of the legal approach mean that in any aftermath situation there will be many primary and secondary perpetrators who continue to move freely in the society. In the reconstructed society, they must find a new role for themselves. How are persons who have occupied roles as perpetrators to find new roles and reacceptance in their own communities and the broader society? If they cannot do so, it is possible that they will resume political violence or resort to criminal activity. Thus arise the challenges of reintegration. Such issues concern not only former perpetrators of abuse but also victims, communities, and the broader society.

The problem of reintegration is a general one that arises in many places. To give some idea of its generality, we may consider just some of the many contexts in which this problem arises.

South Africa, with regard primarily to former fighters in the liberation struggle against the apartheid state.[1]

Iraq: No efforts were made to find new roles for some 350,000 men who had been in Saddam Hussein's army; it is not an exaggeration to say that the results of this omission have been calamitous.

Sri Lanka: Tens of thousands of men and women have been active in the Tamil Tigers, a tightly and oppressively organized terrorist group. If peace comes to Sri Lanka, significant challenges of integration will arise for these people. There is a real chance that other terrorist groups operating in the area will attempt to recruit them.

Uganda: Thousands of children in northern Uganda have been cruelly abducted and forced to fight, brutally and under horrific conditions, for the Lord's Resistance Army. Some such children have escaped, been released, or have been captured and returned to their villages; communities and families face issues about how to reintegrate them.

East Timor: Thousands of persons involved in Indonesian rule or in the post-referendum violence committed by Indonesian militias fled to West Timor and wished to return to East Timor. A major goal of the East Timorese truth commission was to establish community procedures for such persons to return to their communities.[2]

Reintegration is also an enormous challenge in Rwanda, Burundi, Liberia, Ethiopia, Eritrea, Bosnia, Mozambique, Colombia, Angola, Namibia, Afghanistan, Pakistan, New Guinea, the Sudan, and Tajikistan.[3] Discussed in some detail in this chapter will be the contexts of *Mozambique, Northern Ireland*, and *Sierra Leone*.

Obviously, each context has its own specific features. In the cases cited above, the persons requiring reintegration were fighters, leaders of fighters, and their associates. Most will have played the role of primary perpetrators, having committed or been closely involved in such acts as killings, maimings, abduction, and torture. It should not be assumed that people who are primary perpetrators are always members of nonstate groups. The Iraqi army, police, and other state personnel under Saddam Hussein provide just one of many possible examples in which state forces were involved in carrying out serious abuses. The police and army of apartheid South Africa would be another such example; so, too, would Stasi spies and collaborators in East Germany as well as persons in similar roles in other communist or totalitarian societies.

In general, the challenge of reintegration can be described as follows:

1. There has been a significant political shift with regard to the ending of violence and/or oppression.
2. Due to this political shift, roles as agents of violence or oppression that were politically recognized within the previous situation have ceased to be recognized and relevant.
3. Such roles, however damaging, provided a significant number of persons (and, often, their families) with a livelihood as well as a sense of identity and purpose acknowledged in the broader society.
4. Persons who have occupied such roles need to find alternative roles.
5. This need requires adaptation by them and by families, communities, and the broader society.

Obviously there are significant differences between the contexts in which questions of reintegration arise. A relatively young man or woman who has no economic security and has spent much of his or her youth engaging in a violent struggle is in a different position than a middle-aged, upper-middle-class former high-level civil servant who has lost his position in a political transition but retains a good education and resources of wealth and property.

A SMALL DETOUR: LUSTRATION AND NONINTEGRATION

Lustration is the policy of excluding from public office persons deemed to have been complicit with the previous regime and to share responsibility for its political abuses. The term "lustration" is based on the Latin word "*lustrum*," which refers to a ceremony of purification. Ideally, a purification procedure would be accompanied by a process of self-examination. However, lustration in its contemporary sense does not provide for that. In postcommunist Europe, lustration has been adopted as an approach to political and social reconstruction. There is, however, a sense in which lustration seems to be opposed to the goals of reintegration. A number of countries including the Czech Republic, Germany, and Poland adopted lustration policies in the immediate postcommunist period. The underlying idea is that persons who were officials in the previous regime or are deemed to have collaborated with that regime should not be trusted. Such persons must be excluded from public office so that reconstructed institutions may gain the confidence of the public. Lustration is a way of keeping certain categories of people out of certain sorts of institutions and offices, based on their past actions and roles—or alleged past actions and roles. Leading anticommunist dissidents such as Adam Michnik and Vaclav Havel have spoken out against the policy.

While lustration has some degree of plausibility with regard to the desirability of facilitating political change and having trustworthy persons in certain roles and offices, it has proven to be highly problematic in practice. Objections to the practice are many and varied. Accused persons have to prove their innocence and must do so against evidence from files that seem to support charges of collaboration. Such files are typically unreliable since they were maintained by oppressive regimes of little integrity and considerable coercive power. Since many thousands of persons will have been complicit with the previous regime to some extent, lustration will necessarily be selective: not every complicit person can be made to pay for his or her complicity. Persons may be accused as the result of old enmities or for political reasons; thus, lustration, although an attempt to end old corruption, may turn out to facilitate new corruption. In the end, the policy has been shown to victimize innocent people and maintain attitudes of suspicion, thus undermining the very public trust that it is supposed to encourage.[4]

THE SIGNIFICANCE OF POLITICAL CONTEXT

Many persons who commit violations in contexts of oppression, civil war, or other serious political conflict would not do so in ordinary times. On this basis, it may be argued that deeds such as spying, collaboration, torture, killing, looting, and assault do not amount to crimes when they are committed in the context of a politically extreme situation such as a totalitarian regime or civil war. Considerations of context are highly relevant. To begin with, there is a distinction to be made between political violence and criminal violence. This distinction provides the foundation for an ethical response to the fundamental challenge of reintegration. The role of "perpetrator of political violence" is quite distinct from the role of "criminal." A criminal acts for his or her own motives and ends, not for those of a political group or movement. Insofar as they are individual in this way, the motivations for criminal acts are not political.

Sometimes there are fundamental changes in the quality of a governing regime—as is suggested by such expressions as "post-Nazi," "post-Communist," "post-dictatorship," "post-Ba'athist," and "post-apartheid." Societies in transition face questions of transitional justice because they are shifting away from oppressive and violent regimes and constructing new institutions and relationships. During and after the transition, certain roles will become obsolete and disappear. Given that these roles involved wrongful acts, their deletion from the scene is a positive thing. However, the deletion of those roles poses psychological and socioeconomic challenges. Alternative roles are needed, and these alternatives may be hard to find. *Political* perpetrators will have no *political* reason to continue to commit acts of violence or oppression when the political conflict is over. They will, however, have to find their identity, purpose, and livelihood in doing something else.

Needless to say, matters are not always clear in this respect; many complications arise. Notoriously, people can become desensitized and accustomed to lives of violence with the consequence that they may continue violent and brutal acts even when political context has changed. There is a spectrum of cases between violent political activity and just plain criminal activity—as can be inferred from the currency of the term "warlord." There is not always a clear either/or distinction between violence that is criminal and violence that is political. Persons who enjoy or seek violence can find a pretext for it in a political struggle; persons who used violence for criminal purposes can gain a political role; and motives can be mixed.[5]

Furthermore, some defenders of discredited regimes persist even when those regimes are almost universally regarded as having undergone crushing and definitive defeats. Even when a civil war ends, some may be dissatisfied with the political "solution" and may wish to continue the struggle by violent means. Even in contexts in which major players agree that further struggles should be waged by nonviolent means, some radical elements may break away to form new groups that carry on the political violence.[6]

Reintegration requires new roles that can provide not only socioeconomic support but also a sense of identity and purpose. Such roles should provide genuine alternatives to roles of repression and violence and, as such, should not involve criminal activity such as robbery, drug trafficking, extortion, and the like.

VALUES AND ATTITUDES

As we might expect, serious problems arise here. Since violations such as killings, maimings, abduction, torture, and rape are profoundly disturbing and serious, we may expect that those who have committed them will be feared and shunned. To urge their reintegration in the absence of legal trial and punishment will seem a gross moral error. From a practical point of view, the matter may seem clear, given that in many situations of aftermath it is simply not possible to legally try and punish all those who have been perpetrators. But the practical response may seem profoundly inadequate from an ethical point of view. Many will believe that they should not be asked to accept in their midst persons who have played the role of perpetrators, especially when they have been primary perpetrators. They may find these people fearsome and repugnant and doubt that they could ever become trustworthy citizens in a morally decent society.

Issues of Responsibility

With regard to moral responsibility, significant qualifications are often important. Moral responsibility may be individual, shared, or collective—or some combination of these. As an *individual*, a person is morally responsible for an act only if he or she:

(a) has not been coerced into doing that action;
(b) knows what he or she is doing and intends to do it;
(c) causes or plays a role in causing the commission of the act.

Individual moral responsibility involves personal choices about what to do and acting on those choices in a context of relative freedom. This is what we most commonly think of as moral responsibility.

If we consider clause (c) in the above model, we will be led to an understanding of how a person may also *share responsibility* for the commission of some act. Shared responsibility is common in political contexts. Consider, for example, a case in which a group of rebels burn down houses in a village. One person may suggest the act; several others may verbally support it; someone in an informal leadership role may call out an order; and then several individuals go off to find dry wood. Another person may supply the matches with which groups of two or three people go from house to house setting fires. No one in the group opposes the action in any way or does anything to put out the fires. Suppose now that the final result is that all the houses in the village are destroyed. In this context, each person has individually committed certain acts (finding the wood, providing the matches, and so on) and will bear individual responsibility for what he or she has done. But it can also be said that because the action was carried out by the *group* each perpetrator *shares* responsibility for burning down the homes in the village.[7]

As this example also suggests, highly pertinent in political contexts is *collective responsibility*. In its most characteristic form, collective responsibility is the responsibility of an organized group such as a corporation, institution, nation state, or nonstate organized political group. For example, if country A invades country B, then presuming that the invasion was duly authorized within A, that country, as a nation, bears collective responsibility for it. As a collectivity, a state is responsible for its policies; a nation that formulates and implements policies concerning health, schooling, or foreign aid bears the responsibility for those policies and their results. The responsibility of *individual* citizens within A for this act does not follow directly from A's *collective* responsibility.[8] And, as a direct corollary, the fact that individual members of a collective are not *as individuals* responsible for committing some wrong does not prove the absence of *collective* responsibility. Collective and individual responsibility are distinct.

These categories are not, however, mutually exclusive: a person may be individually responsible for some aspects of an action, share responsibility for others, and be a member of a group that is collectively responsible for still further aspects. Insofar as reintegration is about individuals who have played roles as perpetrators, it is individual and shared responsibility that are the most relevant in this context. Both these types of responsibility presume that people know what they are doing and, within reasonable limits, are not coerced or forced. To the extent that people are *forced* to commit actions and *coerced* in such a way that their individual deliberations and choices do not determine what they do, their actions are neither chosen nor free and, therefore, do not reflect their moral character. For such actions, people are not morally responsible. To be morally responsible for what one does, a person must have real options. This requires that there must have been a genuine possibility that that person could have done something other than what he or she did.[9] In other words, a person can be morally responsible for an action only if what was done was avoidable.

This account of moral responsibility has significant implications with regard to political wrongs insofar as many perpetrators do *not* bear full moral responsibility for their actions.[10] The clearest examples here are those of persons who, as children, were abducted by rebel groups and compelled to take on roles in a violent conflict. Though many such persons have played the roles of primary and secondary perpetrators, they cannot be held responsible for what they have done. They have been coerced under severe and brutal conditions and, in many cases, have been threatened with death. Though their actions have resulted in serious and gross damage to persons, because they were vulnerable, forced, and lacking in understanding, they should not be regarded as bearing individual or shared responsibility for their actions.

A qualification is needed at this point. Not all child combatants are members of armies as a result of abduction. Some have joined "of their own choice" as a response to extraordinarily difficult circumstances. In circumstances of violence and war, joining an armed group may present itself as a favorable option to a child who is without security in the form of parents, home, food, and shelter. It is sometimes said of some child combatants, both male and female, that there is a sense in which they have joined fighting units "voluntarily," having decided to do so in order to obtain food or escape an undesirable family situation. One might argue, in such cases, that these children were *willing* recruits and are responsible for what they have done. But despite the appearance of volition, the vulnerability and immaturity of these young people argues against their having been able to make meaningful personal choices in such difficult circumstances.

When communities are urged to accept into their midst former militants who were abducted as children, or even who enlisted "voluntarily" as children, they face severe challenges, because these children may have been brutalized by years of ill-treatment and violence. Among these is one challenge that is more apparent than real. To reintegrate a returned child soldier is *not* a matter of allowing a responsible party to get away with murder, because these children were not morally responsible for their actions.

Similar considerations may apply to some other persons who have played the role of perpetrators, insofar as they have been lured into political violence by rhetorically manipulative leaders or failed to understand the nature of their acts. Burning is burning, looting is looting, rape is rape, and killing is killing—but, in a political context, people may be abnormally open to persuasion that such acts are not only excusable but actually justifiable as means to defend a just and valid cause. If vulnerable people are manipulated to the extent that they are unable to reflect on the nature of their acts, they can be argued to bear diminished responsibility for them.

The Unforgivable?

Quests to reintegrate perpetrators in the community are sometimes met with horror by people who think that these agents of oppression and violence have become moral monsters who should never be reaccepted into their communities. It is often believed that persons who have committed gross violations of human rights have been altered by their actions; that their character is marked, and marked permanently, by what they have done in such a way that they have, in effect, gone beyond the moral pale. Those who have participated in atrocities, mass rapes, or killings have done so as conscious human agents whose very selves have been brutalized. It may be argued that such brutalized persons could never reform their characters so as to become trustworthy citizens. It may be said that such persons are quite simply *unforgivable*.

There are different senses in which a person might be deemed to be unforgivable. One might think that someone ought not to be forgiven under certain conditions but that his unforgivability is *conditional* in the sense that, if he were to express remorse, offer restitution, and show evidence of moral transformation, he might become forgivable. But the word "unforgivable" typically connotes a more absolute and permanent sort of condemnation. That stronger sense is based on the presumption that people who have committed atrocities become moral monsters who could never change for the better. The following ideas underlie that presumption:

(1) The character of the moral agent can correctly be inferred from the character of some of that person's moral acts. One who has committed a monstrous act is a moral monster.

(2) A moral monster cannot become anything other than a moral monster.

(3) Moral monsters should not be accepted back into any decent community.

If accepted and taken literally, these beliefs rule out any reintegration of persons who have committed serious wrongs.

However, a rebuttal is possible. First, it is premature and erroneous to infer the character of an agent from selected acts that person has committed; there is a distinction between an *agent* and his or her *acts*. This point is strengthened if, as explained above, we consider the nature of the political context and the factors that may indicate coercion and diminished responsibility on the part of this agent. Second, the notion of "moral monster" is dehumanizing and, for that reason, objectionable. It is also inaccurate, given that some people have accomplished moral transformation, even in extreme cases. And third, there are fundamental moral objections to the notion that some persons are reducible to monsters who should forever be shunned and ostracized.[11]

However, it is one thing to contemplate these issues from the point of view of a detached philosophical observer and another to reflect on them from the standpoint of persons in a community assigned the task of reintegrating perpetrators. From that perspective, issues of trust are profoundly significant, to say the least.

Issues of Trust

Acts of violence and oppression undermine people's feelings of confidence and security, thus destroying social trust. A major challenge of reintegration, then, is to find means of overcoming feelings of fear and insecurity so that distrust can be replaced with trust. Persons who have participated in serious violations have proven one thing at least: they are capable of grievously harmful acts. They have the experience of what it is to injure, torture, kill, rape, or maim. They have been involved in the brutal imposition of harm on their fellow human beings; they know what it is to do unspeakable things and have probably become desensitized to gross violence as a result of their experiences. It should not be surprising if such people are regarded with deep suspicion as fearsome men and women who could never be relied upon in a reconstructed society. Who, then, would seek to find a place for such people and construct morally decent relationships with them? That there are grounds for distrust cannot be denied. How could some degree of confidence be established?

For communities, the challenge is to open minds and doors so as to receive such persons in the aftermath of a conflict. For those needing reintegration, the challenge is, by word and deed, to show themselves trustworthy and deserving of that reception. Former perpetrators may be able to communicate in words or actions the message that "these acts were wrong; we should not have done them; and we relinquish this past and will not offend again."[12] Failure to acknowledge wrongdoing and express contrition is likely to support suspicion and fear because persons in the community will have little reason to believe that those they are asked to accept have changed their ways.

CONTEXTS AND STRATEGIES

Various approaches can be taken in response to the challenges of reintegration. Common among these are:

(a) *DDR:* This acronym is short for "disarmament, demobilization, and reintegration" and is used in contexts such as those of Sierra Leone, Mozambique, and Liberia in which there has been a civil war. In pursuing DDR, one removes weapons from armed men and women, demobilizes these persons—removing them from the command structure and military context—and, after some amount of education and training, returns them to the communities from which they came.

(b) *Truth Commission Process:* Strictly speaking, a truth commission process is not itself one of reintegration, though it has potential to open doors for reintegration and may, ideally, be expected to do so. A truth commission process is, at root, a process providing for testimony, storytelling, confession, dialogue, exploration, fact-finding, analysis, and recommendations. Truth commissions may be accompanied by an amnesty process through which persons who have served in perpetrator roles may receive immunity from criminal prosecution and civil suit in virtue of their disclosures. Amnesty can be seen as opening the door to reintegration in the sense that perpetrators enter society free of the burden that these legal risks would impose. Whether their reintegration is facilitated in this way will depend on the attitudes of the receiving community.

(c) *Meetings and Workshops:* Truth Commission and DDR processes are conducted at the state level and may involve thousands of individuals. As such, they provide few if any opportunities for persons affected by the conflict to interact with each other on an individual and personal basis. There is a considerable gap between the national (macro) level and the level of persons and their relationships (micro level). Into this gap fall the work of many community and nongovernmental organizations. These initiatives may reflect primarily the talents and energies of particular individuals, as does Father Michael Lapsley's Institute for Healing of Memories in Cape Town, South Africa, or they may reflect the goals of organizations such as the Glencree Centre for Reconciliation, located near Dublin, Ireland. Workshops and meetings provide opportunities for persons who were on different sides and who occupied different conflict roles to share stories and seek mutual understanding.

(d) *Indigenous Rituals and Processes:* In some contexts in which fighters are returning to villages, rituals and traditions of reconciliation can assist in processes of reintegration. For example, in Mozambique a vicious war between 1982 and 1992 was followed by a cease-fire and peace, apparently craved by the people of the region.[13] Even before the cease-fire, displaced people had begun to move back to their communities. More than ten years after the settlement, this peace appears to be stable and sustainable. Several observers have commented favorably on the role of local communities in Mozambique. The country did not have legal tribunals for war criminals; nor was there a truth commission. Instead, there was a blanket amnesty for all who had participated in the brutality of the war, which included vicious killings, sexual slavery, sexual assault, the forced enlistment of children and youth, and forced starvation.

CASES IN POINT

Mozambique

Writing about healing and trauma in Mozambique, Alcinda Honwana emphasized that its peace seemed to be sustainable.[14] Local communities, acting without intervention from outsiders, were doing much of the work of reconciliation, seeking to heal the social wounds of war through ceremonies that sought harmony and the appeasement of spiritual beings. Honwana reports that indigenous rituals included exorcisms, cleansings, and other ceremonies. In a ceremony called *mpfukwa*, the spirits of those killed were to be appeased with the burying of money and cloth. Other ceremonies addressed the issue of abducted children. A returned child would be set in a hut in the clothing in which he or she had returned; the hut would then be burned, together with this clothing; the child would be taken out, bathed, and given medicine to drink. This ceremony was seen as marking for the child and the community a break from a collective traumatic past; the notion was that the ceremony would heal its wounds. In a ceremony called *timbamba*, returning persons would be welcomed home and links with their community and ancestors would be restored; typically this ceremony would involve a meal of goat, chicken, maize, and meal. Returning persons would present themselves to their ancestors at a *gandzelo* tree or other community landmark.[15] Indigenous ceremonies were used to reintegrate child guerrillas, abducted wives, and soldiers who, it was believed, might otherwise have been pursued by the vengeful spirits of those they had killed. Purification rituals involved the entire community, with the idea of separating people from the traumas of the past and sealing the traumas away.[16]

    Carolyn Nordstrom is another scholar who has studied war and its aftermath in Mozambique. Nordstrom was particularly impressed by the work of traditional African healers and their contributions to peace. She interviewed more than one hundred African healers who had been treating the psychic wounds of war. She reported that these healers understood violence as a kind of illness that could overcome people. They considered violence to be the result not of character flaws of individuals but, rather, a symptom of a sickness that had to be healed. In a 1999 presentation, Nordstrom quoted what village elders said to a young soldier during a long and complex cleansing ceremony.

> Time will not erase the fact that you killed people. People we all care about. . . . But you did these acts in a time of war so horrible none of us has been left unscathed. . . . We cannot condemn you for the war, you too were held in its grip. . . . We have to go on now to create a better place for ourselves. Take what you have learned and turn it into good, into rebuilding.[17]

Another commentator, Helena Cobban, interpreted the healing notions in Mozambique as embodying an African conception similar to that of *ubuntu*, a conception of the self as bound up in relationships. The healers, *curandeiros* and *curandeiras*, retained their traditional practices involving spells, rituals, medicines, and other interventions, and, in a situation in which nobody wanted war or the investigation of its many gross atrocities, they were able to work effectively by implementing their interpretation of violence as an antihuman force that can hold people in its grip. Cobban found a "depth of national and social reconciliation" in Mozambique.[18]

It would be incorrect to believe that all the work of reintegration in Mozambique was done through indigenous ceremonies. There were also international agencies, including the United Nations, involved in DDR programs for some ninety thousand fighters. The details of these programs varied, but all included disarmament, demobilized holding camps, literacy and reeducation programs. In some cases there were monthly subsistence payments and the provision of agricultural kits including a hoe, buckets, and seeds.[19] Chris Alden, who studied the effectiveness of reintegration efforts, found that 85 percent of former fighters felt that they had been reintegrated. Alden described ritual ceremonies as an important element of the broader process of reconciliation.[20] NGO workers reported that demobilized soldiers were not a problematic factor in the community. Community leaders were somewhat less optimistic, with some 65 percent stating that they felt former fighters had been successfully reintegrated.

While it is possible to romanticize indigenous traditions, the example of Mozambique serves to illustrate their interest and potential.[21]

Northern Ireland

An excellent study of reintegration in Northern Ireland is that of Brian Gormally, an independent consultant whose work in Belfast deals with policy analysis and community-based organizations.[22] Gormally explains that any peace settlement will eventually require the working out of common values in a society. The role of the fighters in the conflict—many of whom may have been imprisoned for what they did—is a key aspect of the social transformation of a postconflict society. According to the Geneva Conventions, Protocol II, Article 6 (5), at the end of hostilities, the authorities in power should seek the broadest possible amnesty for persons who have participated in the armed conflict or have been deprived of their liberty for reasons related to it. This protocol was ratified by the government of the United Kingdom in 1995. However, that government never accepted that the case of Northern Ireland fell within the scope of the protocol. The language used to describe former fighters in the aftermath of the Good Friday Agreement was somewhat controversial, the terms "combatant," "ex-combatant," and "ex-prisoner" being in common use. Attitudes to persons who had played such roles varied considerably. For example, the British saw members of the Irish Republican Army (IRA) as belonging to a relatively small and highly troublesome group of terrorists while the IRA members saw themselves as Irish soldiers fighting to liberate their country from foreign invaders. It was clear at the time of the Good Friday Agreement that to avoid future violence it would be necessary to accommodate former militants. There would have to be some sort of inclusive winding down process. However, contrary to what some recalcitrant citizens alleged, it was not true that in the aftermath of the Good Friday Accord "criminals" were roaming the streets.

Gormally describes the Good Friday Agreement as one that is *transcendent* in the sense that it provides the basis for new and inclusive definitions of identity, nationality, and civil society. However, this transcendence does not mean that the new conceptions were accepted by everyone. Writing in 2001, Gormally saw the situation of ex-prisoners as one that was central to the peace process in Northern Ireland. Ex-prisoners were the most conspicuous ex-combatants and, for many, the most conspicuous perpetrators. Both Loyalist and Republican prisoners said that they did not go to prison simply in order to be released. Rather, they had fought and made sacrifices for political goals and were resolute in their insistence that they had been *political* prisoners rather than criminals. Many support groups exist for ex-prisoners. Their effectiveness, Gormally argues, is contingent upon voluntary membership, autonomy, transparent management of funds, and effectively addressing economic issues, especially pertaining to barriers to employment. Such barriers are highly significant. For example, persons with criminal connections are ineligible for work in many areas of public service, are exempted from some provisions of equality legislation, and cannot get a license permitting them to drive a bus or taxi. They are also ineligible for many jobs involving access to children.[23]

Considerable funding has been supplied by the European Union for peace and reconciliation work in Northern Ireland, and, in particular, work focusing on the situation of ex-prisoners. By 2001, the European Union Special Support Programme for Peace and Reconciliation (SSPPR) had already supplied some thirty million British pounds for these efforts.[24] Of that amount, one half went to the Northern Ireland government and the other half was distributed more locally, divided between elected councilors and voluntary community organizations. The European Union was determined to get money to local grassroots projects. By April 1998, the SSPPR had funded some eleven thousand projects involving two hundred fifty thousand people. Understood as a bottom-up approach, the SSPPR sought to mobilize local communities in the work of reconciliation and, in particular, the reintegration of ex-combatants and ex-prisoners.[25]

The extent of this funding, the large number of the projects, and the hard work done by many in community organizations does not mean that the problems of reintegration were solved. Former fighters and prisoners continue to suffer social and economic problems, and many victims resent the funds given to persons whom they see as dangerous perpetrators. Some ex-militants continue practices of intimidation and extortion within their communities. Though it has significantly decreased, sectarian violence has not ended.

> The question (of the status of para-military organizations) is related to the more general one of the maintenance of paramilitary structures and power into the future. We cannot ignore the facts that such structures are still very much alive, that prisoner organizations can be a focus for their activities and that weapons have been found in two Loyalist ex-prisoner centers. However, one of the central arguments of this paper is that opening routes for peaceful activism, for productive engagement in the political and social structures of society by ex-combatants is an essential part of the process of reintegration. We would further argue that this process is a much more effective way to gain the goal of a peaceful and inclusive society than simply attacking the existence of paramilitary organizations as such.[26]

Poignantly, Gormally says that "the peace process requires *repeated acts of faith* by all participants."[27] In other words, one would have to hope and persist, even in the face of problems.

The political nature of acts of violence in such contexts and the diminished responsibility of some of those who committed these acts is not everywhere understood. When the British government's Select Committee on Northern Ireland Affairs held hearings in March 2005, it heard extensive testimony from community groups. The committee reached the conclusion that, at that stage, a truth commission process would not be constructive in Northern Ireland. Such a process seemed more likely to be divisive and the committee feared that it would reinforce persisting resentments. According to the extensive testimony presented to this committee, considerable skepticism, insecurity, and doubt about the peace process persisted. Processes of reconciliation were by no means accepted by all, and profound issues of trust remained, particularly—and most significantly—with regard to the police and their role.[28]

In its summary report, the Select Committee noted that the definition of "victim" was highly contested. Some sought to restrict it to those who had been *innocent* victims of *sectarian murder* (a subset of primary victims).[29] Others (including the government and the committee itself) broadened the term to include persons who survived the Troubles but were physically or psychologically injured by the violence; the close relatives or partners of such people were considered victims as well so that, on this account, primary and secondary victims would be included if they continued to suffer from what had happened to them.[30] The Select Committee noted discontent among victims and victim support groups and resentment over resources provided to ex-combatants. Many victims' groups had experienced funding problems. Controversies and issues with regard to apology and acknowledgment were noted. Many former militants refused to accept that they had done anything wrong or even that they were complicit in perpetuating the conflict.

One Loyalist ex-prisoner was quoted as saying that he was not sorry for his actions and that he would not express remorse for things he did some twenty or thirty years earlier because, at the time, he thought they were right. He was willing to concede that violence is not the best way, but he insisted that things were different then and that, in the context in which he had acted, the things he had done were not wrong.[31] Difficulties with regard to the acceptance of personal responsibility on the part of former militants were noted. Yet victims sought such acknowledgment and, when they received it, found it enormously important. The committee also noted that violence and intimidation by some members of paramilitary organizations continued.

In 2005, the Independent Monitoring Commission, established under the Good Friday Agreement, submitted a report that presents a rather gloomy picture with regard to the activities of paramilitary organizations in Northern Ireland.[32] The commission sought to study the compliance of these groups with the terms of the Good Friday Agreement; it investigated whether the groups used violence; whether they had committed crimes such as robbery, drug trafficking, intimidation, and extortion; whether they were seeking to procure arms and new recruits; and whether they continued to exile people.[33] Its report provides evidence of considerable illegal activity in the period from September 1, 2004 through February 28, 2005. Groups described in the report include the Continuity IRA (CIRA); the Irish National Liberation Army (INLA); the Loyalist Volunteer Force (LVF); the Provisional IRA (PIRA); the Real IRA (RIRA); the Ulster Defence Association (UDA); and the Ulster Volunteer Force (UVF) and Red Hand Commando.

Among Republican, or "Catholic" groups, the CIRA was found to have participated in assassination attempts, shootings, some recruiting and training, and some movement of munitions and explosives. The INLA was said to be a significant terrorist group participating in organized crime including drug trafficking, robbery, and coercion. The PIRA was said to maintain a capacity for violence, to be active in organized crime, to exile people, and to participate in shootings, assaults, and the smuggling of fuel and tobacco. In September 2004, police had found ten thousand rounds of ammunition suitable for assault rifles in the hands of the PIRA. In the judgment of the commission, the PIRA sought to continue organized crime activities, exert control in Republican areas, and maintain a capacity for terrorist action. However, the commission did not find evidence of any clear intention to resume political violence as such. It was probably members of the PIRA who were responsible for the January 30, 2005, beating and murder of Robert McCartney.[34] As to the RIRA, there were two factions, both of which were active and were participating in attacks, shootings, exilings, threats, bombings, robberies, and the targeting of police officers. This organization seemed committed to terrorism; however, the commission commented that its ambitions might exceed its capacity in this regard.

Among Unionist/Loyalist or "Protestant" groups, the LVF was found to have participated in drug dealing, shooting, and some recruitment; its activities seemed more criminal than political. Despite having expressed its intent to desist from all "military" activity, the UDA participated in shootings, assaults, arson, abduction, armed robbery, monitoring of persons deemed dissident, and exiling. The UDA was judged to have been responsible for two murders. The UVF and Red Hand Commandoes were said to be active, violent, involved in organized crime and recruiting, and willing to shoot at members of rival groups. The commission observed that Loyalists were committing more violence than Republicans, with four times as many shootings by Loyalist adherents in the period under scrutiny.

The commission further observed that even when these sorts of actions by paramilitary organizations do not result in deaths, they have cruel and harmful effects. Often, they leave people permanently disabled and psychologically scarred. Exiling, in particular, is a gross expression of paramilitary power, one that allows these groups to exercise considerable control over people. To be exiled—in other words, to be coerced at threat of death into leaving home, friends, and community—has a devastating and traumatic impact on individuals. Yet the commission found that, if anything, exiling seemed to be increasing.

The report shows clear evidence of a commonsensical conclusion: if people no longer find a role as militants and are unable to find alternative roles, many will resort to crime. In Northern Ireland, pubs, hotels, security services, and transportation businesses serve as outlets for the monies collected through criminal activities. To address the problem, the commission recommended tax law enforcement and greater rigor in control and licensing regimes.

The violent and criminal activities of paramilitary groups were all the more disturbing since there was also evidence that political parties had not thoroughly dissociated themselves from related paramilitaries. In the judgment of the commission, Sinn Fein still had connections with PIRA and the Progressive Unionist Party had connections with the UVF. The commission urged that these political parties terminate all connections with paramilitary groups engaged in crime and violence. The pervasive sense of fear and suspicion resulting from such activities is profoundly significant. People who live in areas affected by organized crime, drug trafficking, intimidation, assaults, and beatings cannot feel secure. It is an understatement to assert that, under such circumstances, trust cannot develop and efforts to transcend the sectarian conflicts will be seriously handicapped. To state this obvious point bluntly: crime and paramilitary power are obstacles to reconciliation.

The commission has stated emphatically the centrality of nonviolence and the rule of law in working democracies.

> It is axiomatic that anybody in a democracy, and so any political party working within that democracy and publicly committed to exclusively peaceful and democratic means, should accept the definition of crime that the law of that country lays down. There can be no equivocation over this issue, and the increasing focus on paramilitary crime as a whole has raised it in the public consciousness. This is not just an issue for Sinn Fein. It is a fundamental point about the commitment of any

of the Northern Ireland political parties to democratic principles and their readiness to dissociate themselves from illegal paramilitary activities.[35]

Violence, crime, intimidation, trafficking, and exiling by paramilitary groups provide evidence that many former militants have not successfully reintegrated into a postwar society. More than seven years after the peace agreement, paramilitaries in Northern Ireland retain considerable power, which they can—and do—use to intimidating and destructive effect.

Since it is the duty of this commission to monitor crime and violence, it does not attempt to publicize more positive news about reconciliation and nonviolence. Thus, its report will understandably omit reference to successes—whether these stem from community workshops, development groups, or the efforts of third parties. There are many such successes. Ex-combatants have found valuable roles in hundreds of worthy community organizations. Because it does not tell their stories, one might suspect that such a report may be said to offer an unrepresentative picture, one that is unduly bleak and pessimistic.

And yet there are grounds for concern. A worrisome indicator that "reconciliation" in Northern Ireland may be shallow lies in the violence that erupted in September 2005 in Belfast. The immediate cause of this community violence was a dispute over the route of a public march. The deeper cause, apparently, was a sense of alienation from state and police on the part of some Loyalists who feared that widely publicized IRA disarmament was giving Republicans more power, resulting in a situation in which the Loyalist community would be devalued so that there would be nowhere for its members to go.[36] Those events showed that thousands of people were prepared to riot and intimidate, reverting to the bad old ways of troubled Belfast.[37]

Sierra Leone

In Sierra Leone, we can consider four different institutions that play some role with regard to the challenges of reintegration.

1. The *Sierra Leone TRC* was modeled to a considerable extent on the South African TRC, but had less resources and expertise and was required to function in a much more fractured and troubled context. It was clear that a truth commission was needed, as distinct from attempting to deal with the conflict solely through criminal trials. There were far too many who had served as perpetrators; there was a need to acknowledge the stories of victims; and clarification about causes was needed. In addition, it was hoped that a truth commission could indicate promising directions for reforms, promote reconciliation and healing, and pave the way to forgiveness and reintegration.[38]

2. The *Special Court for Sierra Leone* was international in its institutionalization and support but was located within the country in Freetown. It was established

to conduct trials only of persons most responsible for the atrocities committed during the war and, as of winter 2005, had indicted eleven individuals.

3. The process of *DDR* was implemented by the government with the assistance of major NGOs.

4. The fourth resource for reintegration was that of *indigenous ceremonies*, which, in some cases, followed truth commission hearings and, in other cases, were conducted independently.[39]

According to the Lome Peace Accord, the TRC was intended to facilitate genuine healing and reconciliation. According to its October 2004 report, there was an acknowledgment that all parties in the conflict had committed atrocities, including even ECOMOG (Economic Community of West African States Monitoring Group) peacekeepers. The TRC attempted to further reconciliation and, if possible, forgiveness by facilitating exchanges between victims and perpetrators in those cases in which victims wanted the exchange. It took some eight thousand statements, of which 13 percent were given by perpetrators. Some of these persons (about one third) admitted to wrongdoing, often confessing in great detail.[40] At the end of each week, the TRC held a reconciliation ceremony at which victims and perpetrators would sometimes come together. In some cases, ceremonies were incorporated to "wash away evils" from persons who admitted their crimes. Commenting on these events, one observer found them powerful but, unfortunately, limited in number.[41] The TRC in Sierra Leone did not incorporate a model for rehabilitation and reintegration of ex-combatants. It may have been handicapped in its work by the presence of the Special Court, since some feared that what they said could be used against them in the court. Compared to the limited work of the Special Court (which was charged with trying a small number of top persons), the task of reintegrating and—in some sense—reconciling thousands of low-level perpetrators was gargantuan.[42] One commentator referred to it as the task of "integrating into society a teenaged boy whose only skills are operating an AK-47 and mutilating others on order," saying it was simply daunting.[43]

A recent report issued by the United States Institute of Peace gives pause for thought about the truth commission and court in Sierra Leone. Anthropologist Rosalind Shaw traveled in Sierra Leone in the wake of TRC hearings, seeking to explore people's attitudes toward the war and its aftermath. She sought to discover people's preferred mode of coping with traumatic events. On the basis of interview material, Shaw argues that the people of Sierra Leone did not really want a truth and reconciliation commission. On her view, their preferred mode of coping would have been to "forgive and forget."[44] Shaw argues that the notion that telling the truth is helpful and healing is a Western idea and, as such, one that does not fit all cultures. In contrast to Desmond Tutu's thinking in and about the South African case, she states that *nations* cannot be said to *heal* on the basis of *truth telling*. (The argument is that since nations do not have psyches, they cannot heal at all.) Instead, one might seek *social forgetting* in such a context, an approach that would better fit cultural practices in Sierra Leone—or so Shaw maintains.[45]

Shaw reminds her readers that a truth commission is not a form of therapy and that testifying is not necessarily cathartic—even for individuals, and much less for nations. She points out that the truth that is supposedly discovered by truth commissions is open to question; indeed, it is often highly contestable. For these and other reasons, a truth commission is no panacea for reconciliation, and it should not be regarded as such. Furthermore, and still more crucially for Shaw's case, different cultures and regions have their own "memory practices." Rather than adapting a TRC process that was valorized in South Africa, employing confessional practices of a Christian origin and admired by the West, Shaw claims that it would have been preferable for the Sierra Leonese people to employ more locally authentic processes of social forgetting. Shaw states that ethnographic research is necessary because international language, used even by NGO staff who are operating locally, may fail to represent the perspective of local people. She cites as a contrast the traditional practices employed successfully in Mozambique.

On the basis of interviews she conducted in Sierra Leone, Shaw argues that many persons in that country were afraid to testify to the TRC, even if they had not played a perpetrator role. Persons who had been victims were afraid of reprisals from perpetrators, telling her that "it's better to suffer once than to suffer twice."[46] Furthermore, on the part of perpetrators, there was fear of the government and the Special Court, which, it was thought, might use testimony from the TRC to launch legal prosecutions. Shaw found that people were afraid of the TRC, whose Western presumptions were foreign and unhelpful to them. Many former combatants were remaining in the towns in which they had been demobilized because they felt unwilling or unable to return to their former homes. It would have been preferable, Shaw says, to keep these memories out of social space and to separate from them using a cultural ritual. A returning child, for example, might be given a new social identity in a ritual involving the whole community and ceremonial offerings. According to Shaw, people wanted to forget the war and move on with their lives. What they needed was not confession and memory but, rather, some sort of "unmaking" of past violence and "remaking" of combatants as social persons.

Although Shaw does not comment on the point, it is crucial to understand that indigenous rituals *do* involve acknowledgment. These are non-Western forms of acknowledgment. If the ritual is remembered, then the absence and reincorporation of the person into his or her community is remembered as well. The ritual is *not* a form of forgetting; to apply a "forgive and forget" label to it seems simply to be incorrect. To have a ritual incorporating a returning child into the community is not to simply ignore the fact that the child was taken away. Rather, it serves to note and mark the fact of the child's return after an absence, and to do something constructive with that fact. If effective, the ceremony will return the person to the community, ritually cleansing him of the evil involved in his past.

The major program of disarmament, demobilization, and reintegration in Sierra Leone was implemented by the NCDDR (National Committee for Disarmament, Demobilization, and Reintegration). In the disarmament phase, from October 1998 through January 2002, the NCDDR stated that it had collected a total of 42,300 weapons and approximately 1.2 million rounds of ammunition. In this process, some 72,490 combatants were said to have been demobilized. The number is not clear, however, since there are other estimates, a common one being that some 48,000 combatants were demobilized.[47] One analyst cites a figure of 6,904 child soldiers disarmed; however, higher numbers are often given.[48] David Crane, the first prosecutor for the Special Court of Sierra Leone, said that he would not prosecute youth between fifteen and eighteen, deeming that they had been the victims of others who had forced them to commit terrible acts. For this reason, Crane held that they were not morally or legally responsible for what they had done and that they should not be made to suffer further.[49]

In a general discussion of DDR, the Bonn International Center for Conversion explains that effective reintegration must be economic, social, and psychological. Many parties are crucially involved in this process, including male and female ex-combatants (both child and adult), government soldiers, communities, families, militants' associations, and other groups seeking to reintegrate. These would include returning refugees and displaced persons. Parties that will be involved in reintegration will include businesses, government, local and international NGOs, the UN and its agencies, and donors. Particular support will be given to ex-combatants because of the profound importance of turning them away from continued violence or criminal activity.

Raising the question of whether such a focus on assistance for ex-combatants is unfair, a recent account submitted the following reasons for saying it is not: the aid is needed from a humanitarian perspective; ex-combatants often have diminished responsibility; there is a potential for them to make a contribution to the society; and their reintegration is crucial if peace is to be sustainable.[50] The Bonn Center recommends that efforts on reintegration be centralized, start early, attend to the possibility that persons may have more than one weapon, provide good support, pay attention to the needs of women, children, the disabled, and HIV-infected persons, and balance the needs of ex-combatants against those of the larger community, including, of course, victims.

In Sierra Leone, the process of demobilization involved five different phases, these being assembly, interview, weapons collection, eligibility certification, and transportation. Programming for adult ex-combatants included monetary support in the form of reinsertion benefits, a short-term training program, and referral and counseling services. For child ex-combatants, a program established with the cooperation of UNICEF (United Nations International Children's Emergency Fund) provided some schooling and other training. Reintegration is the further process intended to settle former combatants in communities—preferably their own. Socially, the goal is for these persons to be sufficiently well received that they can be trusted and function as normal community members. Economically, the goal is to provide ex-combatants with the means to generate income so as to support themselves through means other than warfare.

Economic reintegration is problematic in Sierra Leone because the civil war had devastated an economy that had never been strong. Even the agricultural sector was affected such that subsistence farming, while highly necessary, was difficult to carry out successfully. Sensitization programs sponsored by NCCDR instructed ex-combatants to strive to understand the effects of the war and the feelings of the people and to use their skills training to provide services to the community. With community involvement, it was more likely that ex-combatants would invest their energy into projects that were genuinely needed; this prospect made acknowledgment of their efforts more likely and lessened the likelihood of victims and community members resenting the opportunities and resources provided to ex-combatants.[51]

Cash payments made to ex-combatants pose certain problems in Sierra Leone and elsewhere. One central problem is that arms may be hard to give up if they have become culturally accepted and are a major source of social identity and physical security. Another is that people might use the money for turned-in armaments to purchase more armaments. In some contexts, including that of Sierra Leone, there are other wars in the region, and ex-combatants who were not faring well could be recruited to fight again. A further problem is that if borders are porous and payments for turned-in armaments are higher in some areas than others, people may move their arms across borders in an attempt to increase their value. Additionally, disadvantages of cash payments for arms include incentives to extravagance and fraud, possible mismanagement, resentment by unarmed persons, the possibility of creating ongoing expectations that cannot be met, and inflation. Nevertheless, there are advantages to monetary payments. Individuals and households can meet their daily needs without resorting to crime or guns; transaction costs are few; there is flexibility; recipients have some power and choice as to how they will use their funds; and accounting is relatively easy.[52]

It is extremely difficult to get a sense, from print sources, of what is happening on the ground in Sierra Leone. It is difficult to credit claims that fifty thousand former fighters have been demobilized and reintegrated. Many of these people were children or were abducted as children, and most of them must have become accustomed to gross and brutal violence as an aspect of daily life. Jeremy Ginifer reported in 2003 that some ex-combatants were not able to acknowledge the reality and significance of their actions and claimed that their violent campaign was one of liberty and sovereignty for the nation.[53] Given the terrible atrocities committed during the war, this lack of acknowledgment must have been profoundly difficult for victims and communities. When one considers, say, persons in a village in which many suffered beating, burning, rape, amputation, and other brutality, it is nearly impossible to contemplate what they would experience when receiving into their midst persons who had committed such acts. Even granting diminished responsibility and a shift away from a war context, the scenario in which such persons return and are reaccepted is hard to envisage. One can only speculate as to how returning persons are received and what the future will hold for them and for their communities. If statistics are to be believed, such reintegration has happened not only a few times, but tens of thousands of times. Yet it seems not only premature but also highly insensi-

tive to pronounce that some forty or fifty thousand ex-combatants have been successfully reintegrated into their communities.

CONCLUDING COMMENTS

In any conflict in which people have engaged in roles calling for violent and oppressive behavior, there will be a requirement for new behavior after the conflict is over.
That requirement poses enormous challenge for individuals, families, communities,
and the state. Clearly, the problem of how to reintegrate ex-combatants has not been
solved. A situation in which reconciliation is sought requires a new basis for physical and social security and, ideally, a reevaluation of what one did in the past. As
we have seen, many dilemmas arise; these vary depending on the context. Solutions,
if found, will similarly vary. One could hardly expect African healing processes,
useful in the context of wide resistance to war in Mozambique, to be effective in
post-communist Poland. Notions of crime and evil, guilt and responsibility,
acknowledgment, reform, and reacceptance will apply in all contexts, but their interpretation and implementation will be different.

One can allude to some plausible pieces of advice about such problems, which
find a basis in logic and common sense. Do not make cavalier generalizations about
what worked in some other context and argue by careless analogy that it will work
somewhere else. Do not put the whole burden on victims by directing them to forgive. Do not reward, or seem to reward, ex-combatants while ignoring victims and
communities. Do not assume that communities will accept militants solely as an
aspect of something abstract like "peace" or "reconciliation." Do not assume that all
combatants are men—girls, boys, and women can be combatants. Do, if possible,
provide resources to communities as such and, again, if possible, engage ex-combatants in work that will benefit the whole community. Do make available a viable
livelihood for ex-combatants that is distinct from crime. Do try to create a police
force and a judiciary that can deal with corruption and crime.

Above all, do remember that reintegration requires a degree of social trust. That
trust may be established in the fresh circumstances of an aftermath, especially if the
war or oppression has truly been transcended and is now viewed by people with
repugnance, as in the case of Mozambique. When these conditions are met, the context is favorable. But social trust still has to be earned—and no one is more likely to
be aware of that fact than victims.

NOTES

1. For details, see appendix 8, South Africa.
2. By March 2006, there was violence in East Timor after some 600 protesting soldiers
were dismissed. For further comments, consult appendix 3, East Timor.
3. Obviously, these cases cannot all be discussed here; however, information about

Mozambique, in which efforts toward reintegration seem to be quite successful, will be included later in this chapter.

4. These points are well known. One useful summary is offered by Gail R. Farley, "Lustration, Decommunization, and European Union Enlargement 2004," http://www.eucenter.scrippscollege.edu/eu_events/papers/paper/panel (accessed September 19, 2005).

5. Surely exemplified in many contexts, of which the Balkans, Somalia, and Afghanistan are three prominent ones.

6. Northern Ireland is a case in point.

7. This is not to say that the responsibility is diminished by being shared. (Responsibility here is not like a pie.) Many complexities arise; suffice it to say that a person may be individually responsible for certain things done by him and may *also* share responsibility for the whole action undertaken by a number of people.

8. To suppose that it did would be to commit the fallacy of division, the mistake of assuming that an attribute of a group must apply to each individual who is a member of that group. Compare appendix 1, Australia, to see how this reasoning has been used in the context of collective apology.

9. The condition "could have done otherwise" is philosophically contested, but this matter cannot be explored in depth here. Suffice it to say that if someone performed an action at gunpoint while drugged by another, while drunk, or in a situation of such vulnerability that resistance would not have been possible, we can assert that that person *could not have done otherwise*. He or she was coerced and should not be held morally responsible. The conditions here are not fanciful. Tragically, they apply to many thousands of child soldiers.

10. Strictly speaking, moral responsibility should be understood in terms of degrees. We can think of degrees of freedom, degrees (conversely) of coercion, and the relative ease or difficulty of resisting the pressures of circumstances.

11. These ideas are developed further in my book *Forgiveness and Revenge* (London: Routledge, 2002), chapter 6.

12. See chapters 3 and 4.

13. African Research Group, "Mozambique: The Achievement of Peace" (Foreign and Commonwealth Office, London, May 1999), http://www.fco.gov.uk/Files/kfile/mozampeace,0.pdf (accessed September 29, 2005).

14. Alcinda Honwana, "Sealing the Past, Facing the Future: Trauma Healing in Rural Mozambique," *Accord* 3 (1998).

15. Honwana reports that such ceremonies were also adapted for urban contexts.

16. "Mozambique: The Achievement of Peace." This approach might be regarded as opposite to those of trials and truth commissions in that there is a sealing off, which amounts to a refusal to focus any longer on the traumatic events of the brutal war.

17. Carolyn Nordstrom, quoted by Jane Lampman, "Taming the Desire for Revenge," *Christian Science Monitor*, November 4, 1999.

18. Helena Cobban, "Religion and Violence," *Journal of the American Academy of Religion* 73, no. 4 (2005): 1121–39. (First presented in 2003.)

19. Chris Alden, "The Reintegration of Demobilised Soldiers in Mozambique," *Journal of Humanitarian Assistance* (January 29, 2003), http://www.jha.ac/articles/a112.htm (accessed September 29, 2005).

20. Alden noted that another approach might be to marry a local woman. Note here the presumption that the person to be reintegrated is male.

21. Joanna Quinn provided a description of some traditional means of acknowledgment

in her paper "What of Reconciliation? Traditional Mechanisms of Acknowledgment in Uganda," presented at the Reconciliation Conference, University of Western Ontario, May 14–15, 2005.

22. Brian Gormally, "Conversion from War to Peace: Reintegration of Ex-Prisoners in Northern Ireland." Bonn International Center for Conversion, Paper 18 (2001).

23. Ibid., p. 21.

24. The amount seems large in the context of funding for local community groups; however, it is small compared to expenditures on military armaments.

25. Gormally, "Conversion from War to Peace," p. 28. Elsewhere, Gormally comments that SSPPR funding of some 3 million pounds went to victims of the Troubles while some 4.5 million pounds went to ex-prisoners. The disparity did *not* go unnoticed and inspired considerable resentment. In his view, the "victim issue" had a considerable destabilizing potential.

26. Ibid., p. 36.

27. Ibid., p. 37. My emphasis.

28. Select Committee on Northern Ireland Affairs, Tenth Report (March 2005), http://www.parliament.the-stationery-office.co.uk/pa/cm200405/cmselectc (accessed September 30, 2005). The Select Committee seems to have simplistically assumed that such conditions did not exist in Northern Ireland but that they had existed in South Africa, where there was a political consensus about reconciliation. See appendix 8 for reasons to believe that assumption was simplistic.

29. Given that "victim" is used to define itself, such a definition is, of course, logically circular.

30. On the first definition, only a subcategory of V1s would be victims; those would be V1s who (a) were killed, (b) were innocent, and/or (c) were victims of sectarian violence. Category (a) excludes persons injured or maimed but not killed; category (b), depending on the definition of "innocence," excludes persons who were injured or killed but also played perpetrator roles; and category (c), given the context, does not seem too inappropriate.

31. Report of the Select Committee on Northern Ireland Affairs, section 55. These comments illustrate the difficulties regarding perpetrator acknowledgment described in chapter 3.

32. *Fifth Report of the Independent Monitoring Commission: Presented to the Government of the United Kingdom and the Government of Ireland under Articles 4 and 7 of the International Agreement establishing the Independent Monitoring Commission* (London: Stationery Office, 2005), http://www.ireland.com/newspaper/special/2005/imc/imc.pdf (accessed October 3, 2005).

33. A person is "exiled" by a paramilitary group if he or she is compelled to leave Northern Ireland due to threats.

34. The widely publicized quest by McCartney's sisters and fiancée for justice by legal means as opposed to acts of violent revenge is commended by the commission.

35. *Monitoring Commission Report*, section 8.11.

36. These events are described in appendix 4, Northern Ireland.

37. The matter is addressed in chapter 10.

38. Elizabeth Evenson, "Truth and Justice in Sierra Leone: Coordination between Commission and the Court," *Columbia Law Review* 104, no. 3 (2004): 730–67. Accessed at \\server05\products\c\COL\104-3\COL308.txt in February 2005. Evenson describes coordination problems between the TRC and the Special Court. These were particularly apparent in the controversial case of Sam Hinga Norman, discussed here in chapter 6.

39. For comments about the Special Court, its role, and its relation to the TRC, see appendix 7, Sierra Leone.

40. Priscilla Hayner, "The Sierra Leone Truth and Reconciliation Commission: Reviewing the First Year" (New York: International Center for Transitional Justice, January 2004), http://www.ictj.org/images/content/1/0/100.pdf (accessed June 9, 2006).

41. Ibid.

42. Evenson, "Truth and Justice in Sierra Leone."

43. Bruce M. McKay, "A View from the Trenches: The Special Court for Sierra Leone—The First Year," *Case Western Reserve Journal of International Law* 273 (2003): 278–85. The quoted phrase is on p. 281.

44. Rosalind Shaw, "Rethinking Truth and Reconciliation Commissions: Lessons from Sierra Leone." United States Institute of Peace, Special Report 130 (2005), http://www.usip .org/pubs/specialreports/sr130.html (accessed September 2005). Shaw repeatedly uses the phrase "forgive and forget." This phrase is seriously misleading since forgiving does not entail forgetting. See chapter 5 for a discussion of this point. However, I repeat the phrase while seeking to explain Shaw's ideas.

45. The logic here is flawed. If it is a mistake to think of nations having minds, then they can no more *forget* than they can *remember.*

46. Shaw, "Rethinking Truth and Reconciliation Commissions," p. 3.

47. Figures cited in Sarah Laing, "Sustainable Reintegration: Considering the Needs of Victims and Ex-combatants in Sierra Leone" (Honors Thesis, Menno Simons College, University of Winnipeg, April 2005). USAID Transition Initiatives cites a figure of 46,480 people demobilized at some two thousand different sites (USAID Transition Initiatives, "Reintegrating Ex-combatants," http://www.usaid.gov/our_work/cross-cutting_programs/transitions_i [accessed February 2005]).

48. Beth Dougherty, "Right-sizing International Criminal Justice: The Hybrid Experiment at the Special Court for Sierra Leone," *International Affairs* 80, no. 2 (2004): 311–28. However, others state larger numbers. For example, Omer Yousif Elagab estimates tens of thousands in "The Special Court for Sierra Leone: Some Constraints," *International Journal of Human Rights* 8, no. 3 (Autumn 2004): 249–73.

49. Dougherty, "Right-sizing International Criminal Justice," p. 324.

50. Peter J. Croll, "Voices and Choices of Disarmament," presented at the Conference on Conflict and Post-Conflict in Bogota, Columbia (December 9, 2002).

51. There are a number of reports of victims and community members resenting the resources supplied to ex-combatants. One such report is contained in Lotta Hagman, Rapporteur, International Peace Academy Workshop Report for June 10–11, 2002.

52. Jeffrey Isima, "Cash Payments in Disarmament, Demobilisation, and Reintegration Programmes in Africa," *Journal of Security Sector Management* 2, no. 3 (September 2004) and UN Development Programme, "Reintegration Briefs: Justification for Providing Reintegration Subsistence Allowance for the Ex-Combatants" (January 26, 2005).

53. Jeremy Ginifer, Evaluation Report EV647. Country/Regional Case Study 3: Sierra Leone. March 2004. Submitted to the United Kingdom Department for International Development by the Bradford University Channel Research Ltd. PARC and Associated Consultants. Accessed June 9, 2006 at http://www.dfid.gov.uk/aboutdfid/performance/files/ev647sleone.pdf.

Chapter Nine

Righting Wrongs?
Reparation, Restitution, and Redress

It is a fundamental moral intuition, enshrined in international law, that those harmed by wrongdoing should receive some form of restitution or redress. It is as though a wrongful action takes something away from victims; what was taken away should be given back, so far as that is possible. In the aftermath of oppression or war, where there is an intended transition to democracy and the rule of law, the loyalty of persons wronged and harmed in the previous conflict cannot be expected if there is no serious attempt to acknowledge and redress these wrongs. Broadly, the goals of reparations extend beyond restoring goods and resources to harmed individuals. Civic trust is involved, as is social solidarity.[1]

One might suppose that the repair or righting of wrongs would require that the wrongs be *undone*, since these things never should have happened in the first place. The conception has a certain poetic appeal but is clearly unsound if taken literally. The notion of undoing past wrongs makes no logical or metaphysical sense. We may begin to think and feel differently about what happened in the past or we may come to interpret past events differently, forming new causal hypotheses and fresh evaluations. But the past cannot be made to "unhappen." Events happened as they did, were what they were, and, as such, cannot be amended.

We may think instead of fixing or restoring the condition of persons harmed. Ideally, victims could be restored to their original condition so that life would proceed as it might have even if the wrongs had not occurred.[2] On this conception of "righting wrongs," when the wrong is righted, it will be *as though* these things had not happened. Wrongs will be "righted" in the sense that the persons harmed are restored to a condition equivalent to what they would otherwise have enjoyed. This conception of righting wrongs is at least intellectually tenable and seems applicable in some cases. If, for example, a person's home was wrongfully taken from him and he was forced to relocate, one might restore to him his property and the legal title to it, including resources needed to return home. If a person's home and the title to it are restored, there is some sense in which the wrongful acts of theft and eviction are terminated.[3] Restoration, in this sense, would not completely fix the harms in question; some effects would persist.

In many contexts, however, such notions of restoration are more problematic. Persons killed cannot be brought back to life; their loss and that of their family, friends, and community is permanent. The same may be said of seriously debilitating injuries such as loss of sight, hearing, or limbs. Nor can we reasonably suppose that persons who have been beaten, raped, abused, or tortured can be healed in such a way that traumatic memories disappear. In such contexts, though the notion of restoration will be appealing, the ideal is unreachable. Restoration, in this sense, cannot be achieved because the damage is too profound and permanent.

Consider, then, the following argument:

1. The wrongs of the past cannot be undone.
2. The most serious wrongs result in permanent harm to those affected.
3. To right a wrong would require restoring a person to his or her prior condition—the condition he or she was in before the wrong was committed.
4. It is not possible to restore seriously harmed persons to their prior conditions.
    Therefore,
5. The most serious wrongs cannot be righted.
    Accordingly,
6. It is pointless to try to provide redress for serious wrongs.

This argument may seem to provide an objection to programs of financial compensation and redress. Its superficial plausibility is probably due to the fact that its premises are true, or at least widely accepted. Premises (1), (2), and (4) are all true. Premise (3) is widely accepted, being, in fact, enshrined in international law. Persons who have been seriously harmed—and, most obviously, those who have been killed—cannot be *fully* restored by any program of reparation or redress. The argument is cogent, but needs to be resisted if we wish to support the idea that redress makes sense. The way to resist it is to qualify the third premise and distinguish redress from the full-fledged "righting" of wrongs. From the fact that one cannot *fully restore* harmed persons to their prior condition, it does not follow that one should do nothing at all in response to their situation.[4]

TERMINOLOGY

Among terms commonly used to explore the topic of *righting wrongs* are: "reparation," "repair," "restitution," "redress," "compensation," "rehabilitation," "remedy," "restoration," and "satisfaction." Here "reparations" will be used as a general term to refer to resources supplied to persons damaged by wrongful acts with a view to some sort of repair. *Reparations*, in this sense, can take various forms. They are often, but need not be, financial in nature. Parties responsible for the wrongs, either the immediate perpetrators or the state in its role of overall responsibility, provide reparations. Questions about reparations will be explored here in the following conceptual framework:

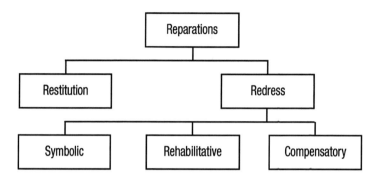

In cases of *restitution*, what was wrongly taken away is (in a fairly literal sense) given back. For example, a person receives *restitution* if her property is given back to her or if her rights of citizenship, taken away under some condition, are restored. A cultural group may receive restitution when its culturally significant and valued objects are returned to it. Clearly, restitution is impossible in many important cases. The beloved husband and father who was killed is gone forever. The childhood spent in misery cannot be replaced; the damaged adult who has emerged has a character and personality deeply affected by his past.

In contexts where restitution is not possible, reparations are referred to as *redress*.[5] With redress, there is an attempt to do something to right the wrong, even though restitution, in the strict sense, is impossible. Within the general category of redress, three elements may be distinguished: symbolic, rehabilitative, and compensatory. *Symbolically*, redress is fundamentally a matter of expressing recognition that what was done was wrong and that it should not have happened.[6] This, in effect, is *acknowledgment* to victims that they deserved better treatment. Symbolic redress or acknowledgment offers vindication to victims.[7] As *rehabilitation*, redress will be directed to improving the physical and mental health of victims and survivors. Persons who have lost limbs may be *rehabilitated* by being fitted with prostheses and given training for suitable occupations. Redress that is neither symbolic nor rehabilitative can be understood as a compensatory response to damages. *Compensation* is often—though not necessarily—provided in the form of financial resources; that is, money transferred to victims and survivors with the intent of compensating them for damages resulting from their losses.[8]

In the context of serious wrongs, the very word "compensation" strikes many people as problematic to the point of seeming offensive. We may ask what could possibly *count* as compensation in the wake of serious wrongs. How could a person be *compensated* for months of torture? For the loss of a beloved family member? For a childhood lost to sexual abuse? Is there some way of estimating the amount of resources that it would take to replace this person? Surely no amount of money—or other resource—could make up for such losses.

THE PARABLE OF THE BICYCLE

In early debates about the activities and deliberation of the South African Truth and Reconciliation Commission, moral intuitions about restitution were often presented in the form of a small story that will be referred to here as "the parable of the bicycle." The story goes like this: Ned takes Tom's bicycle. Then, a year or so after the fact, Ned comes to Tom, acknowledges that he took the bicycle, and tells Tom that now he needs forgiveness. And Tom says to Ned, "But Ned, what about my bicycle?" The point of the story is that there is such a thing as *restitution*, and restitution has been left out of the picture if Ned simply arrives and asks Tom for forgiveness while doing nothing to give back his bicycle.

The parable of the bicycle was used to criticize the emphasis by the South African TRC on forgiveness. Its point is that a wrong is not righted in virtue of the fact that the victim forgives the perpetrator—even in a case where that forgiveness is a response to the perpetrator's acknowledgment and remorse. The perpetrator has to do something to make practical amends; he has to offer the victim some form of restitution or redress. An apology would be a form of acknowledgment and, as such, would amount to an example of symbolic amends. But an apology, as such, does not amount to restitution. In the parable, it is clear what needs to be restored to Tom. It's the bicycle. (The clarity of the case is, of course, what makes it suitable as a parable.) This parable became prominent in debates about reconciliation in South Africa. It was used to illustrate the need for restitution (or redress) by those responsible for the wrongs of apartheid and it was cited in arguments to the effect that forgiveness by victims was premature in the absence of restitution.[9]

The parable is simple and clear. Tom is the primary victim of this wrong; Ned is its primary perpetrator; the bicycle is an easily identifiable physical object; taking the bicycle was an act of theft and clearly wrong from both a moral and a legal perspective. As the story goes, Ned was clearly and simply wrong to have stolen this bicycle. (As the story is told, there is no notion of Ned's having had any excuse or justification for the theft.)[10] Now a bicycle is just the sort of particular and concrete object that can easily be returned to its owner. Ned could offer restitution but does not. The moral response to this paradigm seems clear and intuitive. The wrong has not been righted; it can be righted; it should be righted. Ned should make restitution to Tom by giving back the bicycle.

We can think of a wrong as an event in which something is taken away from the victim. Following through with this conception, something should be given back. One can ask *why* but the question seems so redundant that it almost answers itself.

At the risk of belaboring the obvious, to say that it was wrong for a perpetrator, P1, to take some item, X, away from a victim, V1, is to say that that perpetrator *does not deserve* to have X. P1 should not possess X. Somebody else should have it—namely V1. The clear implication here is that P1 should divest himself of X and give it to V1, the rightful owner. Restitution will be made and the wrong will be righted.

In the debate about the South African TRC, the parable of the bicycle was used as an analogue of the situation of a settler society. For Ned, substitute white settlers taking land and resources from black Africans. For Tom, substitute indigenous black South Africans. For the bicycle, substitute land. For inconvenience due to the lack of a bicycle, substitute lost livelihood, opportunities, wealth, and freedom, all experienced by tens of millions of people over several centuries. For the conclusion that Ned should give back the bicycle, substitute the conclusion that white South Africans should return the land to blacks.

Of course, the analogy is problematic because the differences are enormous—and relevant. The takeover of the lands of South Africa by white settlers in the seventeenth, eighteenth, and nineteenth centuries was a broad process involving millions of people, hundreds of years, enormous historical shifts, and victims, perpetrators, and beneficiaries in many different contexts. As individuals, most primary victims and perpetrators were not alive when debates about reconciliation in South Africa were taking place. Unlike Tom's bicycle, the stolen lands have been greatly changed in the process. There are many people who are descendants and affiliates both of primary victims and of primary perpetrators—South Africans of mixed racial heritage being the most obvious example. One might argue, nevertheless, that the land should simply be returned to black South Africans as a collectivity.[11] But the matter would be messy and complicated—far more so than the return of a bicycle.

THE PERSPECTIVE OF INTERNATIONAL LAW

Reparations have been understood as a central element of respect for human rights. If it is wrong to violate human rights, then such violations should be taken seriously—and a fundamental aspect of taking them seriously is responding, in the aftermath, to the needs and rights of persons harmed.

The most prominent and ambitious program of reparations in the past several decades has been Germany's program of reparations for Holocaust crimes. Other examples include reparations for damages done by Japan during the Second World War and reparations for damages committed against the Armenians by the Turks. There have been prominent actions concerning some cases in US courts, some of which resulted in very substantial awards. Courts in the United States are particularly suitable for such actions due to the Alien Tort Act of 1789, which permits persons of any nationality to sue for damages against individuals or corporations based in the United States—whether the acts in question were committed in the United States or elsewhere.

Influential reports by Theo Van Boven in 1993 and 1996 state that international law provides for a *duty of reparation* that would remove or redress the consequences of wrongful acts and seek to prevent and deter future violations.[12] In these reports, *restitution* is understood to refer to what can reasonably be regarded as restored, whereas *reparations* are taken to involve compensation and rehabilitation.[13] Van Boven points out that states have a duty to make reparations for violations of human rights. As he understands it, this duty arises from customary law, having been consistently affirmed by decisions of international judicial bodies, national and regional human rights courts, and within national and regional law and practice. Van Boven notes that the needs and perspectives of victims are often overlooked and duties of reparation, though officially recognized, are often ignored and regarded as marginal. He notes that Germany, in 1965, offered compensation to residents or former residents during the Nazi era for loss of life, damage to limb or health, or damage to liberty or economic prospects. This and other provisions by the German state were clear acknowledgments of the extraordinarily serious wrongs committed by the German state and its agents during the Nazi era.

Another example is that of *Chile*. There, the truth commission investigated wrongs committed by the military government between 1973 and 1990. Its findings led to the passage of Chilean Law #19.123, which provided for reparations in the form of *pensions* to secondary victims. Other benefits of the reparations package were medical and educational. Secondary victims were deemed to be surviving spouses, mothers, children under the age of twenty-five or handicapped children of any age whose relatives had been killed under the military government. The Chilean reparations were for violations of the right to life and that only.[14] (No provisions have been made for reparations for Chilean victims of torture, of whom there are estimated to be some thirty-five thousand.)

Van Boven's third example is that of Argentina, where financially generous reparations were granted to families of persons killed or "disappeared" in the Dirty War of 1976–1983. There were some nine thousand "disappearances" of opponents of the military regime.[15]

In 2000, Professor M. Cherif Bassiouni submitted to the United Nations a further report on the right to restitution, compensation, and rehabilitation for victims of gross violations of human rights and fundamental freedoms. This report called for the treatment of victims with compassion, dignity, and respect. It defined victims as persons suffering emotional, physical, economic, or legal harm due to violations of human rights or international humanitarian law. Victims could be *primarily* affected individuals or groups, or family members or community members affected indirectly (*secondary* or *tertiary* victims).[16] The Bassiouni Report stipulated that such reparations should be provided in a nondiscriminatory manner, without distinctions based on race, color, gender, sexual orientation, age, language, religion, political belief, wealth, birth, family, or other status. The report maintained that states have a responsibility under international law to make available "adequate, effective and prompt reparation." With regard to human rights, the responsibilities of states were said to be:

(a) to prevent violations;

(b) to investigate such violations as do occur and, if appropriate, take action against the violators;

(c) to provide victims with equal and effective access to justice irrespective of who may be the ultimate bearers of responsibility for any violations;

(d) to afford appropriate remedies to victims; and

(e) to provide for or facilitate reparations to victims.

The victims' right to remedy is understood in a legal frame of reference as involving access to courts and legal institutions of justice. It also includes access to factual information with regard to the violation as well as reparations for the harms suffered.

With regard to reparations, their purpose was said by Bassiouni to be the promotion of justice by redressing violations. States should provide restitution, compensation, rehabilitation, and satisfaction along with guarantees of nonrepetition to victims of violations of human rights and humanitarian law.

Restitution is understood as giving back what was taken away.

Compensation is understood as providing resources to make up for damages.

Rehabilitation is understood as supplying resources to improve mental and physical health and functioning.

Satisfaction and Guarantees of Nonrepetition are understood as efforts to provide assurance and relevant acknowledgment that similar offenses will not be committed in the future.[17]

According to international law, redress should be proportional to the gravity of the violation and the harm suffered by victims. If the violation in question was committed by a state, then it is that state that should provide reparations to victims. If it was committed by an agent other than the state, then that agent should provide the reparations. However, in cases in which the agent in violation cannot or does not do so, the obligation falls to the state. (The agent should, ideally, repay the state at some point.) With regard to reparations, states should enforce their legal judgments and endeavor also to enforce valid foreign judgments. Under international law, a successor state inherits obligations to redress the wrongs of its predecessor.

In cases where the State or Government under whose authority the violation occurred is no longer in existence, the State or Government successor in title should provide reparation to the victims.[18]

This point is highly significant in important cases such as those of the Soviet Union and Russia, East Germany and the Federal Republic of Germany, and South Africa before and after apartheid.

The Rome Statute providing for the International Criminal Court (ICC) recognizes the standing of victims under the jurisdiction of the court to seek reparations. Article 75, paragraph 2 stipulates: "The Court may make an order directly against a convicted person specifying appropriate reparations to, or in respect of, *reparations including restitution, compensation, and rehabilitation*."[19] There is also provision for a trust fund under the ICC to provide funds for reparations to direct victims, whether those are individuals or collectivities, and to surviving family members. The trust fund may receive monies from accountable states, individuals, corporations, or donors. Those funds are to be used on behalf of the victims of the violations. By definition, reparations must go to victims as a response for the violations suffered by them.

SKEPTICAL QUESTIONS

There are many problems that arise concerning reparations and, in particular, the compensatory aspects of redress. The morally intuitive nature of the parable of the bicycle does not automatically or readily transfer to more complex cases. In few political contexts are issues as clear as in the parable of the bicycle. Highly salient differences here are:

(a) It may not be primary victims who receive redress. Often, recipients are secondary or tertiary victims.

(b) Secondary and tertiary victims may be separated from primary victims by decades or longer, sometimes even centuries.

(c) It may not be primary perpetrators who pay the costs of the redress. Those who pay may be citizens who can only tenuously be argued to be tertiary participants, since the wrongs were committed under a dictatorship. (Consider, for example, the reparations owed by Iraq to Kuwait for actions taken by Saddam Hussein in 1990–91.) The party owing reparations may be the state under a successor government quite distinct in ideology and orientation from the state under which the wrongs were committed. Reparations may be paid by international donor groups who shared no responsibility for the original violations.[20]

(d) In the case of successor states, identification with the perpetrating state is likely to be resisted. The responsibility is collective and is the state's responsibility. It would be a fallacy to infer individual responsibility (or guilt) of individuals from collective responsibility.[21] While this logical point is clear, there is nevertheless the fact that financial costs paid by the *state* will usually devolve onto *individual citizens* within it. Often, these individuals shared no responsibility for committing the wrongs and, therefore, politically resist on those grounds.[22] This kind of situation is illustrated in the situations of Australia's Stolen Generation and Canada's residential schools.[23]

(e) Resources may be scarce, and different categories of victims may compete for them. As a social goal, reparations will compete in state budgets with requirements of health, education, and infrastructure. Obligations grounded in international law are all very well, but extremely poor states such as Peru, Rwanda, and Sierra Leone will not be able to fulfill them unless third parties assist.

The factor of *indirectness*, conjoined with factors of *scarce resources, time lag,* and *political resistance* help to explain why the matter of reparations is so often ignored or mishandled.

Assuming consensus that the acts in question were genuinely *wrong*, the symbolic and rehabilitative aspects of redress should be relatively unproblematic. What is called symbolic redress is, in effect, *acknowledgment*. Rehabilitation, such as medical treatment, therapy, or occupational training, applied to primary victims is most often relatively unproblematic. Few would begrudge a prosthesis to a victim of a wrongful amputation or counseling to a victim of torture. The same may be said of some forms of secondary rehabilitation such as assistance with schooling for children whose parent has been wrongfully killed.

Problems will seem most compelling when questions concern compensation and, in particular, financial compensation. A key issue at this point is the (real or apparent) moral taint of money. Many feel a moral taint associated with financial compensation for such severe wrongs as killings, disappearances, torture, internment, or childhood sexual abuse. For money to be awarded as compensation may seem to suggest that money can make up for profound losses and that victims (whether primary, secondary, or tertiary) can, in a sense, be "bought out." This implication will strike many as deeply offensive—especially if there is an implication that victims and survivors who have accepted this money will, accordingly, accept their lot and not ask for anything further in terms of political recognition or financial resources.[24] What is suggested, what is the message, if money is accepted as compensation for profound suffering and loss resulting from abuse, torture, or the killing or disappearance of family members?

While many victims and survivors have accepted compensation in this form, others have resisted it. Disagreements over the symbolic and moral implications of financial compensation have characterized many survivor and victim communities, including Jewish survivors of Nazi camps, native Canadian victims of sexual abuse in residential schools, and the mothers of "disappeared" Argentinean dissidents. In

Argentina, a prominent representative of the long-active and well-known Argentinean *Madres de la Plaza de Mayo* put the point strongly, saying:

> Money cannot make amends for that which justice must repair. It is a very sick society that is built on the acceptance of money as a compensation for death.[25]

In the case of reparations for Holocaust crimes, the process of seeking compensation was extremely repugnant to some victims. Not only was the need to appeal to the co-nationals of the Nazi perpetrators distasteful in itself, there were absurdly cumbersome administrative hurdles along the way. A similar ambivalence about cash settlements is found elsewhere, including in some Canadian Aboriginal groups. Ben Pratt, who sued on the basis of sexual abuse in a residential school, won his case and spent the cash on business debts, gifts, and new kitchen cupboards. He then launched a second lawsuit against another assailant. Pratt admitted to a reporter that there was a certain shame associated with the acceptance of a cash payment as compensation for sexual abuse. "Around here it's called 'arse money.' It's supposed to be dirty," he said.[26]

Although these feelings deserve respect, in the final analysis, arguments from the moral taint of money can be rejected as superficial. Although we should not regard money as providing a tidy quantitative solution to a qualitative problem, it is nevertheless a convenient resource that can readily be supplied to injured persons. Money, given that recipients can choose how to spend it, provides for autonomy. In the modern world, money is the standard means of conducting economic transactions and, as such, a resource that will almost inevitably be used. Financial resources can help victims cope with difficulties resulting from harm due to wrongful actions, which were not their fault. As a fundamental resource, money should not be deemed to be shameful. Those who find it repugnant are of course free to refuse it. If financial resources are supplied in a context in which the dignity of victims and survivors are recognized and acknowledgment is made that what was done to them was wrong, there should be no moral taint associated with it.

Sometimes controversies about the availability of resources arise. Pablo de Greiff cites an especially dramatic case from Peru:

> One of the most notorious . . . involved Leonor La Rosa, a former agent of the security forces who was herself eventually apprehended by another paramilitary group. She was very badly tortured. Eventually her case reached the Inter-American Commission, and the Commission recommended a payment of $100,000 on account of the torture that she suffered. . . . President Toledo went before TV cameras with a huge cheque, like the ones that are common on American TV programs, with $100,000 written on it. Poor Leonor, depending on how you think about her, accepted the cheque in her wheelchair, and of course this was all over the news. The very next day I had meetings with victims' groups in Lima, and of course the attitude was, "Fantastic! We accept that. If she received $100,000, we will as well. This is what we expect." Now, there was absolutely no way that the whole universe of

victims in Peru could receive anything remotely like $100,000 per victim. At that time, and this was very early in the process, we were estimating that there were going to be probably 40,000 beneficiaries in the Peruvian reparations program, so times $100,000 that's $4 billion. Peru's national budget for a whole year is slightly less than $9 billion. So such reparations would have consumed virtually 50 percent of the national budget, which of course is absolutely unthinkable, even if you spread it out over a number of years.[27]

Peru's president had provided what the court had defined as full reparation in the case, but his television gesture was almost certainly undertaken as a cynical attempt to demonstrate the impossibility of providing full restitution to all the forty thousand victims of violence in the Peruvian civil war.

As this example powerfully illustrates, the notion of providing what the law would define as "full restitution" to all victims is often unrealistic.[28] De Greiff argues that when there are thousands of potentially eligible victims, material compensation cannot be approached individually on the basis of cases launched one at a time in the courts. Such an approach will be cumbersome and unfair and will imply unrealistic or impossible burdens. Furthermore, pursuing reparations through court action and getting financial compensation for damages ignores other aspects of redress that are crucially important so far as reconciliation is concerned. These include symbolic reparations (acknowledgment) and the possibility of important collective reparations in such areas as health and education. De Greiff is not arguing against reparations; rather, his point is that individualized approaches through the courts have significant limitations.

In this discussion and elsewhere, De Greiff emphasizes that difficulties should not be understood as amounting to impossibilities. He argues that all too often political expediency underlies claims that resources are insufficient. Nevertheless, for impoverished states such as Peru to provide anything like "full restitution" for thousands of victims is not possible.

A FRAMEWORK FOR REFLECTION

We may reflect on reparations using the following framework of five questions:

1. Who provides reparations?
2. Who receives reparations?
3. What is given as reparation?
4. What is the nature of the processes by which reparations are obtained?
5. What role can reparations play in building positive attitudes and relationships?

In the parable of the bicycle, the transaction of providing reparation is clear, immediate, and direct. The primary perpetrator provides to the primary victim goods equal or equivalent to what was taken away when he committed the wrong. The process is a transaction between these individual parties, and it is reasonable to expect that this process will improve their relationship. There are no third parties or legal or administrative processes; the primary perpetrator simply gives to the primary victim what was taken away from him. The presumption is that the receiving of this restitution will restore the primary victim to his condition before the wrong was committed and that such restoration will *right the wrong* in the sense of undoing the damage.

In the real world in which reparations are debated, we are far removed from restitution in kind and the parable of the bicycle. Moral instincts are less clear, and that comment applies also to legal stipulations. In many real cases, effects are spread out over time and space; issues of individuals and collective harm and responsibility arise; there are complications about group affiliation and collective responsibility; what is given is not what was taken away; resources for the reparations may be provided by persons who bore no responsibility for committing the wrongs.[29] The relevance of the bicycle parable is unclear in a context in which third generation descendents of primary victims claim financial reparations from a successor state in which a minority of taxpayers are third generation descendants of the original primary and secondary perpetrators.[30] To point out relevant differences here is *not* to argue against the granting of reparations. It is simply to say that the force of the bicycle parable will not always be felt and that resistance to it can have a logical basis.

The most provocative questions arise concerning financial compensation. It may appear that resources are too scarce to provide redress for victims, that monies are needed for more general social goals such as education, the building of infrastructure, and the provision of health services. Processes by which reparations are sought and awarded may be cumbersome and promote humiliation and conflict rather than dignity and reconciliation. Financial compensation may inspire resentment on the part of those who do not receive it or may seem tainted even to those who do.

CASES IN POINT

(1) Canada and the Problem of Residential Schools

The most intractable reconciliation problem in contemporary Canada is that of residential schools. These schools, run jointly by the Canadian government and several churches, were in operation between 1880 and the 1950s, with the last ones closing in the 1990s. They were intended to assimilate Aboriginal students into a white, European language and culture; indeed, they had the professed goal of "taking the Indian out of the Indian." In its final report, the Royal Commission on Aboriginal Peoples detailed the inadequacy of health and education in the schools and the extent of cultural, physical, and sexual abuse that occurred. These schools were underfunded and, as a result, staff, food, and conditions were generally poor. As part of attempted assimilation, students were isolated from their families and beaten for speaking their native language. Often, they were subjected to heavy Christianizing propaganda emphasizing their inadequacy as pagan Indians and nonwhites; it was urged that students had to renounce their heritage and race in order to get to heaven. In the 1990s, following revelations by a prominent Aboriginal leader that he had been subjected to sexual abuse in a residential school, there emerged many similar testimonies about physical and sexual abuse.

By the year 2000, survivors of residential schools had begun thousands of lawsuits and some churches were warning that settlements would bankrupt them. The federal government initially sought to put all financial responsibility on the churches, but by 2003 it had stated that it would assume responsibility for 70 percent of the awards made, with churches being accountable for the remaining 30 percent.[31] The extraordinarily large number of legal cases made it clear that some other approach was necessary. After exploratory dialogues involving survivors, lawyers, government officials, and Aboriginal leaders, an alternative dispute resolution (ADR) process was set up. The term "alternative" here is understood as meaning distinct from legal court proceedings. This distinction was intended, given that courts are usually slow and expensive. Furthermore, legal proceedings, being adversarial in nature, often work against the building of better relationships. The ADR process was initially regarded by its supporters as providing for compassion, healing, and respect. The ideals of alternative dispute resolution include equal participation by parties to a dispute.

The shift away from legal litigation in the direction of alternative dispute resolution was praised by several speakers at a prominent conference. They claimed that the Canadian government, adopting an ADR process, had stopped resorting to legal and bureaucratic means of contesting civil cases.[32] It appears, however, that these enthusiastic early commentators did not look below the rhetoric to scrutinize what was actually involved. Survivors who sought to use the process were presented with a highly cumbersome application form some forty pages in length and advised to seek the assistance of a lawyer in order to complete it. To submit claims, residential school survivors had to renounce any claim to legal remedy for losses in other areas such as culture, language, or treaty rights.[33] They were not allowed to make claims about loss of culture or language, isolation from family, or inadequate education and health provisions at the schools. Claims could be submitted only for specific incidents of physical or sexual abuse or for wrongful confinement in a specific location within a school. Specific claims were investigated by private investigators employed by the government. If a claim was accepted in principle, the survivor had to submit documentation about the school, medical treatment, witnesses, employment records, corrections records, and other related matters. There would be further delays. To accept a compensation award at the end of this whole process, a claimant had to submit a Certificate of Legal Advice.

This process departed significantly from the norms of alternative dispute resolution. It was not egalitarian in origin or implementation and it was imposed on Aboriginal claimants by the government. It was not based on consultation and participation. It was not extralegal; it required legal assistance. It involved the submission of applicants to a prescribed bureaucratic process, as distinct from their active and creative participation in that process. It was slow, bureaucratic, cumbersome, and undermining of self-respect. Goals of healing and reconciliation, which had been urged by Aboriginal leaders, dropped out of the picture, as did the historical and political contexts of the residential schools system. In the first year after the allegedly alternative dispute resolution process was established, only eighty cases were settled using it. Yet the total cost was some 125 million dollars, with far more resources going to government investigators and lawyers than to Aboriginal survivors.

Critics estimated that, at that rate, some fifty years and 2 billion dollars would eventually be required to settle the outstanding claims for abuse in Canadian residential schools. Time was passing and survivors of the system were dying. In 1991, there had been some one hundred fifty thousand survivors. By 2005, it was estimated that there were only eighty-seven thousand.[34] There was resentment over delays. Victims and survivors were frustrated with a humiliating and cumbersome process, and hurt by the fact that one could not claim for loss of language or culture. There were quarrels about money, and a sense on the part of some non-Aboriginal Canadians that survivors were cynically out for money and wasting it if they got some. By the spring of 2005, some twelve thousand claims remained unresolved, with a likelihood that more would follow. Aboriginal leaders and other critics predicted that much of the more than two billion dollars that would be spent under the system would go to administrative costs and not to survivors or their descendants.

The Assembly of First Nations argued that the ADR process was not working. It sought a truth commission process, an apology, the allowance of damages for cultural losses, and a genuine partnership role for Aboriginal people in processes of healing and reconciliation. On May 30, 2005, an announcement was made of a landmark agreement between the federal government and the Aboriginal people as represented by the Assembly of First Nations.[35] This agreement was to provide for reconciliation and a new system of compensation.[36] Judge Frank Iacobucci, a former justice of the Supreme Court, was brought in as chief federal negotiator to work with former students in residential schools, the Assembly of First Nations, and representatives of churches and government, with provision for a March 31, 2006 deadline for reaching a new arrangement.[37] (In the interim, the ADR process would remain available for all who wished to employ it.)

Phil Fontaine, leader of the Assembly of First Nations, publicly expressed his optimism. He and other Aboriginal leaders sought a system providing for public acknowledgment and compensatory awards, not only for sexual and physical abuse, but for degradation, loss of language and culture, and isolation from families.[38] In November 2005, the federal government announced a new program to include compensation for all who attended the schools, funding for a truth and reconciliation process, commemorative programs, and projects intended to promote healing in First Nations communities. At an estimated cost of $1.9 billion, the plan was to include a "common experience" payment of up to $10,000 per person plus an additional $3,000 for each year spent in the school and additional payments based on sexual and physical abuse and loss of language and culture. It was estimated that some eighty-six thousand Aboriginal Canadians who attended the schools would be eligible for compensation under the plan. There was to be a speeded-up process for claimants over sixty-five years of age. Victims accepting the package would agree not to sue the federal government or the churches that ran the schools except in cases of sexual or serious physical abuse. Phil Fontaine said he was happy with the offer.[39]

(2) South Africa: Reparations to Victims Testifying before the TRC

The Truth and Reconciliation Commission of South Africa understood itself as pursuing national reconciliation in a context of restorative justice. Selected perpetrators who were granted amnesty by the TRC received immunity from criminal prosecution and civil suit by victims. The understanding was that, as a countermeasure to this amnesty, victims would receive reparations along lines to be recommended by the TRC.[40] Early in the life of the TRC, its amnesty provisions were legally contested in the AZAPO (Azanian Peoples Organisation and Others versus the President of the Republic of South Africa and Others) case. In the ruling of that case, allowing amnesty, reparations to victims were deemed necessary to balance the amnesties given to perpetrators.[41] Furthermore, reparations were promised to those victims who assisted the TRC by testifying before it. They were provided for in the TRC mandate, referred to in the AZAPO case, and part of the general picture of restorative justice.[42] For many, testifying before the TRC meant reliving painful experiences in a public context. The information provided was of great importance; testifying victims performed an essential service to the commission and to South African society more generally. Father Michael Lapsley, heavily committed to post-TRC reconciliation processes and himself a victim of violence, observed that the credibility of the commission hinged on the provision of reparations to the victims who had trusted it enough to come forward.[43] The TRC claimed to be pursuing restorative justice. If the reparations it had recommended were not provided, doubt would be cast on its sincerity and commitment; the process simply would not qualify as one of restorative justice.

Nevertheless, many complex problems have arisen with regard to reparations in South Africa. Under apartheid, every nonwhite South African was victimized. Yet the TRC reparations concerned a particular subgroup: those who had been victims of severe human rights violations (defined as killing, abduction, or severe ill-treatment) and had submitted testimony to the TRC. Not all nonwhites were (in the sense operationally defined by the TRC) victims of *severe* human rights violations, and not all who were in this respect victims provided testimony to the commission.

The TRC recommended the establishment of a president's fund for reparations, suggesting that its source be the national budget, resources from international donors, and interest from those sources. It also suggested taxing wealth as an aspect of broader policies to address extreme socioeconomic inequalities in South African society. The TRC suggested taxing businesses in particular, given that many of these had benefited from apartheid policies resulting in a large pool of low-cost and highly exploitable labor. These recommendations were not popular with wealthy white South Africans or with the business community. (They were not even widely discussed.) In its *Final Report* (1998) the TRC recommended reparations in several broad categories. These were:

- (a) urgent interim relief for some particularly needy victims;
- (b) individual reparations grants for primary and secondary victims who had testified to the TRC—these to be paid in the form of pensions staged over a six-year period;
- (c) symbolic measures;
- (d) remedial measures of an institutional, social, and communal nature.

The total amount for the first two categories would have been some 375 million dollars (US). By the year 2000, about twelve thousand people had received modest funds in category (a). There were no controversies over symbolic measures or collective reparations to communities, categories (c) and (d). It was category (b), that of individual reparations to those victims who had testified to the TRC, that proved controversial and was resisted by the ANC government of Thabo Mbeki.

With regard to these individual reparations, the government dragged its feet. It claimed that this subgroup was not representative of the broader community of victims and that it was opportunistically pursuing financial compensation. It argued that the resources required would be too extensive and reparations would compete for goods to be provided in areas such as social welfare, health, and education. Although the government clearly had a *legal* responsibility to provide these reparations, there was moral unclarity in the case, given that it was an ANC, primarily black government, many of whose members had themselves made sacrifices in the struggle over apartheid.[44] There was also a residual animosity between the ANC and the TRC due to a conflict over the chronicling of human rights abuses by the ANC.[45]

In category (b), the TRC had recommended that 21,700 rand should be paid annually for six years to some twenty thousand victims. If its recommendations had been followed, the cost of these individual reparations would have been 4.864 billion rand.[46] There were claims that such reparations were too expensive. However, the cost per year, according to an analysis by Brandon Hamber and Kamilla Rasmussen, would have only required about .2 percent of the national budget. Hamber and Rasmussen calculated that the amount would have been 3.47 percent of what the national budget allocated to defense and 6.79 percent of what was allocated to education. Thus, in their view, the government's claim that sufficient financial resources were simply not available was not credible. The claim reflected political judgments about priorities, not the availability of absolute amounts of money.

After considerable delay and pressure, President Mbeki announced on April 15, 2003 that individual payments would be made to those victims who had testified before the TRC. These persons would receive a one-time payment of some thirty thousand rand.[47] The amount recommended by the TRC would have been 130,200 rand in total. Thus, what was granted was less than one quarter of what the TRC had recommended. Payment was long delayed, grudgingly provided, and different in structure from what the TRC had recommended. President Mbeki made some dismissive remarks about the recipients in his speech. He said:

> As the TRC itself has underlined, no one can attach monetary value to life and suffering. Nor can an argument be sustained that the efforts of millions of South Africans to liberate themselves were for monetary gain. We are convinced that, to the millions who spared neither life nor limb in struggle, there is no bigger prize than freedom itself, and a continuing struggle to build a better life for all.[48]

These comments are unfortunate at best. Given previous commitments by the TRC and by the courts, victims were owed these reparations. It was insulting and unwarranted to suggest that they were seeking money *instead of* freedom. Given the history of the problem, it is fair to comment that the reparations process in South Africa was cumbersome, controversial, and unsatisfactory in its final result.[49]

The pursuit of reparations for apartheid in South Africa has been taken abroad. Several class action lawsuits were launched in US courts against multinational corporations.[50] The South African government did not participate and, in fact, opposed the suits on the grounds that the problem was to be dealt with by South Africans, not foreigners. The government argued that a foreign court would interfere with South Africa's jurisdiction over its own affairs.[51] The suits for violations against international human rights laws were against businesses that had profited by operating with the South African apartheid system. The government's reluctance may have been due to its wish not to alienate the business community. President Mbeki did acknowledge that individuals and nongovernment groups were free to initiate their own legal actions.

The Alien Tort Claims Act of 1789 provides for persons who are not residents of the United States to sue in US courts for actionable wrongs committed anywhere in the world, provided those wrongs were committed by agents located in the United States. The antiapartheid cases became test cases for the enforceability of international human rights law in contexts in which multinational corporations were, in effect, supporting repressive regimes. Apartheid had been declared to be a crime against humanity according to many resolutions in the UN General Assembly. Wrongs committed under apartheid were clearly violations of international law. Businesses had taken three billion dollars annually out of apartheid South Africa during the period 1985–1993. They were profiting from the system and, at the same time, propping it up, given that their collaboration facilitated its systematic violations.[52] The United Nations Commission on Human Rights had found in 1987 that transnational corporations were complicit in maintaining the apartheid system in the sense that they were accomplices, aiding and abetting a crime against humanity; as such, they ought to have been prosecuted.[53]

One prominent suit is that of the Khulumani Support Group, launched by that group and 108 individual victims of state-sanctioned torture, murder, rape, arbitrary detention, and inhumane treatment. The group represents some victims who testified before the TRC and others who did not. It seeks limited individual relief from foreign multinational corporations on the grounds that they violated international law and colluded with the security apparatus of the apartheid state. Its case states that "with the support of these corporations, the apartheid government committed extrajudicial killing, torture, sexual assault, prolonged arbitrary detention, and multiple crimes against humanity."[54] The defendants in the case are some twenty-three multinational corporations, including Barclay's Bank and IBM. It is alleged that these corporations had aided and abetted a crime against humanity, in the aftermath of which "persistent social damage urgently needs repair."[55] The plaintiffs claim that the corporations had supplied financing, technology, transportation, oil, arms, and so on—all resources that had made possible the crimes of the apartheid state and system. The defending corporations, together with the American and British governments, advised the American court against recognizing that international business must respect the sanctity of basic human rights. They claimed that to do so would infringe on the sovereignty of nations and interfere with free trade.

Along with several other antiapartheid cases, the Khulumani case was thrown out of a US court on September 29, 2004 by a conservative New York judge who argued that there was no violation of the law by corporations having commercial links with apartheid South Africa. The Khulumani case was taken up for appeal.

The success of such cases in US courts is by no means guaranteed. Pertinent factors concern sovereignty, the relative priority of domestic and international law, and opposition by business interests. Judges have almost never authorized settlements under this act; courts have generally not been too friendly to political cases having a broad scope; and many defendants have responded by choosing to leave the United States. In a recent article on the matter, Jeremy Sarkin explains that in such cases it will be legally necessary to show both that the behavior of the multinational corporation led directly to the human rights violations in the state in which they were committed and that activity at the headquarters in the United States led to the violations in question. Sarkin comments that legal cases will be no panacea for victims seeking reparations. In his view, the legal route to reparations is by no means the only one, and political arguments and strategies remain important.

(3) Peru

The Truth and Reconciliation Commission of Peru recommended extensive reparations for some forty thousand people who were victims of torture, killing, disappearance, and other wrongs during its twenty-year civil war. Under the auspices of this commission, an Integral Plan for Reparations was developed.[56] The Integral Plan was thorough in its conception, emphasizing that in the wake of serious human rights violations, both moral and material mending were needed, and these would need to be both collective and individual. Moral mending would be in the form of recognition that the persons wrongly treated were citizens with full rights and had deserved better. Material mending would require that resources would be supplied for better health, education, and quality of life. Under international law and from a moral perspective, the Integral Plan stated that the Peruvian state had an obligation not only to redress the harms brought by its own actions but also the action of non-state actors—in this case the Shining Path, which was extremely brutal in its actions.[57] The status of someone as a primary or secondary victim would not depend on the identity of those who had committed the violations against him or her. Especially vulnerable persons such as the elderly, orphans, widows or widowers, and the disabled would receive additional benefits. Reparations would not go to persons who had already received them from another source.

To leave reparations to legal mechanisms, with victims pursuing claims in the courts, would not be acceptable. Case-by-case court processes would result in variable results. Furthermore, most victims were poor Quecha Indians living in isolated conditions and having little access to the courts. In the courts, people would pursue their cases as individuals; yet many wrongs were systemic. Courts would not be able to address symbolic or collective aspects that were necessary to a complete reparations program. The Integral Plan urged five specific elements that would be necessary in a program of reparations. Such a program should:

- be sensitive from a psychosocial point of view;
- have participatory elements, in the sense that intended recipients would have a part in decision-making;
- be sensitive to cultural needs;
- promote gender equality;
- emphasize the inherently symbolic nature of all reparations.

What was proposed included memorials and commemoration; health facilities; educational resources including scholarships, adult education, the waiving of fees for victims or designated family members; and the restitution of citizen rights in areas such as the legal status of "disappeared" persons, dated arrest warrants, the reissuing of documents, and the expunging of records for political "crimes" during the conflict. In addition, material reparations to victims would be both individual and collective. The Integral Plan stated that individual material reparations were crucial but warned that they should be awarded with care and sensitivity, given the possibility of conflicts over the selection of victims and the amounts awarded to them. Collectively, material reparations were to include the restoration of governing institutions, basic services, and infrastructure in the Andean areas that were so profoundly affected by the conflict. In addition, efforts would be made to develop businesses in the area so as to provide employment.

The Integral Plan offers a framework within which many skeptical questions about reparations are effectively addressed. The (alleged) moral taint of money disappears due to the emphasis on *symbolic reparations* acknowledging the rights and dignity of the victims and *material reparations to groups as well as individuals*, in such crucial areas as health, education, and governance. The presence of a number of *collective* measures would acknowledge the damage the conflict had brought to communities. In recognition of harms to individuals as primary and secondary victims and the difference in particular circumstances and needs, *individual* reparations were also part of the program. The participation of victims in the structure and running of the program would reinforce their status as fully equal citizens in the state, facilitating the recognition of dignity and the restoration of self-esteem. Because the program would be supplied as *reparations*, with the symbolic element highlighted, it would be distinguishable from ordinary government activities in areas of infrastructure or socioeconomic development.

There was only one fundamental problem with Peru's Integral Plan: it was not implemented.[58]

CONCLUDING COMMENTS

Problems such as delayed and acrimonious court processes, humiliating bureaucracy, competition between victims, and the moral taint of money can be avoided if programs of reparations are carefully designed. Reparations should be understood as crucially involving acknowledgment, which—here as elsewhere—is fundamental. While the wrongs of the past cannot be undone and it is nearly always a mistake to think that victims can be restored to their prior conditions, there is much that can be done, both symbolically and materially, to improve their conditions. Not being able to do everything is no excuse for doing nothing—and difficulties should not be construed as impossibilities. Even the shortage of resources should not be understood as an insurmountable problem to reparations. Such shortages are to some extent—often to a considerable extent—the result of lack of political will, which in turn can result from an underemphasis on symbolic aspects, an overemphasis on money, and a general misunderstanding of the nature and purpose of reparations. In addition, resources from donors may supplement the resources of a poor country, and the trust fund being developed by the International Criminal Court will be another resource. As for the issue of collective and individual reparations, prominent in some South African debates, this need not be understood in either/or terms. Given damage to communities, families, and individuals, reparations can benefit the community at large. At the same time, financial reparations to individual primary and secondary victims can assist harmed persons to live with self-respect and some degree of material comfort in the aftermath of violations.

The outstanding problems with reparations seem not to be at the level of moral or legal theory. Nor should they arise at the level of general administrative policy. The outstanding problems with reparations are far more mundane in character. To put the matter bluntly, these problems lie in the area of follow-through. People negotiate, reason, publish reports, and pass laws with regard to reparations, but they do not implement them. Even when plans are thoroughly and coherently developed, there is so often no implementation. That, it would seem, is the most outstanding problem about reparations.

NOTES

1. Pablo de Greiff, a prominent theorist on reparations, emphasizes recognition, civil trust, and social solidarity. These ideas are highly compatible with the interpretation here, according to which reconciliation involves the building or rebuilding of trust in the aftermath of oppression or conflict.

2. In theory and in practice, this notion is oversimplified, even in the most favorable cases. One factor is that during the period between the commission of the wrong and the attempted repair, various things will have happened. Typically, they are adverse; if X is taken away, the restoration of X itself does not mean that correlative damages (incurred by not having X over a period of time) are undone or compensated for. In some cases, it is even more morally complicated: benefits may have resulted from the wrong, benefits going even to the victim. (For example, a person might be forced out of his home, falsely convicted of a crime, and then receive a university education while in prison; an Aboriginal person might be insultingly treated and miserably unhappy in a residential school and yet receive useful language training there, training enabling him to pursue a career as a lawyer.)

3. Which is not, of course, to say that corollary damage is ended.

4. In other words, the inference from (5) to (6) is questioned.

5. When efforts are made to redress wrongs, there is a return to those wrongs. (We might say that, in being "redressed," they are re-addressed, or addressed *again*.)

6. *Symbolic redress* is, in effect, *acknowledgment*, which is explored in detail in chapter 3.

7. Explored in chapter 3 and also discussed in chapter 1 of my *Forgiveness and Revenge* (London: Routledge, 2002).

8. Money can be problematic in some respects, as we will see later.

9. As urged by South Africa's Truth and Reconciliation Commission under the leadership of Archbishop Desmond Tutu.

10. He might have had an excuse had he, for example, been under the influence of a new medication that inhibited his thinking, or a justification had he taken the bicycle in order to ride off quickly to save a life. But these complicating features are not characteristics of the parable.

11. What is said here is said by way of questioning the analogy; I am not arguing that there should be no land transfers, only that the rationale for them, and the effects of them if they occur, will be far more complex than the case for the return of the bicycle.

12. Antonio Buti and Melissa Parker, "International Law Obligations to Provide Reparations for Human Rights Abuse," *Murdoch University Electronic Journal of Law* 6, no. 4 (December 1999), http://www.murdoch.edu.au/elaw/issues/v6n4/buti64_text.html (accessed June 10, 2005).

13. This terminology is compatible with what is used here, which is not coincidental.

14. Such reparations would best be understood as rehabilitation and, to a limited extent, compensation.

15. Excellent background on reparations in the cases of Germany, Chile, and Argentina may be found in Pablo de Greiff, "Reparation Efforts in International Perspective: What Compensation Contributes to the Achievement of Perfect Justice," in *To Repair the Irreparable: Reparations and Reconstruction in South Africa*, ed. Erik Doxtader and Charles Villa-Vicencio (Claremont, South Africa: David Philip, 2004), pp. 321–58. De Greiff is a philosopher and research director for the International Center for Transitional Justice.

16. In other words, the primary victim could be a group as distinct from an individual.

17. "Satisfaction" and "guarantees of nonrepetition" were separated in the report and are compressed here since they seemed to be strongly linked. Both have been dealt with under the topic of "acknowledgment," which was discussed earlier.

18. Bassiouni Report, submitted to the 56th session of the United Nations Committee on Human Rights, January 2000; cited in detail by Conor Foley in *Combating Torture: A Manual for Judges and Prosecutors* (Essex, UK: Human Rights Centre/University of Essex, 2003), appendix 1, http://www.essex.ac.uk/combatingtorturehandbook/manual/app1_11.htm (accessed June 10, 2005).

19. My emphasis.

20. For example, in Argentina, funds for reparations to relatives of persons who were "disappeared" during the military dictatorship between 1976 and 1983 were provided by the United Nations. Third-party resources may indeed be helpful, but one can hardly argue that the intuitive justice that underpinning redress from perpetrators applies in such a case.

21. Compare the objections of John Howard to a state apology. See appendix 1, Australia.

22. In these cases many taxpayers will have been secondary or tertiary beneficiaries of land acquisitions in the process of white settlement and, arguably, of colonizing processes within which the assimilative goals of schooling were located. It is difficult to argue, however, that such people were beneficiaries of the system of residential schools. For some wrongs, there would appear to be few if any beneficiaries. (The Rwandan genocide is a case in point.)

23. For some, this fact has provided a major reason for resisting reparations.

24. This implication is often a feature of such situations and will almost certainly contribute to a sense that there is something shameful about accepting money. I owe this point to Sarah Laing.

25. Hebe de Bonafini, founding member of the Association of Madres de la Plaza de Mayo, Argentina, quoted in Pamela Bone, "Undying Love Gives Birth to Universal Motherhood," *The Age*, http://www.theage.com.au/articles/2002/07/04/10256607033729.html?one clicktrue (accessed June 14, 2005). The group split over this issue.

26. Quoted in David Napier, "Sins of the Fathers," *Anglican Journal* (Canada) (May 2000): 7. Contributing to the sense that there is a moral taint associated with financial compensation for victimization is the fact that money awarded in compensation payments is not always used prudently by those who receive it. Resentment by nonrecipients is another problem.

27. Pablo de Greiff, "The Role of Reparations in Transitions to Democracy," talk presented at the seminar on "Justice and the World Economy: Achieving Global Justice Seminar Series," sponsored by the Carnegie Council on Ethics and International Affairs (May 6, 2004). The quoted passage appears on page 5 of the transcript.

28. When there is full restitution, victims are supposed to be restored to the condition that they would have enjoyed had the wrongs not been committed. De Greiff states that when there is a large number of victims—as, for example, the forty thousand cases in Peru—such restoration is impossible because *resources* are not adequate. However, there would seem to be a more profound problem that applies to the case. Full restitution, in the sense of restoration of the victims, is not possible because of the nature of people and the nature of the damage done to them. One cannot, for example, make a torture or abuse victim the way he would have been had the torture or abuse never occurred; nor can one give a woman the life she would have had with her husband had he not been a victim of extrajudicial execution.

29. It has been argued that such problems arise also with regard to debates about affirmative action if young men lose opportunities because efforts are being made to redress wrongs committed by men in previous generations.

30. The example of Chinese Canadians seeking reparations for the head tax placed on their ancestors illustrates this matter. See appendix 2, Canada.

31. This arrangement was welcomed by some churches but not others. I am indebted for this summary of the problem of compensation for abuse in residential schools to Anna Snyder and Neil Funk-Unrau, "State Defined Alternative Dispute Resolution Applied to Indian Residential Schools Abuse: An Impediment to Intercultural Conflict Resolution?" draft manuscript, June 2005.

32. Conference summary, "Repairing the Past: Reparations and Transitions to Democracy," Ottawa, Canada (March 11–12, 2004). The conference was sponsored jointly by the International Development Research Center and the International Center for Transitional Justice. A more careful observer was Neil Funk-Unrau, whose presentation on the awkward and decidedly nonalternative nature of the process was given at the University of Winnipeg in November 2004. My own awareness of the serious flaws in the ADR procedures in this context stems from his presentation.

33. Snyder and Funk-Unrau, "State Defined Alternative Dispute Resolution." This element was dropped in 2004 after extensive Aboriginal lobbying.

34. Ibid. Snyder and Funk-Unrau cite Canada's Standing Committee on Aboriginal Affairs and Northern Development (2005) for the estimate that it would take about 50 years and 2 billion dollars to settle the disputes.

35. Responses from native leaders varied. Some indication of their initial response may be found in Len Kruzenga, "So Close, Yet So Far: Feds Appoint Former Judge to Handle Residential Schools Settlement," *Drum* (Winnipeg), July 20, 2005. The context for this shift was unfortunate, to the point where one might be cynical about it—as many probably were. At the time, the Liberal Party had an extremely precarious minority government situation and feared defeat at any moment. Prime Minister Paul Martin was seen to be throwing money almost recklessly at various deep problems in an attempt to save his government. Hence, it was quite plausible to interpret the shift in a cynical way.

36. It would, of course, be foolish to assume that an agreement or policy could guarantee reconciliation as such, and by quoting these comments I do not intend to imply that it would.

37. This material was composed in July 2005 and edited in November 2005. See appendix 2, Canada for further details.

38. Bulletin: Minister's Update on Aboriginal and Northern Initiatives, http://www.ainc-inac.gc.ca/ai/bl130605_e.html (accessed July 20, 2005). Information here was also taken from CBC News, July 6, 2005.

39. CBC News, November 23, 2005. Some criticized the offer due to its timing. The Liberal government of Paul Martin was a minority government and had embarked on a phase of spending considerable sums of money, apparently as a quest for support in an imminent election. On November 28, the government fell, having been defeated in a nonconfidence motion. It was replaced by a minority Conservative government.

40. The TRC had the power to grant amnesty. It did not have the power to award reparations but only to recommend that the state do so.

41. For an explanation of the AZAPO case, see Mary Burton, "Reparations: It Is Still Not Too Late," in Dofstadter and Villa-Vicencio, *To Repair the Irreparable*.

42. Sarkin warns, however, that such legal cases will not be a panacea for victims

200   Taking Wrongs Seriously

seeking reparations; the legal route to reparations is by no means the only one and political arguments and strategies remain important.

43. Michael Lapsley and Karin Chubb, "Common Guilt or Common Responsibility? Moral Arguments for Reparations in South Africa," in *From Rhetoric to Responsibility: Making Reparations to the Survivors of Past Political Violence in South Africa*, ed. Brandon Hamber and Tlhoki Mofokeng (Johannesburg: Centre for the Study of Violence and Reconciliation, 2000).

44. For example, Shadrack Gutto argues that the moral responsibility is unclear in ibid., chap. 5, "Constitutional, International and Comparative Law Perspectives on Reparation."

45. Described here in detail in the chapter on mutuality.

46. Brandon Hamber and Kamilla Rasmussen, "Financing a Reparations Scheme for Victims of Political Violence," in Hamber and Mofokeng, *From Rhetoric to Responsibility*, http://222.csvr.org.za/papers/pap247.htm (accessed July 26, 2005).

47. At the time this amount was approximately equal to $4,200 (US).

48. President Thabo Mbeki, "Statement to the National Houses of Parliament and the Nation at the Tabling of the Report of the Truth and Reconciliation Commission," in Doxtader and Villa-Vicencio, *To Repair the Irreparable*, pp. 14–28; quoted passage is on p. 22. Mbeki seems to exploit notions of the moral taint of money to justify the stance of the government.

49. With the conspicuous exception of Mbeki's own speech, the writings in the Doxtader and Villa-Vicencio volume would support that judgment.

50. A thorough and helpful discussion of these attempts is provided by Jeremy Sarkin in "Pursuing Private Actors for Reparations for Human Rights Abuses Committed in Africa in the Courts of the United States of America," in Doxtader and Villa-Vicencio, *To Repair the Irreparable*, pp. 271–320.

51. Former chairperson Desmond Tutu and former commissioner Yasmin Sooka spoke out against this position. Apartheid Debt and Reparations Campaign (Braamfontein 2017, South Africa), "South Africa: Apartheid Reparation Update," July 13, 2004, http://www.africafocus.org/docs04/arep0408.php (accessed July 26, 2005).

52. Dumisa Ntsebeza, speech on "Reparations, the Truth and Reconciliation Commission and Corporate Liability: the Unfinished Business," presented at a dinner marking the first anniversary of the coming into being of Ngcebetsha Madlanga Attorneys, 17 Convention Center Johannesburg, March 6, 2003. (Dumisa Ntsebeza is a lawyer and a former commissioner of the Truth and Reconciliation Commission.)

53. Ibid. In terms of the distinctions developed in this book, multinationals were claimed to be secondary perpetrators.

54. Norman Reynolds, "Khulumani's Reparations Case and the Future of Human Rights," paper disseminated by the Global Policy Forum, January 6, 2005, http://www.global policy.org/intljustice/atca/2005/0106khulumani.htm (accessed August 2005).

55. Sarkin, "Pursuing Private Actors."

56. Summary of the Comprehensive Reparations Plan (PIR), Truth and Reconciliation Commission of Peru, trans. the International Center for Transitional Justice (ICTJ), http://www.aprodeh.org.pe/gem_verdad/informe_final/english/reparations_plan.pdf (accessed July 2005).

57. Background information is provided in appendix 5, Peru.

58. For further details, see appendix 5, Peru.

Chapter Ten

Could This Be Reconciliation?

ollowing the bitter civil war in Lebanon, there were no trials, no truth commissions, and—apparently—no community processes of reconciliation. The
Syrian military remained present in Lebanon to guarantee the peace. This all
happened a mere twenty years ago, and the situation was not unrepresentative.
Although truth commissions had existed before the South African TRC, it was still
common for issues of reconciliation to be ignored. It is fair to say that it was the
prominence of the South African commission, the moral leadership of Archbishop
Tutu and President Nelson Mandela, and the apparently miraculous avoidance of a
civil war in that country that put the topics of reconciliation and forgiveness on the
map. For nongovernmental organizations, governments, and other parties involved
in seeking a sustainable peace, something that should have been obvious suddenly
became obvious. If former adversaries are going to live together, some degree of
social trust is necessary. After violence and oppression, that trust cannot be taken for
granted. It has to be built.

Yet so many gloomy problems have been described in the foregoing chapters that
a person might be excused for asking if reconciliation is possible at all. If there is any
algorithm for solutions in the aftermath of violent conflict, it is not yet known. Indeed,
many of the "lessons" about reconciliation may seem to be negative. Acknowledgment is crucial but may not be forthcoming. The same can be said of mutuality and
evenhandedness. Apologies are a constructive initiative, but only if they are sincerely
offered, understood in that light, and accompanied by appropriate practical amends.
Forgiveness should not be identified with reconciliation, and it should not be directed
from above. Though it may be necessary, amnesty is often problematic. But to question amnesty is not to prove that the proper response to wrongs is penal justice, construed in retributive terms. Seeing the gap here, one may shift to consider restorative
justice, which is often touted as the substitute to retribution. And yet, given the frequent failure to provide appropriate reparations to victims, restorative justice, as a
political reality, often fails. The reintegration of ex-combatants amounts to an enor-

201

mous and challenging problem, one fraught with perils. Efforts can fail, even in what would seem to be highly favorable circumstances.[1]

To a skeptical reader, it might appear that this book has not been characterized by a positive outlook toward reconciliation. It might seem that there are too many tales about animosity, too many accounts of mistakes, and too few stories of success. Taking wrongs seriously is no simple matter.

Efforts toward reconciliation sometimes illustrate flawed thinking. Readers will have noted cases of the importing of institutions from one context to another, with too little attention to relevant contextual differences. Sometimes the needs and expectations of Western governments have led to insensitivity toward local situations. (The ICTR, or International Criminal Tribunal for Rwanda, is a case in point.[2]) There has been a failure to understand the difficulties of acknowledgment in many contexts. The polarized framework of victim and perpetrator can be an obstacle to reconciliation processes. While many observers have commented on the fact that there are victims who are also perpetrators and perpetrators who are also victims, a rethinking of reconciliation processes along lines that do not presuppose the victim/perpetrator dichotomy has barely begun. The significance of gender is a crucial matter that has only begun to be addressed; women have played roles largely unnoticed in conflict and in oppression. Women's needs as survivors, victims, parents, and ex-combatants are highly important from a humanitarian view, and their contributions to family and community life have enormous potential for processes of peace.

One would be hard-pressed to point to a context and confidently assert that "There it is; there is a case of successful reconciliation." This is often done with South Africa; but given the problems about reparations for victims, the high crime rate in the country, remaining racial and socioeconomic divisions, and controversies about amnesty and reparations, that claim is problematic at best.[3] Mozambique, though less known and not as widely cited, is another potential example.[4] Still, the pickings seem slim. Worse yet, there are instances of undue optimism in emerging contexts where harms have been enormous and risks are great.

UNDUE OPTIMISM?

Obtaining a cease-fire and signing a peace agreement do not guarantee that a sustainable peace will be achieved. The rebuilding of societies and communities is not simply a matter of architecture, infrastructure, and formal institutions. It must extend to relationships and the fundamental attitudes that underlie those relationships. Among these attitudes, the most significant is trust. In the aftermath of conflict, people who have harmed and been harmed are likely to feel animosity, resentment, and suspicion. Recognizing that the challenges of reconciliation exist and must be addressed is one thing. Appreciating their seriousness is quite another. In the end, establishing relationships is more difficult than repairing roads and buildings.

(a) Rhetoric and Forgiveness in Sierra Leone

The Reverend Joseph Humper, head of Sierra Leone's Truth and Reconciliation Commission, seems to have sought to emulate the role of Archbishop Tutu in South Africa. Humper stated with confidence that the Sierra Leonese truth commission would "get the perpetrators and the victims to come to terms with their past" through acknowledgment and forgiveness. He commented, "The truth telling is significant in that it *ensures* psychological healing." Asked whether truth and trust were too much to expect in the context, Humper replied that truth telling would "open people's eyes." And as for social trust, he stated that it would have to be manifested in daily life; otherwise, "truth-telling will be meaningless."[5] These statements are misleading to the point of being dangerous. They suggest that the language of reconciliation may become corroded to the point where it loses its meaning and becomes empty rhetoric. Statements like Humper's suggest little awareness of the complexity and depth of the challenges of reconciliation, which lie under a blanket of vagueness and abstraction. A concern here is that people may come to believe their own blithely optimistic comments, leading to tragic—and tragically harmful—self-deceptions.

In the spring of 2003, Laura Skovel, a Canadian researcher, followed the hearings of the Sierra Leone Truth and Reconciliation Commission. She traveled in the country and interviewed people about their attitudes in the aftermath of that country's brutal civil war.[6] Even in the aftermath of amputations and heinous atrocities in their villages, many people said they *forgave* those who had harmed them, explaining that they forgave because they were Christians and, as Christians, they were supposed to forgive. Though people's lives were desperate, the country was rebuilding, and to make that possible, people had to forgive, *reconcile*, and learn to live together again. So they had been taught. The country was under credible leadership, and the rhetoric of the day was forgiveness and reconciliation.

Skovel had the impression that allusions to Christian forgiveness were repeated in a kind of formulaic way. It seemed to her that many persons were saying with implausible lightness that they forgave persons who had committed horrendous acts of violence. Skovel found, however, that when she used a different terminology in posing her questions, she received more differentiated and more cautious responses. The language of *trust* had not been part of the official discourse of reconciliation; religious and political leaders had not told people that they had to learn to trust again. Thus, the language of trust seemed relatively uncorroded. "Do you forgive them? Are you reconciled with them?"—"Oh yes." "Well, do you *trust* those people? Could you *trust* them again?"—"Oh no, we do not trust them, of course not. It will be a long time before we can trust them again." Given the rejection of trust in these contexts, Skovel began to suspect that although people spoke of forgiveness and reconciliation, there had been no genuine shift in their attitudes. There was an unconvincingly automatic character to the rhetoric.[7] Skovel reasoned that people who had genuinely forgiven ought to be willing to trust, at least to some extent. If that was not the case, what was meant by "reconciliation"?

In the context of Sierra Leone, lack of trust often meant that community members remained fearful, careful, and diffident in their dealings with former combatants. Presumably, their suspicions were based on a fear that these people might again resort to acts of violence or abuse. People may say that they have "forgiven" and are "reconciling" with ex-combatants, but if the former combatants are not trusted, they are not yet reintegrated into their communities. Others know their capacity to wreak violence and still regard them as threats.[8] At that point, reconciliation is, at best, barely beginning.

Although people can, of course, *say* that they forgive when they have been urged to do so by persons of authority, emotions, attitudes, and beliefs cannot be simply commanded. If forgiveness is the trend of the day, one promulgated by influential leaders, people may profess to forgive when they do not genuinely do so. When leaders urge forgiveness in the aftermath of serious atrocities, the result is more likely to be verbal gestures than real forgiveness that could bring lasting changes in relationships. The rhetoric may change, but the reality will be unaffected.

(b) Corroded Rhetoric in Rwanda

In the aftermath of the Rwandan genocide, it is rather unbelievable to find people speaking of reconciliation. Nevertheless, President Paul Kagame has said that people will discuss what happened in the genocide and that will bring reconciliation. Even granting that we may not understand just what Kagame means by "reconciliation," the comment seems wildly optimistic. In postgenocide Rwanda, a popular slogan is "The Truth Saves." And yet, twentieth-century Rwandan history is not taught in schools; the history textbooks cannot be written until there is agreement on the details of the history.

Radha Webley, a researcher who visited Rwanda in the summer of 2003, noted a significant disjuncture between allusions to successful reconciliation in government discourse and the realities of people in communities. According to the government, one could find positive indicators that reconciliation was occurring: for example, a once volatile area in the northwest of the country was more secure than previously; soldiers from the former regime had been reintegrated into the armed forces; and various government institutions had been created. Survivors were living together with former perpetrators in villages and communities. The *gacaca*, or community courts, were established as an alternative to judicial institutions that could not meet the challenge of trying over one hundred thousand accused perpetrators, and government officials expressed confidence that these would be an original and effective tool for reconciliation. The government claimed that gacaca courts were already providing a forum in which facts could be established, perpetrators could confess, and victims could forgive them. It was as though they had a blueprint for reconciliation after genocide: a killer would confess, a survivor would forgive him, and people in the community in question would reconcile. (The assignment of a community-service task as some kind of reparation was also part of the plan).[9] And yet, while official sources were optimistic, ordinary people seemed unenthusiastic, if not cynical. Consolate Mukanyiligira, coordinator of AVEGA, a Rwandan widows' group for survivors, said, "We are obliged to reconcile because we are neighbors."[10] One man observed that "we live and work together because we have no choice—killers and victims are all cousins and neighbors. But we don't open our hearts and reveal ourselves any longer. We don't trust one another. We are afraid. We find ourselves alone on an island."[11]

Aimed at both justice and healing, the Rwandan gacaca process was widely supported in the international community as a realistic approach that could be located within communities and had some promising connections with African traditions. There were so many accused killers that national and international courts could not handle the aftermath of the genocide. President Kagame said confidently:

> As soon as the victims of genocide see punishment for the perpetrators of genocide, they are ready to forgive. As soon as those who are in prison are facilitated to get out, to be tried, and to be reinserted into community, to do community service as part of the project, then you are building the bridges for conflict management, you are building the bridges for reconciliation, things have started again. So *gacaca* therefore is tied to the reconciliation process, as soon as both parties to this unfortunate divide see that justice is being done. . . . *Gacaca* therefore is a very big tool, a wonderful [means] for the realization of that dream.[12]

There is a danger here of romanticizing African community practice. Many would like to believe that there is some indigenous method of conflict resolution, one that could prove practical in this gravely difficult context. And it *was* necessary to move outside the courts, which could not address the tens of thousands of cases. And yet, there is a crucial gap in the case. The traditional African gacaca addressed small property offenses and operated in a community in which people had lived together for a long time, knew each other, and expected to go on living together. These conditions are frequently lacking in postgenocide Rwanda because there was considerable mobility after the genocide. In an analysis of the gacaca initiative, Peter Uvin remarked that "in general the degree of distrust that still reigns will make any notion of community a mirage." He added that many factors affect peoples' willingness to participate in these courts, where they might expose themselves to the resentment and fury of their neighbors. Uvin noted that the extent to which people distrust or dislike the government is a factor affecting their participation in the gacaca processes. Gacaca processes have been characterized by the use of poorly educated and trained people as judges, coercion, weak community participation, intimidation of witnesses, suspicion of bias, false confessions, pseudo-forgiveness, and many other problems.

The gacaca process has been slower than expected, and flawed in many respects.[13] Considerable distrust persists among people who suffered in counteroffenses from the Tutsi side or believe the government is biased.[14] In many communities, all the Tutsi were killed so, of necessity, the judges are all Hutus. Persons are given the role of judging suspected genocidaires when they themselves were supporters of the genocide. Another fundamental problem in the process is a failure of mutuality. The mandate of the gacaca is limited in a one-sided way: offenses committed by police or military forces affiliated with the present government do not fall under their jurisdiction.[15] Such selectivity undermines credibility when the governing party refuses to admit its own misdeeds. If accused persons could be trusted to tell the truth, witnesses could be trusted to accurately remember and recount what happened, and community judges could be relied upon to be impartial and competent, a community justice process could have much to offer in some postconflict contexts.[16] But these conditions are often not met, and the postgenocide context is clearly one that is extremely grave and difficult.

The idea that a meaningful sequence of confession, forgiveness, reparation, and reconciliation could emerge from gacaca is optimistic to say the least. In fact, problems are so grave that one suspects that President Kagame was either lying or deceiving himself when he pronounced confidently that gacaca would be a wonderful way of realizing the dream of reconciliation. There is nothing automatic about the sequence: confession, forgiveness, repair, and reconciliation. If Rwanda is to be rebuilt so as to avoid the recurrence of gross civil violence, there must be some kind of reconciliation between Hutus and Tutsis. But with hundreds of thousands of killers and suspected killers, inadequate courts, and limited resources, the challenges are overwhelming and not likely to be met by an ad hoc adaptation. A traditional community process is being used in circumstances vastly different from those in which it functioned before.

In the tragic case of Rwanda, there seem to be illusions—even delusions—so far as reconciliation is concerned. The shift from orthodox legal institutions to gacaca courts in the name of traditional African community justice was a creative move in the extraordinarily difficult circumstances of Rwanda. But the very real problems encountered by those courts strongly suggest that they cannot be adequate tools for bringing about decent relationships in the wake of genocide. Overconfidence and self-deception about the nature and effectiveness of reconciliation processes are dangerous because they support unrealistic beliefs about attitudes and relationships. If—as evidence suggests—institutions such as the Rwandan gacaca courts are functioning imperfectly due to corruption, fear, bias, and coerced participation, then these informal courts cannot provide positive and constructive processes of reconciliation. Instead, they will only serve to inspire cynicism. Resentment, fear, and suspicion will remain; perhaps even to be worsened by a sense that they must remain unexpressed, given that the official rhetoric of the day is one of *reconciliation*. The Rwandan case illustrates the dangers of expecting too much, too soon in the aftermath of atrocities.

MOVING FORWARD

In the light of difficulties, mistakes, and perils, should we give up on reconciliation? Is it a flawed vision? A theologian's dream perhaps—one that persists because some have taken religious texts and applied them in an overly optimistic way to damaged human beings in terribly flawed conditions? We need not go that far.

Generalized pessimism can be resisted because there are positive indicators and achievements. In fact, it would be safe to say that all the means of reconciliation described here have significant benefits, even when there have been flaws and setbacks. Good has come—most conspicuously with regard to acknowledgment, understanding, and the awareness that there is a need to move forward instead of harboring and belaboring grievances about the wrongs of the past.

Truth commissions can considerably increase historical understanding of a conflict and provide a forum for voices to be heard. Many of these voices are those of the rarely heard—marginalized people who have lacked status as citizens and function under difficult circumstances at the geographical or economic fringes of a society. When truth commissions are able to publicize their hearings, broader public understanding and appreciation should result. A truth commission can provide fundamental acknowledgment of violations so that it will be impossible to deny, in the future, that these things did occur. The institution of a truth commission is flexible and adaptable. Truth commissions can allow for event hearings and sector hearings (as in South Africa and Peru), mandate reconciliatory acts (as in East Timor), or provide for healing rituals and ceremonies (as in Sierra Leone). Testimony, systematic research, and careful analysis and writing allow truth commissions to provide final reports that serve as crucial resources for historians and policymakers. In their recommendations, truth commissions can put their understanding to use and offer significant guidelines for needed reform. Truth commissions are fallible and provide no automatic route to reconciliation; slogans like "truth sets you free" and "revealing is healing" are surely simplistic. Nevertheless, it cannot be denied that truth commissions have made enormous contributions to understanding and public acknowledgment. Their contributions would be larger still if their recommendations were more widely followed. However, failures in this area are attributable not to truth commissions themselves but, rather, to the governments that have failed to implement their recommendations.

According to the arguments here, criminal trials should not be seen primarily as a means of reconciliation. Trials of persons accused of genocide and crimes against humanity develop legal expertise, public awareness of the law, and the law itself. In pronouncing atrocities morally and legally intolerable, criminal trials can help to end impunity and introduce the rule of law. Therein lies their value and function.

For all their contentiousness, public apologies initiate a stage of public debate in which acknowledgment has been given, central values have been articulated, and discussion can explore ways of moving forward. If moral apologies are offered after due consideration, by authorized representatives of groups and institutions, and with sensitivity to the needs and expectations of victims, they can provide acknowledgment that moves reconciliation processes into a new stage. Their effectiveness and contribution to reconciliation are, of course, greatly enhanced if they are accompanied by appropriate practical amends.[17]

Community workshops provide a forum for encounters between persons who occupied different roles in a conflict. At their best, they offer occasions in which people can talk, share their stories, break down stereotypes, and begin to understand each other. Friendships established can be invaluable in allowing people to cross social boundaries. At weekend workshops held under the auspices of the Institute for the Healing of Memories near Cape Town, South Africa, black Africans talk to whites about their experiences during the conflict, and whites explain their own sense of loss, frustration, and guilt.[18] With communication in an unthreatening environment, productive contacts can be established, and these may lead to cooperation on further projects beneficial to communities.[19]

Although traditional ceremonies marking cleansing and return may be romanticized and their power exaggerated, such rituals can be sources of power and innovation. They have proven success in some contexts as means of reintegrating ex-combatants and others persons returning to communities. Ritual ceremonies can provide a form of acknowledgment and mark new beginnings for individuals and communities. The notion that violence might be regarded as a feature of situations rather than a character flaw of individual persons is profoundly interesting in this context.[20]

To the notion that reconciliation is some kind of utopian goal, we may reply, first of all, that, rightly understood, it is not a goal at all. Rather, reconciliation is a process of building trusting relationships in the place of resentment and animosity. This building of relationships is crucial for practical reasons. If there is anything unrealistic in discussions of peacebuilding, it is not the urging that reconciliation must be attempted but, rather, the presumption that nonviolent coexistence is sustainable without any such efforts. It is not possible simply to *will* trusting and cooperative relationships into existence. Such relationships must be cultivated over time; time and effort will be necessary, and the processes involved will certainly be difficult for some. Reconciliation should not be understood as some kind of end state that can be quickly reached and painlessly maintained. Changed attitudes and actions will emerge after work has been done, and improved relationships will be sustainable only if there are practices for the handling of fresh conflicts that arise. The challenges of reconciliation are real, and meeting them is no easy matter.

The building of relationships in the aftermath of political conflict is a practical necessity. The need for reconciliation is apparent from plain practical facts about human interdependence and human social life. Its urgency does not emerge from attempts to apply theological or religious beliefs to mundane affairs. To build sustainable peace, people need to cooperate to develop viable social and political institutions. Sustainable cooperation is not possible when relationships are flawed by sentiments of grievance, victimhood, and resentment. If there are no processes of reconciliation, renewed conflict is likely—and such conflict may move around the world, with refugee populations renewing old grievances in receiving countries. The other side of that argument is that if persons learn valuable skills and lessons from reconciliation in their home country, the experience and inspiration acquired may be usable elsewhere.[21] It is absolutely incorrect to think that reconciliation would be a nice thing if possible, but amounts, in the end, to an option and a frill, "soft stuff" removed from the core of hardheaded politics. Far from being a mere aftereffect, reconciliation is the very essence of sustainable peace. It will not happen automatically: it requires attention and effort.

When wrongs are felt in individual relationships, the people involved can sometimes avoid each other, and, in that way, escape the challenges of reconciliation. An alienated couple may, for instance, divorce. Few problems on the larger social level allow for this sort of escape. The zebra is often cited by South Africans to illustrate the fact of interdependence: a zebra could not exist were its black stripes or its white stripes removed. Similarly, the nation of South Africa needs its black and white peoples.[22] Similar points can be made in many political contexts: partition is often simply not a realistic possibility.[23] Northern Ireland, for example, is a small territory within which Protestants, Catholics, and others have to live together. It will undermine their collective future if they commit their talents and resources to violence. In recent years, many people in that region have come to understand this point. Community groups and many individuals have pursued reconciliation with considerable energy—though not without setbacks in the process.

Many of Northern Ireland's leaders and practitioners of peace have been religious believers inspired by personal faith. Faith has enabled them to face the many challenges of reconciliation and to sustain hope for success in the face of many obstacles. No one should wish to turn an effective mediator motivated by faith commitments into a pessimistic skeptic. But while faith and its commitments merit respect, such commitments do not demonstrate that reconciliation must be understood in theological terms. Conceptions of trust, forgiveness, justice, and morally repaired relationships can be given a plausible and practical interpretation that does not presuppose theological commitments.

Whatever its difficulties, it would not make sense to give up on reconciliation. In the sense in which it means building relationships that make cooperation and coexistence possible and providing for some degree of social trust, reconciliation is simply and clearly a prerequisite for sustainable peace. An armchair theorist might take the view that reconciliation processes are fallible at best and sit back comfortably to pronounce that the whole thing will not work. But no such luxury is available for people living in the affected society, whether they are citizens, governments, humanitarian organizations, or interveners.

To appreciate, again, the need for processes of reconciliation, we can revisit the alternatives. These are:

1. Doing nothing at all;
2. Allowing people to take out their frustrations by engaging in acts of revenge;
3. Reverting to the previous war or oppressive regime;
4. Expanding the courts considerably so that a much higher proportion of perpetrators are subjected to criminal trial;
5. Political divorce (partitioning the territory).

In most situations, none of these alternatives is attractive. Sustainable peace presupposes decent relationships between former opponents. Those relationships do not emerge from nowhere and nothing. They require communication, acknowledgment, understanding, and constructive change. Bringing those things about is the work of reconciliation. That work is not easy, and its theory and practice are far from perfect. But the challenges simply cannot be avoided.

There are grounds for optimism that are genuine and not to be found in flawed rhetoric. These lie in the human capacities to be flexible and to learn from experience—to adapt, innovate, synthesize, and create. The themes in this book also illustrate those capacities.

NOTES

1. Northern Ireland seems to be a case in point.
2. This could be alleged in the cases of Rwanda, the former Yugoslavia, Sierra Leone, and East Timor. For further details, see chapter 7 and the relevant appendixes.
3. For details, see appendix 8, South Africa.
4. Discussed in chapter 8.
5. Reverend Joseph Humper, interview by David Busch, *The Religion Report*, Radio National, July 30, 2003, http://ftp.mozilla.org/pub/mozilla/nightly/latest (accessed March 2004).
6. Laura Skovel, interview with the author, Vancouver, March 17, 2004. Skovel reported to me that she was led to inquire about trust by the account of national reconciliation offered in Trudy Govier and Wilhelm Verwoerd, "Trust and the Problem of National Reconciliation," *Philosophy of the Social Sciences* 32, no. 2 (2002): 178–205.
7. Laura Skovel, interview.
8. Distrust, in such contexts, may seem prudent. Its prudence, or otherwise, is not the issue here. The question, rather, is whether, given this residual distrust, it makes sense to suppose that people have *forgiven*, as a shift toward reconciliation. My answer is that it does not.
9. Radha Webley, "Gacaca and Reconciliation in Post-Genocide Rwanda," http://www.222.hrcberkeley.org/download/report_wradha.pdf (accessed March 2004). This well-written and sensitive paper offers excellent observations and I am indebted to it.
10. Quoted by Africa News Network, Integrated Regional Information Network, UN Office for Coordination of Humanitarian Affairs, November 26, 2002.
11. Viateur Itangayenda, quoted in Veronique Mistiaen, "Rwanda's Dead Haunt Survivors," *Pittsburgh Post Gazette*, April 8, 2004.
12. Quoted in Webley, "Gacaca and Reconciliation," p. 4.
13. An Amnesty International press release anticipated such problems, see Amnesty International, "Rwanda: *Gacaca*—Gambling with Justice," press release, June 19, 2002.
14. Peter Uvin, "The *Gacaca* Tribunals in Rwanda," http://www.idea.int/publications/reconciliation/upload/reconciliation_chap07cs-rwanda.pdf (accessed June 14, 2006). Peter Uvin worked extensively in sub-Saharan Africa and is the author of *Aiding Violence: The Development Enterprise in Africa* (West Hartford, CT: Kumarian, 1998).
15. Compare the discussion of mutuality in chapter 3. The RPF, a Tutsi army, also committed abuses; furthermore, government forces in the past decade have been accused by Amnesty International of extensive sexual offenses and assaults.

16. Rosemary Nagy, presentation on Rwanda at a conference on reconciliation, University of Western Ontario (May 13–15, 2005).

17. See chapter 4.

18. I attended one such workshop in June 2000, under the leadership of Michael Lapsley.

19. There are many thousands of such workshops; comments here are based largely on my understanding of the work of the Glencree Centre for Reconciliation, which addresses various conflicts and aftermaths, but primarily the conflict in Northern Ireland. My understanding of this work owes much to conversations with Wilhelm Verwoerd.

20. Described by Carolyn Nordstrom, in the case of Mozambique. For details, see chapter 8.

21. I owe this observation to Sarah Laing.

22. The zebra image is offered here as an illustrative figure of speech, not an argument.

23. This case has been argued effectively by Robert Schaeffer, in *Warpaths: The Politics of Partition* (New York: Hill and Wang, 1990).

Appendix 1, Australia

In 1997, the report *Bringing Them Home* was issued by the Australian government. This report was the result of an inquiry into the practices of separating Aboriginal children from their parents and communities so that they could be raised by white Australians in foster homes or institutions. The report described great suffering and pain, and received an extremely emotional response from the Australian public. It was extremely influential and has set the context of debates, activism, and policies with regard to reconciliation in Australia. There, the removed children are referred to as the "stolen generation." Most of the children who were removed were of mixed Aboriginal-European descent. It was believed that if raised as white, they would seek to pass as white and would be able to do so. In this way, the removal of these children from Aboriginal parents would serve to further goals of assimilation and, eventually, the end of Aboriginality.

The colonization of Australia by European settlers in the nineteenth and twentieth centuries killed more people than the number of Americans killed in the Vietnam War. The Aboriginal culture is believed to be the oldest on earth: it is estimated to have an age of between forty thousand and sixty thousand years.[1] The oppression of the Aboriginal population could be regarded, in fact, as a war of long duration and, given the express intent by Australian governments to eliminate Aboriginality, even as an instance of genocide. During the period when Australia was colonized, there were over three hundred separate indigenous nations on the continent. Given that fact, it is a simplification to speak simply of Aboriginal people or even, as some do, of Aboriginal and Torres Strait Islander people. Issues may vary from one group and location to another; people have moved and they do not always agree on what should be done.

The system of assimilative schools in Australia began in 1839. At first, people were enticed into the system of schools. Adults attended, and attended voluntarily. These schools became, in effect, small communities. They were transformed over time into boarding schools. According to *Bringing Them Home*, the rounding up of "half-castes" so as to compel school attendance began in 1911. The presumption was that the future of Aboriginal children would be better if they were rescued from a "worthless" and "degraded" life among their own people. According to the Aborigines Act of 1911, "neglected" children of mixed descent would be taken from their parents. There was a "chief protector" in each province, and that person was assigned as the legal guardian of all Aboriginal children under the age of twenty-one.[2] In some areas, Aborigines outnumbered white people, and many whites believed them to be a menace. Some worried about "half-castes" beginning a sinister hybrid race. One alarmist figure was Dr. Cecil Cook, architect of Aboriginal policy in Australia's Northern Territory in the 1920s and 1930s. Cook affirmed the goal of breeding out color from people in Australia so that, eventually, one would be able to forget the Aborigines entirely.[3]

The United Nations Convention on Genocide of 1948, Article II(a) defines genocide, stipulating that genocide is occurring if any of the following acts are performed with the intent to destroy in whole or in part a national, ethnic, racial, or religious group:

- killing members of the group;
- causing serious bodily or mental harm to members of the group;
- deliberately inflicting on the group conditions of life calculated to lead to its physical destruction, in whole or in part;
- implementing measures intended to prevent births within the group;
- forcibly transferring children to persons from another group.

By this definition, the policies of the Australian national and state governments would seem to have been genocidal in intent.[4]

The practice of child removal in Australia persisted over some fifty years. This policy was described in *Bringing Them Home* as one presuming astonishing indifference to two of the most fundamental of all human needs—the need for a bond between a child and its mother and the need for individual identity to be rooted in a culture. Often, children were removed and relocated to contexts in which conditions were very poor, featuring overcrowding, poor food, abuse, and limited educational resources. It must be noted that some people did criticize the practices at the time they were being carried out. Their protestations are noted in the report.[5] This fact is relevant to later arguments that it is anachronistic if one judges policies of the past from the moral perspective of the present. After the Second World War, in particular, there were increasing signs of troubled conscience in officials who were administering the policy of removal. The schools were administered by territories, not by the federal government; however, the federal government financed the policies and supported them, at least to the extent that it failed to oppose them. (The federal government could then be termed a secondary and tertiary perpetrator regarding these policies.) By the late 1940s, the United Nations had begun to inquire about the welfare of Aborigines in Australia. The approach of compulsory removal was beginning to seem highly dubious, and many parole officers admitted that they hated removing the "half-caste babies." In 1951, the United Nations World Health Organization stressed that welfare provided to Aboriginal families should emphasize the approach of keeping children within their homes and families. In 1967, the goal of Aboriginal education changed from assimilation to integration. A. R. Driver, who was the administrator of the Northern Territory, conceded that restrictions placed on Aborigines were at variance with the ideals of the Universal Declaration of Human Rights.[6]

The federal government in Australia began to inquire into the policies of the government of the Northern Territory. The administrator allowed that Aboriginals were human beings with the same basic affections shared by other human beings and that Aboriginal mothers really loved their children and would not wish to have them removed. Despite this admission, there was no clear acknowledgement that the policies of removal were wrong. For many years the question of maternal consent was of relatively little interest. Officers taking children from their mothers tried explaining how the policies would benefit children, and a system was established in which a maternal thumbprint was required to authorize the removal of a child. Nevertheless, given the enormous pressure put on mothers, any notion that there was maternal consent to the removals was implausible. The intent to separate children from families and communities remained fundamental, and children who were taken away were forbidden to ever return home.

By the end of the 1950s, officers of Australia's Northern Territory admitted that parental consent had been obtained by pressure and that the children taken away had experienced their separation as an act of force. It was also beginning to be understood that the policy of removals had failed. After children left the institutions to which they had been removed, they still felt themselves to be nonwhite and were regarded as such by the broader society, within which their mixed blood heritage was still a burden. Upon leaving the institutions, some were directed to the southern parts of Australia, where their skin color would be less noticeable, in the hope that they would be able to pass as Italian or Greek.

The assumption behind the policy of removals was that these children needed to be rescued from Aboriginality itself. Aboriginality appeared to policymakers and implementers to be a profound source of harm. Although it appears that many advocating the removals did believe that they were acting in the best interests of the child, they sent these children to institutions of squalor and abuse. To the writers of *Bringing Them Home*, it seemed that supporters of the policy

> simply could not see how terrible was an Aboriginal mother's grief at the loss of her child. They simply could not see how terrible was the pain and bewilderment of Aboriginal children at the loss of mother, family and world. It was in this inability to grasp the depth of Aboriginal suffering that the racism of child removal was most clearly expressed.[7]

Issues of reconciliation in Australia include past racism and discrimination, constitutional provisions with regard to Aboriginal peoples, rights over land, claims to sovereignty by Aboriginal groups, and socioeconomic inequalities. *Bringing Them*

Home recommended that the Australian government offer a formal apology to the stolen generation and their families. This suggestion was roundly resisted by some, including the prime minister and, as a result, reconciliation debates in Australia have focused considerably on apology. A National Sorry Day was established to serve as an expression of the sorrow and regret of non-Aboriginal Australians for racism and the many abuses against the Aboriginal population and, in particular, for the policy of forcible removal. For several years, May 26 marked National Sorry Day in Australia. This annual event commenced National Reconciliation Week (established in 1996), from May 27 until June 3.[8] The first National Sorry Day was commemorated in 1998. In 2005, Sorry Day was replaced by a Day of Healing. The reason for the shift, apparently, is the conviction by some Aboriginal groups that Sorry Day placed too much emphasis on the single issue of national apology.

There seemed to be considerable public grassroots support for Sorry Day events; these included vigils, speeches, demonstrations, marches, and the signing of sorry books, which contain over one million signatures. The *Sea of Hands*, a monument to the tasks and goals of reconciliation, is Australia's largest public art installation. Although some argue that support for reconciliation is largely a middle-class, white phenomenon, some one million men, women, and children have signed their names in sorry books across the country. Thousands more put their names to a *Sea of Hands* outside Parliament House in Canberra. In the wake of *Bringing Them Home* and the discussions about its content, it appears that the Australian mindset has changed. There appears to be a widespread recognition that society only truly works when there is a certain generosity of spirit. One recent commentator on reconciliation in Australia stated that there is no real alternative to it.

> Without reconciliation, we will be a divided nation with racial tension and racial strife because indigenous people will not give up their struggle. They have survived until now, against all the odds, and will continue to fight for their human and legal rights. They see it ultimately as a question of the survival of their culture, a war against cultural genocide. There can be no retreat in such a war, even though some battles may be lost. So, in very stark terms, Australia can either be an inclusive, harmonious nation or one split by race issues. I reject the latter and therefore must embrace the quest for humanity.[9]

In public debates about the issues raised in *Bringing Them Home*, there were also disputes about the term "stolen generation," especially with regard to the issue of what percentage of Aboriginal children were removed from their homes under government policies designed to eliminate Aboriginality. Government statements acknowledge wrongs against the Aboriginal people and support commemorative dates and the articulation of a determination that such things will not happen again. Officially, discriminatory racist attitudes that characterized much of Australia's past have been renounced; hearts and minds have been marked as changed.

Under John Howard's leadership, the Australian government has stated that it wishes to undertake actions of reconciliation; these are understood as practical measures distinct from issuing a formal apology. A $63 million package was established for a four-year time span. The envisaged measures include:

(a) establishing a link-up network to assist members of the stolen generation who wish to connect with their birth families;
(b) creating memorials at Reconciliation Place;[10]
(c) supporting counseling for persons affected by assimilationist policies;
(d) supporting language and culture centers.

In many Australian institutions, there was widespread support for Sorry Day and for apologies. All the state governments have apologized, as have major churches. The most significant gap in the apology process in Australia is that Prime Minister John Howard has not apologized on behalf of the state, even though he has participated in Sorry Day events and has expressed "regret" for the policy of forced removals.[11] Howard does not want to accept without equivocation that the policy and practice of Aboriginal child removal was wrong. He insists that the motivation underlying the removals was basically good. Howard has given the following reasons for his unwillingness to apologize:

1. Saying that one is sorry is an expression of *guilt*. Howard thinks he (as an individual) is not guilty and he does not want the present generation of Australians to feel guilty. As individuals, Australians did not commit these acts; they were responsible for neither the abuses children experienced in institutions and foster homes nor for the problems experienced by Aboriginal people who had lost their families and communities. Howard argues that encouraging *feelings of guilt* would have bad consequences for individuals who were not responsible for the actions. If the state were to apologize, it would (he says) encourage these feelings of guilt on the part of individuals. Furthermore, admitting guilt on the part of the Australian state would probably lead to expensive *compensation* claims. As leader of the state, he does not want to encourage that sort of redress for past wrongs.[12]

2. Past governments pursued these policies and those governments are distinct from his government. Howard argues that his government does not inherit *responsibility* for the acts of past governments.[13]

3. Howard maintains that the cultural assimilation of Aboriginal people seemed to be a correct policy when it was undertaken and that people who were removing these children and placing them in white homes or institutions were doing what they thought was right.

4. Howard maintains that apologies are about the past and, as such, encourage people to focus on the past. He argues that, by contrast, there is a need to

focus on the future, as distinct from the past, and on practical solutions to specific problems of a material and socioeconomic nature.

Howard emphasized *acknowledgment* as distinct from apology, saying that one should acknowledge the wrongs, but could do so without apologizing, implying guilt on the part of individuals, or branding the history of Australia as a history of moral wrongs. National reconciliation, as he understands it, calls for more than recognizing the mistakes of the past. Reconciliation is also about *the future* and, thus, calls for practical policymaking. National reconciliation depends on attitudes and receptiveness to change; it should bring people together. Howard argued that people cannot be brought together if their leaders focus on their inadequacies and on the wrongs of the past. Rather, what is needed is a commitment to raise living standards and increase opportunities for Aboriginal people. Howard contends that reconciliation processes must focus on the future in a principled way. They must be practical and address the profound economic and social disadvantages of many indigenous people in the areas of health, housing, education, and employment.[14]

In August 1999, the Australian parliament considered a Motion of Reconciliation. It reaffirmed the cause of reconciliation, recognized the achievements of the nation, confirmed the notion of working together to strengthen bonds, reaffirmed the central importance of practical matters, and acknowledged that the mistreatment of indigenous Australians was a most blemished chapter in the nation's history. Then it expressed "deep and sincere regret" that indigenous Australians suffered injustices under the practices of past generations, and for the hurt and trauma that many indigenous people continue to feel as a consequence of those practices."[15]

In contexts of settler societies, acts of injustice have come exclusively, or almost exclusively, from one side alone. Australia is one such case. In this context, what is sought is, for all practical purposes, reconciliation between the powerful and the powerless. Such reconciliation requires the powerful to acknowledge, without equivocation, that grave injustices have been committed. Because the situation is asymmetric, it requires from the powerless no reciprocal actions. What is needed is only that the powerless accept "the sincerity of the apology, the appropriateness of the acts of reparation, and that they can find it in their hearts to forgive." It is the powerful who have the primary responsibility. Neither in settler societies nor in other contexts of aftermath should acknowledgment be neglected. The Australian political theorist Robert Manne remarks:

> So long as the political leaders of former enemies after a war resist unpleasant historical truths about their own side reconciliation will not arrive. Similarly while the political leaders of the powerful resist attempts to revise their nation's story in the light of the knowledge of the harm their forebears have done, the prospects for reconciliation with those who have been wronged are dim.[16]

NOTES

1. Grenfell Price, *White Settlers and Native Peoples: An Historical Study of Racial Contacts between English-speaking Whites and Aboriginal Peoples in the United States, Canada, Australia, and New Zealand* (Westport, CT: Greenwood, 1972).

2. Peggy Brock, *Outback Ghettos: Aborigines, Institutionalization, and Survival* (Cambridge: Cambridge University Press, 1993), p. 82. The term "Aboriginal" was defined in a way both seemingly circular and loose enough to permit considerable abuse. It included persons born as Aboriginal natives; persons who were "half-caste," married to Aboriginals, or who habitually associated with Aboriginals; or "half-caste" children under sixteen years. See also Paul Havemann, ed., *Indigenous Peoples' Rights in Australia, Canada, and New Zealand* (Auckland, New Zealand: Oxford University Press, 1999) and Kent McNeil, *Emerging Justice: Essays on Indigenous Rights in Canada and Australia* (Saskatoon: University of Saskatchewan Press, 2001).

3. Human Rights and Equal Opportunity Commission, *Bringing Them Home: Report of the National Inquiry into the Separation of Aboriginal and Torres Strait Islander Children from Their Families*, Australasian Legal Information Institute, 1997, p. 135. *Bringing Them Home* can be accessed at http://www.hreoc.gov.au/social_justice/stolen_children/.

Other relevant material may be found at http://www.journalofhealing.com and http://www.acn.net.au/articles/sorry (regarding "Sorry Day"); http://www.antar.org.au/apology.html (has a link to a Reparations Tribunal); http://www.hansard.act.gov.au/hansard/1998/week03/527.htm (provides access to arguments posed in parliamentary debates; http://www.apology.west.net.au (one can find descriptions of National Sorry Day).

4. This theme is discussed in A. Dirk Moses, ed., *Genocide and Settler Society: Frontier Violence and Stolen Indigenous Children in Australian History* (Oxford: Berghahn Books, 2004).

5. These facts are relevant to the assessment of the claim that it is systematically fallacious to apply to past policies and actions the moral values of the present. The fallacy in question is said to be that of presentism.

6. Human Rights and Equal Opportunity Commission, *Bringing Them Home*, p. 136.

7. Ibid., p. 139.

8. These dates are significant. May 27, 1967, was the Referendum on Aboriginals. And on June 3, 1992, Australia's High Court delivered its decision in the Mabo case on native title rights, in which the notion of *terra nullius* was legally overturned. According to *terra nullius*, Australia was empty and unowned land before the arrival of European settlers in 1788. That doctrine constituted a marked failure of acknowledgment insofar as the very existence of a group of human beings was denied.

9. Rick Farley, "What's the Alternative?" in *Essays on Australian Reconciliation*, ed. Michelle Grattan (Melbourne: Bookman, 2000), pp. 105–12.

10. Some memorials turned out to be highly controversial because the Aboriginal people were not consulted about them and Aboriginal children were insensitively depicted as playing happily.

11. This gap illustrates the distinction between acknowledgment and apology. It is possible to acknowledge that X was wrong *without* apologizing for X. In a moral apology, an individual or spokesperson for a collectivity accepts *responsibility* for X and indicates that it is *sorry* for having done X. In an acknowledgment, it is stated that X occurred and was wrong, but no one accepts responsibility or expresses sorrow for having done X.

12. This response is open to criticism on the grounds that it ignores the possibility of collective responsibility by the state and related institutions as well as the highly relevant possibility of suitably placed and authorized spokespersons issuing public apologies. It also ignores moral and international legal norms pertinent to reparations. An effective philosophical reply to Howard's arguments is offered in Tamara Zutlevics, "Reconciliation, Responsibility, and Apology," *Public Affairs Quarterly* 16 (2002): 63–75.

13. As is explained in the discussion of reparations in chapter 9, this doctrine is counter to international law.

14. John Howard, "Practical Reconciliation," in Grattan, *Essays on Australian Reconciliation*, pp. 88–96.

15. My emphasis. This wording constitutes an important illustration of the fact that an expression of regret is not an apology.

16. Robert Manne, "The Stolen Generations," in Grattan, *Essays on Australian Reconciliation*, p. 130.

Appendix 2, Canada

B roadly speaking, there are four different sorts of contexts in which we can identify issues of reconciliation in Canada. These are:

1. Relations between the Canadian state and society, and Aboriginal Canadians. These issues involve land claims, claims to sovereignty, issues of governance, and apology and compensation for wrongs including, most significantly, physical and sexual abuse in residential schools.

2. Relationships between Francophone and Anglophone Canadians, stemming from the British victory over French forces in 1758 at the Plains of Abraham and the British administration of what had been French territories in Quebec and parts of the Maritime provinces. The Acadian issue discussed in chapter 3 falls broadly within this context.

3. Relationships between the Canadian state and subgroups of varying ethnicities and religions within Canada who have been mistreated by the Canadian state in the past. These groups include Japanese, Chinese, Ukrainian, Doukhobor, German, Italian, African, and Jewish Canadian groups. Jewish Canadian issues concern failure to accept refugees from Nazi Germany. Japanese, Italian, Ukrainian, and German Canadian issues concern internment in times of war. Afro-Canadian issues concern racism and slavery, which was legal in Canada until 1833. In most cases, the Canadian government has adopted an approach of acknowledging wrongs and providing funds for commemoration and education, but not issuing formal apologies or providing redress to individuals. The situations with regard to Japanese, Chinese, Ukrainian, and Doukhobor Canadians are described below.[1]

4. Relationships between Canadians of varied ethnicities in which divisions exist due to conflicts in their lands of origin. These include persons of Croatian, Serbian, or Bosnian origin from the former Yugoslavia; Sikhs and Hindus from the Indian subcontinent; persons of Latin or Central American origin who may have affiliations with victims or perpetrators under military dictatorships; Turkish and Greek Cypriots; Holocaust survivors and victims; persons of Irish origin with affiliations either with the Catholic or the Protestant sides of the sectarian conflict in Northern Ireland; persons from Sri Lanka with Tamil or Sinhalese affiliation; and many others. These issues, though not described here, are mentioned in the interests of completeness.

ABORIGINAL ISSUES

With regard to aboriginal issues, the themes are many. It is no exaggeration to say that these problems pose the most pressing issues of reconciliation in contemporary Canada. There are more than five hundred thousand Aboriginal Canadians and, despite some advances in economic and educational opportunities, many live at a markedly lower socioeconomic status than other Canadians. Issues of land title, treaty rights and interpretation, racism and discriminatory practices, and participation in mainstream Canadian society are many. All these issues are difficult; legal and political processes have been slow. Much has been written about these issues. The present study emphasizes the specific issue of residential schools. Over the past fifteen years, this concern has emerged as the most pressing and intractable problem concerning the aftermath of the colonization and settlement of Canada by non-Aboriginal peoples.

Public awareness of misery and abuse in residential schools began in 1990 when Phil Fontaine, a prominent Aboriginal leader, spoke out about sexual abuse that he and others had experienced in the schools. The existence of schools with assimilationist goals had long been a feature of Canadian society. Even in the early seventeenth century, Catholics in New France had tried—and failed—to assimilate indigenous children to a European way of life. Under the British after 1768, such efforts continued and were again largely unsuccessful. The modern phase of Canadian residential schools dates from the 1880s. Because First Nations people wanted education, understanding it as something that could help them adjust to a changing world, when they signed treaties, these often included a schooling clause. In the prairie provinces in particular, the slaughter of the buffalo by white hunters made pressing the need for a different way of life for Aboriginal people. Initially, they understood schooling as potentially helpful, given the drastically changing situation. In the 1920s, the system of residential schools was at its height. There were some eighty institutions, mostly in the western part of Canada. These schools were instituted and mandated by the federal government but operated by churches—Roman Catholic (some 60 percent), Anglican (about 25 percent), Methodist, and Presbyterian (most of the remainder). Most congregations of Methodists and Presbyterians merged to become the United Church of Canada, which then took on responsibility for the schools run under Methodist or Presbyterian auspices. The intent of the government was to arrange for First Nations people to become economically self-sufficient. The missionaries had the goal of Christianizing the children so that they would fit in to a European culture.

Schools were characterized by a considerable focus on dress, grooming, and behavior appropriate for living in a European-dominated society. Because children were assigned a considerable amount of labor in the fields and in the kitchen, classroom learning occupied, at most, half of each day. Often, children worked for more than half of each day; in some cases, they worked all the time and received virtually no education at all. It would be a significant understatement to say that this system failed to function as intended. The churches were poorly funded by the government and were thus under pressure to overwork the children. Churches proselytized in an extremely aggressive and frightening manner, speaking of indigenous beliefs and practices in highly abusive terms while contrasting the European Christian "way of good" with the Aboriginal "way of evil."

At many schools there was poor physical care and insufficient, low quality food and clothing. This was especially humiliating because the students could see that others—notably staff—were not similarly deprived. In the staff room, furnishing and food were much better; students preparing and serving food to the staff could see this for themselves. There were few facilities for recreation, the atmosphere was cheerless, and the message was that the mostly European faculty and staff devalued the Aboriginal students. There was little emotional support for children in these schools and, given the goal of assimilation, efforts were made to separate children from their families. Because government funding was per capita, there was an incentive to keep children in the school even when they were ill. Poor conditions and overwork often led to health problems, and some children died of tuberculosis. Sexual abuse in the schools was quite widespread. Perpetrators included missionaries, some Aboriginal staff, and even older fellow students.

First Nations groups made efforts to improve the schools, but the federal bureaucracy fought back; Aboriginal efforts were handicapped by the fact that it was difficult for First Nations groups to hire lawyers. However, just before the First World War, an Aboriginal father took a school superintendent to court over poor conditions in the schools and won his case.[2] Some native students rebelled against the harsh treatment in the schools, defying rules about the segregation of the sexes, stealing food, and running away. Some even carried out acts of arson; according to one scholar, residential schools were burned down with surprising frequency.[3] By the 1930s, problems were sufficiently apparent that the federal government had stopped replacing schools that were burned down, and by the middle of the 1940s, activist Aboriginal organizations in western provinces had organized to protest the inadequacy of education, putting the spotlight on mistreatment in residential schools. The Canadian government knew that the system had serious problems and would have to be changed eventually. The United Church, in particular, had wanted to stop running these schools as early as the 1940s, partly for financial reasons.[4]

Because the Second World War was, to a considerable extent, a war against the Nazi ideology of racism, after it ended, the Canadian government officially disavowed racist policies. This fact, in conjunction with the cost of the schools and the high birth rate among First Nations people, led the government to wind down the system of residential schools in the late 1960s. However, a few schools remained open until the early 1980s, with the Catholic Oblate order holding out the longest. In some cases, First Nations children were integrated into public schools, while in others, First Nations communities and groups themselves took over the running of schools for their children.

Although some children benefited from learning English and other skills, the damage to First Nations people as a result of these institutions was extensive and lasting. People emerged from the schools with little sense of indigenous identity, culture, or language, and having lost the connection with their parents, families, and communities. Their skills for the work force were typically poor. They had been educated with low-paying labor, domestic service, or military jobs in mind. Though lacking familiarity and ease in their own culture, they were not accepted as white. Many persons were left with a profound sense of inferiority due to humiliating treatment and denigration of indigenous cultures within the schools. Leaving the schools, they had no obvious place in society and many turned to substance abuse, often in the form of alcoholism. With no experience of family, many experienced difficulty taking care of their own children. Thus, damage from the schools extended over several generations.

In 1986, the United Church issued an apology for practices in the residential schools and for its failure to understand First Nations cultures.[5] The United Church was followed by the Anglican Church and, in 1991, by the Oblate Order.[6] The Catholic Church, as a whole, does not accept institutional responsibility for what happened in schools administered under its auspices and has not issued any apology for emotional, spiritual, sexual, cultural, or physical abuses in schools under its administration. However, in 2002 the Vatican, under Pope John Paul II, issued a generic apology in the Apostolic Letter *Tertio Millenio Adveniente*, in which it said it had an obligation to express regret for the "weakness of so many of her sons and daughters who sullied (the Church's) face."[7] This was an allusion to sexual abuse in various Catholic institutions around the world. Notably, it was a statement of "regret" rather than of apology, and that statement sought forgiveness not from the victims of these assaults, but from God. However, the Pope's statement was, at least, an acknowledgment that bad things had happened.

A discussion of the lasting harm brought about by the residential schools was summarized by the Royal Commission on Aboriginal Peoples, which called for apology and compensation to victims of abuse.[8] In 1998, Cabinet Minister Jane Stewart issued an emotional statement on behalf of the federal government, acknowledging the harms brought by the schooling policies and promising a $350 million healing fund for First Nations people. Efforts by victims were mainly launched through legal claims; some 13,400 claims were made and, as of March 2005, about 2,000 had been settled. In addition, there were class action suits launched by some survivors.[9] Delays and costs of legal procedures were extremely problematic. The government initiated an alternative dispute resolution process, hoping to move cases out of the court system; however, that process was unsuccessful.[10] In November 2005, the Canadian government offered tens of thousands of survivors of abuse up to $30,000 each in a compensation package totaling to $1.9 billion. Another $195 million was to be spent on a truth and reconciliation process, commemoration program, and projects designed to promote healing. Aboriginal leader Phil Fontaine praised the package.[11] The agreement required approval by the courts because of its potential effects on a number of outstanding lawsuits.

ANGLOPHONE-FRANCOPHONE RELATIONS

Until at least the 1960s, Francophone Canadians tended to have lower socioeconomic status than Anglophones, who often looked down on their language, religion, and culture. Resentment over the conquest and this lower status was profound. Since the 1970s, many measures have been adopted to acknowledge the presence and importance of the French language and Francophone culture in Canada. Francophone Canadians participate substantially in government, law, business, education, and other significant institutions. It is fair to say that disparagement and discrimination against Francophone Canadians has dramatically diminished; one might even argue that it has disappeared entirely.

But despite the cultural and economic success of the province of Quebec and the prominence of Francophone Quebeckers in federal institutions, it would be premature to announce reconciliation between Francophone and Anglophone Canadians. Resentment and a sense of threatened culture persist in some circles, and political parties seeking a form of sovereignty for the province of Quebec are prominent. There are two significant political parties active in Canada that have the professed goal of seeking state sovereignty for the province of Quebec. These are the *Bloc Quebecois*, which has a substantial number of members in the federal parliament, and the *Parti Quebecois*, which has several times formed the government in the province of Quebec. For both parties, the prominence of sovereignty in its agenda varies from one time to another, based partly on considerations of expediency and public mood. Sovereignty for what is regarded as a nation of Quebec is by no means their sole political platform. Some might interpret both parties as more nominally than genuinely sovereigntist, especially during periods when public opinion in Quebec seems unlikely to generate referendum support for separation from Canada. It is sometimes plausible to interpret these parties as advocating social democratic policies that exhibit a particular concern for the interests of Quebeckers (as distinct from Canadians in general) but as *not* seeking actual separation from

Canada.[12] A factor that complicates the interpretation of sentiment with regard to separatism is the lack of clarity as to what is sought under terms such as "Quebec sovereignty." The term "sovereignty-association" is often used, and under this conception, persons advocating nationhood and statehood for Quebec typically wish to preserve important associations with the Canadian state, extending even to continued use of the Canadian currency and Canadian passports.

Younger Quebeckers seem less interested in the sovereignty issue than older ones, with the issue of separatism having lost some of its originality and appeal over the forty-year period during which several referenda have been extremely divisive. A highly significant factor here is globalization. Given the growing power of multinational corporations, as rendered official by trade agreements, state power may seem less significant. In addition, the multicultural nature of contemporary Quebec has, for the most part, resulted in leaders of these parties disavowing the ethnic (*pure laine*) form of nationalism.

However, the issue of relations between Anglophone and Francophone Canadians retains the potential to spring to life at almost any given time. For example, on September 27, 2005, Michaelle Jean, a Quebecker of Haitian origin, gave her installation speech as Canada's governor-general. In the speech, she stated that the time of the "two solitudes" that had for too long described the character of Canada had passed. She called for solidarity among all the citizens of Canada.[13] These themes were contested by Quebec separatists who did not appreciate the implication that their cause was, or should be, dead. The ensuing public discussion indicated that French-English polarity has not ceased to be significant in Canadian political life.

ETHNIC COMMUNITIES WITHIN CANADA

Details can be given only for selected cases.

(a) Japanese Canadians

During the Second World War, Japanese Canadians, many of whom were second and third generation citizens of Canada, were suspected of being potentially disloyal to the Canadian state, which was at war with Japan. They were forcibly relocated from coastal areas of British Columbia first to the interior of that province and then, later, to the southern area of Alberta, where many worked in harsh conditions in the sugar beet fields. Physical, mental, and economic hardships suffered during these relocations were severe, and there were significant property losses from which many families recovered only with great difficulty. No Japanese Canadian person was ever found to have committed an act of disloyalty to Canada. In 1988, the Japanese Canadians received a statement of acknowledgment (*not apology*) and financial redress for wrongs committed against them during the Second World War. The financial redress included $21,000 for each individual who had been a victim of relocation.[14]

In addition, there was an allotment of further funds to the Japanese Canadian community, which used these funds to establish a foundation for race relations. The issuance of an acknowledgment rather than an apology may have been intended to avoid any commitment to further compensation.[15]

(b) Chinese Canadians

Chinese men came to British Columbia during the 1860s as part of the gold rush. Most of these men arrived in Canada from California. In the 1880s, another seventeen thousand men came from China to work on the Canadian Pacific Railway. These so-called coolies did difficult and dangerous work, were paid only half the wages given to white people, and were looked down upon. Despite their low social and economic status, their work was essential to the building of this railway which, in turn, was a condition of the joining of British Columbia with the eastern provinces of Canada (and, thus, to the building of modern Canada). When the railway was completed, the governments of British Columbia and Canada decided that they did not want further Chinese immigration and imposed a $50 head tax on all Chinese men who sought to enter Canada to work. When that tax proved an insufficient deterrent, it was raised to $100 in 1900 and then to $500 in 1903. Between 1904 and 1923, some 42,444 Chinese men paid the head tax to enter Canada. It is estimated that between 1885 and 1923 the federal government received some $23 million in head taxes. (This amount would be equivalent to some $1.2 billion in 2005 dollars.)[16]

On July 1, 1923, the Canadian government passed the Chinese Exclusion Act, stipulating that there should be no further immigration of Chinese into Canada. July 1, 1923 is known as Humiliation Day in the Chinese Canadian community. The Chinese Exclusion Act meant that men who had lived and worked in Canada for many years were separated from their families for long periods, often as long as twenty-five years. It was primarily Chinese men who came to Canada to work. Men came to Canada and sent money home, then returned to China to marry and for occasional conjugal visits. With relatively few exceptions, women did not follow them. By 1931, the Chinese Canadian community had 1,240 men for every one hundred women.

Due to its incompatibility with the United Nations Charter of Human Rights, the Chinese Exclusion Act was repealed after the Second World War. In 1947, Chinese Canadians were granted the right to vote in federal elections. In 1967, a point system for immigration was established; this system was not racially discriminatory but was based on other factors such as language, education, and family connections.

Canada has been urged by the United Nations to repay the descendants of those who paid the head tax and to issue an apology for the treatment of these workers in Canada. The redress movement for Japanese Canadians encouraged some Chinese Canadians to lobby for redress; their efforts began in 1984. Their first efforts were resisted on the grounds both that history cannot be rewritten and that government resources were needed to build a more equitable society in the future. In 2001, a class action lawsuit was launched (Shack Jang Mack et. al. v. A. G. Canada) claiming that the head tax should be repaid, with compound interest and additional funds in damages for pain and suffering. This lawsuit was unsuccessful. The Ontario Court judge ruled that the Charter of Rights and Freedoms of 1982 could not be applied retroactively to policies implemented many decades earlier, saying that modern ethics cannot be applied to historical laws.

During the time when Canada sought to restrict immigration from China several other countries had similar policies toward Chinese immigration. These included New Zealand, Australia, and the United States. In 2002, Prime Minister Helen Clark of New Zealand apologized to New Zealanders of Chinese origin for the poll tax there; the apology was accompanied by a fund to restore and maintain the Chinese heritage in New Zealand. No such initiative has been made in the United States, Canada, or Australia.

There is disagreement among Chinese Canadians concerning what should be sought in the aftermath of these wrongs.[17] The precedent of Japanese Canadians is often cited. However, it is generally recognized that there are relevant differences between the cases. The Japanese Canadians were citizens, often citizens born in Canada, who were wronged by their own government. The Chinese, by contrast, were noncitizens who sought to enter Canada to work and improve their economic prospects. There are few surviving Chinese-Canadian persons who paid the tax, and some argue that those who came to Canada were privileged compared to other Chinese persons at the time—even granting that they did have to pay the head tax.

In November 2005, in the wake of negotiations with the National Congress of Chinese Canadians, the Canadian government (under Liberal Paul Martin) agreed to acknowledge the injustice of the head tax and to pay $12.5 million to a foundation. The funds were to be provided for acknowledgment, commemoration, and education programs. They were not to be accompanied by an apology or by redress in the form of compensation payments directly to victims or their descendants. There was considerable controversy over this agreement in the Chinese Canadian community. The Ontario Coalition of Head Tax Payers and Families, representing 4,000 direct and secondary victims, questioned why it was not included in negotiations. In addition, the coalition was unhappy with the offer. It sought apology and compensation for affected individuals and announced an intention to sue the government in order to stop the deal, saying that every Chinese Canadian who paid the head tax and suffered decades of discrimination deserved a chance to be heard.[18] In the spring of 2006, the Conservative government, under Stephen Harper, apologized for the head tax.

(c) Ukrainian Canadians

During the First World War, the Canadian government established internment and work camps under the War Measures Act of 1914. Some 8,579 persons labeled as "enemy aliens" were sent to these camps. Of these people, over five thousand were Ukrainians.[19] Another some eighty thousand persons had to register during the First World War as enemy aliens; the result was the loss of their civil rights. Of these, again, many were Ukrainian. Most detainees were recent immigrants who held Austrian passports and were, as a result, declared aliens of enemy nationality. Although most were men between the ages twenty-eight and thirty-five, there were also women and children. Conditions were quite harsh and by 1920, some 107 persons in the camps had died. These practices resulted from a widespread suspicion that relatively recent immigrants from parts of the Austro-Hungarian Empire would be loyal to their home countries during the war and would thus endanger the Canadian state. Bigotry, exaggerated patriotism, and the desire for cheap labor were also factors underlying the policy. There were some twenty-four internment camps, many of these being in Alberta and British Columbia. In fact, tourist resources in the area of Banff National Park were, in part, developed by the labor of Ukrainian Canadian detainees.[20]

Some members of the Ukrainian Canadian community sought redress for these actions. On August 24, 2005, Prime Minister Paul Martin acknowledged that the internment and stripping of civil rights during the First World War had been wrong, calling it a dark chapter in Canadian history. He signed an agreement providing $2.5 million to Ukrainian Canadian community leaders for markers, plaques, and educational materials to *acknowledge* that these policies and actions were wrong and never should have happened. When the acknowledgment was offered, there was only one survivor. This woman, Mary Marko, had been sent to an internment camp with her family at the age of six and was ninety-seven years old in 2005.[21] There was no explicit apology; nor was there compensation for families of those who had been sent to internment camps. However, leaders in the Ukrainian Canadian community said they were satisfied with the acknowledgment that the internment policies had been harmful and wrong.

(d) Doukhobor Canadians

The Doukhobors, or Spirit Wrestlers, were a pacifist sect experiencing considerable persecution in Russia in the late nineteenth century because of their unwillingness to join the army. Count Tolstoy and the Quakers shared concern for their fate and Tolstoy assisted in financing the relocation of some 8,000 of their members to Canada in 1899. The group arrived under the leadership of Peter Verigin. At this time, the Canadian government felt a need to receive immigrants to populate the western provinces. The coming of the Doukhobors was the largest single migration in Canadian history. The Doukhobor people were promised that they could live in Canada according to their beliefs, which included pacifism, a communal lifestyle, and communal ownership of property. The group first settled in Saskatchewan, where it prospered.

In 1905, Prime Minister Borden passed legislation requiring that land be privately owned. Because their antimaterialistic worldview made them resistant to private ownership, some 5,000 Doukhobors lost their land under this legislation. They were profoundly frustrated by this situation. The conflict between the Doukhobors and Canadian authorities was exacerbated by their unwillingness to swear allegiance to the Crown, a stance based on their fear of being pressed into military service.[22]

In response to these conflicts, many prairie Doukhobors set their animals free and set off on a pilgrimage moving west. The Sons of Freedom, or Freedomites, arrived in the Kootenay Valley of British Columbia around 1910. Once there, they continued to hold radically antimaterialistic views. In fact, their settlement and initiatives comprised the largest experiment in communal living ever attempted in North America. Two of their sayings were "Sons of Freedom cannot be the slaves of corruption" and "the welfare of the world is not worth the life of one child." In the Kootenay region, there came to be some 6,000 Doukhobor Freedomites, who initially fared well. Free from military service, they actually prospered during the First World War. This fact, however, inspired resentment on the part of the larger population—especially among war veterans. Near the end of the war, some people suspected the Doukhobor Freedomites of being Russian spies.

Conflicts between the Sons of Freedom Doukhobors and Canadian authorities were still intense when their leader, Peter Vasilivich Verigin (also called Peter the Lordly), died in a mysterious train explosion in 1924.[23] His son (Peter Petrovich Verigin) took over the leadership of the Sons of Freedom. This man died in 1939 and was, in turn, succeeded by his grandson John J. Verigin.

By the 1950s, conflicts between the Sons of Freedom Doukhobors and the Canadian government and society had become more intense. A major issue was the unwillingness of Sons of Freedom men and women to have their children educated in public schools. Among the reasons for their resistance were fear that the schools prepared people for military service, suspicions of a procapitalist and antiworker bias in schools, and fear of inculcation of nationalist attitudes that would undermine Doukhobors teachings about the brotherhood of all human beings.[24] Many of the Sons of Freedom knew little English and were unwilling to integrate into the broader Canadian society. Some staged nude protests, and violent activists set fire to homes and government buildings as an expression of radical antimaterialism. Burnings and nude protests were meant to emphasize the worthlessness of material goods.

Between 1920 and 1960, there were hundreds of arrests of Doukhobors for public nudity and arson. Antiproperty violence was, in effect, a form of religious terrorism, and the hundreds of people jailed for committing such acts were regarded as martyrs by their fellow religionists. In 1953, the Canadian government decreed that all Canadian children should be in school. As a result of the conflict over schooling, some 170 children of Sons of Freedom Doukhobors were hunted down, arrested, and forcibly placed in a residential school in New Denver, British Columbia. Although some claimed otherwise, there is evidence that these children were not well educated in the school, where they were subjected to physical and psychological mistreatment and permitted to see their families only rarely. Visits took place across fences, children were strapped for speaking Russian, and the treatment was generally poor. These children were released in 1959.

A book by Simma Holt, *Terror in the Name of God*, emphasized the violent nature of Freedomite protest. This book categorized the Sons of Freedom as insane and fanatical terrorists and supported the removal of children from their parents.[25]

Holt cited estimates of 259 bombings and burnings in 1962 alone, with the cost to taxpayers being nearly $3 million. She noted that responding to Freedomite protests had put considerable strain on Royal Canadian Mounted Police forces in the Kootenay area.[26] The conflict between the Sons of Freedom and the Canadian people and state quieted down later in the sixties, due apparently to a moderating of views on both sides as well as mediation undertaken by the Quakers.[27] The Doukhobors were given the right to vote, their marriages were legalized, and they recovered most of the land lost in the period between 1905 and 1910. In addition, they reluctantly agreed to educate their children in public schools.

An important aftermath of this conflict is the damage that was done to the children who were removed. Their situation was investigated by the ombudsman for the province of British Columbia, whose 1999 report found that their childhood suffering had resulted in many of them leading isolated and unhappy lives as adults. This report helped to inspire an expression of *regret* from the attorney general of British Columbia, Geoffrey Plant, in October 2004.[28] A class action lawsuit has been launched on behalf of some of the children, who are seeking a public apology and compensatory funds to support counseling.

NOTES

1. A description of the approach is provided in "Acknowledging Our Past to Build Our Future: Agreement-in-Principle between the Government of Canada and the Italian Canadian Community" Multiculturalism Canada, November 12, 2005, http://www.canadianheritage.ge .ca/progs/multi/pubs/ital/index_e.cfm (accessed November 30, 2005).

2. J. R. Miller, *Shinwauk's Vision: A History of Native Residential Schools* (Toronto: University of Toronto Press, 1997).

3. J. R. Miller, "Residential Schools," presentation at the University of Winnipeg conference Taking Wrongs Seriously, Winnipeg, Manitoba (March 11, 2005).

4. Miller, *Shinwauk's Vision*, p. 257.

5. See chapter 4.

6. Joyce Carlson and Teresa Altiman, *Dancing the Dream: The First Nations and the Church in Partnership* (Toronto: Anglican Book Center, 1995).

7. Pope John Paul II, *"Tertio Millenio Adventiente,"* http://www.vatican.va/hdy_father (accessed September 24, 2005).

8. Royal Commission on Aboriginal People, *Report of the Royal Commission on Aboriginal People* (Ottawa: Royal Commission on Aboriginal People, 1996).

9. J. R. Miller (in "Residential Schools") estimated that there are some ninety thousand survivors of residential schools in Canada.

10. For further details, see chapter 9.

11. CBC News, November 28, 2005. See chapter 9 for further comments.

12. These matters are by no means clear, and commentators would differ. There are many relevant discussions. See, for example, David Taras and Beverly Rasporich, eds., *A Passion for Identity: An Introduction to Canadian Studies*, 3rd ed. (Scarborough, ON: ITP Nelson, 1997), part B.

13. Michaelle Jean, installation speech (September 27, 2005), http://www.gg.ca/media/doc.asp?lang=e&DocID-4574 (accessed October 3, 2005).

14. Discussed in detail in chapter 3.

15. A relevant source is Maryka Omatsu, *Bittersweet Passage: Redress and the Japanese Canadian Experience* (Toronto: Between the Lines, 1992).

16. Vivienne Poy, "The Chinese Head Tax Redress Controversy," lecture at the Koffer Institute for Pharmacy Management, University of Toronto (November 25, 2003), http://www.sen.parl.gc.ca/vpox/english/Special_Interests/speeches/UofT_251103.htm. (accessed May 10, 2005).

17. Representative arguments are presented in Catherine Lu, "Delivering the Goods and the Good: Repairing Moral Wrongs," in *Calling Power to Account: Law, Reparations and the Chinese Canadian Head Tax*, ed. David Dyzenhaus and May Moran (Toronto: University of Toronto Press, 2005), pp. 147–64.

18. CBC News, November 18, 2005.

19. Marina Jimenez and Dawn Walton, "The Last Survivor Finds Peace," *Toronto Globe and Mail*, August 26, 2005.

20. Lubomyr Y. Luciuk, *Righting an Injustice: The Debate over Redress for Canada's First National Internment Operation* (Toronto: Justinian, 1994). This subject was also documented in a film called *Freedom Had a Price* (1994), which was produced and directed by Yurij Lohony under the auspices of the Canadian National Film Board.

21. Campbell Clark, "PM Reaches out to Ukrainians," *Toronto Globe and Mail*, August 25, 2005.

22. Information on the Doukhobors may be found in George Woodcock and Ivan Avakumovic, *The Doukhobors* (Toronto: Oxford University Press, 1968); Margaret Hill, "The Detention of Freedomite Children, 1953–59," *Canadian Ethnic Studies* 18 no. 3 (1986): 47–60; F. Henry Johnson, "The Doukhobors of British Columbia: The History of a Sectarian Problem in Education," *Queen's Quarterly* 70, no. 4 (1967); J. C. Yerbury, "The 'Sons of Freedom': Doukhobors and the Canadian State," *Canadian Ethnic Studies* 16, no. 2 (1984): 47–70; and British Columbia, Office of the Ombudsmen, *Righting the Wrong: A Progress Report*, public report 43, March 2002. Regarding the relationship between Quakers and Doukhobors, some information may be found in Joan Lowe, "Quakers and Doukhobors: Common Ground and Crossing Paths," American Friends Service Committee, http://www.afsc.org/about/hist/2002/doukhobor.htm on May 11, 2005 (accessed May 11, 2005).

23. See Hill, "The Detention of Freedomite Children, 1953–1959"; Johnson, "The Doukhobors of British Columbia: The History of a Sectarian Problem in Education"; and British Columbia, Office of the Ombudsmen, *Righting the Wrong*.

24. William Janzen, *Limits on Liberty: The Experience of Mennonite, Hutterite, and Doukhobor Communities in Canada* (Toronto: University of Toronto Press, 1990), chapter 6.

25. Simma Holt, *Terror in the Name of God: The Story of the Sons of Freedom Doukhobors* (Toronto: McClelland and Stewart, 1964).

26. Ibid., p. 8.

27. I have been unable to find details as to how this religious terrorism was brought to an end. The question strikes me as interesting and potentially relevant to other religiously motivated terrorism.

28. Note that this was a statement of *regret*, not an *apology*.

Appendix 3, East Timor

E ast Timor occupies the eastern half of a small island some four hundred miles northeast of Australia. The island has a mountainous center and swamps and plains near the coast. The climate is hot and humid. The population is primarily Christian, with some practicing animism. A Portuguese colony for some four hundred fifty years, the country has four official languages: Portuguese, Tetum, Indonesian, and English; in addition, there are sixteen local languages. Under the Portuguese colonial rule, from the late sixteenth century until 1974, one could hardly say that conditions were good; however, there was some degree of freedom due to an underlying attitude of benign neglect. East Timor is an extremely poor country, and one with few economically viable activities although there is hope of developing agriculture, fishing, and tourism. In addition, there is some potential for revenues from offshore oil and gas drilling. Presently, unemployment and poverty are substantial problems. The country is small; in 2005, its population was estimated by the United Nations to be 857,000.

In 1974, there was a change of regime in Portugal, which withdrew from all its colonial territory. This meant that East Timor became self-governing suddenly and with little preparation. Within East Timor, there was a struggle for power between various factions. With the unsettled situation as a pretext, Indonesia invaded East Timor, using force to subdue the guerrilla groups and the people who resented its presence. Its rule was repressive and was resented. It is estimated that some two hundred fifty thousand people died under the Indonesian regime.[1] With only a few exceptions, abuses were ignored by the international community.

In 1999, the Indonesian government agreed to allow the East Timorese people to have a referendum to choose between independence and what was called "local autonomy." (In the latter arrangement, the territory would remain part of Indonesia.) The referendum indicated overwhelming support—in the area of 80 percent—for independence. At this point, militias opposing independence went on a rampage of looting, murdering, raping, burning, and destroying buildings and resources. Up to

233

one thousand five hundred civilians were killed by marauding Indonesian soldiers and local militias and some 70 percent of the infrastructure of East Timor was destroyed under a "scorched earth policy." During this period, two hundred thousand people left East Timor and went to West Timor, which remained a part of Indonesia. An international peacekeeping force under the United Nations was sent to halt the mayhem. The peacekeeping mission was followed by a UN mission to assist with the rebuilding of the country. Called UNMISET, it was regarded as a substantial success. UNMISET wound up its activities in May 2005.

A constituent assembly set up under the UN mission provides for a parliamentary system of government with a largely ceremonial president. The parliament has eighty-eight members and is dominated by the former resistance movement, Fretilin. The president is Xanana Gusmao, who was chosen as the first head of state in elections in April 2002.

Given neglect under the Portuguese, hardship and repression under Indonesia, and violence and destruction in the aftermath of the 1999 referendum, East Timor has scarce resources with which to rebuild and develop. There are still some raids by militias across the border with West Timor. As a small country, East Timor wishes to receive back the refugees who fled to the west. It established a truth commission called the Commission for Reception, Truth and Reconciliation in East Timor. That commission was to have a truth-seeking role, hear testimony, report on findings, facilitate community reconciliation, and make recommendations for further action. As the name suggests, one of its major aims was to receive and reintegrate into their original communities those who returned to the country.

East Timor sought to combine goals of justice and reconciliation through its truth commission, community processes, and court procedures. A distinction was made between the most serious crimes, including killing and sexual crimes, and less serious ones such as theft, arson, killing of livestock, destruction of crops, and assault. Persons accused of the less serious crimes were allowed to go through a community process in which they could confess before victims, community members, and elders, and agree on "acts of reconciliation" that they would perform for the victim or community. (These acts could be such things as apologizing, cleaning a church, returning stolen goods, or helping to rebuild the house of a victim). The idea was to seek the truth through perpetrators' admissions, see that perpetrators accepted responsibility for what they had done, and then achieve forgiveness and reacceptance. After completing this process, perpetrators would be received back into the community. The process was understood as providing a kind of accountability, acceptance of responsibility, and, in that sense, justice, while, at the same time, providing for reintegration and reconciliation. It was not understood as amounting to *amnesty* for perpetrators; they were held accountable and had to acknowledge what they had done. The community process was not intended to provide for the most serious crimes; for those, court proceedings were deemed to be appropriate.[2]

Fausto Belo Ximenes, who has studied the community processes in East Timor, has argued that these processes effectively supported the reception and reintegration of persons who had left their communities. In addition, in 1999, the proceedings facilitated the return of some refugees who had not committed crimes but were afraid to return home, fearing an atmosphere of punishment and revenge. Ximenes has argued that the community proceedings provided information, diminished fear, prevented acts of vengeance, and encouraged participation, face-to-face dialogue, and empathy based on the sharing of suffering. Given the overloading of the court system, these proceedings were especially important as a complement to the regular justice system.

Accountability under the courts was a complex matter, particularly since both East Timor and Indonesia were involved. In the 1999 violence, court buildings were destroyed, and there was an almost complete judicial void, since nearly all qualified judicial personnel had fled the country. In late 1999, the UN Transitional Administration in East Timor created a Serious Crimes Investigation Unit (SCIU) to provide for the investigation and prosecution of cases in front of two Special Panels for Serious Crimes in the Dili District Court. The SCIU was later placed under the authority of East Timor's prosecutor general. The SCIU has responsibility for preparing indictments against persons responsible for crimes against humanity and other serious crimes committed in East Timor in 1999, and has exclusive jurisdiction over murders and sexual offenses committed between January 1, 1999 and October 25, 1999. It also has jurisdiction over crimes of genocide, torture, war crimes and crimes against humanity committed before 1999. The two panels consist of three judges each, with two being international and one national. There is also a mixed panel as part of the appeals court system. The prosecution is staffed completely by international prosecutors, funded by the UN, and managed by an international professional, who has the title of deputy general prosecutor; he reports to East Timor's general prosecutor.[3] Under the auspices of the SCIU, some lower-ranking members of the East Timorese militia have been successfully prosecuted.

However, there is an important anomaly: the Indonesians, who led and encouraged the 1999 violence, remain at large in Indonesia. Attempts to extradite these persons have been unsuccessful. As a result, the Special Panels in East Timor seem to carry out only "small fry" prosecutions, a form of selectivity that has inspired cynicism and lack of confidence. Legal personnel, funds, and resources for translation into four official languages and multiple local dialects have not been adequate. In addition, given that East Timor is a small and vulnerable country bordering on a far larger neighbor that must be accommodated, its situation works against pressing too vigorously for extradition and prosecution of suspected human rights abusers. Commentators on the criminal processes within East Timor have noted many difficulties and setbacks, but have generally commended the efforts made under the circumstances.

> Considering all the factors that have hindered the justice process in East Timor, it is highly commendable that the UN prosecutors and judges have managed to perform as effectively as they have. By formulating and issuing up to 400 indictments the prosecutors have contributed significantly to establishing the truth and historical background of the human rights crimes. The judgments of the Special Panels will

remain an important and objective source for judges, prosecutors and historians in East Timor and around the world.[4]

Between 2000 and 2005, a total of 440 persons were indicted by the Special Panels. Some eighty-seven defendants were tried, of which eighty-four were convicted. However, of the 440 indicted persons, 339 (nearly three quarters) were outside the jurisdiction.[5]

The Indonesian government had promised to hold its own military personnel responsible. Indeed, an ad hoc Human Rights Court was established for that purpose in Jakarta. But the results of these proceedings were slim indeed. Only eighteen persons were brought to court, and of these only six were convicted. One spent just a few weeks in prison before the Supreme Court overturned his sentence, and several others had their sentences overturned or drastically reduced. Some of the most prominent suspects were never indicted in the Indonesian court at all. In addition, its jurisdiction was limited to the time frame of the referendum period. It did not extend to the period of occupation from 1974 to 1999, during which many serious violations were committed.[6] One key suspect, General Wiranto, who was the Indonesian minister of defense at the time of the 1999 atrocities, was actually a top contender for the presidency of Indonesia in the electoral campaign of 2004.

Disappointment with the processes in Indonesia led the UN Secretary-General to form an independent commission of experts to review the prosecution of crimes of serious human rights violations in East Timor. This commission was resisted both by Indonesia and East Timor. (In the latter case, the resistance was probably due to the vulnerable small country's efforts to make a good relationship with its neighbor a higher priority than the prosecution of human rights violators.) Instead, a Timorese-Indonesian Truth and Friendship Commission was established on December 21, 2004 to look into referendum-related violence, to name perpetrators, and to encourage them to apologize. On its founding, Jose Ramos-Horta, the foreign minister for East Timor, expressed the hope that the work of this commission would close the door on this chapter of the past, resolving once and for all the work of 1999. The proposal was, however, met with skepticism by observers concerned for international law and human rights. Their concern was the result of the fact that the Truth and Friendship Commission would have no mandate to investigate any crimes committed during the Indonesian occupation, its processes would not lead to prosecution, it would provide for amnesty for some offenders who revealed the truth, and it sought rehabilitation of human rights violators, apparently in cases when such persons would not have undergone any trial.[7]

Human rights analysts and activists generally opposed the idea of a Truth and Friendship Commission. They urged some form of international commission under which the most serious violators would be prosecuted. They argued against impunity for persons suspected of having committed grave offenses such as crimes of war and crimes against humanity, saying that it is "politically unwise to close the door to the right of victims under the assumption that little can be done currently" and stating categorically that *"only judicial mechanisms best fulfill victims' desire and right to see justice done."*[8] On this view, certain serious violations of international law such as genocide, crimes against humanity, and war crimes should never go unpunished. If there was insufficient resolve to prosecute perpetrators in Indonesia and East Timor, the international community should fill that gap. It was therefore argued that the UN should continue its efforts and extend further support for criminal prosecutions in connection with the Indonesian role in East Timor. It was suggested by some that a possibility would be to restructure the Special Panels for Serious Crimes along the model of the Special Court for Sierra Leone.[9] It was presumed that an international, independent institution would be needed to ensure that the right sorts of cases could be brought to trial under the right sorts of conditions, which would be difficult to realize either in East Timor or in Indonesia.

In June 2005, the UN Commission of Experts submitted its report to the Secretary-General. It found the Indonesian prosecutions manifestly weak, saying that "the work of the prosecutors was inadequate, verdicts were inconsistent, and perpetrators were not held accountable." It called on Indonesia to reopen cases and consider trying General Wiranto. The Commission of Experts expressed serious reservations about the Truth and Friendship Commission, arguing that legal justice was profoundly important.[10]

East Timor's president, Xanana Gusmao, disagreed with many international commentators with regard to the relative priorities of reconciliation, on the one hand, and legal justice in the form of prosecutions, on the other. In interviews, he called for healing the wounds of the occupation and referendum period so as to look to the future. He explained that one reason for this view was that his own group, Fretilin, which had begun as a Marxist group, had also committed wrongs. Gusmao urged reconciliation as distinct from revenge and wanted to bury hatred and make reconciliation a priority over justice. He urged the reintegration both of former freedom fighters and of persons who served in the Indonesian militia and police—and forgiveness even of persons who committed serious crimes.[11] Gusmao has also said that East Timor needs good relations with its large neighbor, that it is an independent country, and that the international community should not try to force this small and young nation to pursue a criminal justice approach. He pointed out that prosecuting lawyers paid by the United Nations were receiving a lot of money; in fact, their salaries were higher than his presidential salary. Resources spent on prosecuting crimes could, in his view, be put to a better use. Gusmao felt that Indonesia faced its own challenges and would not invade again. He emphasized his stance of mutuality, saying that his own side had committed crimes before 1975 and that punishing themselves would threaten their existence as a community.[12]

On this issue, East Timor's foreign minister, Jose Ramos-Horta (a Nobel Peace Prize winner in 1996), also expressed skepticism about full trials, though for somewhat different reasons. He believed that the UN Security Council would not make criminal trials of Indonesian military figures a high enough priority to sponsor them under its auspices and that if it did so, it would not pay for them. Although international human rights advocates called for a war crimes tribunal if Indonesia did not hold credible trials, there was a general feeling that prospects for an international tribunal were not promising. It would be costly; prospects for extradition were poor; and the costs paid would yield few economic benefits either to East Timor or to Indonesia itself.[13]

The situation in East Timor provides a vivid illustration of a context in which reconciliation and (penal) justice present themselves as contending values. We can reflect on this problem at four levels.

(a) At the *community* level, given the facilitation of truth commission staff and provisions for confession, apology, restitution, and forgiveness, the dilemma seems to be largely resolved. Early in the truth commission process, one could find quoted comments from people in East Timor who said they were willing to lure back refugees with promises of amnesty and forgiveness and then subject them to criminal processes. And, indeed, some in refugee camps in West Timor have feared to return due to reports of violence and vengeance circulated by pro-Indonesian militias.[14] Yet there is evidence that community processes are working to diminish the conflict between (retributive) justice and reconciliation. These processes apply to lesser offenders and not to leaders or persons charged with committing serious crimes of murder and sexual violence.

(b) At the *national* level, many suspected of serious crimes have been indicted, prosecuted, and sentenced, and are serving time. At that level, we could say that reconciliation has not been given priority over justice, or at least that it was not given that priority during the period from 2000 to 2005. The goal was to reject impunity for these crimes and, with international assistance, serious efforts were made. But the fact that those bearing the most serious responsibility for the crimes—leaders and instigators—were in Indonesia and were not taken seriously by courts there made it seem as though Dili courts were dealing only with the "small fry" cases. The effort to end impunity was not credible because, to a substantial extent, impunity continued to exist—at least for the "big fry."

(c) At the *binational* level, we find Indonesia and East Timor opting for a kind of truth commission process that would apparently avoid prosecutions and, instead, adopt a kind of amnesty orientation. We could say, then, that at this level, reconciliation is being valued over (penal) justice. However, in the case of East Timor, which is a small and vulnerable country in need of positive relations with a large and powerful neighbor, one might suspect a certain lack of free choice in opting for the "truth and friendship" approach.

(d) At the *international* level, we find nongovernmental organizations such as Human Rights Watch, Amnesty International, and the Commission of

Experts appointed by the United Nations pushing for trials of Indonesian leaders and rejecting the idea of a "truth and friendship" commission. At this level, there is a strong tendency to value the trial and punishment of perpetrators more highly than reconciliation and improved relationships between East Timor and Indonesia. So justice (construed in this sense) is given priority over reconciliation. This priority may be more rhetorical than practical, however. The chance of the concerned international groups actually funding long and expensive trials, given the reluctance of Indonesia, is small.

In a context where the involved parties would prefer to pursue reconciliation through a process other than legal trials, it is questionable whether the international community should press for prosecutions. When the countries in question have limited resources and when one of them is highly vulnerable, such pressure seems unwise. At the very least, it seems fair to say that *if*, in the interests of "ending impunity," establishing deterrents, and cementing the rule of law, the international community embarks on a serious campaign of systematically prosecuting war crimes and crimes against humanity, then the United Nations, along with donor countries and organizations, should staff and fund the process.

In the spring of 2006, violence erupted in East Timor and approximately one hundrd thousand civilians fled their homes. An important contributing cause was the dismissal of some six hundred servicemen. Violence between pro-government and pro-rebel forces had increased to the point of street antagonism. Soldiers from Australia, New Zealand, Malaysia, and Portugal arrived at the government's request. In this context, one could hardly claim that reconciliation processes in East Timor had been effective.

NOTES

1. Leonie von Braun and Monika Schlicher, "Rethinking Justice for East Timor: Position Paper on the Reform of the International Justice Process in East Timor and Indonesia," Watch Indonesia! http://home.snafu.de/watchin/Rethinking-Justice.htm (accessed February 2005).

2. For an account of community justice in East Timor, see Fausto Belo Ximenes, "The Unique Contribution of the Community-Based Reconciliation Process in East Timor," paper prepared under the Transitional Justice Fellowship Programme, cohosted by the International Center for Transitional Justice and the Institute for Justice and Reconciliation, http://www.easttimor-reconciliation.org/jsmpReport-prk-summary.html (accessed August 2005).

3. Von Braun and Schlicher, "Rethinking Justice."

4. Ibid., p. 6.

5. Tiago A. Sarmento, "The Future of Serious Crimes: Cooperating with Timor Leste: Ideas for Good Development Practice," paper presented under the auspices of the Judicial System Monitoring Programme, Victoria University, Melbourne, Australia (June 16–18, 2005).

6. Ibid. The International Center for Transitional Justice published a report in August

2003 called "Intended to Fail," in which it argued that Indonesia never intended to fulfill its promise of holding perpetrators accountable for the violence during the 1999 referendum in East Timor.

    7. Sarmento, "The Future of Serious Crimes."

    8. Ibid., p. 6.

    9. Described in chapter 8 and in appendix 7, Sierra Leone.

    10. International Center for Transitional Justice press release, June 27, 2005.

    11. Xanana Gusmao, interview by Andre Vitchek, Znet News, April 12, 2002, http://www.zmag.org/content/Interviews/vltcheck_eastimor.cfm (accessed August 2005).

    12. Xanana Gusmao has frequently been interviewed about his stance on justice and reconciliation. It is clear that he values and seeks both; however, he generally prefers reconciliation over justice if justice is interpreted as the trial and punishment of perpetrators. Relevant comments may be found in Margo Cohen, "East Timor: A Lot to Forgive," March 28, 2000, http://www.easttimor-reconciliation.org/feer.htm (accessed August 15, 2005); Allene Masters, "H. E. Xanana Gusmao: October 3, 2002," http://www.usindo.org/Briefs/h.h.%Xanana%20 Gusmao.htm (accessed August 15, 2005); and Xanana Gusmao, "A Leader's Dream for Peace and Prosperity," interview by Peter Mares, Australian Broadcasting Corporation, October 10, 2001, http://www.etan.org/et2001c/october/07-13/10xanana.htm (accessed August 15, 2005).

    13. Ellen Nakashina, "Indonesia Attempts to Avert Tribunal to Probe East Timor," *Washington Post*, July 16, 2005.

    14. Ximenes, "The Unique Contribution."

Appendix 4, Northern Ireland

In the sixteenth century, the British began to subjugate Ireland. Large numbers of Scottish Protestants came to the north to the so-called plantation of Ulster and were instrumental in consolidating British rule. Understandably, there was a rise of Irish nationalism in response. Nationalism among indigenous Irish Catholics inspired, in turn, the rise of a kind of Protestant nationalism in Ulster. Protestants who had settled in Ireland, called Unionists or Loyalists, favored the union of Ireland and Britain. They feared that any independent rule in Ireland would threaten their cultural and religious identity as well as their economic interests. Current divisions between Catholic Republicans and Protestant Loyalists involve not only religious differences but also differences in cultural aspirations and economic circumstances. The divide between these groups is sectarian, but the term "sectarian" has to be understood, in this context, as involving more than differences about theology and religious tradition.[1]

By the late nineteenth century, there was already a deep conflict between Unionists and Republicans—Catholic Irish, who favored Irish independence. In 1914, the Ulster Volunteer Force (UVF) was formed with the goal of defeating the Irish home rule that was favored by Republicans. The UVF vowed to use military force if necessary. There were one hundred thousand members of this group. At the same time, the Irish volunteers of the Irish Republican Army formed; this group dedicated itself to the achievement of Catholic nationalist goals, by violent means if necessary.[2] Easter 1916 marked a violent uprising by the IRA. This uprising failed, but the imposition of martial law on Ireland did much to inspire the nationalist cause. Sinn Fein ("ourselves alone") was founded to pursue republican nationalist goals by political means.

After years of Republican (Catholic) protest, by 1919 the British were prepared to withdraw from Ireland. However, Protestants, who were a relatively prosperous and well-positioned ruling class, opposed their withdrawal. There came to be an intense conflict between Catholics, who opposed British rule in Ireland, and Protestants, who favored it. This conflict led to the partitioning of Ireland, which was intended to be a compromise solution to the problems of the sectarian divide and incompatible political goals. The southern parts of Ireland become an independent state on the basis of the Anglo-Irish Treaty, signed in December 1921. In 1922, the Irish Free State came into existence. It became a republic in 1932. The northern provinces remained British and became known as "Northern Ireland" or "Ulster." The two political entities, south and north, were divided by religion, culture, and different interpretations of both the history of Ireland and the British role in its history.

This partition of the island of Ireland left a sectarian division within Northern Ireland because in that territory there remained a substantial Catholic minority. In the six counties that constituted Ulster, there were 820,000 Protestants and 430,000 Catholics.[3] Although Protestants constituted a majority of the population in the area, it was not a large majority.

The 1920 Government of Ireland Act provided for a separate northern Irish government to rule the six counties in the North. Given the centuries of disputes between Protestants and Catholics, the partition seemed sensible and even, to many, inevitable. However, the partition set the stage for conflicts still not resolved. The role of Britain was, and was understood to be, maintaining the division of Ireland and upholding the position of the Unionists. The Catholic population of Ulster was not happy with the settlement. Furthermore, even the Protestants, whose interests were supposedly protected by this arrangement, did not feel secure; they tended to regard the Catholic population as an enemy within. In 1954, the IRA adopted the official policy of seeking to drive the British out of Northern Ireland.

There were some relatively tranquil years in Northern Ireland between the mid 1920s and the late 1960s. Economic conditions, which had been poor, especially for Catholics, began to improve in the 1950s. The IRA, with its policies of violent opposition to Britain and the Ulster government, seemed, for some years, to have relatively little support from the Catholic population of the North. Observers might have been excused for concluding that the partition of Ireland had provided a successful solution to conflicts between Protestants and Catholics. Nevertheless, there was a deep unresolved problem, given that the territory of Northern Ireland included two very different national and cultural identities with sharply differing political goals. In particular, Protestants and Catholics in Northern Ireland differed on the issue of the role of mainland Britain in that territory.[4]

In the 1960s, a civil rights movement was initiated among Catholics in Northern Ireland. This movement was originally nonviolent, being modeled to some extent on the civil rights movement that had advanced the cause of blacks in the southern United States. Grievances among Catholics in Northern Ireland included discrimination in housing, employment, and education as well as a pronounced lack of political power. At the time, the Northern Irish government, under the leadership of Terence O'Neill, had actually taken steps in the direction of tolerance, reform, and modernization. His initiatives caused some in Unionist groups to believe that he was going too far. They came to fear that changes favoring Catholics would work against them. A particularly intense and influential anti-Catholic leader emerging during this period was the fundamentalist Baptist preacher, Ian Paisley. Paisley preached against the Pope and "the Roman way," inciting Protestant opposition to proposed reforms that would result in improvements in opportunities for Catholics. The Loyalist UVF armed itself in response to Catholic activism and, in 1966, declared war on the IRA, engaging in sectarian killings of IRA militants. Prime Minister O'Neill outlawed the UVF in 1966. At that point, the organization went underground. Although not all Northern Irish Protestants supported the tactics of the UVF, there was a pronounced and fearful anti-Catholicism in this community. "Northern Irish Protestants as a group had one defining quality—the entrenched siege mentality which had developed *vis-à-vis* the Catholics since 1921."[5]

What became known as "the Troubles" in Northern Ireland began with a civil rights march in Londonderry in October 1968. The march was policed by the Royal Ulster Constabulary (Protestant) and a riot squad (also Protestant). Protesters were treated very roughly. Contrary to the intentions of its organizers, this march was not nonviolent. Prime Minister O'Neill announced some reforms and suspended the Londonderry council. This move inspired an angry counterprotest under the leadership of Ian Paisley. In January 1969, the civil rights protestors staged another march, from Belfast to Derry. On that occasion, they were ambushed by a group of Protestants who were assisted by Ulster police. In the same period, IRA violence was occurring in the form of stone throwing and petrol bombing. The Provisional IRA (PIRA), or "Provos," arose as a more intense revival of the IRA movement. This group was dedicated to getting Britain out of Ireland, unifying Ireland (thereby ending the status of Northern Ireland as a separate unit), and establishing a socialist republic in Ireland.[6] The PIRA regarded itself as the legitimate army of the island of Ireland. In 1972, the official IRA signed a cease-fire and, after that time, the name "IRA" came to refer to the PIRA or Provos. The activities of this group came to include bombings, assassinations, kidnappings, extortion, robberies, and punishment beatings.[7]

Prime Minister O'Neill resigned in May 1969 and was replaced by a man less determined to bring reforms. Meanwhile, violence between civil rights protestors and Protestant groups continued. Policing was a major issue, since the police were largely Protestant and were regarded by Catholic civil rights protesters as hostile. The Catholic minority in Northern Ireland continued to have problems with regard to discrimination, lack of political power, and socioeconomic inequalities. The Protestant majority there had a problem too: they feared that changes in the name of reform would eliminate their community. In 1968 and 1969, there was a sharp reaction as people who were accustomed to tradition were confronted by change. As violence continued, the authority and legitimacy of the government came increasingly into question, and it appealed to the British government to uphold its authority. In August 1969, British troops were sent to Ireland to support the contested authority of the government.[8]

Within a short time, British troops themselves were subject to attacks by paramilitary groups on both sides. Originally, the British Army had been understood as a force protective of the Catholic minority, whose nonviolent quest for civil rights had provoked a violent response from Protestants. However, as the conflict developed, the British Army sought to counter violence by the IRA, which opposed connections to Britain and understood itself as pursuing justice for Catholics. The British Army came to seem an enemy of the Catholics of Northern Ireland.

It was initially expected that British troops would be able to calm things down, protect the Catholics, and monitor some sort of peace. However, the IRA and PIRA opposed the presence of the troops, as did Protestant paramilitaries. The British government began to define the problem in Northern Ireland as one of a violently rebellious Catholic minority. The army imposed a curfew and began an extensive campaign of door-to-door searches in Catholic communities. These practices alienated the Catholic population. In addition, suspected violent activists were imprisoned without trial and, in some cases, interrogated brutally. Employing violence against terrorists only increased support for them, resulting in further terrorist activity. Troop levels were increased. On Sunday, January 30, 1972 there was a Civil Rights march in Londonderry. British soldiers opened fire on the crowd and killed thirteen people. This event, known as Bloody Sunday, is still contested. The British army claims that soldiers shot in self-defense, but the coroner at the inquest accused the army of outright murder. The event gave the IRA a massive propaganda victory. As the Troubles continued, the British government announced in March 1972 that Northern Ireland would be ruled directly from Westminster. (This was called Direct Rule.)

Under Direct Rule, there were considerable departures from the rule of law and extensive brutality as the British Army sought to quell terrorism and paramilitary activity, particularly that of the PIRA. The activity of the PIRA in cities diminished as a result of army activity. However, the PIRA moved to rural areas where it still enjoyed power. In addition, the PIRA adopted the policy of taking the battle over Northern Ireland to the mainland, and began bombing campaigns there.

The Troubles in Northern Ireland are sometimes referred to as an intimate conflict. The numbers of fatalities, over thirty years, were in the area of 3,700; some forty thousand people were seriously injured.[9] In absolute terms, these numbers may not seem large, especially when the situation of Northern Ireland is compared to those of other areas such as the Balkans, West Africa, and Rwanda. In those contexts, tens or hundreds of thousands of people have been killed and millions have been subject to compulsory relocation. In fact, during the 1970s, when there was racial violence in some cities in the United States, it was often observed that annual deaths in Detroit exceeded those stemming from the political violence in Northern Ireland. Nevertheless, the numbers of deaths and serious injuries in Northern Ireland was substantial relative to the size of the population of the territory. Northern Ireland had a population of about 1.5 million in 1991 and 1.7 million in 2001.[10]

The civilian population was greatly affected by the political violence. As one response, Betty Williams and Mairead Corrigan, whose sister lost three of her young children as a result of the violence, founded a peace movement. Under the leadership of Williams and Corrigan, some thirty thousand women of Northern Ireland joined the "Peace People," decrying the aggressiveness and violence on the part of boys and men claiming, on both sides of the civic conflict, to be fighting for justice. The Peace People pronounced war to be a senseless evil that could not solve political problems.[11] Although Corrigan and Williams were awarded the Nobel Peace Prize for their efforts in 1976, the movement later lost momentum, appearing to die out.

In the mid-1970s, the PIRA came under new leadership. With Martin McGuinness and Gerry Adams in leadership roles, the PIRA proclaimed its intent to use political methods as well as violence in the struggle over Northern Ireland. Its approach would be to contest both local government and parliamentary seats. If elected, the PIRA candidates would take local seats but refuse to occupy seats in parliament.[12] The British government began to seek out a solution to the greatly vexing problem of Northern Ireland. In the 1990s, under the influence of Prime Minister Tony Blair, negotiations were energetically pursued.

With regard to the suppression of political violence by paramilitaries and terrorists, the practices of the British Army in Northern Ireland turned out to be seriously counterproductive. House-to-house searches uncovered armaments, but alienated those whose houses were searched. Imprisonment, rough interrogation techniques, and other repressive policies similarly alienated the population. When repressive measures managed to squeeze the PIRA agents out of cities, they went elsewhere—to rural areas and mainland Britain—to continue their violence. The British sought to "Ulsterize" the policing, seeking to diminish the controversial role of the British Army and the extensive commitment of troops. However, Catholic communities had little confidence in the Royal Ulster Constabulary or the Ulster Defence Regiment, which were Protestant in identity and affiliation. These groups had no better claim to be unbiased than the British Army itself. There was hope of turning the work over to police; however, those hopes were never realized. The original expectation had been that British troops would be needed only for a few weeks. However, they were involved in Northern Ireland for nearly three decades.[13]

Counterterrorism measures continued to be problematic in the 1980s, with the British Army being accused both of having a "shoot to kill" policy and of conducting secret and provocative operations. The Royal Ulster Constabulary (predominantly Protestant) was accused of corruption and incompetence. Informers or "supergrasses" were used with some success, but this policy caused more internal violence within the PIRA and other paramilitary groups. In 1984, the PIRA launched an attack at a Conservative party conference. Five people were killed and Prime Minister Margaret Thatcher barely escaped death. There were many other attacks, including car bombings, attacks with nail bombs, and an attack in 1991 on Prime Minister John Major at his home at Ten Downing Street, London. By 1996, the British Army had assigned 16,500 troops to Northern Ireland and, in addition, had had to take many counterterrorism measures in mainland Britain.[14]

The apparently intractable challenge for the British government was to repress violent activities, but do so in a way that would not alienate Catholic opinion. In 1976, the policy of imprisoning suspects without trial was ended. At the same time, however, the British government announced that all persons convicted of crimes related to the Troubles would be treated as ordinary criminals. In other words, the category of "political prisoner" would be abolished and acts of political violence would be defined simply as criminal acts. This shift in policy resulted in an extreme response. Political prisoners had been given special status and privileges including, for example, the right to wear their own clothes instead of prison uniforms. When the changes were announced and concessions by the British were deemed too trivial, a wide campaign of protest, including hunger strikes, began. On May 5, 1981, the (Catholic) prisoner Bobby Sands died due to a hunger strike. His death was followed by nine others. Eventually, the British government made further concessions and the hunger strike ended.[15] In the meantime, Bobby Sands had been elected to parliament and had achieved the status of a hero and a martyr. The whole phenomenon amounted to a propaganda victory for the IRA.[16] PIRA leader Gerry Adams was elected in June 1983 as the member of parliament for West Belfast and was received as a guest of Ken Livingstone, the leader of the Greater London Council, shortly thereafter.[17] Despite continuing use of violent means, the IRA was gaining political appeal and power.

Discussions with the government of the Republic of Ireland resulted in the Hillsborough Agreement of 1985, which emphasized the need for reform in the North, required majority approval for any change in the status of the North, and acknowledged that reform would require input from the Republic of Ireland as well. The Republic of Ireland (the South) ratified the European Convention for the Suppression of Terrorism, which meant that there would be a greater degree of cooperation regarding the extradition of accused persons. But this agreement provoked anger and resentment on the part of Unionists in the North. They began to riot to stay within Britain and attacked British security forces. In 1986, there were some 10,200 British soldiers stationed in Northern Ireland.[18] Violence was unremitting between 1985 and 1990.

However, there were more positive trends developing. Sinn Fein was increasingly emphasizing a political approach, and there was increased cooperation between the governments of the Republic of Ireland and Great Britain. Although the PIRA still hoped for a military victory that would drive the British out of Ireland, and had received considerable shipments of arms from Libya, the Catholic people of Northern Ireland were increasingly alienated by its violent approach. Fortunately, some cross-community contacts were developing. In August 1994, the IRA declared a cease-fire, citing as their motivation both war-weariness and their fear that their use of violence was alienating the population. The Loyalist paramilitaries declared a cease-fire in September, announcing that they were terminating military operations. The IRA bombing attack on Canary Wharf in 1996 constituted a major break in this cease-fire, seriously undermining the credibility and trustworthiness of the IRA as an organization resolved to move away from violent methods.

On April 10, 1998, the Good Friday Accord was reached, providing for a cease-fire to be observed by all paramilitary groups and setting out the terms for the nonviolent political mechanisms that were intended to move Northern Ireland into a state of sustainable peace. Within the terms of this agreement, the peace-building process in Northern Ireland was to include *reconciliation*, empowerment through education, the shifting of the sectarian conflict into the political domain, the transfer of power over the future of the territory to its own people, and the engagement of young people and other stakeholders in community relations. On April 11, 1998, the *Times* of London provided a summary of the Good Friday Accord. It provided for the resolution of differences by political means and not by the use of threat of force, noting Northern Ireland's sovereignty and right of self-determination, and stating that the governments of the United Kingdom and Ireland would recognize the will of the Northern Irish people as to their future political affiliation. It stated a commitment to human rights including freedom of political thought, freedom of religion and the expression of religion, the right to choose one's place of residence, and the right of all persons to equal opportunity in all social and economic activity, regardless of class, creed, disability, gender, or ethnicity. Women were stated to have the right to full and equal political participation.

With regard to victims, the Good Friday Accord stated that, for reconciliation, it was essential to acknowledge and address their suffering. The agreement stated a commitment to provisions for the decommissioning of arms held in the hands of paramilitary groups, so that they would be totally disarmed within two years. As for prisoners, there were provisions for the accelerated release of those convicted in connection with the political violence and a commitment to try to facilitate their reintegration into society by providing support prior to and after release, particularly in areas of retraining and employment opportunities. The vast majority of these prisoners were released by the year 2000. (In fact, most had served their terms and had been released prior to the signing of the Good Friday Accord.)

Since the establishment of the Good Friday Accord, violence by paramilitaries has decreased dramatically, although it has not altogether ceased. Many outstanding issues remain, including the status of former prisoners or "ex-combatants," the allocation of resources for victims and survivors, competition between different groups of victims and between victims and survivors; the decommissioning of armaments, and the inability of the parliament of Northern Ireland to function, which led to the British government again ruling the area directly. The number of nongovernmental groups working on community development and reconciliation processes is large, and there are opportunities for generous funding by the European Union, the British government, and expatriate Irish groups.[19] In the aftermath of September 11, 2001, there was an increased and intense repugnance for terrorist methods in many circles, and this affected those IRA affiliates who continued to endorse violent methods, making funding and acceptance outside of Ireland far more difficult.

What is known in Northern Ireland as marching season is a time of stress and sectarian conflict. Even in the aftermath of the Good Friday Accord, demonstrations, jeers, riots, and violence still occur during this season. The biggest day is July 12, which, for Protestants commemorates that victory of the Protestant William of

Orange over the Stuart Catholic King James at the Battle of the Boyne in 1690. Marching routes are a matter of controversy, since tradition calls for members of the Protestant Orange Order to parade triumphantly through predominantly Catholic areas. Police often restrict routes to avoid riots and violent demonstrations, but when they do that, controversies arise due to resentment on the Protestant side.

Between September 9 and September 12, 2005, there was considerable violence in connection with one such restriction. The mayhem and violence at that point seemed to constitute a serious blow to confidence that sustainable peace had really come to Northern Ireland. Some seven hundred Protestant rioters attacked police with petrol bombs and missiles on September 10. In fact, several thousand persons, including children, had participated in riotous demonstrations during several previous days. In various areas of Belfast, men with revolvers halted traffic and rampaging mobs hijacked and set fire to cars, blocked roads, and threw stones at police. Police tried to hold back rioters with water cannons and plaster bullets. Two buses were hijacked, and many were damaged.[20] Officers were shot at, and it was only by good luck that none died. And yet, the ostensible cause for these violent and disturbing disruptions was the rerouting of a relatively small march. The march of junior members of the Protestant Orange Order had been rerouted by less than one hundred meters so as to be moved away from Catholic homes. In addition, a gate in a peace wall between two communities had been welded shut so that it could not be forced. (The march had been delayed three months because controversies about the route could not be resolved.) The Orange Order was held responsible for the riots. The affiliation of the rioters seemed particularly clear, since many wore the Order's orange sashes while attacking police.[21] The radical Loyalist politician Ian Paisley gave a rousing speech saying (approvingly) that this particular parade could provide a spark, kindling a fire that could not be put out.

The deeper causes of this Protestant violence seemed to be a sense by many that Loyalists were losing in the peace process. Many radical Loyalists felt that the police were no longer on their side and that the government was all too ready to place confidence in the IRA, believing that it had decommissioned all its arms and was committed to politics by peaceful means. Loyalist rebels felt that the IRA had won influence by its violence, showing that people would only be heard, in the political process, if they used violence. It is also likely that gangsterism and hooliganism were factors in these events.[22]

In addition to its intimacy—the fact that a substantial proportion of a small population was intensely affected by the political violence in the context of a deeply sectarian history—the conflict in Northern Ireland has other distinctive characteristics. With Britain both party to the conflict and a mediating influence on it, there is a significant outsider role. That role is seen further in the influence of the European Community, both through its legal judgments and through its extensive resources for community development and reconciliation activities. The aftermath of the Good Friday Accord powerfully illustrates issues of reintegration of militants, revealing the spectrum of acts ranging from political violence to ordinary crime, and the policing and prison issues that that spectrum poses. These issues, accompanied by debates about whether former militants are "terrorists," "criminals," "ex-prisoners," "soldiers," or "ex-combatants," have a considerable impact on reconciliation processes. The status of ex-combatants, and even the language used to describe them, is hotly contested. These issues significantly affect opportunities and attitudes. In addition, many victims of the Troubles feel that too many resources have gone to perpetrators.[23]

NOTES

1. An excellent account of sectarianism in Northern Ireland is that of Joseph Liechty and Cecilia Clegg, *Moving Beyond Sectarianism: Religion, Conflict, and Reconciliation in Northern Ireland* (Dublin: Columba, 2001). See also John Magee, ed., *Northern Ireland: Crisis and Conflict* (London: Routledge and Kegan Paul, 1974).

2. Caroline Kennedy-Pipe, *The Origins of the Present Troubles in Northern Ireland* (London: Longman, 1997).

3. Ibid., p. 21.

4. Ibid., p. 30.

5. Ibid., p. 39.

6. Tim P. Coogan, *The IRA: A History* (Boulder, CO: Roberts Rineheart Publishers, 1993).

7. From "Irish Republican Army (IRA), Provisional Irish Republican Army (PIRA), Direct Action against Drugs," http://www.globalsecurity.ort/military/world/para/ira.htm (accessed August 31, 2005).

8. Kennedy-Pipe, *Origins of the Present Troubles*, p. 48.

9. British House of Commons Northern Ireland Affairs Committee, *Ways of Dealing with Northern Ireland's Past: Interim Report—Victims and Survivors*, Tenth Report of Session 2004–05, vol. 1, April 14, 2005, www.parliament.the-stationery-office.co.uk/pa/cm 200405/cmselect/cmniaf/303/303ii.pdf (accessed August 2005).

10. In 1991, the population of Northern Ireland was 1,577,836, according to a census cited in John Darby, *Northern Ireland: Managing the Difference* (London: Minority Rights Group International, 1995). In 2001, it was 1,685,267, according to government statistics provided at www.statistics.gov.uk/census2001/pyramids/pages/152.asp.

11. See Mairead Corrigan Maguire, *The Vision of Peace: Faith and Hope in Northern Ireland* (Ossining, NY: Orbis Books, 1999). The presentation speech for the Nobel Peace Prize can be read at http://nobleprize.org/peace/laureates/1976/press.html.

12. Kennedy-Pipe, *Origins of the Present Troubles*, pp. 85–6.

13. Parallels with the situation in Iraq are striking.

14. Coogan, *The IRA*. Regarding bombs in Britain, see chapter 30.

15. The status of former prisoners and the significance of the political status of their acts remains an important issue in efforts toward reconciliation to this day.

16. Kennedy-Pipe, *Origins of the Present Troubles*, p. 88.

17. Ibid., p. 109.

18. Ibid., pp. 125 and 138.

19. For relevant details, see the discussion about reintegration of former militants in Northern Ireland in chapter 8.

20. Shawn Pogatchnik, "Seven Wounded in Irish Riots," *Globe and Mail* (Toronto), September 10, 2005; "50 Police Officers Injured in Belfast Riots," *Guardian Unlimited* (London), September 12, 2005; Angelique Chrisafis, "Riots Rain on Belfast's Parade," *Guardian Unlimited* (London), September 12, 2005.

21. Angelique Chrisafis, "Riots Rain on Belfast's Parade," *Guardian Unlimited* (London), September 12, 2005, http://www.guardian.co.uk/Northern_Ireland/Story/o,2763 ,1568318,00.html (accessed June 19, 2006).

22. This comment was made in early October 2005.

23. These issues are discussed in chapter 8.

Appendix 5, Peru

Between 1980 and 2000, the Peruvian state was engaged in a bitter war against the Maoist Shining Path guerrilla group. This extraordinarily brutal group was founded by a philosophy professor, Abimael Guzman Rienoso. When the conflict began, the Peruvian state was basically democratic, allowing for free speech and free elections. The Shining Path guerrillas employed extremely violent methods in its attempt to revolutionize the state. The indigenous people of the Andes areas did not submit to this revolutionary group as the group had anticipated they would; their resistance to recruitment brought extreme brutality by the Shining Path in response. State authorities at first failed to understand that few of the Andean people were supporters of the Shining Path. State troops and police commenced violations against these people, whom it assumed were in support of the rebellion. The war ended after the capture of the Shining Path leader and his major supporters; terrorist attacks diminished, but did not cease entirely.

In June 2001, a Truth and Reconciliation Commission was established in Peru and given the tasks of discovering the root causes of political violence between 1980 and 2000. The Peruvian TRC was to assign responsibility for human rights abuses committed during this civil war and, in addition, set forward proposals for prosecutions, reparations, and reforms needed for human rights protection in the future. It was also assigned the task of establishing mechanisms to assure that its recommendations would be acted upon. In the TRC hearings, which sought to dignify and heal victims of the violence, some seventeen thousand testimonies were collected. Hearings were held at many remote locations in the Andes, with the purpose of acknowledging and helping to heal victims of violence. Witnesses were seated with commissioners, listened to without interruption, and treated with respect. There were eight victim hearings, five thematic hearings, seven public assemblies, and fifteen citizen dialogues and meetings.[1]

The Peruvian TRC was unusual in several respects. It was the first Latin American truth commission to incorporate public meetings. It held thematic hearings as well as victim hearings, investigating such topics as antiterrorism legislation and its relation to due legal process; violence against women; the role of the judiciary and churches; and educational practices. In addition, the Peruvian TRC was unique in that it investigated human rights abuses that had been committed under democratically elected governments for much of the conflict. The Peruvian TRC was designed with advice from experts with the International Center for Transitional Justice. The idea was that its work would not stop with the issuance of its report; there was to be a special effort to follow up on recommendations in the areas of reparations and systematic change. The Peruvian TRC had a connection with Peru's national criminal justice system and recommended prosecutions of some key figures. It worked with the International Committee of the Red Cross in a campaign to get more information on the "disappeared." It recommended a comprehensive reparations package that would combine symbolic and material reparations and synthesize individual awards with collective benefits.[2] The suggestion was that the proposed reparations should be financed by the Peruvian state, civil society, and international donors. Reparations were understood in a comprehensive way—as symbolic, as providing material compensation to individuals and collectives, and as having some deterrent effect.[3] The Peruvian TRC was cited as a model and studied for its relevance in other places such as Sierra Leone, East Timor, and Ghana.

In its *Final Report*, released on August 28, 2003, the Peruvian TRC estimated that some sixty-nine thousand people had died or "disappeared" in the twenty-year guerrilla war. Of these deaths, approximately 50 percent were attributed to the Shining Path guerrillas and approximately 30 percent to government security forces. The remainder were unaccounted for or were attributed to smaller groups: the Tupac Amaru guerrillas, local militias, and peasant self-defense units. The Peruvian state had been seriously limited in its ability to guarantee public order and security during the guerrilla war. The report emphasized that the victims of political violence were disproportionately Quechua-speaking Indians of the Andean regions. These people were the poorest and most exploited segment of Peruvian society. Thus, the violence fell unequally on the people of Peru: it was severe among poor and poorly educated peasants living in Andean regions, but not much felt by the rest of the country. Due to the violence in the Andean regions, some four to six hundred thousand villagers fled their homes and were displaced.[4] The Peruvian TRC found that racism and scornful attitudes in Peruvian society allowed many to think that violence against these Indian people was of slight importance.

The Shining Path guerrillas were judged by the commission to have practiced and recommended extreme violence and cruelty. The group had a fundamentalist Maoist ideology, disdained the value of human life and human rights, and advocated a notion of the unfolding of history that led to a violent and disproportionate response from the Peruvian state. The Shining Path movement was said to show a tragic blindness, seeing society as composed not of individuals but only of social classes. It encouraged fanaticism and pursued notions of paying the blood toll, deliberately inducing genocide so as to arrive at a revolutionary "triumph." This supposed achievement was believed to require at least a million deaths. The slaughter was deemed necessary in order to destroy the old state. The fundamentalist communism of this group led it to regard even persons of modest means as class enemies. Moderately successful shopkeepers or barbers, who had just slightly more economic success than others, would be regarded as rich and, therefore, as enemies of the poor. The Peruvian TRC found that the Shining Path, and *especially* its leaders, bore direct responsibility for the commission of crimes against humanity. Crimes against humanity took the form of armed attacks against the civilian population, whether carried out on a grand scale or as specific maneuvers. The Shining Path had started the violence of the twenty-year war; had a bloody strategy; was employing that strategy against a democratic state; used violence to control people and territory; had a terrorist character; and advocated mass killing as an explicit policy. It was clear that the actions and policies of this group amounted to grave violations of the Geneva Conventions.

The TRC found that many young people had been at one stage seduced by propaganda of the Shining Path, which in its initial phases was able to exploit university resources and credibility. (Its leader, Abimael Guzman, was a professor of philosophy at Ayacucho University and used his position to influence vulnerable young people.) Many young people joined the Shining Path movement under pressure from apparently authoritative figures, with no real understanding of what sort of rebellion was being pursued. They were then locked into an abusive and totalitarian group and became victims themselves. This situation provides a vivid illustration of the syndrome in which people can be victimized, become perpetrators as a result of their victimization, and then, as perpetrators, be subject to further victimization.

The Peruvian TRC also found that the Peruvian state was responsible for serious political violence and human rights violations. Three different governments were involved. The first two were democratic, at least in the sense that they had been democratically elected. The third, after the 1992 coup by President Fujimori, was authoritarian. Initially, according to the TRC, the Peruvian state had lacked understanding of the Shining Path movement. The Peruvian military had, in the first years of the conflict, not grasped the gravity of the situation. For example, it had sent marginally competent agents on missions to the affected territories as a means of punishing them and with no real concern for the effect of their activities on the conflict. In seeking—oppressively but ineffectively—to counter the Shining Path, agents of the government (police and army) became alienated from the Andean people. Their authoritarian and repressive practices, which had existed and been resented before the civil war, were only reinforced in this new and difficult situation. In struggling ineptly against the Shining Path, state agents often engaged in cruel practices against the very same people who were being viciously victimized by the rebels, practicing extrajudicial executions, torture, forced disappearances, cruel and inhuman treatment, and extensive sexual violence against women.

After 1985, and especially after the capture of Guzman in 1992, there was better understanding within the government of the Shining Path movement and the nature of indigenous responses to it; there were some improvements in the state's response. Nevertheless, indiscriminate excesses and systematic violations of human rights still occurred. The commission found that the military high command bore the greatest responsibility for these and urged that the Peruvian judiciary pursue prosecutions of some top people. (In this context, some 120 names were provided to the judicial authorities by the commission.) Although the commission found that actions directed against peasant people had become less numerous after 1989, it concluded that later abuses were nevertheless still deliberate. Death squads appeared, and there were allegiances between drug traffickers, the army, and the police. After 1992, the government-sponsored Colina Group was engaged in corruption, blackmail, the persecution of dissenting military officers, and political espionage within the ranks of the armed forces. Guzman was tried under Peru's antiterrorist legislation, found guilty after a ten-day trial, and sentenced to life in prison.

By this time, attacks had diminished—though there was a bomb that exploded on a street in Lima in 1992, killing more than forty people. Despite the lessening of violence, there was not much improvement in terms of the material condition of indigenous people.

In 2003, Peru's antiterrorism legislation was struck down by its Constitutional Court on the grounds that both life imprisonment and the use of military courts to try civilians were unconstitutional. This legal judgment necessitated retrials of all persons tried between 1992 and 1997 by the so-called faceless judges (those judges whose identities were kept secret for their protection). This development necessitated the retrial of Shining Path leader Abimael Guzman.[5] His second trial, held in a special bulletproof room, had to be suspended after chaotic courtroom scenes in November 2004. Guzman had cleaned himself up for this trial, and no longer gave the impression of being a raving fanatic. His grey hair was neatly cut and combed and he appeared wearing thick-rimmed tinted glasses and looking like the philosophy professor he had once been. He and his long-term partner Elena Iparraguirre showed no repentance for their murderous campaigns, shouting slogans such as "Glory to Marxism, Leninism, Maoism" and "Long live the Peruvian People." If this trial is able to proceed to the point of conviction, Guzman will be able to appeal its ruling to the Inter-American Court of Human Rights. One expectation was that, in that context, Guzman would be able to contest the definition of "terrorism."[6]

The Peruvian TRC was subject to serious criticism within Peru even before its *Final Report* was issued. In addition to its criticisms of some military officers, there were continuing issues about the funding of its deliberations. At one point, a Lima prosecutor opened an investigation to decide whether to charge twelve commission members for advocating terrorism, which was a serious crime. This initiative was launched by a legislator sympathetic to former president Alberto Fujimori. The legislator objected to the production of a video in which four former members of the Shining Path were shown expressing remorse for their actions.[7] Opposition legislators called for the commission to be investigated, for its findings to be kept secret, and even for it to be disbanded.

The response to the Peruvian TRC report was fury on the part of political parties who were deemed to share responsibility for some 30 percent of the deaths during the terrible civil war. Leaders of these parties rejected the report, saying that they were very disappointed in it and commenting that it primarily reflected the left-wing views of the commissioners. Although a poll indicated that most Peruvians supported the work of their TRC, one congressman called for an inquiry to investigate commission members. Others accused the commission of favoring the rebels, adopting this interpretation because the TRC report contained criticisms of the actions of persons who had fought against the rebels. Not willing to accept any criticism, party spokespersons responded to the report by accusing the commissioners of left-wing bias.[8] (There is an analogy here with criticisms of the South African TRC by members of the ANC, who interpreted the TRC criticisms of its actions in the 1998 Report as amounting to an endorsement of the other side).[9] Conservative politicians especially attacked the commission, criticizing it for "digging up the past." Archbishop Ciprani of Lima criticized the report at a mass that was attended by the president of Peru, saying that he did not accept the report because it was simply not true.

Former military officers denied any wrongdoing and accused the commissioners of being terrorists or communist sympathizers.[10] Many military officers were incensed at the criticisms. They understood themselves to have served in the highlands areas where they had been given extraordinary powers, which they were to use to control a volatile situation. Those charged with human rights violations were quick to defend themselves. They understood themselves as having done something of great value to the state and as having protected it against Marxist rebels.

Peru's president, Alejandro Toledo, issued a formal apology for the actions of the state and announced that the government would spend some 800 million dollars on social programs for the communities most affected by the violence.[11] He rejected calls for individual economic reparations, arguing that Peru had insufficient resources. However, the sincerity of this stance was questioned by many since, at the same time, President Toledo had made some 64 million US dollars available to compensate twenty-eight thousand civil servants who had been unjustly fired.[12] Toledo's proposed Peace and Development Plan called for some 800 million US dollars for reconstruction in the areas most affected by the conflict. However, commentators pointed out that a *redevelopment* plan does not amount to *reparations*; the two are different. Development, as such, is distinct from reparations because it has no necessary connection with restitution, compensation, or rehabilitation in the wake of harm to individuals. Nor does it involve acknowledgment of responsibility for harms inflicted on individuals or groups.[13]

The Truth and Reconciliation Commission of Peru had put forward a plan for integrated reparations to help victims regain personal dignity, security, health, and tranquillity. This plan recommended that reparations should be offered to any individual or group that had suffered acts or omissions that amounted to human rights violations under international human rights law. Such violations included forced disappearance, kidnapping, extrajudicial execution, murder, enforced displacement, arbitrary detention, violation of due process, enforced recruitment, torture, and rape. The plan recommended inclusion of reparations for persons wounded, injured, or killed as a result of attacks by armed opposition groups—regardless of who the perpetrator was.[14] It envisaged symbolic reparations and reparations in such fields as health, education, legal status, institutional reform, and financial compensation to those left with physical or mental disabilities.[15]

In March 2004, the Inter-American Human Rights Commission said that the conclusions of the Peruvian TRC *Final Report* were fundamental and lauded actions taken to apply its recommendations as exemplary. It said that the government of Peru was absolutely committed to unrestricted respect for human rights. A representative of President Toledo attended the meeting of the Inter-American Human Rights Commission held between February 23 and March 12, 2004. The president of this commission, Jose Zalaquett, spoke favorably of the progress Peru had made in securing both justice for victims and their families and funding for reparations, while noting that there was still much to do regarding the latter. International observers paid close attention to the follow-up work after the release of the commission's report.

In Lima, there is a museum dedicated to victims of the vicious civil war. It is the only museum yet initiated by a truth commission, and was established to pay permanent homage to the victims of Peru's political violence. This museum had received one hundred thousand visitors by the summer of 2004. In other respects, however, follow-up to the work of the Peruvian TRC has been slow at best. By the summer of 2004 there had been few trials, no legislation providing for institutional reform, and no program of reparations.[16] An Amnesty International report on Peru stated that the government had established a system of prosecutors' offices and courts, but that it had only commenced trials in three out of the recommended forty-three cases presented by the Truth and Reconciliation Commission. Although there had been several initiatives to offer reparations to victims and their families, and to commence development efforts in areas affected by violence, only a few people had received compensation by the end of 2004.[17]

There were several groups established to act on matters relating to peace, reparations, and reconciliation. Some progress was made on providing documents to persons who had none, and there was a commencement of health and mental health problems in some of the areas most affected by the violence. In August 2004, the government of Peru announced that part of the next year's budget would be assigned to fulfil obligations for collective and individual reparations, as recommended by the TRC. In the collective area, plans included improvement of road infrastructure, programs of scholarships, and perhaps provision for integral health insurance for victims. Individual reparations were not yet envisaged.[18] However, Salomon Lerner Febres, the former president of the Peruvian TRC, stated that little progress had been made in the areas of trials and reparations.[19] Follow-through on the commission's recommendations has been halfhearted at best, and issues related to human rights abuse and reparations did not receive much attention in the elections of May 2006.

NOTES

1. Description provided by Minnesota Advocates for Human Rights, http://www.mn advocates.org/Peru.html.

2. The Program of Integral Reparations was particularly sensitive and careful. It is discussed in chapter 9. See also Lisa Laplante, "Reparations for Justice," December 18, 2003, http://www. latinamericapress.com. See also Walter Chiara and Lisa J. Laplante, "Prosecutors in Peru: Testing the Limits of Impunity," *Reparation Report* 3 (April 2004) and Lisa J. Laplante, "Peru: Reparations in the Post Truth Commission Era," *Reparation Report* 3 (April 2004), http//:www.redress.org/reports/april/2004.pdf (accessed June 24, 2005). The *Reparation Report* is published by the Redress Trust, third floor, 87 Vauxhall Walk, London, UK, SE11 5HHJ.

3. Discussed in chapter 9 in greater detail.

4. Joanna Crandall, "Truth Commissions in Guatemala and Peru: Perpetual Impunity and Transitional Justice Compared," *Peace Conflict and Development* 4 (April 2004).

5. Amnesty International: Peru (covering events from January–December 2004).

6. BBC news report, http://news.bbc.co.uk/2/hi/americas/3987741 (accessed June 21, 2005).

7. Human Rights Watch, Division de las Americas, "Peru: Truth Commission Under Pressure," http://www.aprodeh.org.pe/sem_verdad/comission/verdad/12ago2003 (accessed May 2004).

8. Lucien Chauvin, "Peru: Truth but No Reconciliation," *World Press Review* (November 2003).

9. Discussed in detail in chapter 6.

10. Dennis Jett, "Dirty Wars Cast Shadow on Virtues of Patriot Act," *Christian Science Monitor*, September 29, 2003. The author is a former US Ambassador to Peru.

11. Alan Farrington, "Moment of Truth: Peru's Struggle to Recover Its Moral Memory Is a Remarkable First Step in Remaking the Society." Ford Foundation Report, Spring 2004, http://www.fordfound.org/publications/ff_report/view_ff_report_detail.cfm?report_index+484.

12. Paulo de Greiff, "What Reparations Contribute to the Achievement of Imperfect Justice," presented at the Symposium on Repairing the Past: Reparations and Transitions to Democracy, Ottawa, Canada, March 12, 2004. The symposium was held under the joint auspices of the International Development Research Center and the International Center for Transitional Justice.

13. Ibid.

14. Amnesty International, "Peru: The Truth and Reconciliation Commission—A First Step Towards a Country without Injustice," http://web.amnesty.org/library/index/engamr 460032004 (accessed August 26, 2005).

15. Discussed in chapter 9.

16. Hannah Hennessey, "Peru's Lessons from the Past," BBC News, UK Edition, August 27, 2004, http://news.bbc.co.uk/1/hi/world/americas/3604550.stm (accessed June 24, 2005).

17. Amnesty International: Peru, http://web.amnesty.org/web/web.nst/print/DIA9C 4A6E66156C780 (accessed July 2005). The information on this Web page covers events from January–December 2004.

18. Information provided by Minnesota Advocates for Human Rights, "Peru," http:// 222.mnadvocates.org/Peru.html. The Minnesota Advocates for Human Rights is based at 650 3rd Avenue South, #550, Minneapolis, MN, 55402-1040.

19. Ibid.

Appendix 6, Rwanda

Between March and July 1994, between eight hundred thousand and one million people were killed in Rwanda by advocates of Hutu power. Most of the victims were Tutsis although some were Hutus unwilling to participate in the killings. These killings were mostly committed with the use of machetes; they involved close physical contact and were often carried out by people who knew their victims. Rape, brutality, and torture were frequent. The Rwandan genocide was one in which outside parties failed to intervene despite knowledge of what was going on and warnings about its likelihood just prior to the commencement of the killings. Unlike the Holocaust, this was not a genocide planned and executed by centrally placed administrators who disguised their activities from the public at large. Rather, it was overt and everywhere, and the brutal killings were carried out by vast numbers of people.

At the root of the supposed racial and ethnic difference between Hutus and Tutsis lies a strange history in which Belgian colonial practices and attitudes are highly significant. In a colonial situation, there is a dichotomy between the (superior) settler and the (inferior) native. To settle his territory effectively, the settler will seek to eliminate the native or at least render him powerless. Colonial occupation is a violent process based on a polarization of roles. Emerging from this process, the opposition to colonialism tends to be similarly polarized. The central polarity is that between those who have come to a territory from elsewhere and those who are indigenous to it; the significance of origin comes from the fact that colonial settlers are not indigenous. Natives, by contrast, are indigenous. In most anticolonial struggles, they assert their rights on that basis.

In Rwanda, colonial history and settler/native polarity played a crucial role in the construction of Hutu/Tutsi identities.[1] Its significance arose from a mythology about the Tutsi, according to which Tutsi people were not indigenous to the Rwandan territory because they had a distinctive racial origin. The Tutsi had been construed by the Belgian colonizers as nonindigenous persons in Africa. They were thought to be "Hamites" who had migrated into the region of Rwanda at some time in the past. Given this mythology of migration, the Tutsis were not regarded as natives. Thus, in postcolonial Rwanda, their status was insecure; they were on the "wrong side" of the settler/native polarity.

Under the Belgians, the Tutsis had been considered to be black but not exactly negroid. The Tutsis were supposed to be a superior black race with oval faces, large eyes, and high noses; they were thought sometimes to be a kind of black master race, coming originally from Ethiopia and resembling Europeans more than did other African peoples.[2] This hypothesis originated with John Hanning Speke, a racist European author. The Belgians believed that the Tutsis were a nobler and more aristocratic people, while the Hutus were coarser and more bestial. One might compare the roles of the groups with the fundamental division in Belgium itself between dominating Francophone Walloons and "coarser" Flemish.[3] Tutsis were thought by the Belgians to be designed for rule.[4] They were seen as a superior people, having distinctive non-Bantu origins. The hypothesis was taken very seriously, to the point where it was invoked to explain all signs of "civilization" in Africa.

Hutu and *Tutsi* are not true racial, ethnic, or even tribal identities. It is argued that these identities are best understood as political and historical. The roles of Tutsi and Hutu were sociopolitical and based on mythologies and functions enforced by the state. These people spoke the same language and, outside Rwanda and Burundi, did not divide into Hutu and Tutsi. The colonial state constructed these "tribal" identities in racial terms. They construed the Hutu/Tutsi distinction as one between people indigenous to the area of Rwanda (Hutus) and persons who had come to it from elsewhere some time in the mythic past (Tutsis). It would be an exaggeration to say that the Belgians arbitrarily invented the distinction between Hutu and Tutsi; the distinction did exist before colonization. However, both European racism and the administrative exploitability of the distinction led to a *racial* interpretation of the Hutu/Tutsi distinction.

In precolonial times, kings were considered sacred, and all were Tutsi. The brutal and demanding Belgian colonial regime used the Tutsis to administer affairs to the enormous suffering and disadvantage of the Hutus. The King, through the Tutsis, imposed corvée labor on the Hutus. One man explained the situation as one in which "you whip the Hutu or we will whip you."[5] After the 1933 census, the identities of Hutu and Tutsi were enforced.

In 1959, there was a social revolution that resulted in the reversal of Tutsi/Hutu political roles. In this Hutu Revolution, democracy was supposed to replace feudalism. Resisting the colonial system, many Hutus were also resisting the Tutsi who, as supposed superiors, had helped to administer and enforce it. The Bahutu Manifesto called for the liberation of Hutus from white settlers and the (supposedly) nonindigenous Tutsis, who were regarded as a privileged ethnic minority. This political shift gave rise to the development of a Hutu counterelite. Most Tutsis, and in particular those who were well educated and had played roles in running Rwanda, went into exile. A Hutu form of racialized nationalism victimized the Tutsis, many of whom became refugees in surrounding states, notably Uganda. There commenced a movement of armed Tutsi guerrillas called *inyenzi* (cockroaches).

Many Tutsis were not living in Rwanda, but rather in surrounding states; however, in these states, they were also regarded as nonindigenous and had no right to citizenship. The lasting influence of the Hamitic hypothesis meant that the Tutsis were regarded as ethnic strangers everywhere in Africa. In effect, there was a Tutsi diaspora. The situation of the Tutsis has been compared to that of the Jews in Europe. With limited opportunities and no citizen rights in Uganda, many Tutsis sought to return to Rwanda. Understood as racial strangers who had enjoyed privileges under colonialism, the Tutsi were targeted as victims.

During the 1970s, there was some recognition of the Tutsis as a minority group within the Rwandan state. As a minority group, Tutsis were granted some rights. However, the presumption was that political power would have to remain with the Hutus.[6] It was not the dominance of Hutus, as such, that caused these killings and the eventual bloodbath but rather the fact that Tutsis wished to return to Rwanda and regain power there. Hutus feared this and sought to repress and repel these efforts. There were killings in 1959–1963, 1973, and in the period 1991–1994. This last conflict was, in effect, a civil war prior to the 1994 genocide. It has been estimated that between 1959 and 1990 at least 750 to 5,000 Tutsis were killed. Thus, the animosity between Tutsi and Hutu was serious, even extreme, before 1994. There were expulsions and even massacres. None of these, however, amounted to genocide.

With little ethnic violence, Rwanda enjoyed comparatively good times in the 1970s and 1980s. There was socioeconomic progress and the country was regarded as efficient, stable, and open to the world. During this period, the Tutsis who lived in Rwanda were not involved in politics or the military; generally, however, they were safe, and many thrived in the private sector. In the late eighties, this situation changed. The prices of tea and coffee, major exports of Rwanda, dropped considerably. This market situation contributed to further economic difficulties, including inflation, unemployment, land scarcity, and a lack of opportunities for young men in particular.[7] The International Monetary Fund imposed financial conditions on the Rwandan government, compelling it to devalue the Rwandan franc by two thirds. There was a pronounced resource crunch, and the Gross Domestic Product fell by 40 percent.

In 1990, despite a shortage of resources, President Habyarimana had announced that Tutsi refugees had a right to return to Rwanda. In 1991, he signed a new constitution that provided for an end to the system of identity cards, multiparty politics, and the banning of political parties based on ethnic or religious affiliation. At that time, although there had been talk of reconciliation since the seventies, there was only one Tutsi member in a nineteen-member cabinet; one Tutsi ambassador, two Tutsi deputies in a seventy-seat national assembly, and two Tutsis in the central committee of the country's only political party. By 1993, Habyarimana had agreed to power sharing with the RPF (a Tutsi-Rwandan army). However, both on the Hutu and on the Tutsi sides, there were many people who opposed these accords.

In October 1990, the RPF invaded Rwanda from Uganda. One motivation was to allow the Tutsis, who had been exiled from Rwanda, to return to their own country. Some of these forces had assisted Uganda's President Museveni in coming to power in Uganda, and his government was willing to assist them in their return to Rwanda. The RPF invasion resulted in a civil war. The Habyarimana regime had been pledged to ethnic reconciliation but, after the invasion, it shifted its position and instead pledged to uphold Hutu power in Rwanda. The fear of Hutus was that if the RPF was successful in gaining the reentry of tens of thousands of Tutsis, the Tutsis would resume their previous positions of privilege and would expel Hutu peasants from the Rwandan state. In the invasion, the RPF did commit killings, but not massacres, and not genocide.[8]

In the context of this civil war, Hutu propaganda against the Tutsi became extreme. Radios broadcast that the country was in danger of being taken over by a foreign race. In the "Hutu Ten Commandments," the Hutu were instructed to stop having any mercy on the Tutsi and to refuse to engage with them in any way—whether sexually, in business relations, or in governmental affairs. All Tutsis were said to be dishonest, and any Hutu having financial dealings with them was said to be an enemy of his own people.[9] Hutu men were warned that all Tutsi women were Tutsi agents; even if one's own wife was a Tutsi woman, she was a threat and one should kill her. The constant message was that "they are coming back and they will bring feudalism with them." This framework was an extreme version of an *us-or-them* mentality; "We must exterminate them or we will die." Radio Rwanda, in March 1992, had announced that the Tutsi planned to massacre the Hutu. Later, Radio Mille Collines broadcast to Hutus, urging more killings of the Tutsis, and using vicious sayings such as "The grave is only half full. Who will help us fill it?" Underlying the brutal Hutu propaganda was a genocidal line of thinking according to which the Tutsis were an absolute menace and the only appropriate response was to eliminate them. In that struggle, the weapon was to be the Hutu people themselves. The Hutus saw themselves as victims; they had been victims of colonial and Tutsi power in the past, and could be victims of a Tutsi takeover in the future. Any internal dissent was regarded as treachery.

When the 1994 genocide occurred, United Nations peacekeeping forces were in the country, under the leadership of a Canadian general, Romeo Dallaire. Dallaire appealed repeatedly to UN headquarters in New York for a strengthening of his mandate and for additional forces, feeling his men virtually powerless to do anything to stem the intense and appalling violence. His messages were ignored.[10]

A fundamental challenge when seeking to understand the Hutu/Tutsi conflict and the genocide of 1994 is how the shifting and essentially contrived identities of Tutsi and Hutu, with no racial basis and a questionable historical foundation, could have become so polarized and deeply entrenched as to give rise to genocide. One possible explanatory factor is that when Hutu propaganda urging extermination of the Tutsi enemy was commenced, it was in a context in which there was already a civil war in Rwanda. Hutus were told that in such a war no one could be neutral, and anyone not willing to kill Tutsis to save his country was on the side of the attackers. The context was one of diminishing resources, increasing population, fear of authority, state incentives to kill, a history of racist doctrine, and a definition of the enemy that seemed credible. The taking of enemy lives was defined as a political necessity. To kill was supposed not to be criminal in the context; rather, it was argued to be political—and necessary for the very survival of the Hutu people.[11] Given the civil war, the history of the Tutsis and Hutus under Belgian imperialism, and the quest, in that context, for Hutu power, the Rwandan genocide cannot be said to have come out of nowhere. However, no amount of historical background really suffices to make such mass brutality comprehensible.[12]

There were deep inequalities between Tutsi and Hutu emerging from precolonial times and reinforced by the Belgian administration. The expulsion of Tutsis in 1959, their lack of citizenship elsewhere, their desire to return, and the resultant civil war of 1990–1994 were also important factors in the immediate context of the 1994 genocide. There were killings in the period between 1990 and 1994 (sometimes called "practice massacres") and there was a massive importation of arms. Reviewing all these conditions, Philip Gourevitch has asked, "Was it waiting to happen?" It appears that the question is rhetorical; he anticipates an answer of "yes." Nevertheless, Gourevitch does refrain from saying that even all of these conditions make the genocide intelligible.[13]

The genocidal killings stopped because the Tutsi RPF forces took over Rwanda. In so doing, it was the only military force in the world to live up to the requirements of the 1948 Genocide Convention. The RPF was an organized and disciplined fighting force of some 14,000 men, directed by Paul Kagame, who was proclaimed as a highly effective military leader and became the president of Rwanda after the military victory. The notion of a military victory in this context is, however, somewhat misleading. The Hutu genocidaires and their supporters fled the country.[14] In their invasion, the RPF forces were hardly faultless; there were reprisal killings and some atrocities against Hutu civilians. There was also some forced recruitment of boys and men to serve as porters and cattle herders. In addition, hundreds or perhaps even thousands of unarmed civilians and captured opponents were killed by the RPF in the period between April and August 1994. Still, these forces were not implementing genocide. They were fighting—with ultimate success—against it.

The Tutsis came to power by a military victory that ended the genocide. They took over the country, in which they were a minority. Since so many of the Tutsis who had lived in Rwanda prior to 1994 were killed, many postgenocide Tutsis were returnees from Uganda. Others were genocide survivors who had witnessed horrors and had many family members killed. Tutsi survivors told amazing stories. Some Hutus sheltered Tutsis and assisted them in various ways only to go on to kill others. One Tutsi survivor estimated that 10 percent of the Hutu helped Tutsis, 30 percent were forced to kill under extreme threat, another 20 percent killed with some reluctance, and 40 percent killed enthusiastically.[15] The Catholic Church in Rwanda, and much of its medical profession, participated directly in the genocide. In fact, some of the largest massacres occurred in churches where people had gone seeking refuge. So much of the population was involved in these killings that in the aftermath millions could be regarded as guilty. Postgenocide recovery was an extraordinary challenge of building a democratic and equitable society in a context in which a military power became the governing authority and had the challenge of ruling over an aggrieved, fearful, and guilty majority.

In the aftermath of 1994, Paul Kagame became the leader of Rwanda. Kagame announced a program of reconciliation in which tribal identity cards would be abolished. There would be no talk of Tutsi and Hutu, and moderate Hutus would be brought into the government. However, Kagame's apparently well-intentioned beginnings later gave way to repression, censorship, accusations of "divisionism" on the part of opponents, and efforts to co-opt or silence civil society.[16] There came to be increasing authoritarianism in the government, and international guilt about the failure to intervene made it difficult for outside groups to criticize the government. A moderate Hutu, Pastor Bizimungu was the first postgenocide president. He later opposed Kagame on some points, winding up in jail. Even given evidence of increasing censorship, repression, and exclusion of Hutus from the government, outside donors did not wish to criticize Tutsis; they had been the victims of genocide. As ultimate victims, they were presumed to be beyond criticism. It has been said that Kagame has been given a victim's license; the genocide was so terrible that people are reluctant to criticize the victim group. This reluctance to object to censorship and repression in contemporary Rwanda means that outside parties, who made the mistake of uncritically supporting Hutu domination, may lapse into an analogous mistake with regard to the Tutsi-dominated regime. The presumption seemed to be that good governance would require a strong state, one that would be identity neutral—and, in this context, so far as Hutu and Tutsi were concerned, "identity neutral" seems to have been interpreted as "identityless."[17]

The Kagame government faced extraordinary challenges of physical and social reconstruction. Its response was increasingly coercive. It decreed that there are no Hutus and Tusis: "We are all Banya-Rwanda," *one* Rwandan people. The very names "Hutu" and "Tutsi" became taboo in postgenocide Rwanda. This policy was aimed against ethnic and racial prejudice, but it made it impossible to publicly reflect on what had happened.[18] Even research centers in Rwanda assimilated the taboo, with the effect that they could not acknowledge the situation as it had been or as it was. People were not even supposed to use the language of Hutu and Tutsi, and if they did, they would be accused of divisionism and of having a genocidal mentality, a charge against which there was no good defense. One victim willing to speak out said, "I am a Tutsi. I didn't know I was a Tutsi until they came to kill me. Now they want me to say I am not a Tutsi. I won't."[19] People were compelled to speak pleasantly, say "good morning" in the name of national unity, and pretend that crimes had not been committed against them.

The horrifying Rwandan genocide was motivated by fears of Tutsi power. Ten years later, there is a new set of inequalities, and Tutsi power has become a reality. The situation of Rwanda can scarcely be said to be stable, especially in light of the many thousands of Hutu militia active in neighboring areas such as the Congo.[20] There has been considerable rhetoric about forgiveness and reconciliation, but that rhetoric corresponds badly with the reality on the ground. People will say they forgive, but explain that they have been compelled to do so. The phenomenon seems to be an example of directed forgiveness.[21]

In the area of punitive justice, practical problems were enormous. There were so many persons accused of killing and other crimes during the genocide that the international tribunal (ICTR, in Arusha, Kenya) and the Rwandan national courts could not have tried all of them in less time than two hundred years. Accordingly, a system of community courts, the *gacaca*, was legally established in 2001. Each of some ten thousand villages was to have its own court to deal with persons who had committed certain sorts of crimes. The idea was to have confession, apology, restitution, and reintegration of the offenders into the community, which was envisioned as a way of dealing with the past together in an informal, popular, and comparatively inexpensive process.[22] However, the problems have been many. The indigenous traditions on which the *gacaca* were based was not devised to handle crimes of genocide.

NOTES

1. Mahmood Mamdani, *When Victims Become Killers: Colonialism, Nativism and the Genocide in Rwanda* (Princeton, NJ: Princeton University Press, 1998), chap. 1.

2. Philip Gourevitch, *We Wish to Inform You That Tomorrow We Will Be Killed with Our Families* (New York: Farrar, Straus, and Giroux, 1998), pp. 52–3.

3. Ibid.

4. There were deep contradictions in the notion of the Hamitic (roughly white-like African) race, as several commentators have noted.

5. Mamdani, *When Victims Become Killers*, p. 99.

6. Ibid., p. 140.

7. Organization for African Unity, "Executive Summary of 'Rwanda: The Preventable Genocide,'" ReliefWeb, July 7, 2000, http://www.reliefweb.int/rw/rwb.nsf/AllDocs-ByUNID/f52bc6c855bfb3388525691800527bb6 (accessed June 2, 2005). See also Gourevitch, *We Wish to Inform You.*

8. Mamdani, *When Victims Become Killers,* pp. 180–94.

9. Gourevitch, *We Wish to Inform You,* p. 87 and following.

10. These events are described in Romeo Dallaire, *Shake Hands with the Devil* (Toronto: Random House, 2003) and Samantha Power, *"A Problem from Hell": America and the Age of Genocide* (New York: Harper Perennial, 2002), pp. 340–82.

11. These conditions are cited not as excuses, but as partial explanation.

12. Andrew Rigby, review of Mamdani, *When Victims Become Killers, Peace News* 2445 (December 2001–February 2002).

13. This summary owes much to Gourevitch, *We Wish to Inform You.*

14. Ibid., p. 220.

15. Mamdani, *When Victims Become Killers*, p. 224. See also Gourevitch, *We Wish to Inform You*, p. 130 and following.

16. James Astill, "Rwanda's Electoral Charade," *Guardian Unlimited* (London), August 27, 2003, http://www.guardian.co.uk/comment/story/0,,1029776,00.html (accessed June 20, 2006).

17. Stephen Brown, presentation at the "Reconciliation" conference, University of Western Ontario, May 14, 2005.

18. Ibid.

19. Ibid.

20. The very considerable and important international dimensions of this problem cannot be explored here.

21. Discussed in chapter 5.

22. Rosemary Nagy, presentation at the "Reconciliation" conference, University of Western Ontario, May 14, 2005. The *gacaca* courts are also described in chapter 10.

Appendix 7, Sierra Leone

by Sarah Laing

The history of Sierra Leone exemplifies the struggles faced by many West African nations. This African subregion was previously exploited by Portuguese, French, and British colonial rule and was the historical dumping ground for freed slaves. While the colonial aspects of Sierra Leone's history are shared by many other nations, the civil war that would plague the nation is particularly noteworthy from a conflict perspective. Sierra Leone's war grew out of corruption and exploitation and had no ethnic, racial, or religious groundings. This feature is distinctive, since so many other wars have been based upon religious, ethnic, or racial prejudices and divisions. Unfortunately, this type of civil war may become more common; many African nations face similar issues of corruption in the context of previous colonial domination.

Sierra Leone gained independence from the United Kingdom in 1961, at which time the people of Sierra Leone were granted the freedom of democratic governance as an independent nation.[1] However, the nation would continue to be economically exploited due to the discovery of massive diamond deposits. Unfortunately, this discovery would sow the seeds of a government plagued by corruption, leading to cycles of coups. Sierra Leone's political elite would control and profit from the lucrative diamond trade. In the early 1930s, an agreement had been signed between the government of Sierra Leone (then still under British rule) and the DeBeers diamond company, granting DeBeers a monopoly over the diamonds within Sierra Leone.[2] In essence, the government received payment for the land that DeBeers used and received little, if any, compensation for the mined diamond wealth. The people of the nation gained no benefit from this deal between their government and DeBeers. Even with the newly granted independence in 1961, the diamond wealth was still under contract to DeBeers, and no direct benefits from the mineral wealth were allotted to the people of Sierra Leone. As a result, the country has been plagued by an ongoing struggle to gain control of the government and the profits from the DeBeers agreement.[3]

Seven years after the country gained independence, the governing Sierra Leone

People's Party (SLPP) was overthrown by the African People's Congress (APC). Once in power, the APC, led by Siaka Stevens, abandoned the concept of participatory democracy and launched what would be a reign of dictatorship, characterized by corruption and the suppression of rights and freedoms. Factions developed as a result of political disagreements within the APC and violence became common between developing oppositions. The APC attempted to guard its government power and wealth by declaring Sierra Leone a republic in 1971, subsequently creating almost limitless powers for the self-declared executive president, Siaka Stevens. Stevens knew that by maintaining a centralized government he and the APC maintained control over the proceeds from the DeBeers agreement. In order to maintain this control, the ruling APC banned any publications by the United Democratic Party (UDP), which had separated from the APC. At the same time, imprisonment and other oppressive tactics were used to suppress UDP members and their democratic initiatives. [4]

The new executive president became aware of a plot by the UDP to overthrow his government. In 1991, he had several officers executed and he ordered the imprisonment of a corporal by the name of Foday Sankoh.[5] Later released, Foday Sankoh would go on in 1991 to lead the rebel war against the central government.[6]

The people of Sierra Leone, exploited by the self-proclaimed dictatorship, witnessed the dissolution of public services such as education and health care, especially in rural areas.[7] They knew of the diamond wealth, given that many worked in the mines, but they did not experience the benefits of this wealth. The nation's mineral wealth was being exploited not only by the ruling dictator but also by smugglers, who would transport the pocketed diamonds to Liberia, where the diamonds would be sold. This ongoing and far-reaching exploitation of the nation's resources was compounded by further state corruption, which reserved opportunities, education, and privileges for the single-party government, producing an atmosphere in which civil unrest might have been deemed inevitable.

In March 1991, civil unrest became a reality. Led by Foday Sankoh, rebel forces, calling themselves the Revolutionary United Front (RUF), began waging a civil war on the government of Sierra Leone. Their war was declared against the APC government, now ruled by Major General Joseph Saidu Momoh. The RUF proclaimed support for true democracy and equal rights and freedoms.

Paradoxically, though, their war primarily targeted the powerless civilians for whom they claimed to be fighting. Only a few months prior to the initial attack on Sierra Leone, Charles Taylor, the leader of the National Patriotic Front of Liberia (NPFL), had publicly condemned the neighboring country for supporting the efforts of the Economic Community of West African States (ECOWAS), which sought to quell the NPFL's violent uprising in Liberia.[8] Charles Taylor, who would later become the president of Liberia, publicly threatened Sierra Leone, saying that it and its people "would taste the bitterness of war."[9] He had already begun preparing to follow through on this threat when he made this statement. The RUF troops in Liberia had been receiving substantial support and training in guerilla warfare in preparation to attack Sierra Leone.

Charles Taylor provided support for the RUF because it presented an opportunity to punish Sierra Leone for its involvement in peacekeeping operations that had hindered his party's activities in Liberia. Moreover, Taylor believed that by aligning himself with the RUF he could gain further access to diamond wealth if the RUF succeeded in seizing control of Sierra Leone's mining regions. Deplorably, he sought to further exploit an already abused nation. Taylor's close connections with Foday Sankoh, leader of the RUF, would play a horrifying role throughout the rebel war.

Although the RUF was primarily backed and trained by this violent Liberian warlord, it is important to recognize that its original motives and declarations were not directly aligned with those of the NPLF leader. Primarily, the RUF was reacting to frustration and resentment toward conditions in Sierra Leone: corrupt government officials, disparity between the elite and the civilians, and the lack of educational and employment opportunities. Originally, the uprising in Sierra Leone was focused on achieving an honest democratic government and equal access to education. Unfortunately, the means that were used by the RUF embraced values that were absolutely contrary to those goals. The RUF's campaign of terror swept across the country, sacrificing the lives of civilians as a means of gaining the attention of the government. Brutal amputations, mass rape, and abductions became common rebel tactics. Fear and the need for protection became the motivating factors for the formation of other groups. Evolving factions included the Civil Defense Forces, and the Armed Forces Revolutionary Council, along with several smaller factions like the Kamajours[10] and the West Side Boys.

The Civil Defense Force (CDF) was created with the support of President Kabbah and was intended to provide local security for the people of Sierra Leone. However, the CDF became known for targeting and torturing anyone suspected of supporting the RUF. The CDF came to commit human rights abuses and war crimes in its attempts to prevent similar atrocities committed by the RUF. The Kamajours were a smaller militia associated with the CDF. This group consisted mostly of local farmers, who became known for intercepting humanitarian aid and extorting various means of payment at roadblocks. The Armed Forces Revolutionary Council (AFRC) was largely comprised of former soldiers of the Sierra Leone Army (SLA) and was responsible for launching numerous attacks against the government of Sierra Leone. The West Side Boys were also stemmed from the SLA, as many former soldiers joined this faction. This smaller militia was responsible for hostage situations as well as extortion of humanitarian aid, primarily for the purposes of feeding and protecting themselves. They were a small militia that served to assist in the individuals' survival, as opposed to fighting for a specific larger goal.

Enemies and alliances fluctuated as the civil war transitioned into a brutal pursuit of survival. Trust and security became practically extinct as the roles of allies, enemies, civilians, and soldiers grew to be almost indistinguishable. "Sobels" began to emerge. These were men who were government soldiers by day and brutal rebels by night.[11] These sobels plundered communities and villages in search of money, food, and valuables. This phenomenon exemplifies the difficulties with identifying clear roles during the war. Soldiers were supposed to be protecting the people of Sierra Leone from the RUF attacks, but many participated in rebel activities such as looting in what may have been attempts at survival. The soldiers were not receiving their pay from the government and sought other, often brutal, ways of meeting their needs.

In 1992, the Sierra Leone Army overthrew President Momoh in response to his failure to pay the forces.[12] During the same year, the RUF gained control of the Kono region and the vast diamond wealth in that area. Massive disorder and anarchy continued to spread as the various factions fought for control and influence by targeting civilians. In 1996, the nation held an election that resulted in the naming of Ahmed Tejan Kabbah as the new President.[13] During the election period, the RUF began vicious campaigns to prevent the people of Sierra Leone from voting. These campaigns involved the amputation of limbs, particularly arms and hands, and the delivery of these dismembered parts to the steps of the government buildings. Without their hands, the civilians were seen as unable to vote. The RUF made sure that the government was aware of these campaigns.

Also in 1996, the Sierra Leone People's Party established the Ministry of Reconstruction, Resettlement and Rehabilitation. After two transformations and reconstitutions, this ministry became the National Committee for Disarmament, Demobilization and Reintegration (NCDDR). The commission's general goal was to consolidate existing short-term security so as to provide the foundation for sustainable peace. [14] Consistent with Sierra Leone's history, the new government was quickly overthrown by the AFRC, led by J. P. Koroma. He, in turn, rerouted some of his newly acquired power to the RUF. This consequently interrupted the plan for establishing peace. The years to follow would continue to be characterized by horrific RUF campaigns such as "Operation No Living Thing" and "Operation Pay Yourself."[15]

Atrocities involving the forced recruitment of extremely young children, gang rape of women and girls, slavery, torture, brutal amputations, and mutilations continued. After many failed attempts to negotiate peace, the RUF and the newly reinstated President Kabbah signed the Lomé Peace Accord on July 7, 1999.[16] This agreement granted an "absolute and free pardon and reprieve of all combatants," including those in the RUF.[17] The issue of amnesty was addressed by United Nations Secretary General Kofi Annan, who submitted a written disclaimer, which stated that amnesty should not (and would not) apply to war crimes and human rights abuses.[18] Although the Lomé Peace Accord was not able to establish a sustainable peace, it did provide the legislation that was later used to establish the Truth and Reconciliation Commission of Sierra Leone.[19]

Following the Lomé Peace Accord of 1999, instability and rampant violence continued to stain the nation. The RUF, clearly not committed to the agreement, maintained its terrifying operations, targeting civilians.[20] Over half a million people fled the country.[21] During this time, the United Nations Mission in Sierra Leone (UNAMSIL) became the target for further attacks. In May 2000, over five hundred UN peacekeepers were taken hostage by RUF rebels.[22] It was this event that resulted in the arrival of Indian troops under UN auspices, further military action, and the eventual release of the remaining peacekeepers. The prolonged unrest resulted in the Sierra Leone government's request for a Special Court to try persons bearing the most responsibility for serious crimes of war. The Special Court was instigated in 2002.

CONTEXTUAL COMPLEXITIES

Certain complexities of the situation in Sierra Leone play important roles in both the violent conflict and efforts toward reconciliation in its aftermath.

i)   The civil war was distinctive in the sense that it was not based on perceived ethnic, religious, racial, or ancestral divisions. Rather, the source of the conflict lay primarily in corruption and the inequality that resulted from it, leading rebels to resort to desperate measures. Although there was interference by individuals such as Charles Taylor, who had other motives for war, the predominant motivator was that of inequality resulting from corruption.

ii)   Even though the civil war in Sierra Leone involved unimaginable atrocities, including child abduction, amputation, rape, and sexual slavery, it did not receive adequate attention from Western nations until the violence had spun completely out of control.[23] "Affected ignorance," or the willful refusal to acknowledge, by outside persons and, in particular, world powers was a factor in allowing atrocities to spread extensively.[24]

iii)   The civil war involved fighting between people who were part of the same communities and resulted in the formation of several distinct factions that fought against the government of Sierra Leone as well as several distinct factions that fought against rebel forces. Antagonistic groups were not easily separated. In the current aftermath situation, ex-combatants, internally displaced persons, and victims are often forced to live within the same cities, villages, and communities. This situation increases the need for immediate attention to reintegration strategies.

iv)   The number of displaced persons is amplified by the fact that the country is also occupied by some sixty thousand refugees from neighboring countries.[25] Sierra Leone is not only a nation from which refugees flee; it is also a nation into which refugees from neighboring nations seek asylum. Many such refugees, as well as other internally displaced persons, have been seriously victimized by various factions. The existence of these suffering people presents another population that requires attention, services, and resources.

v)   The instability that causes these incoming refugees to flee surrounding nations such as Guinea, Cote D'Ivoire, and Liberia creates another problem. This western region of Africa, as a whole, has experienced immense instability, which, in turn, compounds the anxiety and tensions already existing within each nation. Sierra Leone has also been the center of territorial disputes involving all three nations. An example of this is the dispute between Guinea and Liberia, which has resulted in the two nations fighting across the eastern regions, directly affecting the citizens of Sierra Leone who reside in the area.

vi)   The close proximity to other conflicts also raises a major concern in terms of reconciliation because such proximity impacts hopes for reintegration and disarmament in Sierra Leone. These surrounding conflicts provide alternate sources of "employment" for combatants because it is relatively simple for a combatant to cross the border to Liberia or Guinea and continue his or her "career" as a combatant. Further, there is an increased possibility that former RUF combatants will return to the base of their movement's first attack, Liberia. Charles Taylor lived for several years in exile in Nigeria, temporarily protected from the efforts of the Special Court for Sierra Leone. There was a fear that Charles Taylor's presence within the West African region could draw combatants into another conflict under his leadership, even though he had been indicted by the Sierra Leone Special Court. The previous relationship between the NPFL and the RUF raises suspicions about possible new collaboration. In March 2006, Taylor was arrested and removed to Freetown. In June 2006, he was taken to The Hague for trial, the understanding being that he would be tried according to the rules for the Special Court of Sierra Leone.

vii) The "ex-combatants" of Sierra Leone include children. This situation calls for alternative reintegration strategies and specifically designed support systems.[26] Thousands of children were reported to have been kidnapped and forced into combat through the use of drugs, alcohol, and threats.[27] When RUF forces entered a community, they often forced children to commit atrocities against their own community, resulting in a profound alienation from any community members that may have survived. These appalling acts served to deter the abducted children from attempting to run from their captors because they would no longer be welcome in the communities that had been their homes. Furthermore, many of the abducted were mutilated by forced tattoos and scarring that depicted the RUF name. This branding practice served to ensure that if the abductees escaped, other opposing forces, such as the government, would kill them. Once children were inducted into a militia, their alcohol consumption was virtually continuous. Some combatants were supplied with bonuses; drugs and alcohol were often provided both before attacks and as rewards after successful attacks. Cocaine and gunpowder mixtures were pressed into open wounds to provide the child combatants with a high that could allow them to fight for days on end.[28] A person's age and mental state at the time of actions are criteria used to determine criminal responsibility, which means that many who have committed atrocities are not eligible to stand trial. [29]

viii) The fact that many of the ex-combatants in Sierra Leone were children and that obvious drug and alcohol abuse were prevalent raises issues in regards to whether or not recruitment and involvement with the factions could be viewed as voluntary. Even in situations where youths were not kidnapped, it would be difficult to say that they had joined militias voluntarily. In order to claim that a choice had been made, in this case the choice to join a militia, it is required that there were distinct options from which to choose. If a young person was faced with a surrounding world of terror, had no means to feed or protect him or herself, and knew that he or she could be (and probably would be) attacked at any time, he or she had no realistic alternative to aligning with a militia for some form of protection. The sheer depravity and terror involved in the circumstances of most youth can be seen as reducing their capacity to make a conscious rational decision to enter into combat. Overall, there has been considerable debate about responsibility in this context—and not only with regard to children.[30]

ix) Among the abducted were many women and girls. Primarily serving as *bush wives* or sex slaves, these women were kidnapped and forced into subservience by the various factions. Initially, their circumstances were not considered in the design of programs for disarmament, demobilization, and the initial stages of reintegration. Furthermore, some women were only *girls* (as young as ten or eleven). Girls and women of varying ages had become mothers to children of the rebel soldiers who had enslaved them.[31] The incidence of sexual abuse, rape, and unwanted pregnancy results in a heightened need for programs specifically for women and programming sensitive to their experiences.[32] Appallingly, it was not until midway through the reintegration process that the women were allotted services and support. [33]

x) The unfortunate economic situation of Sierra Leone played a role in fermenting the conditions for civil war. In addition, a weak economy inhibits the nation's capacity for establishing and funding programs, services, and processes to recover from the war. According to the CIA

World FactBook, 68 percent of the population of Sierra Leone lives below the poverty line, and the average income of an individual citizen is a mere five hundred dollars per year.[34] It is for this reason that some of the training provided for the ex-combatants can be deemed inadequate. Because of widespread poverty, there was simply not sufficient demand for the services that they were trained to provide.

STEPS AND PROCESSES OF RECONCILIATION

Sierra Leone provides a unique example in regards to the processes utilized in the immense task of national recovery. It is one of the few nations to have employed the processes of both a special court and a truth and reconciliation commission.[35] In addition to these two central bodies, the National Committee for Disarmament, Demobilization, and Reintegration (NCDDR), numerous NGO operations, as well as active grass roots community programs and projects have been involved in the project of national recovery.

The coexistence of a truth and reconciliation commission and a special court has been the focus of analysis and debate. Coordination between the two bodies stands out as a problem. While these bodies were operating at about the same time, they were not requested or established simultaneously. They differ in status: the Special Court for Sierra Leone is considered a body of the international community and the United Nations, while the Truth and Reconciliation Commission for Sierra Leone is a domestic or national body requested and established through national legislation in Sierra Leone. A leading criticism of the two processes' coexistence is that there were no concrete guidelines for cooperation and interaction. The TRC was established before the Special Court and as a national entity, not an international body. The Special Court was established through international agreement. The separate establishments and dissimilar jurisdictions have made for coordination difficulties, with many persons concerned that testimony offered at the TRC could be used against them in the Special Court. The primary concern relating to the coexistence of the two bodies is centered on their cooperation and the necessary preparations that would provide for less antagonistic coordination. It is possible that these administrative difficulties could have been avoided.

The fact that the Truth and Reconciliation Commission for Sierra Leone was established by domestic legislation affected that body insofar as it was not equipped with international powers or jurisdiction.[36] The Truth and Reconciliation Commission was launched in July 2002 and given a mandate to "address impunity, break the cycle of violence, provide forum for both victims and perpetrators of human rights violations to tell their story, [and] get a clear picture of the past in order to facilitate genuine healing and reconciliation."[37]

The Sierra Leone TRC proceedings included over six thousand statements and numerous hearings and activities. Its *Final Report* was released in October 2004.

Establishing a truth and reconciliation commission was a plausible option, given the clear impossibility of prosecuting all perpetrators of mass abuses, especially in a country in which the judicial system was unreliable. A somewhat idealized perception of the success of the South African TRC was also a factor in inspiring the creation of the Sierra Leone TRC.[38] The *Final Report* released by the Sierra Leone TRC states that "[Special] Courts do not reach the wider truth."[39] (The clear implication was that a truth and reconciliation commission was more likely to do so.) When the Special Court was established in the summer of 2002, its mandate was to try "only those who bear the greatest responsibility." In total, thirteen perpetrators were indicted, three from each of the major factions (the Civil Defense Forces, the Revolutionary United Front, and the Armed Forces Revolutionary Front) and four other primary accused.[40] The trials for each faction remain separate. However, the indictments of the individual leaders of each faction have been consolidated to create joint trials.

Sam Hinga Norman, Moinina Fofana, and Allieu Kondewa, as leaders of the Civil Defenses Forces, were indicted on "eight counts of war crimes, crimes against humanity and other serious violations of international humanitarian law." After the prosecution concluded its case, the defense filed a motion for acquittal, which was denied in October 2005.[41] The prosecution of Sam Hinga Norman is controversial and may have serious political implications, since many Sierra Leoneans consider him a hero who defeated the rebels.[42] Foday Saybana Sankoh, Sam Bockarie, Issa Hassan Sessay, Morris Kallon, and Augustine Gbao have been indicted for crimes and violations under the name of the RUF, with seventeen counts against them. The indictments against Foday Saybana Sankoh and Sam Bockarie have been withdrawn due to their deaths. The trial against the remaining three RUF leaders began on July 5, 2004. Alex Tamba Brima, Brima Bazzy Kamara, and Santigie Borbor Kanu of the AFRC have been indicted on seventeen counts of war crimes, crimes against humanity, and other violations of international humanitarian law. The trial of these three began on March 7, 2005. Charles Taylor is charged with war crimes including murder, pillage, outrages on human dignity, cruel treatment, and terrorizing civilians; crimes against humanity including murder, mutilation, rape, enslavement, and sexual slavery; and other serious violations of international humanitarian law including the use of child soldiers. The whereabouts and fate of former AFRC leader Johnny Paul Koroma is unknown, and it is suspected that he is dead.

While the Special Court concentrates on the prosecution and accountability of only a few key individuals seen to bear the most responsibility for crimes of war, the TRC attempts to hear the stories of thousands and establish accountability through full disclosure and admittance. It has been said of the Special Court and the Sierra Leone TRC that their "common denominator . . . is that they aim at ending impunity."[43] This common denominator indicates that the two processes have an important common goal. If the Special Court is able to provide genuine retributive justice to an acceptable extent, it is possible that incidents of vigilante action will be diminished. The existence of the TRC provides an additional outlet for the sharing of testimonies as well as an arena for public accountability and healing; all of which are integral to a national transition from civil war to sustainable peace.[44] Given a lack of public confidence and a distrust of the judicial system, the TRC may have the greatest likelihood of gaining the respect and attention of the masses. In a context where people have no faith in the only judicial system they have ever known, it seems unlikely that support for an international special court would be easily cultivated. Perhaps if the TRC and the Special Court are understood to jointly represent the rule of law and enforce accountability, the two processes will come together to mutually generate some degree of public confidence and trust that perpetrators of horrendous crimes will be held accountable and future atrocities will be prevented.

In addition to the TRC and the Special Court a major program aiding in reconciliation is the National Committee for Disarmament, Demobilization, and Reintegration (NCDDR). Since its establishment in 1998, its programs and organization have seen considerable changes, the least of which have been two successive amendments to the organization's name. However, the ability of the NCDDR to respond to changing demands and manage fluctuating complexities within Sierra Leone has been a superior quality of the organization. In 2002, the NCDDR became aware that its assistance programs were inadequate and that enhancements had to be implemented quickly. This awareness grew from publications by human rights groups such as Human Rights Watch and the Women's Commission and reports of ex-combatants failing to complete programs or selling off the tool kits obtained through apprenticeships. In June 2000, the NCDDR held a conference for all "stakeholders in the Peace Process," which included government, UNAMSIL, donors, civil society, nongovernmental organizations, and partnership organizations as well as ex-combatants.[45] This conference allowed for discussion of current and potential problems with programs and implementation and resulted in distribution of services to areas previously unreached and initiatives to provide programming for women and victims.[46]

Programming for adult ex-combatants included the provision of post discharge support in the form of reinsertion benefits; "short-term reintegration" for employment, skills training, formal education, and other possibilities within a Training and Entrepreneurial Program (TEP); and referrals and counseling support services for assistance in building relationships with their families and communities.[47] Due to the substantial number of child ex-combatants, a separate program was established with the cooperation of UNICEF. This program entailed short-term care services, family tracing, counseling, health care provisions, and reunification efforts. In addition, the opportunities for child ex-combatants include two alternate reintegration programs. The first is the Community Education and Investment Program (CEIP), which provides support for formal education in the communities by means of placement within schools as well as financial support during attendance. For example, St. Michael's Lodge in Lakka Town is a home for reintegrating youth where schooling is provided to help the children develop important social skills until they are ready to be reintegrated with their families.[48] The second is the Training and Employment Program (TEP), which funds skills training programs for youth between the ages of fifteen and seventeen who are unable to return to formal school. Training in agriculture, mechanics, construction, and civic duties are provided in various communities throughout the nation. As noted above, the TEP also provides training for adult ex-combatants, but specially designed courses have been implemented for the younger generation of ex-combatants.

In addition to special courses for youth, impromptu programs have been developed for women. USAID has been flexible in providing support for women affected by enslavement, abuse, and resulting pregnancies. Training programs in cooperation, self-esteem, parenting, and skill development have been implemented, although, unfortunately, on a very small scale. Various organizations such as Human Rights Watch and the Women's Commission have alerted programmers to potential inadequacies. The programs have been designed, refined, and implemented within the country.

As these programs indicate, the NCDDR is aspiring to provide substantial support and assistance to cultivate economic and social reintegration of ex-combatants. These two conceptions of reintegration are tightly connected, especially in the situation of Sierra Leone. The nation's economy has been limited by corruption and poverty, which eventually led to the eruption of the civil war. Even today, the economic circumstances limit the abilities of reintegration programs. As of 2002, the reinsertion packages of $150 (US) were valued at 60,000 national Leones, illustrating the diminished value of Sierra Leone's currency and market.[49] The civil war only worsened the weak economy; destruction of infrastructure, towns, farms, and businesses were the result of chaotic rebellion, further diminishing the nation's ability to sustain itself.

The disarmament phase spanned from October 1998 to January 2002, with the NCDDR reporting the collection of a total of 42,300 weapons and approximately 1.2 million rounds of ammunition; this disarmament is said to have resulted in 72,490 demobilized combatants.[50] However, it should be noted that there have been other somewhat contradictory estimates claiming only 48,000 demobilized ex-combatants.[51] The process of demobilization involves five phases for each combatant: 1) assembly; 2) interview; 3) weapons collection; 4) eligibility certification; and 5) transportation.[52] On January 18, 2002, a symbolic ceremony of the burning of arms was held to commemorate what is considered the end of the eleven-year war.[53] Following the closing stages of disarmament and demobilization was the immense undertaking of initiating the process of reintegration. Reintegration is the final and most challenging mandate of the NCDDR. The support services previously discussed were fulfilled by other partnership organizations.[54] Reintegration support programs were officially commenced in January 2000, although on a rather limited basis. At that time, the frameworks for assistance were burdened with significant problems and were initially only available in less than half the country. The estimated time of operation for the NCDDR programs was to be from 1998 until 2004. President Ahmad Tejan Kabbah declared the official end of the DDR period to be effective March 31, 2004, on completion of final wrap-up activities. While he noted that the National Commission for Social Action (NCSA) would continue to deal with the related social issues, Kabbah announced that the government's official programming for reintegration had come to a close.[55]

Another important effort in Sierra Leone has been that of the Talking Drum Studio. This radio programming is broadcast throughout Sierra Leone on eleven stations.[56] There are programs for all varieties of people but "their messages all have the same goal: to promote peace and reconciliation."[57] Individual programs range from children's news and phone-in hours (*Golden Kids News*) to magazine style feature stories "depicting interests and issues that are shared by conflicting groups" that are known as Common Ground Features.[58] There are regular discussions of reintegration efforts in addition to features designed to educate ex-combatants about the efforts of, and opportunities provided by, the NCDDR.

Ceremonies have also played a key role in reconciliation processes. In addition to the arms-burning ceremony previously mentioned, other public events have been held. One of particular interest was the opening of the Koindu International Market. Located in the eastern region of Sierra Leone, where the nations of Sierra Leone, Guinea, and Liberia meet, this area has seen many territorial disputes, an influx of refugees, as well as the horrors of civil war. The president of Sierra Leone, Dr. Kabbah; Cellou Dalein Diallo, prime minister of Guinea; and Charles Gyude Bryant, chairman of the National Transitional Government of the Republic of Liberia were all present at the opening ceremony. Each nation provided chickens and sheep to be sacrificed for an enormous feast. Spanning four days, the ceremony included feasting, consideration of the historical background of the Kissi people, discussion of the plight of refugees, as well as publicly facilitated conversations regarding the wrongs committed by the various groups in attendance. The MARWOPNET (Mano River Women's Peace Network) attended in full traditional dress and were presented with funding from the United States Agency for International Development (USAID). Although the United Nations Development Program was responsible for funding the ceremony, it was the creation of the local people.

> The occasion was the first opportunity for the Kissi people of the three countries to come together and it was regarded by all present as the first step to building people-to-people regional cooperation and solidarity in the sub-region. The official launching of the market also provided the Kissis an opportunity to celeberate their common heritage and culture after several years of mutual suspicion and fear fed by events of the war in the sub region. [59]

A twelve-person subregional committee known as the "Koindu Resolution" was formed to represent the collective interest of the Kissi people. This committee is designed to deal with issues of cross-border disputes, economic concerns, the promotion of cultural values, and collective security. It also put forth suggestions to include women in decision making and contributed to a plan for cross-border trips for Kissi children to help them grow more connected with their culture, a culture that spans the areas of three separate nations.[60]

CURRENT SITUATION

Although numerous steps have been taken in Sierra Leone as aspects of reconciliation efforts, the nation still faces enormous challenges. The poor economic situation in Sierra Leone plays an inhibiting role in the ongoing recovery of the nation. Human rights organizations such as Amnesty International and Human Rights Watch have made public announcements regarding their concerns about the treatment of women, the protection of women's rights, and, more specifically, the practice of female genital mutilation. The murder of Fanny Ann Eddy, a female activist and founder of the Sierra Leone Gay and Lesbian Association, is, sadly, a reflection of the hostility that remains toward activists in some areas.

With the remaining 2,515 UN Troops only mandated to remain in Sierra Leone until December 30, 2005, concerns arose.[61] One recommendation was the suggestion of a permanent human rights panel, put forth by the Office of the United Nations High Commissioner for Human Rights (OHCHR). The OHCHR also urged for prompt comprehensive law reforms in addition to further initiatives promoting human rights.[62]

Sierra Leone faces an intimidating history of exploitation. Colonial powers exploited the people and resources of Sierra Leone by declaring it a colony, reaping the rewards of the colony's resources, and then using it as a dumping ground for freed slaves. The mineral resources were then exploited by the DeBeers diamond company. The subsequent funds received from the DeBeers contract were then exploited by corrupt government officials. The mineral wealth was further exploited by diamond smugglers. The rebels that had demanded democracy, equal access to power, and free and equal education were exploited by Charles Taylor, as he used them and their cause to gain control of diamond-rich regions. Charles Taylor then further exploited Sierra Leonese rebel combatants by using them in his own profit-motivated wars. For a nation of people to recover from these many levels of exploitation and the extreme violence that ensued is indeed a daunting task.

NOTES

1. The Central Intelligence Agency (CIA), *World Factbook*, Sierra Leone, http://www.cia.gov/publications/factbook/geos/sl.html (accessed June 21, 2006).

2. Greg Campbell, *Blood Diamonds: Tracing the Deadly Path of the World's Most Precious Stones* (Boulder, CO: Westview, 2000).

3. This struggle for control over mineral wealth was, in essence, a struggle for the profits of renting the land in which the mineral wealth was found, not for the mineral wealth itself. Ironically, and pitifully, the government that was exploiting its nation for financial gain was, in turn, being exploited by the DeBeers corporation, which was only leasing the land and, therefore, paying nothing for the vast wealth it was reaping from the mines.

4. Joe A. D. Alie, "Background to the Conflict (1961–1991): What Went Wrong and Why?" in *Bound to Cooperate: Conflict, Peace, and People in Sierra Leone*, ed. A. Ayissi and R. Poulton (New York: UNIDIR, 2000).

5. This would be one of many attempted coups that would arise in 1971. It should also be noted that Foday Sankoh has been spelled in different ways, such as Fodah Sanko.

6. Alie, "Background to the Conflict."

7. At one point in time, Sierra Leone was viewed as having one of the top education systems in Africa.

8. This ECOWAS mission was known as the ECOWAS Cease-fire Monitoring Group (ECOMOG).

9. Quoted in Alie, "Background to the Conflict," p. 16.

10. "Kamajours" is also sometimes spelled "Kamajors."

11. Beth K. Dougherty, "Right-sizing International Criminal Justice: The Hybrid Experiment at the Special Court for Sierra Leone," *International Affairs* 80, no. 2 (March 2004): 315.

12. Elizabeth M. Evenson, "Truth and Justice in Sierra Leone: Coordination between Commission and Court," *Columbia Law Review* 104, no. 3 (2004): 730–67.

13. Ibid., p. 735.

14. Thokozani Thusi and Sarah Meek, "Children in Armed Conflict Review and Evaluation Workshop," Institute for Security Studies, http://www.iss.co.za/AF/Arms/ (accessed March 2005). See also Institute for Security Studies, "Sierra Leone—Building the Road to Recovery," http://www.iss.co.za/Pubs/Monographs/No80/Chap1.html.

15. M. Ragmoolie, "Prosecution of Sierra Leone's Child Soldiers: What Message Is the UN Trying to Send?" *Journal of Public and International Affairs* 12 (2001).

16. President Kabbah was reinstated with the military intervention of Nigerian-led ECOMOG. These ECOWAS/ECOMOG troops (primarily Nigerian) were also accused of committing atrocities during the time that they were on their peacekeeping mission in Sierra Leone.

17. Evenson, "Truth and Justice in Sierra Leone," p. 737.

18. M. O'Flaherty, "Sierra Leone's Peace Process: The Role of the Human Rights Community," *Human Rights Quarterly* 26, no. 1 (February 2004).

19. Evenson, "Truth and Justice in Sierra Leone," p. 737.

20. This lack of commitment to the peace accord may be related to the denouncing of amnesty by UN Secretary General Kofi Annan.

21. Omar Yousif Elegab, "The Special Court for Sierra Leone: Some Constraints," *International Journal of Human Rights* 8, no. 3 (2004): 250.

22. Evenson, "Truth and Justice in Sierra Leone," p. 738.

23. Even when Sierra Leone started to receive international attention, the response was inadequate. Funding for the Special Court was especially weak in comparison to the funding received by other courts (like the International Criminal Tribunal for the Former Yugoslavia).

24. Affected ignorance is the inverse of acknowledgment; see chapter 3.

25. CIA, *World Factbook*.

26. It has been estimated that the average duration of rehabilitation provided to child ex-combatants was a mere thirty to ninety days before they were expected to fend for themselves. Douglas Farah, "Children Forced to Kill," *Washington Post*, April 8, 2000, http://www.globalpolicy.org/security/issues/sierra/childarm.htm (accessed October 31, 2005).

27. Ibid. According to Farah, as many as ten thousand children were abducted during the war in Sierra Leone.

28. Ibid. I owe the mention of specific abusive tactics to a conversation with John Pohl, October 29, 2005. He reminded me of some of the grave atrocities committed against the children and of the reasons for using children as soldiers: they are easy to manipulate because they do not have strong ideologies, they provide cheap labor, and they are agile.

29. See chapter 8.
30. See chapter 8.
31. Specific information regarding victims is available on the TRC Web site at http://www.sierraleone.org/drwebsite/publish/index.shtml, where two lists of victims are provided.
32. A preliminary study by Physicians for Human Rights in 2000 found that 70–90 percent of rape victims tested positive for sexually transmitted diseases. It also noted that both men and women fell victim to the "explosion" of sexually transmitted infections such as gonorrhea in men and pelvic inflammatory disease in women. Retrieved from http://www.reliefweb.int/library/documents/2002/sc-seven-dec.01.pdf (February 2005).
33. Discussed in Susan McKay and Dyan Mazurana, *Where Are the Girls? Girls in Fighting Forces in Northern Uganda, Sierra Leone, and Mozambique: Their Lives during and after War* (Montreal: Rights and Democracy, 2004).
34. CIA, *World Factbook*. This measure is in American dollars.
35. East Timor is another example of a nation that has utilized both a TRC and a Special Court. More information is available in appendix 3, East Timor.
36. The South African TRC was also established through domestic legislation.
37. Evenson, "Truth and Justice in Sierra Leone," p. 737. This quote is taken from the Peace Agreement between the Government of Sierra Leone and the Revolutionary United Front of Sierra Leone, July 7, 1999.
38. Patricia Hayner, *Unspeakable Truths: Confronting State Terror and Atrocity* (New York: Routledge, 2001), chap. 3, outlines five of the foremost motivations for the use of a TRC: "to clarify and acknowledge the truth" and establish an accurate record of the events, "to respond to the needs and interests of the victims," "to contribute to justice and accountability," "to outline institutional responsibility and recommend reforms," and "to promote reconciliation and reduce tensions resulting from past violence."
39. *Witness to Truth: Report of the Sierra Leone Truth and Reconciliation Commission* (Freetown, Sierra Leone: Truth and Reconciliation Commission of Sierra Leone, 2004), p. 82. The topic of a "wider truth" is addressed here in chapter 7.
40. Retrieved from http://www.sc-sl.org in February and March of 2005. This selection of indicted individuals seems rather tokenistic. However, the court originally indicted five leaders of the RUF. The number was reduced to three after the death of two of the accused, Foday Sankoh and Sam Bockarie. In addition, J. P. Koroma was indicted separately even though he was a former leader of the AFRC. He has not been tried because his fate is unknown and it is suspected that he is dead.
41. http://www.sc-sl.org.
42. The controversial issues surrounding the prosecution of Sam Hinga Norman are further discussed in chapter 6.
43. Elagab, "The Special Court for Sierra Leone," p. 250.
44. Sarah Laing, "Sustainable Reintegration: Considering the Needs of Victims and Ex-Combatants in Sierra Leone" (undergraduate thesis, University of Winnipeg, 2005).
45. National Committee for Disarmament, Demobilization, and Reintegration (Executive Secretariat), "The DDR Program: Status and Strategies for Completion" (2002), p. 4.
46. Ibid., p. 4.
47. Ibid.
48. Retrieved from http://www.cryfreetown.org (accessed March 2005).
49. NCDDR, "The DDR Program."
50. Thusi and Meek, "Children in Armed Conflict," p. 2.

51. Institute for Security Studies, 2005.

52. Thusi and Meek, "Children in Armed Conflict," p. 4.

53. The civil war in Sierra Leone has been (somewhat arbitrarily) defined as spanning from March 1991 to 2002.

54. See chapter 8 for more on the challenges of reintegration.

55. Yusuf Alghali, *Sierra Leone's Disarmament, Demobilisation and Reintegration Programme End*, The Republic of Sierra Leone State House Online, February 3, 2004, http://statehouse-sl.org/ddr-end-feb3.html (accessed November 2005).

56. Talking Drum Studio also has programming in Cote D'Ivoire and Liberia.

57. http://www.sfcg.org/programmes/sierra/sierra_talking.html (accessed November 2005).

58. Ibid.

59. United States Agency for International Development, "Kissis Unite to Address Cross-Border Issues," April 20, 2005, http://www.usaid.gov/sl/sl_democracy/news/050420_kissisinkoindu.index.htm (accessed November 2005).

60. Ibid.

61. Peace and Security Section of the Department of Public Information (United Nations), UNAMSIL, http://www.un.org/Depts/dpko/missions/unamsil/ (accessed November 2005).

62. UN News Service, "Sierra Leone: UN Rights Body Calls on Government to Establish Rights Panels," Ocober 24, 2005, http://allafrica.com/stories/200510240977.html (accessed November 2005).

Appendix 8, South Africa

Apartheid in South Africa resulted in a political struggle to achieve a social framework characterized by nondiscrimination and a respect for human rights. It was in the wake of this struggle over apartheid that South Africa's Truth and Reconciliation Commission was established.

Apartheid itself emerged from the history of the country.

Human beings have probably lived in southern Africa for some one hundred thousand years. The early known inhabitants of the region that is now the Republic of South Africa were the San, or Bushmen, who were hunter-gatherers, and another group of pastoral people known as the Khoikhoi, sometimes referred to as the Hottentots. Contact with Europeans began after the arrival in 1652 of Jan van Riebeeck and ninety others. This contact soon proved to be seriously harmful to the indigenous people. Although relationships were at first based on fairly amiable bartering, conflicts developed concerning such issues as cattle thefts. The Europeans brought with them smallpox and others diseases, which the African people had little capacity to resist. As early as 1657, the white people began to bring slaves into the area. Some of the enslaved people were black Africans from eastern Africa, while others were Muslims from the East Indies, including a significant minority of Malays.[1]

By the early 1700s, some white settlers, called *trekboers*, had become independent farmers in the Cape region. There had been some intermarriage between white people, Africans, and descendents of slaves. This group became known as "coloreds," and included some persons of Islamic faith. During the second half of the eighteenth century, more colonists came to South Africa, especially to the area of the eastern Cape. These included people of Dutch, German, and French Huguenot origin. It was these people who formed the beginning of the Afrikaner nation. In 1795, Britain took the Cape area away from Holland in a military victory. Although the area was returned to the Dutch, it came under British control again in 1806. There was also military conflict between British forces and those of the African Xhosa people. The Boers had achieved a victory over the Zulu leader, Shaka, in the

early eighteenth century, and that victory gave them some confidence in their conflicts with the British. The British made some efforts to improve conditions for servants; however, these efforts were not popular with Afrikaner residents.

In 1820, some five thousand British settlers arrived in the eastern Cape, in the
area around Port Elizabeth and Grahamstown; their arrival resulted in intense military conflict with the Xhosa residents. A Xhosa leader prophesied that if the people
were to kill all their cattle, the whites would go away, returning to the sea, allowing
the Xhosa people to possess the kind of wealth enjoyed by the English. Due to wide
acceptance among the Xhosa of these messages, they killed many cattle, destroyed
grain, and refrained from sowing seed. Despite the efforts of some, such as Charles
Brownlee, to stop the slaughter by purchasing Xhosa cattle, these practices continued. In October 1857, some one hundred and fifty to two hundred thousand cattle
were killed. Thousands of Xhosa starved to death as a result, despite the efforts of
some missions and hospitals to help. Ironically, due to these self-imposed hardships,
the Xhosa people became more dependent on whites; thousands moved into the English colony to take employment in order to sustain themselves.[2]

In 1834, slaves were emancipated within the British Empire. Some European
missionaries working in southern Africa were philanthropically minded and sensitive to the condition of black and colored Africans. That fact exacerbated conflict
between the British and the Afrikaners, leading to the Great Trek, in which some
fourteen thousand Afrikaner farmers (Boers) moved inward and northward in order
to live independently from British rule. One of many issues dividing the British and
the Afrikaners was the treatment of nonwhite people. The Afrikaners resisted the
idea of equality before the law, believing that racial egalitarianism was not justified.
The Great Trek was, in effect, a rebellion against the British government. The Boer-
trekkers left their original homes in order to found their own state and govern it in
their own way. Although they were never fully independent, they were largely free
of British control and broke certain British laws with impunity. In 1854, the British
recognized them as free people.[3]

By the mid-1800s, there were white settlements over practically all of what is
now South Africa. The Cape Colony had a legislature by 1853 and was largely self-
governing by 1872. Voting rights were restricted by economic qualifications as distinct from race. However, because most black African and colored individuals were
too poor to qualify to vote, the result was a pronounced absence of representation for
black African and colored peoples. In the area of Natal, there were reserves for black
people, who were placed under the authority of chiefs. Britain annexed the Trans-
vaal in 1877 and this region was given internal autonomy in 1884. Paul Kruger, an
intensely pro-Afrikaner and conservative figure, became its leader. When gold was
discovered, the British came into conflict with the Afrikaners, leading to the Anglo-
Boer War, which lasted from 1899 until 1902. The Boers used some guerilla tactics
in this conflict. At one point, General Jan Smuts had moved his troops to within 190
kilometers of Cape Town. In this bitter struggle, brutal policies were adopted. The
British gained the highly dubious distinction, in this context, of establishing his-

tory's first concentration camps for civilians. Although some officials recognized that the situation in camps was dreadful and was causing deaths, it was argued that the internment was needed.[4] Some twenty-six thousand Boer women and children and fourteen thousand black and colored people died in appalling conditions in these camps, which were racially segregated. The barbaric treatment and the large number of deaths at the hands of the English are often cited by Afrikaners as evidence that they were a victimized people and (by implication) not perpetrators.[5] The Anglo-Boer War ended with the Peace of Vereeniging in 1902. South Africa was then within the British Empire.

The former Boer state maintained a whites-only franchise. Resistance to its racist policies was growing among nonwhite South Africans and in 1909 a delegation went to London to plead the nonwhite case. Mohandas Gandhi was active with innovative nonviolent campaigns in South Africa on behalf of the Asian population; he lived in South Africa between 1893 and 1914, a period that was crucial to the development of his ideas on nonviolent action and political leadership.[6]

In 1910, South Africa became a republic. Within it, only the Cape area had a nonracial franchise and, even there, blacks could not be members of parliament. At the time, there were some six million South Africans. Of these, 87 percent were black, 9 percent were colored, and 2.5 percent were Asian. In order for the white minority to retain its power, the state apparatus adopted repressive policies.

The African National Congress was formed on January 8, 1912 and joined other anticolonial movements that formed around the globe after the First World War. At the same time, Afrikaner nationalism was growing in strength and intensity. Afrikaners opposed South Africa's participation in the Second World War. As Afrikaner nationalism developed, the African National Congress continued its antiracist activities. By the mid-1940s, Nelson Mandela and Oliver Tambo, later to be prominent leaders, were already involved in the youth wing of this movement Nonviolent efforts against racism were unsuccessful, and the Afrikaner nationalist National Party continued to gain strength. It came to power in 1948 and began to institutionalize racial discrimination and white power. In 1950, the National Party government passed the Population Registration Act, creating apartheid, and the Group Areas Act, which established racial division of land ownership and residency.[7] In 1952, the Pass Laws were implemented; these severely restricted the movement of nonwhite persons within South Africa. In 1953, the Separate Amenities Act established segregation on buses, beaches, and in post offices and other facilities. (These policies were known as petty apartheid.)

In 1955, the African National Congress (ANC) adopted the Freedom Charter, which was signed at a Congress of the People held in Soweto. This Charter stated that South Africa belongs to all who live in it, *black and white*, and that nonwhite Africans had been robbed of their birthright to land, liberty, and peace by a form of government founded on injustice and inequality. It also stated that the only resolution that would be acceptable to the people of South Africa would be the establishment of a democratic state based on the will of all, a state that would not differentiate between persons on the basis of distinctions of color, race, sex, or belief. It was argued that the people should, through their chosen representatives, govern the country and share its wealth, with all groups and individuals having equal rights. The Freedom Charter called for the return of the wealth of South Africa to its people, and for the land to be shared among those who work it. Under this plan, all would enjoy equal human rights and stand as equals before the law. The ANC and its supporters campaigned nonviolently against the racist policies of the National Party government. These campaigns involved acts of civil disobedience and dissent, including mass boycotts.[8]

In 1958 H. F. Verwoerd became prime minister of the Republic of South Africa. H. F. Verwoerd, who is widely known as the architect of apartheid, established policies of separate education, development, and living for black, colored, and white South Africans. Under the government of his National Party, the representatives of black Africans were removed from Parliament. These initiatives were found strongly objectionable by the ANC and by the PAC (Pan-African Congress), another resistance group that formed at the time. In March 1960, the PAC sponsored a passive resistance campaign against the system of passes. In response, the South African police killed sixty-nine unarmed protesters in what came to be known as the Sharpeville Massacre. The government introduced a state of emergency; declared the ANC, the PAC, and other resistance groups to be illegal; and instituted a policy of detention without trial. These groups went underground. In 1961, H. F. Verwoerd took South Africa out of the British Commonwealth. In the same year, the ANC formed *Umkhonto we Sizwe* (the Spear of the Nation), a wing dedicated to sabotage and violence as means of resistance. Its formation was due to the extreme repression that seemed to make nonviolent resistance to the apartheid state impossible. Nelson Mandela was a member of this branch of the ANC and traveled on its behalf in the early sixties, aiming to make and develop contacts. He was arrested for these activities in Natal in 1962. About his trial, Mandela later said, "I was a symbol of justice in the court of the oppressor, the representative of the great ideals of freedom, fairness and democracy in a society that dishonored those virtues."[9] Mandela represented himself at his trial and wore traditional Xhosa dress so as to embody the history, culture, and heritage of his people. Speaking in his own defense, he called no witnesses. Instead, he used the occasion to make a moving political speech.

At the end of the trial, the prosecutor said, "For the first time in my career, I despise what I am doing. It hurts me that I should be asking the court to send you to prison."[10] Nevertheless, the minister of justice, John Vorster, argued that persons who had been banned should not be able to use the courts as a forum for political speech. As a result, many of Mandela's statements were not covered in the press. Mandela was eventually sentenced to life imprisonment. He began to serve his sentence at the age of forty-six. A powerful consolation was that he did not find himself alone; some of his closest friends accompanied him. Just before the sentencing, the United Nations General Assembly called on its members to implement sanctions against South Africa because of its racist apartheid policies.

H. F. Verwoerd was assassinated in Parliament in 1966. B. J. Vorster, another National Party politician dedicated to upholding the system of apartheid, replaced him. Resistance from the nonwhite population continued. In June 1976, the youth in the Soweto township rose up in protest on the grounds that they did not wish to receive their education in the Afrikaans language, as required by law. Police fired in response. Following this, a period of considerable violence began and continued through the 1980s. A Black Consciousness movement was founded by the influential leader, Steve Biko, who died in detention in 1977 after being captured by police.[11] The UDF (United Democratic Front) was founded and initiated an influential program of consumer boycotting, the purpose of which was to demonstrate to white retailers that they needed the business of black South Africans. In pursuit of "separate development" policies, black "homelands" were established by the government. The land reserved for black Africans was poor and scattered, and the pretense that they were being given equal resources for their development lacked all plausibility. By the 1980s, violence in the black townships and elsewhere had escalated to the point where South Africa was becoming ungovernable.

By 1989, the crisis had developed to the point where Prime Minister P. W. Botha initiated negotiations with the ANC through the person of Nelson Mandela, who remained in prison. Botha resigned due to poor health and lack of support within his party. He was replaced by F. W. de Klerk, who was determined to work out a solution to the serious conflict over apartheid. In December 1989, the de Klerk government released Walter Sisulu and several other persons who had been imprisoned for activities against apartheid.[12] In February 1990, it lifted restrictions on thirty-three opposition groups, including the ANC, the PAC, the Inkatha Freedom Party (IFP), and the Communist Party. After further negotiations, Mandela himself was released on February 11, 1990. On Mandela's release, the ANC agreed to refrain from acts of violence and to work for a peaceful transition in South Africa.

Nelson Mandela's reappearance as a spokesperson on the South African and global political scenes marked a moment of striking importance in twentieth-century history. Mandela emerged from prison with messages of forgiveness and reconciliation and an attitude of generous acceptance, blaming the system of apartheid, rather than white people as individuals or even as a group, for the suffering undergone by his people and himself.[13] This moving approach, by a man who had spent twenty-seven years of his adult life in prison, inspired many thousands of people. It was an important factor in building interest among activists, citizens, and scholars in the topics of political forgiveness and reconciliation and their potential for breaking cycles of violence.

Regrettably, despite positive initiatives, violence continued after the release of Mandela and other political prisoners. In fact, between 1990 and 1994, it actually increased. This increase in violence was the result of conflicts between the ANC and the Inkatha Freedom Party (IFP), under the leadership of Chief Gatsha Buthelezi.

In 1993, representatives of the ANC, National Party, IFP, and other groups agreed to form a Government of National Unity, to be formed after elections in which black and colored South Africans would be fully enfranchised. In April 1994, South Africa held its first ever democratic elections. The turnout was massive. Pictures of long lines of black Africans waiting patiently to vote for the first time in their lives were shown around the world. The ANC won the election; Nelson Mandela became the first president of non-apartheid South Africa. F. W. de Klerk and Thabo Mbeki were deputy presidents. The Government of National Unity was charged with the task of developing a constitution for the South African state. It established the Truth and Reconciliation Commission in the Promotion of National Unity and Reconciliation Act.[14]

THE TRUTH AND RECONCILIATION COMMISSION

The Truth and Reconciliation Commission of South Africa was established in recognition of the fact that victor's justice would not be possible, even if some believed it to be desirable. In effect, there was no clear victor; there had been a military stalemate in South Africa between state forces and those of the liberation groups. The settlement was a negotiated one, and members of the state security establishment would not have supported a negotiated settlement if they had anticipated, within its terms, running the gauntlet of trials followed by long jail terms. The TRC was authorized to give amnesty on an individual basis to persons found to have committed serious human rights violations, provided that those persons had committed acts for political motives and fully disclosed them to the commission. The incentive to disclose was *amnesty*, which was understood as essential to the fact-finding activities of the commission. Only if perpetrators revealed their actions would the TRC and the people of South Africa gain information about what had really happened during the long struggle, and amnesty would give a strong incentive to disclose.[15] Courts of law were not regarded as the best way to find out what had gone on. The understanding needed was broader than what could be achieved in criminal trials and in any event, courts were suspect, since they had served a repressive function under apartheid. Furthermore, legal standards of proof were so high that many guilty persons could not have been convicted.[16] The TRC sought to acknowledge victims and facilitate their healing; it was thought that legal proceedings would be harrowing experiences for victims, given the extensive cross examination that is often necessary in courts of law. The TRC saw itself not as giving up on justice in order to achieve peace but, rather, as pursuing justice in a nonretributive sense. It viewed itself as seeking restorative justice, which was understood as concerned with correcting imbalances, healing, and restoring broken relationships.[17]

As suggested by its name, the South African Truth and Reconciliation Commission sought *truth as a path to reconciliation*. In its *Final Report*, the South African TRC stated that the state had used considerable resources to wage a war against its citizens, a war that included deception, torture, murder, and death squads. The liberation groups were not models of virtue either; they had sometimes egged people on, encouraging them to behave in uncontrollable and irresponsible ways. There had been a campaign to make the country ungovernable. Given that the apartheid government denied human rights to the vast majority of people of the society, this response seemed justifiable. In the aftermath of apartheid, the TRC observed that moral standards in South Africa were disastrously low.[18] Disrespect for the law had been warranted and encouraged, and the cost of widespread lawlessness was later felt. After apartheid fell, South Africa experienced a high crime rate, one that could with some plausibility be attributed to disrespect for the law encouraged in the liberation struggle.

Some 21,300 persons filed petitions with the TRC, regarding gross human rights violations. The TRC investigated some fifty thousand serious human rights violations.[19] Nevertheless, that was a small reflection of the suffering that the racist regime had imposed on nonwhite South Africans, for whom apartheid was a grim daily reality. At least 3.5 million had suffered compulsory relocation (which involved the seizing, bulldozing, or gutting of their homes) and removal into rural ghettoes, resulting in increased poverty and desperation. In a context of entrenched racism, extensive violence, abuse, and animosity, it became apparent that the national reconciliation sought by the TRC, as mandated by Parliament, was not to be achieved quickly or easily. It was recognized that reconciliation had to be understood as a long-term process, one that would have to continue long after the work of the TRC had been completed. Archbishop Desmond Tutu, head of the TRC, urged victims to forgive, but emphasized that reconciliation should not be understood as anything easy and facile.

Many other truth commissions preceded the South African TRC; however, these lacked funds, were less ambitious, and were less well publicized. The South African TRC has become the main reference point for subsequent truth commissions. It is distinctive in many respects. It is the best-known truth commission. Its hearings have been the most public, with results echoing around the world. Its amnesty process was individual rather than blanket. Its leadership was morally respected. And it was focused to an unusual extent on reconciliation and the achievement of a sustainable peace for the country.[20] The South African TRC was also distinctive in providing for special hearings with regard to key events. Special hearings were also held to consider the roles of such institutions as business, the health sector, and the clergy. The South African TRC allowed for direct contributions by human rights and other nongovernmental organizations and it was the first truth commission to have a witness protection program. Furthermore, it was several times larger in terms of staff and budget than any commission before it.

The TRC was committed to dealing evenhandedly with victims, regardless of their group or political affiliation. It took the stance that those with the greatest power carried the most responsibility for abuse. In effect, that perspective implicated the state, which had a range of powerful institutions and resources at its disposal. The goal of the TRC was to provide a historic bridge between the past and the future; that was a task that would require as complete a picture as possible of the injustices committed in the past. Reconciliation was understood to include individual, community, and national levels. Within communities (and between them), there were many conflicts associated with the struggle over apartheid. There were divisions between men and women, young and old, and different ethnic and political groups, all of which needed attention.

THE ACCOUNT OF TRUTH ADOPTED BY THE SOUTH AFRICAN TRC

(1) *Factual.* Factual truth involves the determination of what happened, where and when it happened, and to whom it happened. It is a matter of verifying and corroborating to make sure claims are correct. Also in this category are contexts, causes, and patterns of violations; thus, some inferences from information are involved. Research of a social-scientific kind may be required, and some secondary sources may be used. About such work, Michael Ignatieff famously stated that it could only serve to reduce the number of lies in circulation.[21] However, the word "only" may be misplaced here. Reducing the number of lies in circulation is highly important and is no trivial matter. For example, after the testimony at the TRC, one could not deny that state security forces widely and systematically used torture. One could not say, either, that there were only a few rotten eggs or bad apples who were involved in gross human rights violations. One could not say that the chemical and biological warfare program was only defensive, that slogans yelled by sections of the liberation movement did not contribute to killings of farmers, or that accounts of gross human rights violations in the ANC camps were only the consequence of state disinformation. These sorts of claims have entirely lost credibility as a result of the publicized TRC hearings and the commission's *Final Report.* Fundamental facts about these things have been acknowledged, and that is a fact of great political significance.[22]

(2) *Personal and Narrative Truth.* The commission wanted to attend to unheard voices, especially those of victims, and provide persons who testified with an opportunity to tell their stories from their own perspectives. The conception of storytelling, in this sense, can be understood as related to African oral traditions. The TRC proceedings were based on a conception of restoring the human and civil dignity of victims by granting them an opportunity to relate *their own accounts* of the violations of which they were victims.[23] Victims and survivors could tell their own stories from their own perspectives and in their own languages; when they did so, they would be listened to with respect. This endeavor was intended to help create a "narrative truth" and to contribute to reconciliation by providing for a sense of validation of the individual subjective experiences of people who had previously been silenced or voiceless. The goal was to obtain the widest possible record of people perceptions, stories, myths, and experiences, and to use certain cases as sources of insight into further experiences.

(3) *Social Truth.* Social truth is considered to be the truth that emerges from discussion and dialogue. There is a sense here of *experience*, but not of simply individual experience. The experience underlying social truth is the experience of interaction, dialogue, and debate.[24] The TRC tried to attend to perspectives of individuals from various walks of life, faith communities, nongovernmental organizations, and political parties. "The process whereby the truth was reached was itself important, because it was through this process that the essential norms of social relations between people were reflected. It was, furthermore, through dialogue and respect that a means of promoting transparency, democracy and participation in society was suggested as a basis for affirming human dignity."[25]

(4) *Healing and Restorative Truth.* The notion of healing truth alludes to process and to acknowledgement. It includes notions of how information is acquired, why, and what purpose it will serve:

> Acknowledgement refers to placing information that is (or becomes) known on public, national record. It is not merely the actual knowledge about past human rights violations that counts; often the basic facts about what happened are already known, at least by those who were affected. What is critical is that these facts be fully and publicly acknowledged. Acknowledgement is an affirmation that a person's pain is real and worthy of attention. It is thus central to the restoration of the dignity of victims.[26]

The notion here, then, is that testifying and being acknowledged will restore one's dignity and lead to healing.

FURTHER COMMENTS ON THE TRC

The TRC *Final Report* calls for the emergence of a responsible society, which requires acceptance of some individual responsibility by all those who supported the system of apartheid or allowed it to continue functioning by failing to oppose it. Apartheid political structures condemned millions of people to lives of suffering and violence solely on the basis of their birth, a matter over which an individual has no control. By definition, apartheid was based on systematic racial discrimination. The lemming-like behavior that people so often exhibit—going along with the crowd—made apartheid possible. People bear some responsibility for their own thoughtless submission. As an inquiry into the past, the TRC sought to establish the foundation against which present and future governments would be judged.

Institutional as well as individual responsibilities were noted. Institutional responsibilities included those of professions, industries, financial institutions, banks, churches, schools, universities, and media. Complicity was shown in many ways: by obeying commands, by denial, or by being seduced by personal advantages that could be obtained by cooperating with the system. There was, then, a many-layered situation, providing for multiple and complex forms of responsibility. It is these sorts of behaviors that make possible large-scale, systematic human rights violations in modern states. Noteworthy in South Africa, of course, was the role of the enfranchised white community, who voted National Party governments into power time after time, with ever-increasing majorities. In its *Final Report*, the TRC stated that to shift the country away from racism and its bitter heritage, "what is required is a moral and spiritual renaissance capable of transforming moral indifference, denial, paralyzing guilt, and unacknowledged shame into personal and social responsibility."[27]

To manage its work, the TRC had to specify a mandate providing focus on a restricted range of human rights violations; these were gross violations of human rights, including killing, torture, abduction, and severe mistreatment.[28] But violations that were, in this sense, severe were by no means the only harms wrought by the apartheid system. That system profoundly and adversely affected the lives and opportunities of all nonwhite South Africans. Because there was a narrowing of focus on victims in the work of the TRC, there was a corollary narrowing of focus on perpetrators. Perpetrators were those who committed the severe violations—and, of course, most white South Africans did not literally do so. That narrowing was problematic in the sense that many white South Africans failed to appreciate the significance of their own role in propping up apartheid by various forms of complicity and collusion. They did not see themselves in those represented by the TRC as perpetrators and failed to recognize their own responsibilities as tertiary perpetrators. In the words of the *Final Report*, a key pillar of the bridge between the divided past and the future based on human rights is "a wide acceptance of direct and indirect, individual and shared, responsibility for past human rights violations."[29] It should be understood, the report urged, that *beneficiaries* of apartheid still benefit from a wide range of unearned privileges. For that reason, beneficiaries have a role to play in national reconciliation and should accept an obligation to contribute to the reconstruction of the society. With regard to broad responsibility, the *Final Report* stated that "it is only by recognizing the potential for evil in each one of us that we can take full responsibility for ensuring that such evil will never be repeated."[30]

President Nelson Mandela stated that all people in South Africa shared shame, given the society's demonstrated capacity for inhumanity, and that all should share the commitment to a renewed nation in which that inhumanity would never be manifested again.

AFTER THE TRC: A BRIEF OVERVIEW

An interesting anomaly about the South African TRC is that its reputation is far stronger abroad than at home. This disparity was evident even before the *Final Report* was published.[31] The moral and intellectual leadership of Archbishop Desmond Tutu and Nelson Mandela was highly inspiring to many international observers, who had expected South Africa to lapse into a generalized bloodbath in which blacks would rise up in fury to slaughter their white oppressors. Against the background of this expectation, the well-funded and highly serious hearings and deliberations of the TRC were hailed as nearly miraculous. The fact that black South Africans did not engage in acts of revenge and, instead, shifted in the direction of forgiveness struck foreign observers as stunning and as offering hope to the world. In the mid and late nineties, the South African TRC was nearly always discussed abroad in highly positive terms. Indeed, to this day, its illustrious reputation has contributed to the conviction that truth and reconciliation commissions provide a sound third path, a constructive alternative between doing nothing whatsoever and dealing with perpetrators through the criminal justice system.[32]

In fact, there is a sense in which the international reputation of the South African TRC abroad has become problematic. Some judge its success prematurely and then hastily conclude that a similar process would function well in another country, even one characterized by a quite different set of conditions.[33] There are problems in this reasoning. Both the premise of TRC success and the inference that the approach would work in a quite different environment require scrutiny. In fact, the belief that reconciliation, under the TRC, was some kind of uncontested success in South Africa is simplistic and unrealistic. In addition, the analogy between South Africa and other emergent democracies is often flawed. With the exemplary moral leadership of Tutu and Mandela, a well-developed infrastructure in some regions, and resources far exceeding those of most postconflict countries, South Africa is a singular case.[34]

It is noteworthy that the enormously positive reputation that the TRC enjoys abroad is not enjoyed within South Africa. Liberal whites and many blacks decry the amnesty policies. Some non-Christian observers think there was too much talk about Christian forgiveness and too much injection of religion into what should have been a primarily political process. Victims and survivors complain about the delays and inadequacies regarding reparations. The ANC government resents the account of human rights violations in the liberation struggle. Conservative whites claim that the TRC was a "witch hunt," biased against Afrikaners, who themselves were victims of the English in earlier struggles. The IFP delayed the publication of the last two volumes of the *Final Report* because it objected to discussions of its violent activities and regarded the TRC as conducting a witch hunt against its members.[35]

To assess the success of the South African TRC is a highly complex matter. Given the size of the country, presently estimated to have a population of some 40 million people, the complexity of its problems, and the contestable aspects of the concept of "reconciliation," it is both careless and premature to make definitive pronouncements on the issue. One enormously serious problem in contemporary South Africa is a high crime rate. South Africa has one of the highest murder rates and lowest conviction rates in the world. An estimate for January through September 2001 stated that some 32.5 percent of the crimes reported were violent; in this period, there had been 1,844,000 crimes reported to South African police.[36] Some commentators who opposed the policy of amnesty argue that amnesty has been a factor in causing crime. Their argument is that amnesty implied impunity and thus supported an attitude of profound disrespect for the law. One might equally well attribute the crime rate to extreme socioeconomic inequalities, disrespect for apartheid law, and a high rate of unemployment. The causes of the high crime rate are debatable.

A high rate of infection with HIV/AIDS is another serious problem in contemporary South Africa. The HIV/AIDS problem affects many adults of working and parenting age, resulting in orphaned children and greatly overburdened grandparents and communities. Clearly, it would be unreasonable to attribute the ravages of AIDS to the activities of the TRC and its policies relating to reconciliation. A UNICEF report in 2003 claimed that there were some twenty-four thousand adults with HIV/AIDS and fifteen thousand AIDS orphans.[37] Another estimate was that some 5.7 million children could lose one or both parents to HIV/AIDS by 2015 and that by that date, 30 percent of all South African children between the ages of fifteen and seventeen would have lost their mothers to the disease. This estimate was based on predictions of a continuation of sexual behavior without interventions.[38] The relevance of the HIV/AIDS situation to reconciliation is unclear. However, HIV/AIDS does constitute a profoundly serious problem in South Africa, one that restricts socioeconomic progress in the many affected areas. Thabo Mbeki's idiosyncratic theories on HIV/AIDS are another matter, compounding the problem for several years and costing Mbeki credibility in the international community.[39]

Problematic aspects of South African society that relate more specifically to activities and recommendations of the TRC include: (a) delays in awarding reparations to victims of human rights abuse;[40] (b) the failure of beneficiaries of apartheid, most particularly businesses and relatively wealthy white South Africans, to support programs directed against continuing gross socioeconomic inequalities; (c) the continuation of gross socioeconomic inequalities in the country; and (d) pressures for amnesty by persons who failed to apply to the TRC for it until after the Amnesty Committee of the TRC had finished its activities and completed its report. In the light of these many problems, it is a mistake to baldly assert—as many outside commentators do—that South Africa is a country in which people are "reconciled" to each other and to their past and are proceeding into the future in an atmosphere of harmony and constructive trust.

This is *not* to say that the South African TRC should be deemed a failure, or that there is no such thing as reconciliation in contemporary South Africa. The activities of the TRC, most notably its extensive and widely publicized victim and sector hearings, make it impossible to deny that apartheid was a brutal and unjust system that unfairly oppressed many millions of black and colored South Africans. Its inequities and cruelties were broadcast loud and clear, as were the crimes of assault, abuse, torture, and murder that were committed in its defense. This publicity constituted *acknowledgement*, consolidated in the ambitious and carefully reflective *Final Report*. After the TRC, it would be impossible to deny the wrongs and crimes of apartheid. The voices of many victims were heard, and their testimonies contributed to the historical record, not to be erased.

Several surveys of racial attitudes in South Africa were conducted as elements of a project under the auspices of the Institute for Justice and Reconciliation, called the Reconciliation Barometer. In these surveys, approximately three thousand five hundred people were questioned during three different time periods: March–April 2003, October–November 2003, and April–May 2004. Subjects were interviewed face to face in the language of their choice by an interviewer of the same race as themselves; both rural and urban areas were studied. Some results were less than encouraging.[41] For example, more than one third of those interviewed reported having no contacts with persons of other population groups during an average day. More than one half reported that they never socialized with persons belonging to a different population group. Two thirds said that they experienced difficulty in understanding people of other races and (dramatically, in terms of reconciliation) about 45 percent stated that they found persons of other races *untrustworthy*. In that area, though, there was a positive finding in that the sense of untrustworthiness declined among white, colored, and Indian populations during 2003–2004.

There were some grounds for optimism. Over half the people interviewed said that they would have no problem accepting integrated neighborhoods, with 48 percent of whites and 80 percent of colored persons approving. A substantial 68 percent of all South Africans favored mixed schools. And between November 2003 and April 2004, there was an increase of 20 percent over previous rates, in the number of whites favoring mixed schools.

NOTES

1. M. Wilson and L. Thompson, eds., *The Oxford History of South Africa*, vol. 1, *South Africa to 1870* (Oxford, UK: Clarendon, 1969), p. 231.

2. Ibid., p. 258.

3. Ibid., pp. 292–408.

4. Terence Keith Surridge, *Managing the South African War 1899–1902: Politicians versus Generals* (Rochester, NY: Boydell, 1998), p. 152.

5. Note that this line of reasoning presupposes that the roles of victim and perpetrator are mutually exclusive. See chapter 2 for arguments against this presupposition.

6. See "Gandhi in South Africa," chap. 3 of B. R. Nanda, *In Search of Gandhi: Essays and Reflections* (New Delhi, India: Oxford University Press, 2002), pp. 31–7.

7. David M. Smith, *Apartheid in South Africa*. 3rd ed. (Cambridge, UK: Cambridge University Press, 1990).

8. Ibid., p. 76.

9. Quoted in Anthony Sampson, *Mandela: The Authorized Biography* (London: HarperCollins, 1999), p. 172.

10. Ibid., p. 175.

11. Norman Etherington, ed., *Peace, Politics, and Violence in the New South Africa* (London: Hanz Zell Publishers, 1997).

12. L. Boule and others, eds., *Malan to De Klerk: Leadership in the Apartheid State* (New York: St. Martin's, 1994).

13. Sampson, *Mandela*.

14. Johnny de Lange, "The Historical Context, Legal Origins, and Philosophical Foundation of the South African Truth and Reconciliation Commission," in *Looking Back, Reaching Forward*, ed. Charles Villa-Vicencio and Wilhelm Verwoerd (London: Zed Books, 2000).

15. Ibid.

16. *South African Truth and Reconciliation Commission*, Final Report, 1:6.

17. A helpful description of the South African TRC is found in Priscilla B. Hayner, *Unspeakable Truths: Facing the Challenge of Truth Commissions* (New York: Routledge, 2002), pp. 40–5.

18. *South African Truth and Reconciliation Commission,* Final Report, vol. 1.

19. According to the *TRC Final Report* (vol. 1), the racial configuration of persons who testified with regard to human rights violations was as follows: African, 89.9%; Colored, 1.7%; Asian, 0.2%; White, 1.1%. (By contrast, estimated percentages of the general population are: African, 76.1; Colored 8.5; Asian 2.6; and White 12.8.) Among Africans, women dominated, with 55.9% of persons coming to the TRC being women. A partial explanation of this phenomenon is that proportionately more men were killed in the violence. Women were testifying mainly as secondary victims.

20. Priscilla Hayner, "Same Species, Different Animal: How South Africa Compares to Truth Commissions Worldwide," in Villa-Vicencio and Verwoerd, *Looking Back, Reaching Forward*.

21. Michael Ignatieff, "Wounded Nations, Broken Lives: Truth Commissions and War Tribunals," in *Index on Censorship* 5 (1996): 110–22.

22. *South African Truth and Reconciliation Commission*, *Final Report*, 1:111–12.

23. Ibid.

24. The notion of social truth is sometimes attributed to Albie Sachs.

25. *South African TRC, Final Report*, 1:114.

26. Ibid.

27. Ibid., p. 132.

28. For an explanation of this focus, see Alex Boraine, *A Country Unmasked* (Oxford, UK: Oxford University Press, 2000).

29. *South African TRC, Final Report*, p. 133.

30. Ibid., p. 133.

31. I experienced the phenomenon myself during a visit to South Africa in March 1997 and in many discussions after that time.

32. The amnesty policies of the South African TRC remain controversial and are often referred to dismissively, despite what ought to be recognized as an obvious fact. It was not politically, logistically, or financially possible to subject all suspected perpetrators of human rights violations to a criminal trial. For a discussion of amnesty, see Ronald Slye, "Justice and Amnesty," in Villa-Vicencio and Verwoerd, *Looking Back, Reaching Forward*, pp. 174–83.

33. In "Toward a Response to Criticisms of the South African Truth and Reconciliation Commission," Wilhelm Verwoerd explains some of the criticisms of the commission to an international audience, using political cartoons to illustrate his comments. In Carol A. L. Prager and Trudy Govier, eds., *Dilemmas of Reconciliation* (Waterloo, ON: Wilfrid Laurier University Press, 2003), pp. 245–78.

34. These facts are, of course, obvious to informed observers and commentators such as those working through the highly influential International Center for Transitional Justice in New York.

35. Human Rights Watch, "South Africa: Human Rights Developments," *Human Rights Watch World Report, 1998,* http://www.hrw.org/worldreport/Africa-11.htm (accessed October 2005).

36. Martin Schonteich, "2001 Crime Trends: A Turning Point?" *South African Crime Quarterly* 1 (July 2002). A somewhat more optimistic outlook is provided by Ted Legett in "Is South Africa's Crime Wave a Statistical Illusion?" in *South Africa Crime Quarterly* 1 (July 2002). Leggett argues that statistics might reflect increased reporting of crime.

37. http://www.unicef.org.uk/press/news_detail.asp?news_id=25 (accessed October 2005).

38. Health Systems Trust, "South Africa: Number of Children Orphaned by AIDS to Increase," http://news.hst.org.za/news/indexphp/20020620/.

39. Helen Epstein, "The Mystery of AIDS in South Africa," *New York Review of Books,* July 20, 2000.

40. The topic of reparations is discussed in detail in chapter 9.

41. Karin Lombard, "Race Relations: Is There Hope?" in *South Africa Reconciliation Barometer: Tracking Socio-Political Trends* (October 2004).

Index